MICROPROCESSOR AND MICROCONTROLLER

AUTHOR(s)

Prof. Saurabh Chaudhury
Professor,
Department of Electrical Engineering, National Institute of Technology, Silchar, Assam

Dr. Risha Mal
Assistant Professor,
Department of Electrical Engineering, National Institute of Technology, Silchar, Assam

REVIEWER

Dr. Hariharan Seshadri
Associate Professor,
Department of ECE, Indian Institute of Information Technology, Kanchipuram, Chennai

All India Council for Technical Education

Nelson Mandela Marg, Vasant Kunj, New Delhi, India

Dear Readers,

To prevent the piracy, this book is secured with HIGH SECURITY HOLOGRAM on the front title cover. In case you don't find the hologram on the front cover title, please write us to at contact@khannabooks.com or whatsapp us at +91-99109 09320 and avail special gift voucher for yourself.

Specimen of Hologram on front Cover title:

Moreover, there is a SPECIAL DISCOUNT COUPON for you with EVERY HOLOGRAM.

How to avail this SPECIAL DISCOUNT:

Step 1: Scratch the hologram

Step 2: Under the scratch area, your "coupon code" is available

Step 3: Logon to www.khannabooks.com

Step 4: Use your "coupon code" in the shopping cart and get your copy at a special discount

Step 5: Enjoy your reading!

ISBN: 978-93-5538-511-6

Book Code: UG425EN

Micoprocessor and Microcontroller

by Saurabh Chaudhury, Risha Mal

First Edition: 2026

Originally Published by:

All India Council for Technical Education, Ministry of Education, GOI

Exclusively Published & Distributed by:

Khanna Book Publishing Co. (P) Ltd.

4C/4344, Ansari Road, Daryaganj,
New Delhi (INDIA)

Visit us at: **www.khannabooks.com**

Write us at: **contact@khannabooks.com**

To view complete list of books,
Please scan the QR Code:

Printed in Bharat.

प्रो. टी. जी. सीताराम
अध्यक्ष
Prof. T. G. Sitharam
Chairman

अखिल भारतीय तकनीकी शिक्षा परिषद्
(भारत सरकार का एक सांविधिक निकाय)
(शिक्षा मंत्रालय, भारत सरकार)
नेल्सन मंडेला मार्ग, वसंत कुंज, नई दिल्ली–110070
दूरभाष : 011–26131498
ई–मेल : chairman@aicte-india.org

ALL INDIA COUNCIL FOR TECHNICAL EDUCATION
(A STATUTORY BODY OF THE GOVT. OF INDIA)
(Ministry of Education, Govt. of India)
Nelson Mandela Marg, Vasant Kunj, New Delhi-110070
Phone : 011-26131498
E-mail : chairman@aicte-india.org

FOREWORD

Engineers are the backbone of any modern society. They are the ones responsible for the marvels as well as the improved quality of life across the world. Engineers have driven humanity towards greater heights in a more evolved and unprecedented manner.

The All India Council for Technical Education (AICTE), have spared no efforts towards the strengthening of the technical education in the country. AICTE is always committed towards promoting quality Technical Education to make India a modern developed nation emphasizing on the overall welfare of mankind.

An array of initiatives has been taken by AICTE in last decade which have been accelerated now by the National Education Policy (NEP) 2020. The implementation of NEP under the visionary leadership of Hon'ble Prime Minister of India envisages the provision for education in regional languages to all, thereby ensuring that every graduate becomes competent enough and is in a position to contribute towards the national growth and development through innovation & entrepreneurship.

One of the spheres where AICTE had been relentlessly working since past couple of years is providing high quality original technical contents at Under Graduate & Diploma level prepared and translated by eminent educators in various Indian languages to its aspirants. For students pursuing 2nd year of their Engineering education, AICTE has identified 87 books, which shall be translated into 12 Indian languages - Hindi, Tamil, Gujarati, Odia, Bengali, Kannada, Urdu, Punjabi, Telugu, Marathi, Assamese & Malayalam. In addition to the English medium, books in different Indian Languages are going to support the students to understand the concepts in their respective mother tongue.

On behalf of AICTE, I express sincere gratitude to all distinguished authors, reviewers and translators from the renowned institutions of high repute for their admirable contribution in a record span of time.

AICTE is confident that these outcomes based original contents shall help aspirants to master the subject with comprehension and greater ease.

(Prof. T. G. Sitharam)

ACKNOWLEDGEMENT

The authors are grateful to the authorities of AICTE, particularly Prof. T. G. Sitharam, Chairman; Dr. Abhay Jere, Vice-Chairman; Prof. Rajive Kumar, Member-Secretary and Dr. Amit Kumar Srivastava, Director, Faculty Development Cell for their planning to publish the books on **Microprocessor and Microcontroller**. We sincerely acknowledge the valuable contributions of the reviewer of the book Dr. Hariharan Seshadri, Associate Professor, Department of ECE, Indian Institute of Information Technology Kancheepuram for reviewing each chapter minutely, pointing out the errors and for his useful suggestions to enrich the write up and as a whole in giving a better shape of the book.

Further, I would like to thank NIT Silchar for giving a conducive environment to perform the task of writing this book. I express my sincere gratitude to my teachers, mentors in building up a sound knowledge of the subjects like, Digital Electronics, Computer Architecture, Microelectronics, DSP etc. which helped me in writing this book.

I sincerely acknowledge the helping hand of my co-author Dr. Risha Mal for contributing a few chapters and Mr. Jayanta Kar, Md. Sheikh, for their support in verifying the lab experiments through physical connections through microprocessor and microcontroller kits, also, in listing the content of the book. Special thanks to my family members, specially my mother, Kiron Bala Choudhury for her constant encouragement, my wife, my son and my daughter Subhashree for their constant support and inspiration towards the completion of the book.

This book is an outcome of various suggestions of AICTE members, experts and authors who shared their opinion and thought to further develop the engineering education in our country. Acknowledgements are due to the contributors and different workers in this field whose published books, review articles, papers, photographs, footnotes, references and other valuable information enriched us at the time of writing the book.

Prof. Saurabh Chaudhury

Dr. Risha Mal

PREFACE

The book titled "Microprocessor and Microcontroller" is an outcome of the rich experience of our teaching the subject and exposure to various other fundamental courses. This book aims at giving the readers specially, the second-year undergraduate students a thorough knowledge of microprocessors and microcontrollers in a best possible way. It is written in a very lucid manner so as to understand the underlying concepts easily. Keeping in mind the purpose of wide coverage as well as to provide essential supplementary information, we have included the topics recommended by AICTE, in a very systematic and orderly manner throughout the book. The book begins with a brief history on the evolution of computers and processors for making the subject interesting. Further, starting from the very basic microprocessor 8085 and the basic microcontroller 8051, the book gradually progresses towards advanced microprocessors and microcontrollers in the most appropriate manner. Looking into the level of maturity of students, the contents are covered in depth, explained in a reader-friendly manner with explanatory examples and designed appropriately. The book gives a comprehensive view of microprocessors and microcontrollers which would be also useful for self-study purposes.

During the process of preparation of the manuscript, we have considered the various standard text books and accordingly we have developed sections like critical questions, solved and supplementary problems etc. Apart from illustrations and examples as required, we have enriched the book with numerous solved problems in every unit for proper understanding of the related topics. Under the common title "Microprocessors and Microcontrollers" there are many books. However, most of the books have given emphasis to one particular microprocessor or microcontroller and none is complete in the sense of current book, where, we have included the basic microprocessor, 8085 and progressed through 8086 to some of the advanced microprocessors such as Pentium. Similarly, starting with 8051 microcontroller we have given coverage to ARM based microcontrollers which is the core component of any embedded system today. Further, we have included the relevant laboratory practicals and presented it in the form of a manual in appendix which the students will find easy to perform experiments. Annexure includes the hex code corresponding 8085 assembly language.

As far as the present book is concerned, it is meant to provide a thorough understanding on microprocessors and microntrollers on the topics covered. This book will prepare students to apply the knowledge in solving engineering challenges and many real-life problems. The subject matters are presented in a constructive manner so that an Engineering degree prepares students to work in different sectors or in research centres at the very forefront of technology.

We sincerely hope that the book will inspire the students to learn architectural innovations and programming skills of various microprocessors and microcontrollers which will surely contribute to the development of a solid foundation of the subject. We would be thankful to all beneficial comments and suggestions which will contribute to the improvement of the future editions of the book. It gives us immense pleasure to place this book in the hands of the students. It was indeed a big pleasure to work on different aspects of coverage in the book.

Prof. Saurabh Chaudhury

Dr. Risha Mal

OUTCOME BASED EDUCATION

For the implementation of an outcome based education the first requirement is to develop an outcome based curriculum and incorporate an outcome based assessment in the education system. By going through outcome based assessments evaluators will be able to evaluate whether the students have achieved the outlined standard, specific and measurable outcomes. With the proper incorporation of outcome based education there will be a definite commitment to achieve a minimum standard for all learners without giving up at any level. At the end of the programme running with the aid of outcome based education, a student will be able to arrive at the following outcomes:

PO1. **Engineering knowledge:** Apply the knowledge of mathematics, science, engineering fundamentals, and an engineering specialization to the solution of complex engineering problems.

PO2. **Problem analysis:** Identify, formulate, review research literature, and analyze complex engineering problems reaching substantiated conclusions using first principles of mathematics, natural sciences, and engineering sciences.

PO3. **Design / development of solutions:** Design solutions for complex engineering problems and design system components or processes that meet the specified needs with appropriate consideration for the public health and safety, and the cultural, societal, and environmental considerations.

PO4. **Conduct investigations of complex problems:** Use research-based knowledge and research methods including design of experiments, analysis and interpretation of data, and synthesis of the information to provide valid conclusions.

PO5. **Modern tool usage:** Create, select, and apply appropriate techniques, resources, and modern engineering and IT tools including prediction and modeling to complex engineering activities with an understanding of the limitations.

PO6. **The engineer and society:** Apply reasoning informed by the contextual knowledge to assess societal, health, safety, legal and cultural issues and the consequent responsibilities relevant to the professional engineering practice.

PO7. **Environment and sustainability:** Understand the impact of the professional engineering solutions in societal and environmental contexts, and demonstrate the knowledge of, and need for sustainable development.

PO8. **Ethics:** Apply ethical principles and commit to professional ethics and responsibilities and norms of the engineering practice.

PO9. **Individual and team work:** Function effectively as an individual, and as a member or leader in diverse teams, and in multidisciplinary settings.

PO10. **Communication:** Communicate effectively on complex engineering activities with the engineering community and with society at large, such as, being able to comprehend and write effective reports and design documentation, make effective presentations, and give and receive clear instructions.

PO11. Project management and finance: Demonstrate knowledge and understanding of the engineering and management principles and apply these to one's own work, as a member and leader in a team, to manage projects and in multidisciplinary environments.

PO12. Life-long learning: Recognize the need for, and have the preparation and ability to engage in independent and life-long learning in the broadest context of technological change.

COURSE OUTCOMES

After completion of the course the students will be able to:

Students will be able to:

CO-1: Understand and Compare Fundamentals of Microprocessors and Microcontrollers

CO-2: Illustrate Architecture of AT 8051Microcontroller

CO-3: Implement Assembly Language Programs for Data Manipulation

CO-4: Interface I/O and Peripheral Devices with AT 8051 Microcontroller

CO-5: Implement Communication Standards and Protocols

CO-6: Understand Architecture of ARM (RISC) Microcontroller

GUIDELINES FOR TEACHERS

To implement Outcome Based Education (OBE) knowledge level and skill set of the students should be enhanced. Teachers should take a major responsibility for the proper implementation of OBE. Some of the responsibilities (not limited to) for the teachers in OBE system may be as follows:

- Within reasonable constraint, they should manoeuvre time to the best advantage of all students.
- They should assess the students only upon certain defined criterion without considering any other potential ineligibility to discriminate them.
- They should try to grow the learning abilities of the students to a certain level before they leave the institute.
- They should try to ensure that all the students are equipped with the quality knowledge as well as competence after they finish their education.
- They should always encourage the students to develop their ultimate performance capabilities.
- They should facilitate and encourage group work and team work to consolidate newer approach.
- They should follow Blooms taxonomy in every part of the assessment.

Bloom's Taxonomy

Level	Teacher should Check	Student should be able to	Possible Mode of Assessment
Create	Students ability to create	Design or Create	Mini project
Evaluate	Students ability to justify	Argue or Defend	Assignment
Analyse	Students ability to distinguish	Differentiate or Distinguish	Project/Lab Methodology
Apply	Students ability to use information	Operate or Demonstrate	Technical Presentation/ Demonstration
Understand	Students ability to explain the ideas	Explain or Classify	Presentation/Seminar
Remember	Students ability to recall (or remember)	Define or Recall	Quiz

GUIDELINES FOR STUDENTS

Students should take equal responsibility for implementing the OBE. Some of the responsibilities (not limited to) for the students in OBE system are as follows:

- Students should be well aware of each UO before the start of a unit in each and every course.
- Students should be well aware of each CO before the start of the course.
- Students should be well aware of each PO before the start of the programme.
- Students should think critically and reasonably with proper reflection and action.
- Learning of the students should be connected and integrated with practical and real life consequences.
- Students should be well aware of their competency at every level of OBE.

ABBREVIATIONS AND SYMBOLS

List of Abbreviations

General Terms			
Abbreviations	**Full form**	**Abbreviations**	**Full form**
A/D	**Analog to digital**	**ALU**	**Arithmetic/logic unit**
ARM	**Advanced RISC Machines**	**ALE**	**Address Latch Enable**
BTB	**Branch target buffer**	**ASCII**	**American Standard Code for Information Interchange**
CISC	**Complex instruction set computer**	**BIU**	**Bus interface unit**
CPI	**Cycles per instruction**	**BCD**	**Binary coded decimal**
CU	**Control Unit**	**CWR**	**Control word register**
CPU	**Central Processing Unit**	**CSMA**	**Career sense multiple access collision avoidances**
DMA	**Direct Memory Access**	**IR**	**Instruction Register**
DTE	**Data terminal equipment**	**I2C**	**Inter-Integrated Circuit Bus**
DCE	**Data Communication Equipment**	**LIFO**	**Last in first out**
EU	**Execution unit**	**LSB**	**Least significant bit**
FPU	**Floating point unit**	**FPGAs**	**Field programmable gate arrays**
GPU	**Graphics Processing Unit**	**INTR**	**Interrupt Request**
I/O	**Input/output**	**ICs**	**Integrated Circuits**
MAC	Media Access Control	**NMI**	**Non-maskable interrupt**
MMU	**Memory management unit**	**MCU**	**Microcontroller unit**
SU	**Segmentation Unit**	**SoC**	**System on Chip**
PC	**Personal computer**	**ROM**	**Read only memory**
PU	**Paging unit**	**RAM**	**Random access memory**
UART	**Universal Asynchronous Data Receiver &Transmitter**	**MPU**	**Microprocessor unit**
SCADA	**Supervisory Control and Data Acquisition**	**MIPS**	**Million instructions per second**
WPAN	**wireless personal area networks**	**RISC**	**Reduced instruction set computer**
SPI	**Serial Peripheral Interface**	**SFRs**	**Special function registers**
MOS	**Metal-oxide semiconductor**	**SR**	**Status Register**
VLSI	**Very large-scale integration**	**PSW**	**Program status word**
TLB	**Translational look-aside buffer**	**MSB**	**Most significant bit**

List of Symbols

Symbols	Description	Symbols	Description
t_H	Data hold time	T	T-states
t_{DSW}	Data set up time	f	Clock frequency
t_{PWH}	Enable pulse width		

LIST OF FIGURES

CONTENTS

List of Tables

Chapter 1

Fundamentals of Microprocessors and Microcontrollers

Key Features of Module-1

- Definition and significance of microprocessors and microcontrollers
- Brain vs Computer
- History, growth and evolution of computers
- Overview of 8085 and 8086 processors
- Fundamentals of microcontrollers
- Comparison of 8-bit, 16-bit and 32-bit microcontrollers
- Microcontrollers for Embedded Systems design

Pre-requisites

- Fundamentals of Digital Electronics
- Basics of Computers

Module-1 Outcomes

- Students should be able to understand the fundamentals of 8085 and 8086 processors specifically, the architecture, addressing modes and instruction set
- Students should be able to write assembly language programs for 8085 and 8086 processors
- Should be able to understand the fundamentals of microcontrollers, difference between microprocessor and microcontroller
- Should be able to understand embedded systems and its characteristics and the role of microcontrollers in the embedded systems applications

This chapter gives an overview of general structure of microprocessors and microcontrollers, an analogy between the human *brain versus computer*, history, growth and *evolution of computers*. Progress in microprocessors and advances in semiconductor technology, *microcomputer systems* and the classification of computers are then illustrated. It further introduces the readers about representation of data and how the binary data in the form of 0 and 1 are manipulated by the processor when written in *machine language*, *assembly language* (abbreviated form of instruction or mnemonics) or *high-level languages* such as FORTRAN, BASIC, C, C++ or Java. The major component of the chapter is the overview of **8085** and **8086** microprocessors. It covers the architecture, instruction set, addressing modes, interrupts, instruction cycles. The chapter also encompasses the fundamentals of microcontroller architecture beginning with 8-bit microcontroller such as **8051** and then a comparison of it with the other *microcontrollers* namely, 16-bit and 32-bit is also illustrated. Lastly, at the end of the chapter a brief introduction is given to *embedded systems* and its characteristics. Also, on how microcontrollers can be used to design an embedded system.

1.1 Introduction

Microprocessor can be considered as the brain of a digital computer. It plays a significant role in our day to day life in today's digital era. It can be viewed as a programmable logic device that can be used to control processes or can be used to turn on/off any mechanical, electrical or electronic devices. Microprocessor can also be viewed as data processing or computing unit of a computer or any other digital systems. It is a programmable integrated circuit capable of computing and decision making similar to the **central processing unit (CPU)** of a computer. Many a times the term microprocessor and CPU are used synonymously. Every computer, like human brains, contains a processor able to interpret and execute programs; has a memory for storing the programs and the data it processes; and has input output devices for transferring the information from the computer to the outside world and vice-versa. Today we find the uses of microprocessor enormous. Apart from the general computing systems, it is being widely used in consumer products, medical equipment, smart cars and many other embedded applications.

1.1.1The Brain versus the Computer

From the time immemorial humans relied on their brains to perform calculations, as if they were the computers. As the civilization progressed through many generations, a variety of computing tools were invented but could not replace manual computations. But if the size and complexity of the calculation increases, two major limitations of human computation that become apparent.

- The speed at which human brains can compute is limited
- Humans are so badly prone to error.

Even with these limitations, we can make an analogy between the human brain and the computer. Consider the course of actions needed by human brain in order to manually fill up an income tax return form. First of all, human need paper to store information. The information that can be stored include a list of instructions—more commonly known as *programs, algorithm or procedure* (in the sense of digital computers) to carry out the calculation, as well as numbers or *data* to be used. Some relevant information can be gathered either from radio, television, newspaper, internet etc. We can consider them as input devices. Data processing takes place in human brain which acts like the *processor or CPU.* During the process of calculation human need to store intermediate results as well as final results on the paper (like a *memory* or *storage device*). It is quite apparent that human brain performs two distinct functions. First, it interprets the instructions and *controls* the flow of processing the instructions and ensures that they are executed in a proper sequence. Secondly, the *execution* function that includes some specific tasks such addition, subtraction, multiplication and division. Usually, a calculator aids in doing such calculations to the brain. After the completion of the task, the results may be uploaded over the internet or may be furnished to an organization which can be considered as the output devices. Figure 1.1 illustrates, the analogy between the brain and the computer.

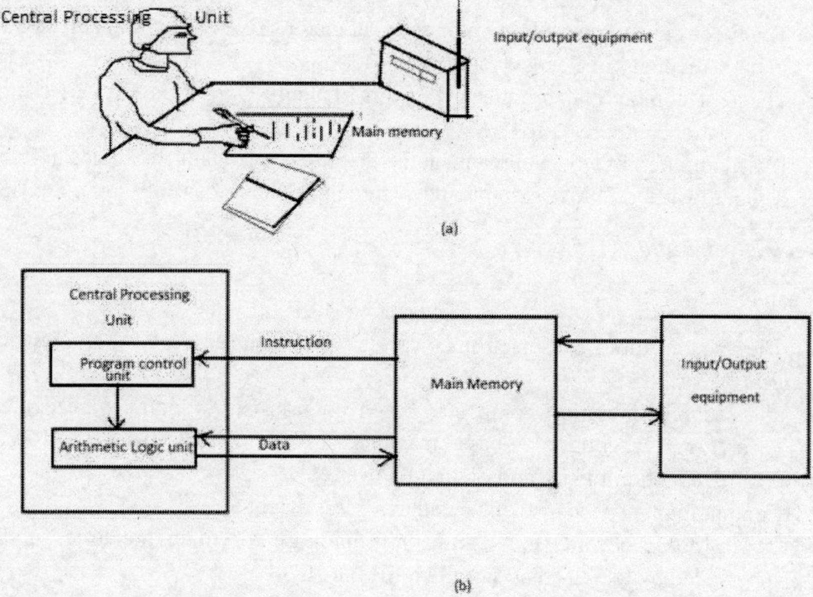

Fig.1.1: Brain Vs. Computer

1.1.2 History and Evolution of Computers

Like human civilization computers also have evolved through centuries for many generations to reach to the level of today. People thought of computation and performing some elementary operations such as addition, subtraction, multiplication and division long back in 16th century or even earlier [1]. In those days these were some clever mechanical devices designed with gears, levers, wheels and the like.

1.1.2.1 The Mechanical Era

- Blaze Pascal [1623-62], a French philosopher first invented an early, influential mechanical calculator that could add or subtract decimal numbers.
- Gottfried Leibniz [1946-1716], in Germany extended Pascal's design to perform multiplication and division.
- Charles Babbage's difference engine in the 19th century to perform multistep operations automatically without human intervention at every step.
- Some later developments in the design of general-purpose program-controlled computer includes Z1 in 1938 (still a mechanical computer from Germany), Z3 in 1941,
- an automatic calculator known as Harvard Mark I in 1944 from Harvard University.

1.1.2.2. Electronic Age

The mechanical computers suffered from two serious limitations: it is inherently slow in computation because of its movable parts and the transmission of information by mechanical means is unreliable. Moreover, the size is also very large. With the development of electronic valves and vacuum tubes in early 1900, permitted the processing and storage of digital data at a much higher speed than that of any mechanical device.

The first generation (1940-1950)

- First by John V. Atanasoff (1903-95), at Iowa State University, in late 1930s

- The Electronic Numeric Integrator and Calculator (ENIAC) by Mauchly and Eckert in the University of Pennsylvania, 1943-46
- The first commercial product by Eckert-Mauchly Corp was UNIAC (Universal Automatic Computer) in 1951.
- IAS Computer, by von Neumann, at the Institute for Advanced Studies in Princeton began to work on the design of a new stored program electronic computer, 1947

***The second generation* (1954-64)**

Key Features

- The vacuum tubes and electronics valves were soon replaced by *bipolar junction transistors*, in 1947
- the second-generation computers based on transistors soon replaced the first-generation of vacuum tube-based machines
- drastic reduction in size and cost and power.
- Computational speed also enhanced to a great extent.
- *ferrite cores* became the dominant technology for main memories until it is superseded by the all-transistor memories in 1970s.
- Magnetic disks became the principal technologies for secondary memories since then.
- With the introduction of *index* registers, it is possible to have indexed instructions, which increments or decrements the designated index I.
- Another innovation in second generation was the introduction of program-control instructions: *call* and *return* which allow the linking of programs.
- It allowed to perform operations on *floating point numbers,*
- With the introduction of *compilers* in has become possible to write instructions in high level language.
- For system management, *batch processing* came into existence. Batch processing makes use of supervisory program known as *batch monitor* which is a rudimentary version of *operating system,* which is a system program designed to manage computer's resources efficiently.

***The third generation* (1965-75)**

Key Features

- introduction of silicon based integrated circuits (ICs) in the design of computer hardware, in 1961
- This replaced all the second-generation computers designed with discrete transistors,
- reduced size, cost and enhanced the speed.
- The most significant event during this period was the recognition of the need to *standardize the computers*,
- more and more software were developed and used more efficiently.
- IBM developed the most influential third-generation computer, the System/360 which was announced in 1964 and came in the year 1965.
- Since then System/360 became the *de-facto* standard and all the models in the series are *software compatible* with each other (share common instruction set).
- Introduction of *status register* (SR) to save the *program status word,* for any exceptional conditions, errors, divide by zero or any urgent service requests such as interrupts.

- ***The VLSI Era***

With the advent of integrated circuits (IC) in 1959 at Texas Instruments [2] and its commercialization in1961, the dominant technology for manufacturing the computer logic circuits and memory has been the ICs. Initially, the ICs started with few transistors (less than 100) and gradually progressed through technology advancements allowing more and more devices to be accommodated in a single chip with the advent of *metal-oxide semiconductor* (MOS) ICs. This has resulted in medium scale (MSI), large scale (LSI) and *very large scale integrated* (VLSI) circuits containing 1000, 10000 and millions of transistors, respectively. This allowed to fabricate CPU, main memory, *multichip module* or even all the electronic circuits of a computer on a single chip at a very low cost [3]. This is an enormous advancement allowing to develop a wide range of machines starting form portable personal computers, microcontrollers to supercomputers containing thousands of CPUs.

1.1.3 Growth in IC

With the invention of CMOS devices in 1960s there was a rapid growth in silicon-based ICs. An enormous growth in processor design and in the design of memories had been observed. Looking into pattern of growth in IC, Gordon Moore, a co-founder of Intel 1965 prophesies that growth in ICs will double in every 24 months, popularly known as *Moore's law* [4]. Fig. 1.2 shows the growth in ICs in processor hardware and future trend up to 2025. It initially followed a linear rate, but after mid-1990s it deviated from Moore's law and followed an exponential growth rate. However, Moore's law still remains a business standard in other design fronts such as, in number of processor cores, in the design of pipelining stages or in selecting the clock frequency for next generation computers.

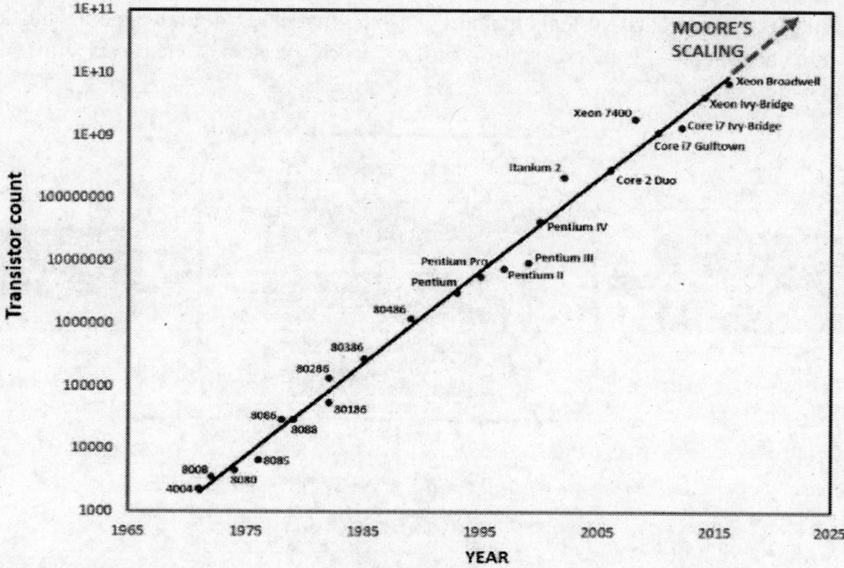

Figure1.2: Growth in IC (processors) in terms of transistor counts over the years (Courtesy- ResearchGate)

1.1.4 Microprocessor versus Microcontroller

Microprocessor is a programmable logic device, built on electronic circuit, which is capable of taking binary instructions from a storage device called *memory*, operates on binary data (*input*) according to the instructions and produces results (*output*). Usually, microprocessor is the essential part of a general-purpose computing system. A typical programmable computing system consists of four components: microprocessor, a high-speed memory, input and output devices as shown in Fig.1.3. Any users program can be carried out using these four components often known as the *hardware*. Users *program* is nothing but a set of instructions. A group of programs is commonly known as *software*. Such a system can be used to carry out any mathematical function or it can be used to design traffic light control. Depending upon the type of applications, such a system can be simple or highly sophisticated (high performing). Accordingly, the microprocessor can be implemented to design reconfigurable processors, domain specific processors and application specific processors apart from general purpose. However, we can in general classify the microprocessors into two categories-*reprogrammable systems* and *embedded systems*. In reprogrammable systems such as microcomputers, the microprocessor is used for computing and data processing. Such a system includes a general-purpose processor, a mass storage device, such as disk and CD-ROMs and peripheral devices such as, printers, scanners: personal computer (PC) is a perfect example for this. While in embedded systems, the microprocessor is used for specific task and it is not reprogrammable to the end users. It is a part of the consumer product. Microprocessors used in such a system are categorised as *microcontrollers,* which includes the components as shown in Fig.1.4. Microcontroller is essentially an entire computer on a single chip which houses, memory, I/O interfacing circuits, A/D converters, serial I/O and timers. While embedded systems can be viewed as products or systems that use microprocessor or a microcontroller to perform a specific task. Examples of embedded systems include, Washing machines, digital cameras, traffic light control, automobile dashboard control, antilock braking system in smart cars, cruise control and many more.

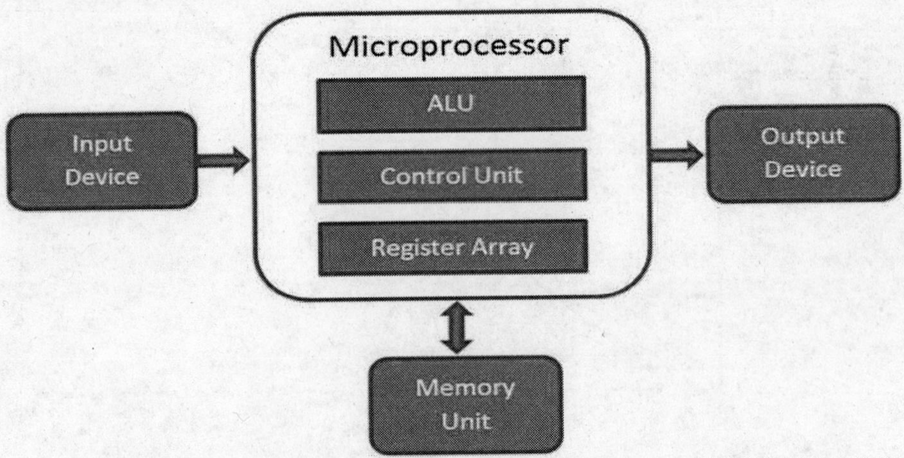

Fig.1.3: General-purpose computing system with microprocessor as CPU

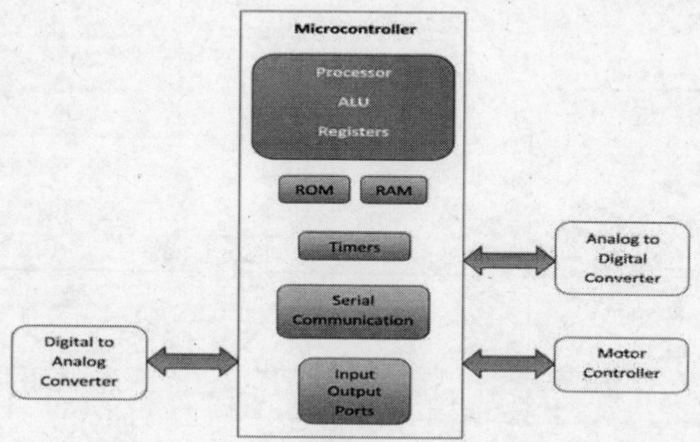

Fig.1.4: Basic architecture of Microcontroller

1.2 The Microcomputer and the Microprocessor based System

The computers that are designed with microprocessor are known as microcomputers and is one among many microprocessor-based systems. The general organization of such a system is shown in Fig. 1.5. It has three major components, the *microprocessor*, *I/O* (input/output) and the *memory* (read/write memory and read only memory). These components are connected by a high-speed communication path known as *bus.* Each of these components are called sub-systems and the entire unit is referred to as a system or a *microcomputer system.* Thus, microprocessor is only one component of the microcomputer whereas, the microcomputer is a complete system like other computers, except that the function of CPU is performed by the microprocessor. As it is apparent from the Fig. 1.2 that 4-bit and 8-bit microprocessors came around 1975-80. Initially they were used in the area of machine control and instrumentation. However, as the price went down with the advancement in technology, microprocessors began to use in many application areas, such as for video games, word processing, small-business applications. Early microcomputers were designed with 8-bit microprocessor. As the technology progressed through, other higher bits microprocessors (16-bit, 32-bit and 64-bit) such as 8086,80286/386/486, Pentium, Pentium-Pro, Pentium 4, Motorola 68000 and Power PC became available and the present microcomputers are built around these microprocessors.

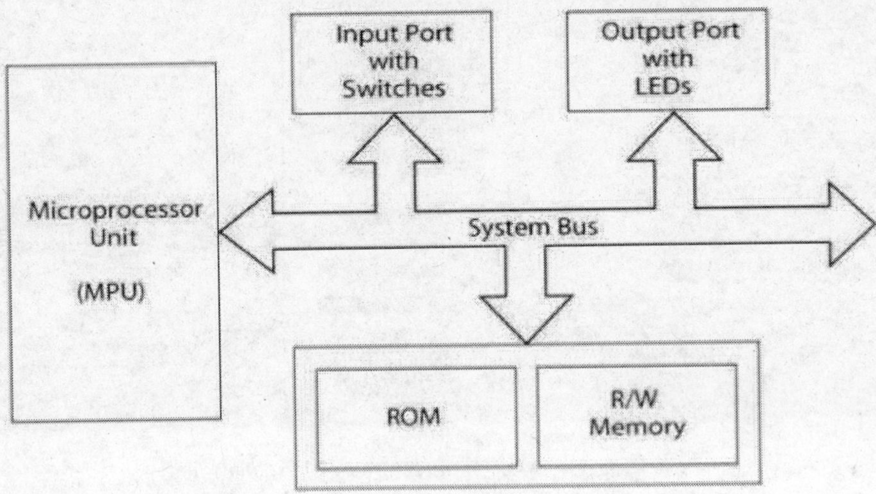

Figure 1.5: General organization of a Microprocessor based System

The Central Processing Unit (CPU)

We have seen so far microprocessor as the essential component of a digital computer. The structure of a computer is represented in the form of block diagram as in Fig.1.3. It has four major components: memory, input, output and the central processing unit (CPU). The CPU is comprising of an arithmetic/logic unit (ALU) and the control unit. It also contains some internal registers to store data temporarily.

The Arithmetic/Logic Unit (ALU)

The ALU performs the basic arithmetic operations such as addition, subtraction, multiplication, division and the logical operations such as AND, OR, NOT.

The Control Unit

The control unit generates a set of control signals which enters into the ALU unit (commonly known as data-path unit) at appropriate point and time and controls the sequence of events for the task to be completed faithfully by the ALU. In other words, the synchronisation and timing for communication is carried out by the control unit. It consists of instruction decoder, counters and a control unit that generates control signals.

Basic functions of CPU

The CPU fetches instructions from the memory, decodes the instructions and performs (executes) the task specified in the instructions. It also communicates with input and output devices to receive or send data. Various steps involved are

- It fetches instructions from the memory
- Determines what function it has to do (i.e. decodes the instruction)
- Performs the function in ALU unit (execution)

While execution some major tasks are need to be carried out. These are as follows:

- Transfer of data from register to register in CPU itself
- Transfer of data between CPU register and specified memory location
- Performing ALU operation on data from a specific memory location or designated CPU register

- Directing CPU to change the sequence of fetching instruction if the processing of data identifies a specific condition
- It looks for special control signals such as interrupts and provides appropriate responses

With the advent of IC technology, it is possible to build CPU on a single chip. A computer designed with a microprocessor acting as its CPU is known as microcomputer. The term, *microprocessor* and the *microprocessor unit (*MPU) are often used synonymously. Again, a computer may have a single processor acting as a CPU or it can have multiple processors acting as the CPU. Thus, many a times, microprocessor and the CPU are used synonymously to mean the same.

Address Bus

It consists of set of connected wires known as bus which carries the address, to identify a memory location or an I/O port. It is usually a binary pattern of 0s and 1s. For example, an 8-bit address bus has eight lines thus it can identify $2^8 = 256$ different locations. So, the locations in hexadecimal format can be written as 00H – FFH. It is unidirectional.

Data Bus

The data bus is used to transfer data either between memory and processor or between I/O device and processor and vice-versa. For example, an 8-bit processor will generally have an 8-bit data bus and a 16-bit processor will have 16-bit data bus. It is bidirectional.

Control Bus

The control unit in the processor generates the control signals and the control bus carry those signals, which consists of signals for selection of memory or I/O device from the given address, selecting and controlling the appropriate functional units also for direction of data transfer and synchronization of data transfer in case of slow devices.

1.2.1 Classification of Computers

Computers can be broad classified into following three categories: *Large/main frame*, *mini* and *micro-computers*.

Large general-purpose computers are usually owned by a big organization with multi-user and multi-tasking capabilities designed to perform complex scientific and engineering problems and also for handling records of big organization or government agencies. These are categorised into two: *the main frames* and *supercomputers*. Examples of these include IBM *main frame* computers, System/390 series, Fujitsu GS8800 and the Hitachi MP5800, Cray-2. [5]

Whereas, medium-size computers or the *minicomputers* are usually a departmental level computer or the computer of a small factory, with relatively lesser size, reduced computational capability and less cost than the main frame computers. A typical example of this is Digital Equipment PDP 11/45.

Micro-computers again can be classified into: Personal computers (PC)-desktops/laptops, Workstations, single board and single chip microcomputers (microcontrollers).

1.2.2 Microprocessor Instructions and Programming Languages

Microprocessor understands only binary language. Each microprocessor has its own binary words, meaning and language. A binary word is defined as the number of bits the microprocessor can recognize and process at a time. Accordingly, there are 4-bit (small), 8-bit, 16-bit, 32-bit and 64-bit (large) microprocessors. Every computer has its own set of instructions depending upon the design of its CPU or of its microprocessor. However, to communicate with the computer, it is necessary to give instructions in binary form which is commonly known as **machine language**. For example, 8085 microprocessor uses 8-bit words to write instruction. Thus, its instruction set is composed of various combination of these eight-bit words. Following are the two examples of 8085 instructions:

0011 1100 = an instruction to increment the number in the accumulator by 1

1000 0000 = an instruction that adds the number in the register B with the content of the accumulator and keep the sum in the accumulator

But it is difficult for most of the people to write programs using binary instructions. Programmers prefer to write instructions and programs using a much simpler and short form symbolic codes **(mnemonics)** known as **assembly language.** For example, if we would like to represent the earlier binary code 0011 1100 (or in Hex code, 3CH) in mnemonic is INR A,

INR A: INR means increment and A stands for accumulator. The symbol indicates the operation of incrementing the accumulator content by 1.

ADD B: ADD means addition, and B represents the content in register B. This symbol indicates to add the content of register B with accumulator content and keep the result in accumulator.

However, the instruction written in assembly language are machine dependent. So they cannot be transferred from one machine to the other. To get rid of this problem, some machine independent languages such as BASIC, FORTRAN, PASCAL, C, C++, JAVA are evolved. These are referred to as **high level languages**, which are English-like, taking symbols and conventions from English. The instructions are written in statements rather than mnemonics. But the English-like languages the machine cannot understand, so there is need for translator translating these languages to machine language. So, there is a need either for a **compiler** or an **interpreter.** The compiler or the interpreter is essentially a program that takes high level language as input or source code and converts into machine specific object code understandable by that computer only. During the process of conversion, it also checks for syntax errors etc. if any in the source code. While a compiler reads the entire source code or program first and then translates or converts into machine code that is executable by the processor. The interpreter takes one instruction at a time and produces an object code and executes it before taking another instruction. Writing programs in high level language has an obvious advantage that the designing the code and debugging is very easy. Finding an error is easier when written in high level language rather than the assembly language.

1.3 Overview of 8085 Microprocessor

8085 microprocessor is an 8-bit processor developed by Intel corporation in the year 1976. Although it is the most basic processor but it has all the important features of today's higher bit microprocessors. So, to understand the internal architecture of a microprocessor it is better to start with a simple processor.

Key Features of 8085

- It is an 8-bit processor
- It is a single chip MOS device with 40 pins

- It has 8-bit data bus and 16-bit address bus. However, the lower order address and data are multiplexed (AD0-AD7)
- It works on +5V DC power supply
- It has a maximum clock frequency of 3MHz where the minimum frequency is 500 KHz
- It has five addressing modes
- It can address up to 64 k memory locations
- Its instruction set consisting of 72 instructions
- To address an I/O or peripheral device it uses both memory-mapping as well as IO mapped IO. It uses 16 bit addresses for memory-mapped IO and 8 bit addresses for IO mapped IO
- It is a CISC processor and uses five stage execution unit

1.3.1 PIN Diagram and Architecture of 8085

The 8085 microprocessor is an IC having 40 pins. The layout of which is shown in Fig. 1.6 and Fig.1.7. The signals which are connected to these pins can be classified into six groups. These are

- Address bus
- Data bus
- Control & status signals
- Power supply and frequency signals
- Externally initiated signals
- Serial I/O signals

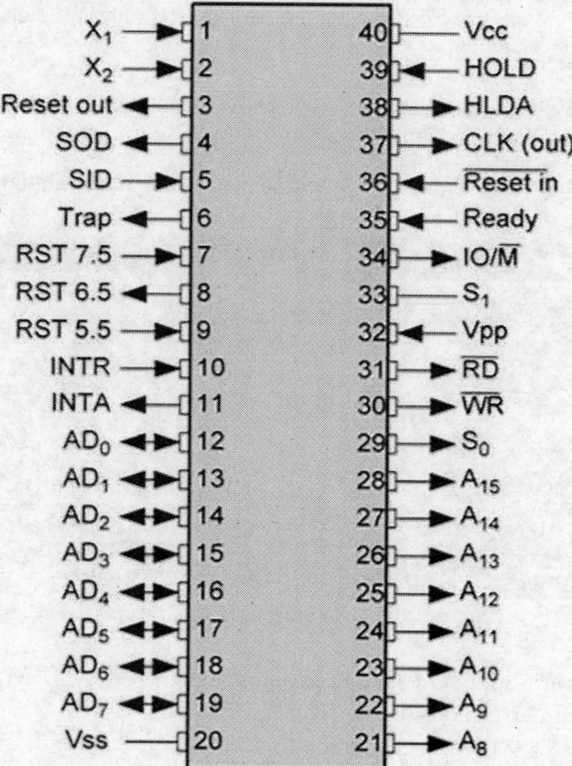

Figure 1.6: 8085 Microprocessor Pin layout and associated signals

1.3.1.1 The address bus and Data bus

Address bus is 16-bit wide and consists of 16 signal lines/wires for communication. Higher order address bus consists of bit lines (A8-A15) which is unidirectional. Usually goes to tri-state/high impedance state during HOLD and HALT mode. Lower order address consists of bit lines (A0-A7) is multiplexed with data bus. Thus, we have multiplexed address/data bus (AD0-AD7) and is bidirectional. It behaves as address bus during first clock cycle. In the subsequent clock cycles (3rd and 4th) it acts as data bus. These 8 signal lines goes to tri-state/high impedance state in HOLD and HALT mode.

1.3.1.2 Control and Status signals

This group consists of the following signals,

- ALE : Address Latch Enable
- $\underline{RD}$: Read control signal
- $\underline{WR}$: Write control signal
- IO/$\underline{M}$, S1 and S0 : Status signal

ALE occurs during the first clock cycle of a machine state and enables the address to get latched. The falling edge of ALE guarantee the setup and hold times for the address information. ALE can also be used to strobe the status information. It is never tri-stated.

IO/$\overline{M}$ is a status signal used to differentiate between I/O and memory operations. When this signal goes high it indicates an I/O operation and when it is low indicates a memory operation. This signal is usually combined with $\overline{RD}$ and $\overline{WR}$ signals to generate control signals for I/O and memory.

S1and S0 are the status signals similar to IO/$\overline{M}$, however, they are rarely used in small systems. The following table shows various machine cycles and associated status signals.

Table 1.1: Machine cycles and status signals

Operations	IO/$\overline{M}$	S_0	S_1
Opcode Fetch	0	1	1
Memory Read	0	1	0
Memory Write	0	0	1
I/O Read	1	1	0
I/O Write	1	0	1
Interrupt Ack.	1	1	1
Halt	High Impedance	0	0

1.3.1.3 Power Supply & Clock Frequency Signals

Again, this group consists of four signals,

□ Vcc : +5 V DC power supply

□ Vss :Ground

□ X1, X2 : Crystal Oscillator with a frequency of 6 MHz is connected to these two pins

□ CLK : Clock output

1.3.1.4 Externally Initiated Signals and Interrupts

- $\overline{RESETIN}$: When the signal on this pin goes low, the PC is set to 0 and the buses are tri-stated and the processor is reset.
- RESET OUT: This signal indicates that the processor is in reset state. The signal can be used to reset other devices.
- READY: When this signal goes low, the processor waits for an integral number of clock cycles until it goes high.
- HOLD: This signal indicates that a peripheral such as DMA (direct memory access) controller is requesting for the use of address and data bus
- HLDA: This signal acknowledges the HOLD request
- INTR: Interrupt request is a general-purpose interrupt
- $\overline{INTA}$: This active low signal is used to acknowledge an interrupt
- RST 7.5, RST 6.5, RST 5,5 – restart interrupt: These are vectored interrupts and have the higher priority than other interrupts i.e. INTR
- TRAP: This is a non-maskable interrupt and has the highest priority

1.3.1.5 Serial I/O Signals

This group consists of only two signals,

- SID: Serial input signal. Bit on this line is loaded to D7 bit of register A using RIM instruction.
- SOD: Serial output signal. Output SOD is set or reset by using SIM instruction

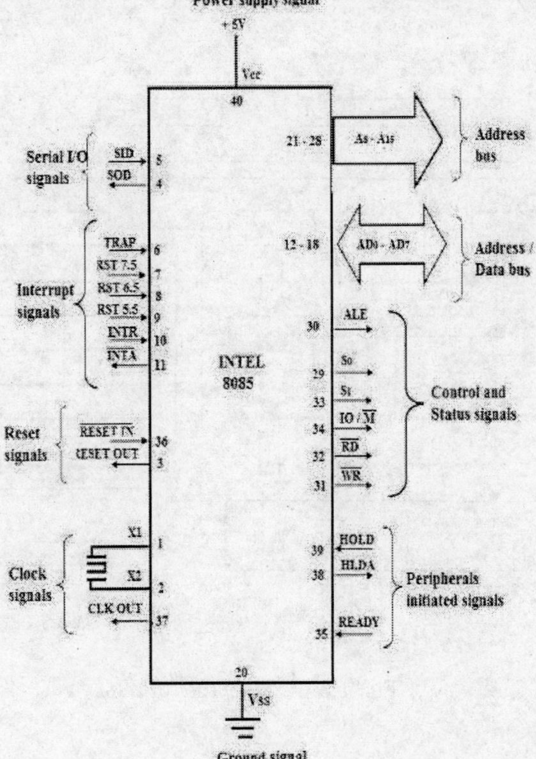

Fig. 1.7: Pin layout of 8085 according to Signal Groups

1.3.2 Architecture of 8085 microprocessor

A microprocessor's architecture is often specified with its instruction set, addressing modes, data types and their formats, design of its CPU, main memory and IO subsystem. The logic design of the microprocessor is usually called as the **architecture**. Microprocessor is a programmable logic device designed with registers, flipflops and timing circuitries. It has a set of instruction to manipulate data and communicate with peripherals. The microprocessor can be programmed to perform various tasks on a given data by selecting necessary instruction from its set. It can also respond to external signals. Various functions of microprocessor can be classified into:

- Microprocessor-initiated operations
- Internal operations
- Peripheral or externally initiated operations

Microprocessor needs a group of logic circuits and a set of control signals to perform all these functions. Today's microprocessors have all these modules housed in a single chip whereas earlier processors did not have all the necessary components in one chip. The complete unit were made up of more than one chip. Thus, the term *microprocessing unit* (MPU) is often used to represent these group of devices to perform all these functions like a CPU. Therefore, the term *MPU* and *microprocessor* are often used synonymously.

The architectural diagram of 8085 microprocessor is shown in Fig.1.8. It consists of the ALU (the arithmetic/logic unit), PC, control unit, instruction register and instruction decoder, register array and the busses. The address and data bus are already illustrated in earlier section. Rest of the modules will be discussed here briefly.

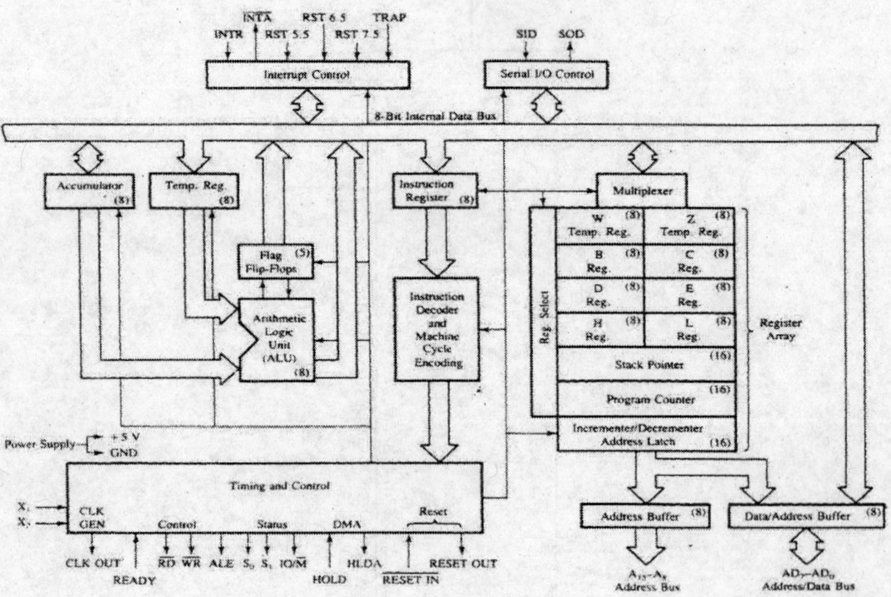

Fig. 1.8: Architecture of 8085

The ALU

The arithmetic/logic unit or the ALU performs various computing functions. These are basically the arithmetic operation such as addition, subtraction and logic operations such as

AND, OR, XOR. For data manipulation, it takes help of Accumulator and a temporary register which are considered as a part of ALU.

The Register Array

It is consisting of various registers identified as B, C, D, E, H, L. These are primarily used to store data temporarily during program execution and are accessible to the user through instructions. They can be used singly either to store 8-bit data or can be used in pair (such as BC, DE or HL) for 16 bit-operations. The register pair HL is also used as data pointer (holds memory address).

The 8085 microprocessor also has an accumulator and a temporary register for the data processing by the ALU, which not accessible by the user. The accumulator is used to store 8-bit data and also to store the result of an ALU operation.

Flag Registers

The ALU also contains a 8-bit flag register to accommodate 05 flags. These flags set or reset according to the program operation, i.e. data condition in A or other registers. These are

- *Zero (Z)* : it is set if the result of an arithmetic operation is zero
- *Carry (CY)* : is set if there is a carry/borrow after arithmetic operation
- *Sign (S)* : is used to indicate the sign of data in the accumulator
  - is set to 1 if negative and set to 0 (reset) if positive
- *Parity (P)* : is set if the number is even and reset if the number is odd
- *Auxiliary Carry (AC)*: is set if there is a carry out from bit 3 position

Most commonly used flags are-Zero, Carry and Sign. Microprocessor uses these flags to test data conditions before jumping.

The Control Unit

It provides necessary timing and control signals to all the operations. Also control flow of data between microprocessor and main memory/peripherals. A bit pattern usually called micro-program initiates execution of an instruction. By setting a sequence of control signal, it selects appropriate logic circuits in ALU and performs the task. Control signals are communicated through the control bus.

Program Counter and SP

The program counter (PC) is a16 bit registers to hold memory addresses. Memory addresses are of 16-bit. The PC is used to sequence the execution of instruction. It points to memory address where from next byte to be fetched.

The stack pointer or SP is a memory pointer to point memory location in R/W memory, called stack. It is also a 16-bit register. Beginning of stack is defined by loading a 16-bit address in SP. Stack is an area of memory used to hold data that will be retrieved soon. The stack is usually accessed in a Last in First out (LIFO) fashion.

Instruction Register (IR) and Decoder

These are some non-programmable registers. Instructions are stored in IR after being fetched by the processor. Decoder decodes the instruction in IR.

1.3.2.1 Addressing Modes

It specifies the way to represent the data to be operated on by the instruction. In other words, the addressing modes indicates the formats of specifying the operands. The 8085 microprocessor has the following five different types of addressing modes.

- Immediate addressing
- Memory direct/Direct addressing
- Register direct addressing
- Indirect addressing
- Implicit (or implied) addressing

Immediate Addressing

In immediate addressing the operand is present in the instruction itself. The operand (either a byte or a word) will be either transferred to a register or a memory location. For example,

MVI A, 32H : means the immediate operand 32H is to be transferred to the register A.

MOV A, #6AH: means copy the immediate operand 6AH to accumulator.

The format of immediate addressing is shown in Fig. 1.9a, while program memory and immediate data, how is being transferred to accumulator is shown in Fig. 1.9b.

(a)

Immediate Addressing Mode

Instruction	Opcode	Bytes	Cycles
MOV A, #6AH	74H	2	1

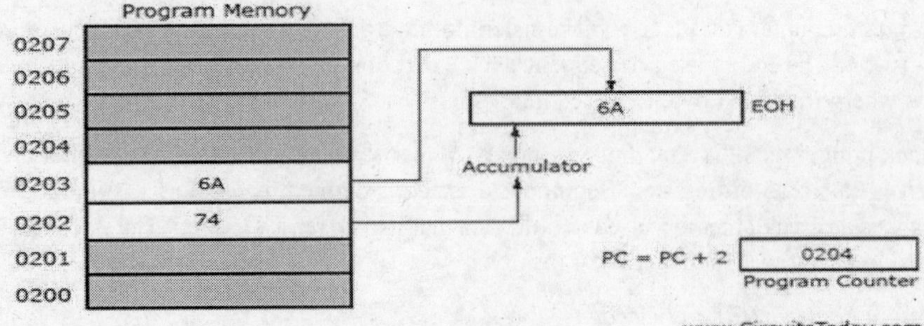

Fig. 1.9 (a) Format of immediate addressing and (b) Program memory and immediate data

Memory direct/ Direct addressing

This type of addressing indicates that data transfer operation is direct. The address of a memory location where the operand is stored is directly specified in the instruction. For example,

LDA 2051H : it means load the content of the memory location specified by 2051H into accumulator register (A). A pictorial representation of this mode of operation is shown below in Fig.1.10.

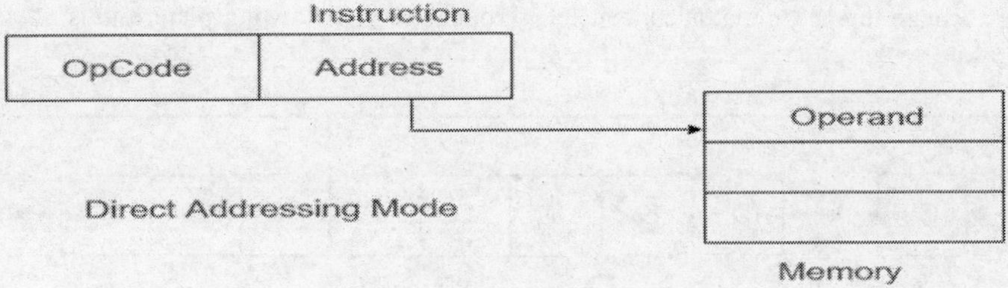

Fig.1.10: Direct Addressing Mode

Register Direct Addressing

This type of addressing refers to transfer of the data byte or a word directly from one register to the other. For example, MOV A, C: it means copy the content of register C to register A. Fig.1.11 depicts the pictorial representation of this mode of operation. For more on addressing scan the QR code:

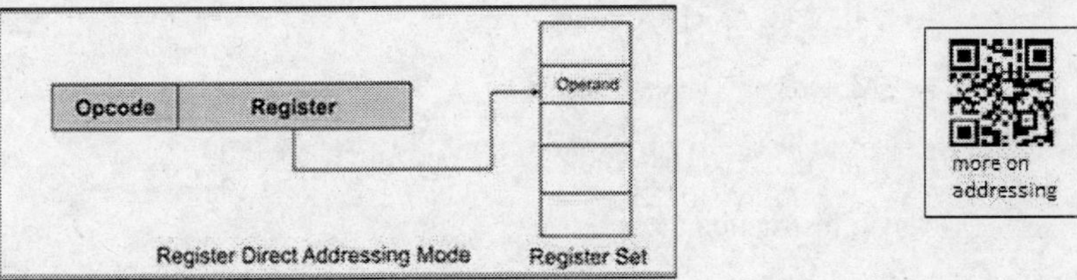

Fig.1.11: Register Direct Addressing process

Indirect Addressing

Indirect addressing refers to data transfer (byte or a word) between a register and a memory location specified by register pair. For example,

MOV B, M : copy the data byte into register B from the memory location specified by the address in the register pair HL. Fig.1.12 represents indirect mode of addressing.

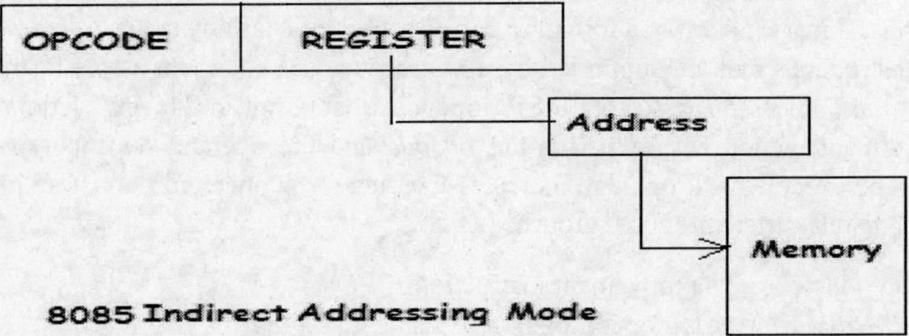

Fig.1.12: Indirect Addressing process

Implied or Implicit Addressing

In this type of addressing no operand is needed. The operand is implicitly present there in the opcode/ instruction itself. For example,

CMA : complement the content of the accumulator,

RAL : Rotate the content of accumulator to the left

RLC : Rotate the accumulator content left through carry. Following picture illustrates the same.

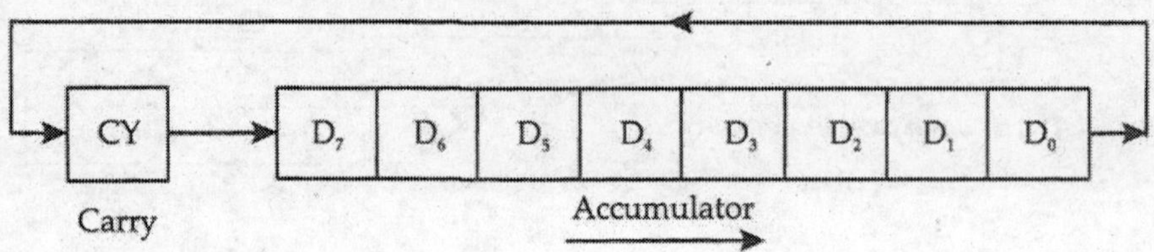

Again, there may be one byte, two byte or three bytes in an instruction which will correspond to equal number memory addresses where they will be stored. As such, processors dealing with corresponding such instructions are known as *1-Address, 2-Adress or 3-Adress* machines. Examples of which are as follows:

- One byte Instruction
  - MOV C, A (Hex code: 4FH)
  - ADD B (Hex code: 80H)
  - CMA (Hex code: 2FH)---Implicit operand
- Two-byte Instruction
  - MVI A, 32H (Hex 3E : first byte, 32 : second byte
  - MVI B, F2H (Hex 06: first byte, F2 : second byte
- Three-byte Instruction
  - LDA 2050H (Hex code: 3A:first byte, 50:second byte, 20: 3rd byte)
  - JMP 2085H (Hex code: C3: 1st byte 85: 2nd byte 20: 3rd byte)

1.3.2.2 Instruction Set

Instruction is a binary pattern or a format to perform a specific task by the processor. The entire group of instructions that are supported by a microprocessor is known as the instruction set. The 8085 microprocessor has a total of 74 opcodes that result in 246 instructions (with all variants). An instruction has two parts-the *opcode* and the operand. Opcode specifies the function to be executed and operand indicates the data to be operated on. These instructions can be broadly classified into three groups.

- Data transfer or data movement instructions
- Data Processing (ALU operations)
  - Arithmetic instructions
  - Logic instructions

- Program Control
  - Branch instruction
  - Machine control instructions

Data Transfer Instructions

These are a group of instructions used to copy data from one location (source) to another (destination). Such an operation does not modify the source register content. Following are the various types of instructions under data processing depending upon the type of source and destination.

- Instruction Types:
  - Between registers (example, B to D)
  - A specific data byte to a register or a memory location (example, load B with 32H)
  - Between a memory location and a register (example, from location 2000H to B)
  - Between I/O device and accumulator (example: Keyboard to accumulator)
  - Between registers and stack memory

Some illustrating examples are given in the following table.

Mnemonics	**Examples**	**Operation**
MOV, Rd, Rs	MOV B, A MOV C, B	Copy data from source register Rs to destination register Rd
MVI R, 8-bit	MVI A, 8FH	Load 8-bit data (immediate) into a register
LXI Rp	LXI D, 2051H	Load 16-bit data (immediate) into the register pair, DL
IN 8-bit	IN 01H	Read the data from an input device (port) and place it in the accumulator
OUT 8-bit	OUT 08H	Write the 8-bit data from accumulator to an output device (port)
LDA 16-bit	LDA 2050H	Copy the data byte into A from the memory specified by 16-bit address
STA 16-bit	STA 2075H	Copy the data byte from A to the memory location specified by 16-bit address
LDAX Rp	LDAX B	Copy the data byte into A from the memory location specified by address stored in the register pair BC
STAX Rp	STAX H	Copy the data byte from A to the memory location specified by the address in the register pair HL

MOV R, M	MOV B, M	Copy the data byte into register B from the memory location specified by the address in register pair HL (indirect address)
MOV M, R	MOV M, A	Copy the data byte from the register to the memory location specified by the address in the register pair HL (indirect address)
LHLD 16-bit address	LHLD 2040H	This instruction copies the data byte from the memory location specified by the address into L and copies the content of next memory location to H
SHLD 16-bit address	SHLD 2032H	This instruction stores the data bytes from L registers into the memory location specified by the address and from H to the next memory location by incrementing the operand
SPHL none	SPHL	Stores the content of register pain H and L into the stack pointer register. H provides the higher order address while L stores the lower order address
PUSH Rp	PUSH B	Content of the register pair are copied into stack. Stack pointer register is first decremented and content of higher order register is copied. Again, stack pointer is decremented and the content of lower order register is copied there.
POP Rp	POP H	Content of the memory location pointed out by the stack pointer register is loaded into the register C, E or L (lower order byte). The stack pointer is then incremented by 1 and the content of that memory location is copied to register B, D or H (higher order byte)

Data Processing (Arithmetic and Logic) Instructions

This group includes all the instructions needed for arithmetic operations and logical operations which comprise of the following instruction types.

- Arithmetic Operations
  - Addition (any 8-bit number, contents of register or contents of memory location can be added with accumulator content)
  - Subtraction (performed in 2's complement)
  - Increment/Decrement: contents of a register or register pair can be incremented/decremented by 1
    - Deals with one register or one location

- Logical Operations
  - AND, OR, Exclusive-OR
    - any 8-bit number, contents of register or contents of memory location can be logically ANDed, ORed or XORed with accumulator content
  - Rotate: each bit of accumulator can be shifted left or right
  - Compare: for equality, greater than or less than
  - Complement: Each bit of accumulator contents

Some of the important instructions under this are shown next in the table.

Mnemonics	Instruction/Example	Operation
ADD R	ADD B	Add the content of register B with the content of A
ADI 8-bit	ADI 4FH	Add the 8-bit data (immediate) with the content of A
ADD M	ADD M	Add the content of the memory location specified by register pair HL with the content of A
SUB R	SUB D	Subtract the content of register from the content of A
SUI 8-bit	SUI 32H	Subtract the data byte from the content of A
SUB M	SUB M	Subtract the content of the memory location specified by register pair HL from the content of A
INR R	INR B	Increment the content of register
INR M	INR M	Increment the content of memory location specified by register pair HL
DCR R	DCR C	Decrement the content of the register
DCR M	DCR M	Decrement the content of memory location specified by register pair HL
INX RP	INX B	Increment the content of the register pair
DCX Rp	DCX H	Decrement the content of the register pair
ANA R	ANA B	Logically AND the content of register B with that of A
ANI 8-bit	ANI 4DH	Logically AND the data-byte with the content of A
ANA M	ANA M	Logically AND the content of memory location specified by the register pair HL with that of A
DAD Rp	DAD H	16-bit content of the specified register pair will be added with the content of H and L register and the result will be saved in HL pair.
ORA R	ORA C	Logically OR the content of register with that of A
ORI 8-bit	ORI 4FH	Logically OR the 8-bit data with that of A
ORA M	ORA M	Logically OR the content of memory location specified by the register pair HL with that of A
XRA R	XRA D	Logically XOR the content of register with that of A

XRI 8-bit	XRI 7BH	Logically XOR the 8-bit data with that of A
XRA M	XRA M	Logically XOR the content of memory location specified by the register pair HL with that of A
CMP R	CMP B	Compare the content of B with that of A for less than, Equal to or greater than
CPI 8-bit	CPI 4FH	Compare 8-bit data with the content of A for less than, equal to or greater than

Program Control Instructions

This group includes all the instructions needed for branching operations as well as for machine control operations. These can be further classified as follows:

- Jump:
  - Conditional Jump
    - Test for certain condition (e.g. zero or carry flag)
  - Unconditional jump
    - Call, Return and Restart: change the sequence of instruction execution
  - By calling a subroutine
  - Returning from a subroutine
- Machine Control Operation
  - Halt, Interrupt or do nothing

Following are typical program control instructions.

Mnemonics	**Instruction/Example**	**Operation**
JMP 16-bit address	JMP 2050H	Change the sequence of program execution form the specified 16-bit address
JZ 16-bit address	JZ 2070H	Change the sequence of program execution form the specified 16-bit address when Zero Flag is set
JNZ 16-bit address	JNZ 2080H	Change the sequence of program execution form the specified 16-bit address when Zero Flag is reset
JC 16-bit address	JC 2025H	Change the sequence of program execution form the specified 16-bit address when Carry Flag is set
JNC 16-bit address	JNC 2030H	Change the sequence of program execution form the specified 16-bit address when Carry Flag is reset
CALL 16-bit address	CALL 2175H	Change the sequence of program execution to the location of a subroutine
RET None	RET	Return to the calling program after completing the execution in subroutine
HLT None	HLT	Stop processing of instructions and wait
NOP None	NOP	Do not perform any operation

DI None	DI	Disable or reset the interrupt enable flip-flop and all the interrupts except the TRAP are disabled
EI None	SI	Set the interrupt enable flip-flop and all the interrupts are re-enabled except the TRAP

These are some of the typical and most widely used instructions. There are many other instructions in the set of 8085 instructions which includes other 16-bit operations, additional jump instructions and conditional Call and Return instructions. Interested readers are advised to go through the QR link for further details.

more on 8085

Example 1

Write a program to subtract two numbers 49H from 4FH already stored in two memory location 2051H and 2052H respectively and save the result in memory location 2053H. Instructions begin at 2030H.

Mnemonics	Memory location	HEX code
LDA 2051H	2030	3A
	2031	51
	2032	20
MOV B, A	2033	47
LDA 2052H	2034	3A
	2035	52
	2036	20
SUB	2037	90
STA 2053H	2038	32
	2039	53
	203A	20
HLT	203B	76
//Manual load	2051	49
	2052	9F
	2053	00

1.3.2.3 Instruction Timing diagram and Machine Cycle

Microprocessor runs with a *global clock*. Every action of the processor is initiated with reference to this clock either at leading/trailing edge. Any operation involving read/write operation or data transfer with the action of control signals, IO/$\overline{M}$, S1 and S0 can be displayed in the form of a timing diagram.

A *machine cycle* is the time taken by the microprocessor to complete the task of accessing memory or I/O devices. Various operations like opcode fetch, memory read, memory write, I/O read, I/O write etc. are performed in a machine cycle. Each cycle of the clock is known as *T-sate*. Thus, a machine cycle will have many states. As both the instruction and data are stored in memory, so the microprocessor fetches the instruction first to read the instruction or data and then executes the instruction.

An *instruction cycle* thus consisting of two step operation: fetch and execute. This may take typically 1-5 machine cycles involving 3-6 T-states. For example, the first machine cycle in every instruction is the opcode fetch which requires at least 4T states as in Fig. 1.9.

Example 2

Illustrate the steps involved and timing diagram of data flow when the instruction MOV C, A (Hex code: 4FH) stored in 2005H is being fetched.

Step 1: Microprocessor places 16-bit address from the PC on the address bus

- This is accomplished in T1 cycle
- ALE goes high
- IO/M-bar goes low

Step 2: Control unit sends RD-bar control signal to enable the memory chip

- Initiates it in clock cycle T2 and continues up to T3

Step 3: Byte from the memory location is placed on the data bus (AD7-AD0)

- RD-bar signal goes high
- Bus goes to high impedance state

Step 4: The byte is placed in the instruction decoder and the task is carried out as per instruction

- The task of decoding and execution is performed in T4 clock (if data is one byte)

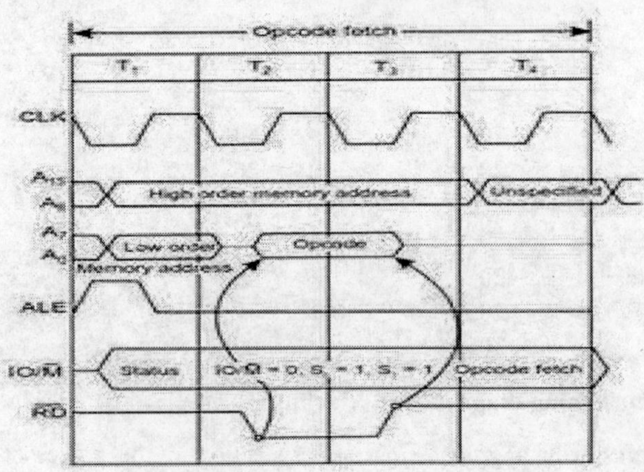

Fig 1.8 Opcode fetch machine cycle

Fig. 1.13: Opcode Fetch Machine Cycle

Similarly, the instruction cycle for the instruction MVI A, 32H is shown below which consists of two machine cycles M1 and M2 with opcode fetch (M1) and memory read (M2). Opcode fetch takes 4T states whereas, memory read requires 3T states as shown in Fig. 1.10.

Execution of an Instruction: MVI A, 32h

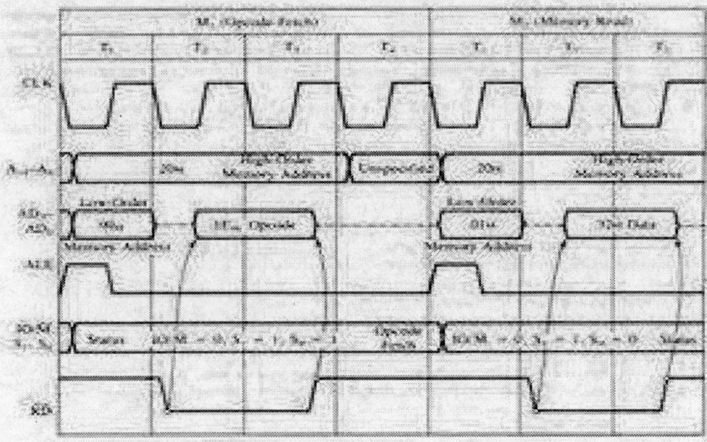

Fig. 1.14: Execute cycle

If we assume a clock frequency of 2MHz, then the execution time for memory read cycle and the instruction cycle can be calculated as follows:

- Clock frequency = 2MHz
- T-state = 1/2MHz = 0.5μS
- Execution time for Opcode Fetch = 4T = 2 μS
- Execution time for Memory Read = 3T =1.5μS
- Execution time for the Instruction =7T = 3.5μS

Example 3

Program to add two 8-bit numbers with a provision of Carry.

Program

MVI C, 00 //Clear Reg C for carry

LDA 4100 //Load accumulator with the data byte from memory location 4100H

MOV B, A //Transfer the data to register B

LDA 4101 //Load the second data from memory location 4101H

ADD B // Add the content of register B with that of accumulator

JNC L1 //If no carry is generated jump to step 8 levelled L1

INR C //else, increment register C by 1 to indicate a carry

L1 STA 4200 // Store the result in the memory location 4200H

MOV A, C // Transfer the content of register C to accumulator

STA 4201 //Store the carry to memory location 4201H

HLT/RST //End the program with Halt (HLT) or go back to monitor program with

//Restart (RST)

Example 4

Reverse a string of numbers.

Program:

```
MVIB, 06      // Initialize one register (Reg B) with the length of the string
LXI H, 8100 // Initialize one register pair (HL) with the starting address of the source array
LXI D, 8205 // Initialize one register pair (DE) with ending address of the destination array

L1: MOV A, M  //Move the memory content to accumulator
STAX D  // Store the accumulator content in DE pair
INX H    // Increment HL pair
DCX D  //Decrement DE pair
DCR B  // Decrement the counter register – Reg B
JNZ L1  //Check for zero, if not zero, go to step 4
RST1    //Stop
```

//Some sample data input and output

Input		Output	
8100	0A	8200	0F
8101	0B	8201	0E
8102	0C	8202	0D
8103	0D	8203	0C
8104	0E	8204	0B
8105	0F	8205	0A

1.4 8086 Microprocessor-An Overview

Key Features

- First 16-bit processor introduced by Intel in 1978
- It is a 40-pin DIP IC, works on 5MHz clock
- Consists of 29,000 transistors
- Have more powerful and high-speed computational resources
- Have more powerful instruction set compared to 8085 processor
- 20-bit Address bus
- 16-bit Data bus
- Addressed memory size is 1M
- Can address up to 4 segments of 64KB
- 8088 is a less expensive version of 8086 that uses 8-bit data bus

1.4.1 **PIN Diagram of 8086**

The pin-diagram 8086 processor is shown in Fig. 1.11. It is a 40-pin dual-in-line (DIP) package IC and works on 5MHz clock with a +5V dc power supply. 8086 is designed to operate in two modes, Minimum and Maximum. It can prefetch up to 6 instruction bytes from memory and queues them in order to speed up instruction execution. Various groups of signals associated with the pins are described next.

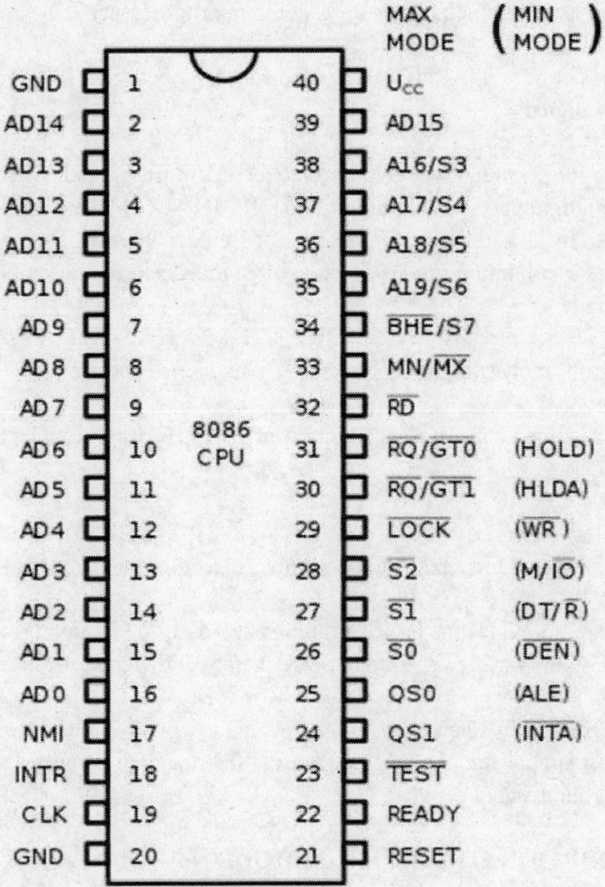

Fig.1.15: Pin Diagram of 8086 Microprocessor

AD0-AD15

These signal lines are associated with pins [16-2 & 39] These are. multiplexed bidirectional address/data bus. In T1 cycle, they carry lower order 16-bit address. In the remaining clock cycles, they carry 16-bit data. Lower order data byte is carried by AD0-AD7 while AD8-AD15 carry the higher order byte of data.

A19/S6, A18/S5, A17/S4, A16/S3

These signal lines are associated with the pin [35-38]. These are unidirectional multiplexed address and status bus. During T1 cycle, they carry higher order address (4-bits) while in the remaining clock cycles, they carry status signals.

BHE / S7

BHE stands for Bus High Enable. It is associated with Pin 34. BHE signal is used to indicate the transfer of data over higher order data bus (D8 – D15). 8-bit I/O devices use this signal. It is multiplexed with status pin S7.

READY

Pin 22 is associated with this signal. This is an acknowledgement signal from slower I/O devices or memory. It is an active high signal. When it goes high, it indicates that the device is ready to transfer data. When it goes low, microprocessor is then in wait state.

RESET

Pin 21 is associated with this signal. It is a system reset and active high signal. When it goes high, microprocessor enters into reset state and terminates the current activity. It must be active for at least four clock cycles to reset the microprocessor.

RD (Read)

This signal is connected to Pin 32. It is used for read operation. It is an output signal. It is an active low signal

MN / MX

Connected to Pin 33. 8086 works in two modes: **Minimum Mode, Maximum Mode.** If MN/MX is high, it works in minimum mode. If MN/MX is low, it works in maximum mode. Pins 24 to 31 issue two different sets of signals. One set of signals is issued when CPU operates in minimum mode. Other set of signals is issued when CPU operates in maximum mode.

INTR

It is an interrupt request signal connected to Pin 18. It is active high. It is level triggered

NMI

It is a non-maskable interrupt signal connected to Pin 17. It is an active high, edge triggered interrupt.

TEST [at Pin 23]

It is used to test the status of math coprocessor 8087. The BUSY pin of 8087 is connected to this pin of 8086. If low, execution continues else microprocessor is in wait state.

CLK [at Pin 19]

This clock input provides the basic timing for processor operation. It is symmetric square wave with 33% duty cycle. The range of frequency of different versions is 5 MHz, 8 MHz and 10 MHz

VCC and VSS [at Pin 40 and Pin 20],

VCC is power supply signal connected to Pin 40. +5V DC is supplied through this pin. VSS is the ground signal

PIN DESCRIPTION FOR MINIMUM MODE

INTA

The signal associated with [Pin 24] is an interrupt acknowledge signal, INTA. It is active low output signal. When microprocessor receives INTR signal, it acknowledges the interrupt by generating this signal.

ALE

The signal at [Pin 25] is ALE, which is called Address Latch Enable signal. It indicates that a valid address is available on bus AD0 – AD15. It is an active high output signal and remains high during T1 state. It is connected to enable pin of latch 8282.

DEN

[Pin 26] is DEN signal or a Data Enable signal. This is an active low output signal. This signal is used to enable the transceiver 8286. Transceiver is used to separate the data from the multiplexed address/data bus.

DT / R_bar

[Pin 27] is a DataTransmit/Receive signal. It decides the direction of data flow through the transceiver. When it is high, data is transmitted out. When it is low, data is received in.

M / IO

[Pin 28] is a signal issued by the microprocessor to distinguish memory access from I/O access. When it goes high, memory is accessed. When it goes low, I/O devices are accessed.

WR

[Pin 29] is a Write signal. It is an active low output signal. This is used to write data in the memory or output device based on the status of M/IO signal.

HLDA

HLDA is attached to [Pin 30]. It is a Hold Acknowledge signal. It is issued after receiving the HOLD signal. It is an active high output signal.

HOLD

[Pin 31] is for HOLD signal. In DMA mode of data transfer when the DMA controller needs to use address/data bus, it sends a request to the CPU through this pin. It is an active high input signal. When microprocessor receives HOLD signal, it issues HLDA signal to the DMA controller.

DMA stands for Direct Memory Access which allows I/O devices to directly access memory with less participation of the processor. It is a hardwired-controlled data transfer technique. In this mode, the external hardware which is the DMA controller, takes over the charge of processor busses for data transfer. Suppose, disk controller is ready to transmit the information from the disk, it transfers a DMA request (DRQ) signal to the DMA controller. The DMA controller then sends a HOLD signal to the processor's HOLD input. The processor in reply to this signal suspends the buses and transfers an HLDA acknowledgment signal. When the DMA controller gets the HLDA signal, then the DMA controller gains the control of the buses, it transfers the memory address where the first byte of information from the disk is to be written. It also transfers a DMA to acknowledge (DACK) signal to the disk controller device to signal it to get ready for transferring the output byte. However, in this mode, the device can make only one byte or word transfer. After each transfer, DMAC gives the control of all buses to the processor. HOLD signal will be reasserted when the I/O device is ready again to transfer next byte or word.

PIN DESCRIPTION FOR MAXIMUM MODE

QS1 and QS0

These two signals are assigned to [Pin 24 and 25]. These pins provide the status of instruction queue. For example, when QS1 QS0 = 00, means no operation, for 01, it indicates 1st byte of opcode from queue, 10 means Empty Queue and 11 means subsequent byte from queue.

S0, S1, S2

[Pin 26, 27, 28] are for three status signals (S0, S1, S2) which indicate the operation being done by the microprocessor. This information is required by the Bus Controller 8288. Bus controller 8288 generates all memory and I/O control signals. With S0, S1 and S2 there can be 8 possible combinations. These are as follows.

0 0 0 => Interrupt Acknowledge
0 0 1 => I/O Read
0 1 0 => I/O Write
0 1 1 => Halt
1 0 0 => Opcode Fetch
1 0 1 => Memory Read
1 1 0 => Memory Write
1 1 1=> Passive

LOCK

[Pin 29] is for the signal LOCK. This is an active low output signal and it indicates that other processors should not ask CPU to relinquish the system bus. When it goes low, all the interrupts are masked and HOLD request is not granted. This pin is activated by using LOCK prefix on any instruction.

RQ/GT1 and RQ/GT0

[Pin 30 and 31] are associated with these two signals. They are bi-directional. These are Request/Grant pins. Other processors request the CPU through these lines to release the system bus. After receiving the request, CPU sends acknowledge signal on the same lines. RQ/GT0 has higher priority than RQ/GT1.

1.4. 2 Architecture of 8086

8086 provides an improved architecture over 8085. It is a 16-bit processor supported by 16-bit ALU, a set of 16-bit registers. It has a segmented memory addressing capability. It also includes a rich instruction set with a powerful interrupt structure and fetched instruction queue for overlapped fetching and execution. The internal architecture of 8086 is shown in **Fig. 1.12**. 8086 has a pipeline architecture. Entire architecture of 8086 can be divided into two separate processing parts--*bus interface unit* (BIU) and *Execution Unit* (EU). **The *bus interface unit*** consists of circuits for physical address translation and a pre-decoding instruction byte queue (6 bytes long). Bus interface unit is responsible for establishing communication between peripheral devices (external) including memory via the bus. Moreover, 8086 can address segmented memory. So, the complete physical address which is 20-bit long is generated by adding the segment and offset register, each of which are 16-bit long.

To generate the physical address, the content of the segment register, also known as segment address is left-shifted four times and then the content of offset register also known as the offset address is added to produce a 20-bit address. For further explanation with examples refer [6]. More on memory mapping techniques will be described in Chapter 6.

The segment addressed by a segment value of 1005H can have the offset values ranging from 0000H to FFFFH i.e. a maximum of 64K memory locations can be accommodated by a segment. Thus, the segment register essentially indicates the base address of a particular segment and the offset indicates the distance of the required memory location from base address in the segment. As the offset is a 16-bit number, so each segment can have 64K locations. The bus interface unit has a separate adder to perform this address translation to obtain the physical address of peripheral device or a memory location. The segment address value is taken from an appropriate segment register depending on whether a code, data or stack to be accessed. While the offset may be the content of IP, BP, SP, SI, DI, BX or an immediate 16-bit value depending upon the type of addressing mode.

In 8085 microprocessor, instruction is first fetched and decoded and then goes to execution unit to perform the arithmetic or logic operation, during which the external bus remains idle. While in 8086, this time-slot is utilized to perform overlapped fetch and execution. While the fetched instruction is decoded and executed internally by the processor, the external bus is used to fetch next machine/instruction and arrange them in a buffer queue, known as pre-decoded instruction byte queue. It is a 6-byte long first-in first-out buffer queue. While the opcode is being fetched by the bus interface unit, the execution unit executes the pre-decoded instructions concurrently. Thus, the BIU and the EU forms the

pipeline architecture. Branch interface unit therefore manages the complete interfacing of execution unit with I/O devices or memory under the control of timing and control unit.
The execution unit contains the register set of 8086 except the segment registers and IP. It has a 16-bit ALU to perform the arithmetic and logic operations. It has also 16-bit flag registers which reflect the results of execution performed by the ALU. The decoding unit decodes the instructions issued by the instruction byte queue. The control unit provides the necessary timing and control signals for execution. The execution unit may pass the result to bus interface unit for saving them to external memory.

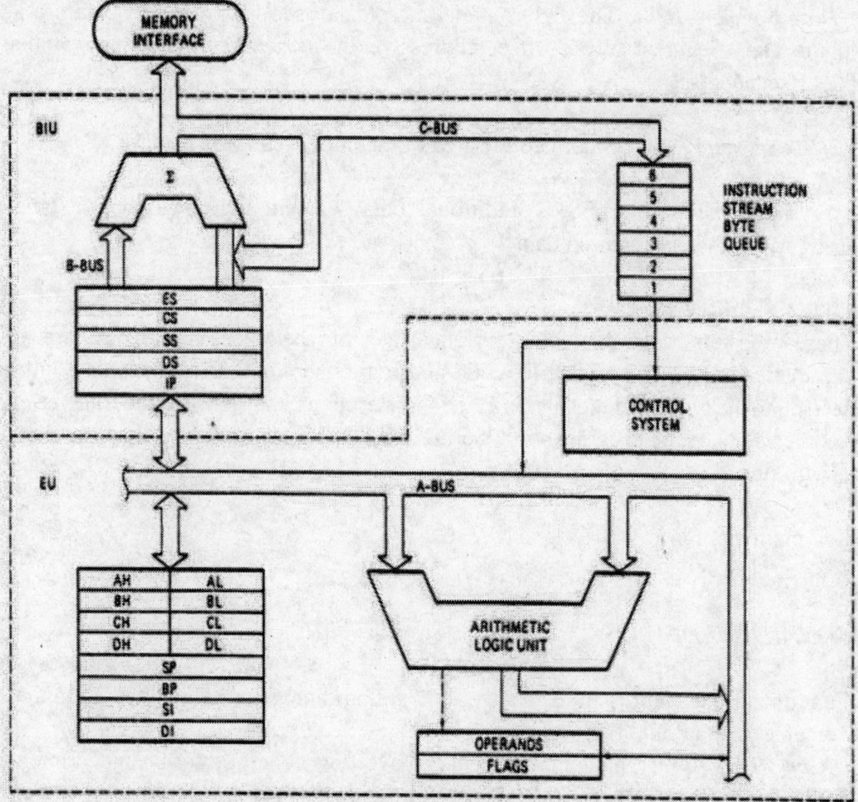

Fig. 1.16: Internal Architecture of 8086 Microprocessor {Courtesy: EEEGUIDE [7]}

1.4.2.1 GENERAL PURPOSE REGISTERS OF 8086

There are 14 user addressable registers altogether in 8086, each of which are 16-bit. Four general purpose registers- AX, BX, CX, and DX can be used as 8-bit registers individually or can be used as 16-bit in pair.

- AX Register: AX register is also known as accumulator register that stores operands for arithmetic operation like divided, rotate.
- BX Register: This register is mainly used as a base register. It holds the starting base location or the base address of a memory region within a data segment.
- CX Register: It is defined as a counter. It is primarily used in loop instruction to store loop counter.
- DX Register: DX register is used to contain I/O port address for I/O instruction.

1.4.2.2 SEGMENT REGISTERS

There are some additional registers called segment registers to generate memory address when combined with other (offset) in the microprocessor. In 8086 microprocessor, memory is divided into 4 segments as follows:
Code Segment (CS): The CS register is used for addressing a memory location in the Code Segment of the memory, where the executable program is stored.

- *Data Segment (DS):* The DS contains most data used by program. Data are accessed in the Data Segment by an offset address or the content of other register that holds the offset address.

- *Stack Segment (SS):* SS defined the area of memory used for the stack.

- *Extra Segment (ES):* ES is additional data segment that is used by some of the string to hold the destination data

1.4.2.3 Flag Registers

These registers determine the current state of the processor. They are modified automatically by CPU after arithmetic and logic operation operations. They allow us to determine the type of the result, and also to determine conditions for the transfer of control to other parts of the program. In 8086 there are 9 flag registers and they are divided into two groups:

1. Conditional Flags
2. Control Flag

CONDITIONAL FLAGS

Conditional flags represent the status of the last arithmetic or logical operation that is executed. Conditional flags are as follows:
1. *Carry Flag (CF):* This flag represents an overflow condition for unsigned integer arithmetic operation. It is also used in multiple-precision arithmetic.
2. *Auxiliary Flag (AF):* If any arithmetic operation performed in ALU results in a carry/barrow from the lower nibble (i.e. D0 – D3) to the upper nibble (i.e. D4 – D7), then the AF flag is set i.e. carry given by D3 bit to D4 is AF flag. This is not a general-purpose flag, it is used internally by the processor to perform Binary to BCD conversion.
3. *Parity Flag (PF):* This flag is used to indicate the data bits parity in the result. If the lower order 8- bits of the result contains even number of 1's, the Parity Flag is set and it is reset for odd number of 1's.
4. *Zero Flag (ZF):* This flag is set if the result of any arithmetic or logical operation is zero else it is reset.
5. *Sign Flag (SF):* In sign magnitude notation of a number, the sign of number is indicated by MSB. Usually 0 for positive and 1 for negative number. If the result of an operation is negative (i.e. MSB = 1) then sign flag is set.
6. *Overflow Flag (OF):* This occurs when signed numbers are added or subtracted. When this flag is set it indicates that the result has exceeded the capacity of machine.

CONTROL FLAGS

Control flags are set or reset deliberately by the CPU to control the operations of the execution unit. Control flags are as follows:

1. Trap Flag (TP):

- This is used for single step control.
- It allows user to execute one instruction of a program at a time for debugging purpose.
- When trap flag is set, program can be run in single step mode.

2. Interrupt Flag (IF):

- It is an interrupt enable/disable flag.
- If it is set, the maskable interrupt of 8086 is enabled and if it is reset, the interrupt is disabled.
- It can be set by executing instruction sit and can be cleared by executing CLI instruction.

3. Direction Flag (DF):

- This is used for string operation.
- If this is set then the string bytes are accessed from higher memory address to lower memory address.
- When it is reset, the string bytes are accessed from lower memory address to higher memory address.

1.4.3. ADDRESSING MODES OF 8086

The different ways in which a source operand is denoted in an instruction is known as addressing modes. There are specifically 8 different addressing modes in 8086 programming. However, considering I/O, memory locations and type of data, there are more variations. These are as follows:

Addressing Modes for Register and Immediate Data

- Register Addressing mode
- Immediate Addressing mode

Addressing modes for memory data

- Register Indirect Addressing mode
- Direct Addressing mode
- Based Addressing mode
- Indexed Addressing mode
- Base Relative Addressing mode
- Base Indexed Addressing mode
- String Addressing Mode

Addressing modes for I/O port

- Direct I/O port Addressing
- Indirect I/O port Addressing

Relative Addressing

- Implied Addressing Mode

Immediate addressing mode

The addressing mode in which the data operand is a part of the instruction itself is known as immediate addressing mode.

Example,

- MOV CX, 4929 H * ADD AX, 2387 H, * MOV AL, FFH

Register addressing mode

In this mode, the register is the source of an operand for an instruction.

Example,

```
MOV CX, AX   // copies the contents of the 16-bit AX register into
             // the 16-bit CX register),
ADD BX, AX
```

Direct addressing mode

In this addressing mode, the effective address of the memory location is written directly in the instruction.

Example

MOV AX, 1592H, MOV AL, 0300H

Register indirect addressing mode

This addressing mode allows data to be addressed at any memory location through an offset address held in any of the following registers: BP, BX, DI & SI.

Example

```
MOV AX, [BX]  //Suppose the register BX contains 4895H, then the contents
              //4895H are moved to AX
ADD CX, {BX}
```

Based addressing mode

In this addressing mode, the offset address of the operand is given by the sum of contents of the BX/BP registers and 8-bit/16-bit displacement.

Example

MOV DX, [BX+04], ADD CL, [BX+08]

Indexed addressing mode

In this addressing mode, the operands offset address is obtained by adding the contents of SI or DI register with 8-bit/16-bit displacements.

Example

MOV BX, [SI+16],
ADD AL, [DI+16]

Base-indexed addressing mode

In this addressing mode, the offset address of the operand is calculated by summing the base register with the contents of an Index register.

Example

ADD CX, [AX+SI],
MOV AX, [AX+DI]

Base Relative (displacement)addressing mode

In this addressing mode, the operands offset is obtained by summing the base register contents, with a constant offset.

Example

- MOV AX, [BP + 1],
- ADD CX, [BX+16],
- JMP [BX+1]

I/O DIRECT ADDRESSING MODES

Here the port number is a 8 bit immediate operand. This allows fixed access to ports numbered 0 to 255.

Example: OUT 05H, AL //outputs [AL] to 8-bit port 05H

INDIRECT ADDRESSING MODE

The port number is taken from DX allowing 64K 8-bit ports or 32K 16-bit ports.

Example: IN AX, DX //If [DX]=5040, Inputs the 8-bit content of port 5040 into AL and 5041 into AH.

RELATIVE ADDRESSING MODE

In this mode, the operand is specified as a signed 8-bit displacement, relative to PC (Program Counter).

Example: JNC START // if carry=0, PC is loaded with current PC contents plus the 8-bit signed value of START, otherwise the next instruction is executed.

IMPLIED ADDRESSING MODE

Instructions using this mode have no operands.

Example: CLC //This clears the carry flag to zero

1.4.4 8086 Instruction Set

The 8086 microprocessor supports 8 different classes of instructions. These are,

- Data Transfer Instructions
- Arithmetic Instructions

- Bit Manipulation Instructions
- String Instructions
- Program Execution Transfer Instructions (Branch & Loop Instructions)
- Processor Control Instructions
- Iteration Control Instructions
- Interrupt Instructions

Let us now discuss each of these instruction sets in detail along with examples.

1.4.4.1 Data Transfer Instructions

These instructions are used to transfer the data from a source to the destination. Following are the list of instructions under this group.

Instruction to transfer a word

- **MOV** – This instruction is used to copy a byte or word from a given source to a specified destination. For example,

MOV CX, 037AH, MOV AX, BX or MOV DL, [BX]

- **PUSH** – This instruction is used to put a word at the top of the stack. For example, PUSH BX, PUSH DS. The SP is decremented by 2 after PUSH operation.
- **POP** – This is used to get a word from the top of the stack to a given location. For example, POP DX, POP DS. After POP operation SP is incremented by 2.
- **PUSHA** – This is used to put all the registers into the stack.
- **POPA** – This instruction is used to get words from the stack to all registers.
- **XCHG** – This is used to exchange the data between two locations. For example, XCHG AX, DX or XCHG BL, CH
- **XLAT** – This instruction is used to translate a byte in AL using a table in the memory.

Instructions for input and output port operations

- **IN** – This is used to read a byte or word from a given port to the accumulator. For example, IN AL, OC8H or IN AX, 34H
- **OUT** – This is used to send out a byte or word from the accumulator to the intended port. For example, OUT 3BH, AL or OUT 2CH, AX.

Instructions to transfer the address

- **LEA** – This instruction is used to load the address of operand into a given register.
- **LDS** – This instruction is used to load DS register and other specified register from the memory
- **LES** – It is used to load ES register and other specified register from the memory.

Instructions to transfer flag registers

- **LAHF** – This instruction is used to load AH with the lower-order byte of the flag register.
- **SAHF** – This is used to store AH register to low-order byte of the flag register.
- **PUSHF** – This is used to copy a word in the flag register to two memory locations in the stack pointed by the stack pointer. Decrements the stack pointer by 2
- **POPF** – This is used to copy a word from two memory locations at the top of the stack to the flag register and increments the stack pointer by 2.

1.4.4.2 Arithmetic Instructions

These instructions are used to perform arithmetic operations like addition, subtraction, multiplication, division, etc.

Following is the list of instructions under this group.

Instructions to perform addition

- **ADD** – This instruction is used for the addition of the provided byte with a byte or a word with a word.
- **ADC** – This is used for addition with a carry.
- **INC** – This instruction is used for incrementing the provided byte/word by 1.
- **AAA** – This instruction is used to adjust ASCII after addition.
- **DAA** – This instruction is used to adjust the decimal after the addition/subtraction operation.

Instructions to perform subtraction

- **SUB** – This instruction is used to subtract the byte from a byte or the word from a word.
- **SBB** – This is used to perform subtraction with borrow.
- **DEC** – This instruction is used to decrement the provided byte/word by 1.
- **NPG** – This is used to negate each bit of the provided byte/word and add 1's or 2's complement.
- **CMP** – It is used to compare 2 provided byte/word.
- **AAS** – It is used to adjust ASCII codes after subtraction.
- **DAS** – This instruction is used to adjust decimal after subtraction.

Instruction to perform multiplication

MUL – Instruction to multiply unsigned byte by byte/word by word. For example,

  - MUL BH ---Multiply AL with BH; result in AX
  - MUL CX--Multiply AX with CX; result in DX (higher word) and AX (lower)

- **IMUL** – Instruction to multiply signed byte by byte or word by word. For example,
  - IMUL BH -- Multiply signed byte in AL with signed byte in BH; result in AX
  - IMUL AX --Multiply AX times AX; result in DX and AX
- **AAM** – Instruction to adjust ASCII codes after multiplication.

Instructions to perform division

- **DIV** – This instruction is used to divide the unsigned word by byte or unsigned double word by word. For example,
  - DIV BL -Divide word in AX by byte in BL; Quotient in AL, remainder in AH
  - DIV CX - Divide down word in DX and AX by word in CX; Quotient in AX, and remainder in DX.
- **IDIV** – This instruction is used to divide the signed word by byte or signed double word by word. For example, IDIV BL //Signed word in AX/signed byte in BL.
- **AAD** – This instruction is used to adjust ASCII codes after division.
- **CBW** – This is used to fill the upper byte of the word with the copies of sign bit of the lower byte.
- **CWD** – This is used to fill the upper word of the double word with the sign bit of the lower word.

1.4.4.3 Bit Manipulation Instructions

These instructions are used to perform operations where data bits are involved, i.e. operations like logical, shift, etc.

Following is the list of instructions under this group:

Instructions to perform logical operation

- **NOT** – This instruction is used to invert each bit of a byte or word.
- **AND** – Used for adding each bit in a byte/word with the corresponding bit in another byte/word. For example, AND BH, CL AND BX, 00FFH etc.
- **OR** – This instruction is used to multiply each bit in a byte/word with the corresponding bit in another byte/word. For example, OR AH, CL OR BP, SI OR BL, 80H etc.
- **XOR** – Used to perform Exclusive-OR operation over each bit in a byte/word with the corresponding bit in another byte/word.
- **TEST** – Th is used to add operands to update flags, without affecting operands.

Instructions to perform shift operations

- **SHL/SAL** – This instruction is used to shift bits of a byte/word towards left and put zero(S) in LSBs.
- **SHR** – Used to shift bits of a byte/word towards the right and put zero(S) in MSBs.

- **SAR** – This instruction is used to shift bits of a byte/word towards the right and copy the old MSB into the new MSB.

Instructions to perform rotate operations

- **ROL** – This instruction is used to rotate bits of byte/word towards the left, i.e. MSB to LSB and to Carry Flag [CF].
- **ROR** – Used to rotate bits of byte/word towards the right, i.e. LSB to MSB and to Carry Flag [CF].
- **RCR** – Used to rotate bits of byte/word towards the right, i.e. LSB to CF and CF to MSB.
- **RCL** – This is used to rotate bits of byte/word towards the left, i.e. MSB to CF and CF to LSB.

1.4.4.4 String Instructions

String is a group of bytes/words and their memory is always allocated in a sequential order.

Following is the list of instructions under this group –

- **REP** – This instruction is used to repeat the given instruction till $CX \neq 0$.
- **REPE/REPZ** – Used to repeat the given instruction until CX = 0 or zero flag ZF = 1.
- **REPNE/REPNZ** – Used to repeat the given instruction until CX = 0 or zero flag ZF = 1.
- **MOVS/MOVSB/MOVSW** – This instruction is used to move the byte/word from one string to another.
- **COMS/COMPSB/COMPSW** – Used to compare two string bytes/words.
- **INS/INSB/INSW** – This is used as an input string/byte/word from the I/O port to the provided memory location.
- **OUTS/OUTSB/OUTSW** – Used as an output string/byte/word from the provided memory location to the I/O port.
- **SCAS/SCASB/SCASW** – This is used to scan a string and compare its byte with a byte in AL or string word with a word in AX.
- **LODS/LODSB/LODSW** – Used to store the string byte into AL or string word into AX.

1.4.4.5 Program Execution Transfer Instructions (Branch and Loop Instructions)

These instructions are used to transfer/branch the instructions during an execution. It includes the following instructions –

Instructions to transfer the instruction during an execution without any condition –

- **CALL** – This is used to call a procedure and save their return address to the stack.
- **RET** – This is used to return from the procedure to the main program.
- **JMP** – This is used to jump to the provided address to proceed to the next instruction.

Instructions to transfer the instruction during an execution with some conditions –

- **JA/JNBE** – This is used to jump if above/not below/equal instruction satisfies.
- **JAE/JNB** – This is used to jump if above/not below instruction satisfies.
- **JBE/JNA** – This is used to jump if below/equal/ not above instruction satisfies.
- **JC** – This is used to jump if carry flag CF = 1
- **JE/JZ** – This instruction is used to jump if equal/zero flag ZF = 1
- **JG/JNLE** – This is used to jump if greater/not less than/equal instruction satisfies.
- **JGE/JNL** – This instruction is used to jump if greater than/equal/not less than instruction satisfies.
- **JL/JNGE** – This is used to jump if less than/not greater than/equal instruction satisfies.
- **JLE/JNG** – Used to jump if less than/equal/if not greater than instruction satisfies.
- **JNC** – This is used to jump if no carry flag (CF = 0) is set.
- **JNE/JNZ** – This is used to jump if not equal/zero flag, ZF = 0
- **JNO** – This is used to jump if no overflow i.e. OF = 0
- **JNP/JPO** – This is used to jump if not parity/parity odd PF = 0
- **JNS** – This is used to jump if not sign SF = 0
- **JO** – This is used to jump if overflow flag is set i.e. OF = 1
- **JP/JPE** – This is used to jump if parity/parity even, PF = 1
- **JS** – This is used to jump if sign flag, SF = 1

1.4.4.6 Processor Control Instructions

These instructions are used to control the processor action by setting/resetting the flag values.

Following are the instructions under this group –

- **STC** – This instruction is used to set carry flag CF to 1
- **CLC** – This is used to clear/reset carry flag CF to 0
- **CMC** – This is used to put complement at the state of carry flag CF.
- **STD** – This instruction is used to set the direction flag DF to 1
- **CLD** – This is used to clear/reset the direction flag DF to 0
- **STI** – This is used to set the interrupt enable flag to 1, i.e., enable INTR input.
- **CLI** – This is used to clear the interrupt enable flag to 0, i.e., disable INTR input.

1.4.4.7 Iteration Control Instructions

These instructions are used to execute the given instructions for number of times. Following is the list of instructions under this group –

- **LOOP** – This is used to loop a group of instructions until the condition satisfies, i.e., CX = 0
- **LOOPE/LOOPZ** – This is used to loop a group of instructions till it satisfies ZF = 1 & CX = 0
- **LOOPNE/LOOPNZ** – This is used to loop a group of instructions till it satisfies ZF = 0 & CX = 0
- **JCXZ** – This is used to jump to the provided address if CX = 0

1.4.4.8 Interrupt Instructions

These instructions are used to call the interrupt during program execution.

- **INT** – This instruction is used to interrupt the program during execution and calling service specified.
- **INTO** – This is used to interrupt the program during execution if OF = 1
- **IRET** – This instruction is used to return from interrupt service to the main program

1.4.5 8086 Interrupts

Interrupt is a method of making a temporary halt during program execution and allowing peripheral devices to access the microprocessor. The microprocessor responds to that interrupt with an **ISR** (Interrupt Service Routine), which is a short program that instructs the microprocessor on how to handle the interrupt.

The following figure (Fig. 1.13) shows the types of interrupts that are there in a 8086 microprocessor.

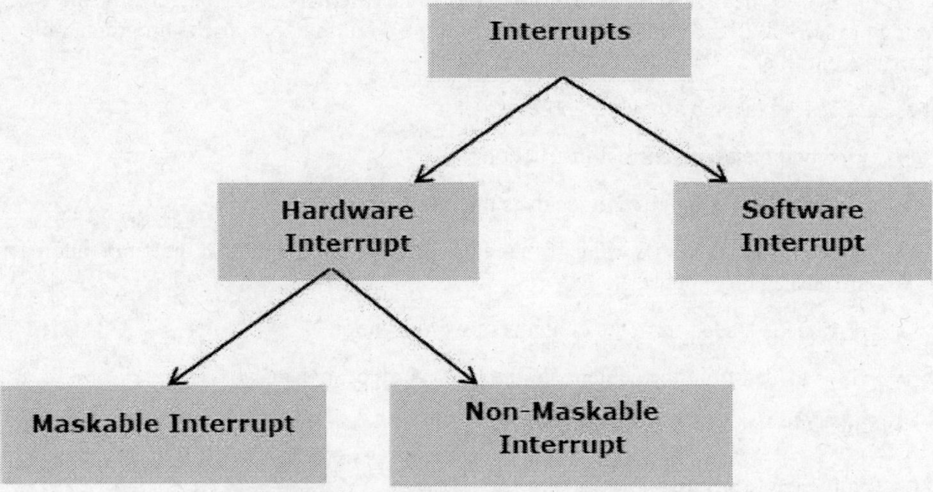

Fig. 1.17: Classification of 8086 Interrupts

1.4.5.1 Hardware Interrupts

Hardware interrupt is caused by any peripheral device by sending a signal through a specified pin to the microprocessor.

The 8086 has two hardware interrupt pins, i.e. NMI and INTR. NMI is a non-maskable interrupt and INTR is a maskable interrupt having lower priority. One more interrupt pin associated is INTA called interrupt acknowledge.

NMI

It is a single non-maskable interrupt pin (NMI) having higher priority than the maskable interrupt request pin (INTR)and it is of type 2 interrupt.

When this interrupt is activated, these actions take place –

- Completes the current instruction that is in progress.
- Pushes the Flag register values on to the stack.
- Pushes the CS (code segment) value and IP (instruction pointer) value of the return address on to the stack.
- IP is loaded from the contents of the word location 00008H.
- CS is loaded from the contents of the next word location 0000AH.
- Interrupt flag and trap flag are reset to 0.

INTR

The INTR is a maskable interrupt because the microprocessor will be interrupted only if interrupts are enabled using set interrupt flag instruction. It should not be enabled using clear interrupt Flag instruction.

The INTR interrupt is activated by an I/O port. If the interrupt is enabled and NMI is disabled, then the microprocessor first completes the current execution and sends '0' on INTA pin twice. The first '0' means INTA informs the external device to get ready and during the second '0' the microprocessor receives the 8 bit, say X, from the programmable interrupt controller.

These actions are taken by the microprocessor –

- First completes the current instruction.
- Activates INTA output and receives the interrupt type, say X.
- Flag register value, CS value of the return address and IP value of the return address are pushed on to the stack.
- IP value is loaded from the contents of word location X × 4
- CS is loaded from the contents of the next word location.
- Interrupt flag and trap flag is reset to 0

1.4.5.2 Software Interrupts

Some instructions are inserted at the desired position into the program to create interrupts. These interrupt instructions can be used to test the working of various interrupt handlers. It includes –

INT- Interrupt instruction with type number

It is 2-byte instruction. First byte provides the op-code and the second byte provides the interrupt type number. There are 256 interrupt types under this group.

Its execution includes the following steps –

- Flag register value is pushed on to the stack.
- CS value of the return address and IP value of the return address are pushed on to the stack.
- IP is loaded from the contents of the word location 'type number' × 4
- CS is loaded from the contents of the next word location.
- Interrupt Flag and Trap Flag are reset to 0

The starting address for type0 interrupt is 000000H, for type1 interrupt is 00004H similarly for type2 is 00008H and ……so on. The first five pointers are dedicated interrupt pointers. i.e. –

- **TYPE 0** interrupt represents division by zero situation.
- **TYPE 1** interrupt represents single-step execution during the debugging of a program.
- **TYPE 2** interrupt represents non-maskable NMI interrupt.
- **TYPE 3** interrupt represents break-point interrupt.
- **TYPE 4** interrupt represents overflow interrupt.

The interrupts from Type 5 to Type 31 are reserved for other advanced microprocessors, and interrupts from 32 to Type 255 are available for hardware and software interrupts.

INT 3-Break Point Interrupt Instruction

It is a 1-byte instruction having op-code is CCH. These instructions are inserted into the program so that when the processor reaches there, then it stops the normal execution of program and follows the break-point procedure.

Its execution includes the following steps –

- Flag register value is pushed on to the stack.
- CS value of the return address and IP value of the return address are pushed on to the stack.
- IP is loaded from the contents of the word location 3×4 = 0000CH
- CS is loaded from the contents of the next word location.
- Interrupt Flag and Trap Flag are reset to 0

INTO - Interrupt on overflow instruction

It is a 1-byte instruction and their mnemonic **INTO**. The op-code for this instruction is CEH. As the name suggests it is a conditional interrupt instruction, i.e. it is active only when the overflow flag is set to 1 and branches to the interrupt handler whose interrupt type number is 4. If the overflow flag is reset then, the execution continues to the next instruction.

Its execution includes the following steps –

- Flag register values are pushed on to the stack.

- CS value of the return address and IP value of the return address are pushed on to the stack.
- IP is loaded from the contents of word location 4×4 = 00010H
- CS is loaded from the contents of the next word location.
- Interrupt flag and Trap flag are reset to 0

1.5 Microcontroller and Its Architecture

A **microcontroller** is a small, low-cost microcomputer which is designed to perform the specific tasks of embedded systems like, cruise control, ABS in Cars, displaying microwave's information, washing machines, printers and many more. In general, the microcontroller consists of the processor, the memory (RAM, ROM, EPROM), Serial ports, peripherals (timers, counters), etc. in a single chip.

A **microcontroller** (**MCU** for *microcontroller unit*) can also be defined as a small computer on a single MOS VLSI chip. A microcontroller contains one or more CPUs (processor cores) along with memory and programmable input/output peripherals. Program memory in the form of ferroelectric RAM, NOR flash or ROM is also often included on chip, as well as a small amount of RAM. Microcontrollers are designed for embedded applications, in contrast to the microprocessors used in personal computers or other general purpose applications (such as, Pentium, Motorola 68000 series) consisting of RAM, ROM, timers, I/O ports, bus interface, cache memories etc. are added externally and comes in various discrete chips.

In modern terminology, a microcontroller is similar to, but less sophisticated than, a system on a chip (SoC). An SoC may connect the external microcontroller chips as the motherboard components, but an SoC usually integrates the advanced peripherals like graphics processing unit (GPU) and Wi-Fi interface controller as its internal microcontroller unit circuits. By reducing the size and cost compared to a design that uses a separate microprocessor, memory, and input/output devices, microcontrollers make it economical to digitally control even more devices and processes. Today, mixed signal microcontrollers are common, integrating analog components needed to control non-digital electronic systems. In the context of the internet of things, microcontrollers are economical and popular means of data collection, sensing and actuating the physical world as edge devices.

1.5.1 Types of Microcontrollers

Microcontrollers are divided into various categories based on memory, architecture, bits and instruction sets. Following are their types.

Bit Based

Based on bit configuration, the microcontrollers are further divided into three categories.

- **8-bit microcontroller** − This type of microcontroller is used to execute arithmetic and logical operations like addition, subtraction, multiplication division, etc. For example, Intel 8031 and 8051 are 8 bits microcontroller.
- **16-bit microcontroller** − This type of microcontroller is used to perform arithmetic and logical operations where higher accuracy and performance is required. For example, Intel 8096 is a 16-bit microcontroller.
- **32-bit microcontroller** − This type of microcontroller is generally used in automatically controlled appliances like automatic operational machines, medical appliances, etc.

Memory Based

Based on memory configurations, the microcontroller is further divided into two categories.

- **External memory microcontroller** – This type of microcontroller is designed in such a way that they do not have a program memory on the chip. Hence, it is named as external memory microcontroller. For example: Intel 8031 microcontroller.
- **Embedded memory microcontroller** – This type of microcontroller is designed in such a way that the microcontroller has all programs and data memory, counters and timers, interrupts, I/O ports are embedded on the chip. For example: Intel 8051 microcontroller.

Instruction Set Based

Based on the instruction set configuration, the microcontroller is further divided into two categories.

- **CISC** – Stands for complex instruction set computer. It allows the user to insert a single instruction as an alternative to many simple instructions, thereby reducing total number of executable instructions in a program (N).
- **RISC** – Stands for Reduced Instruction Set Computers. It reduces the execution time by shortening the cycles per instruction (CPI).

1.5.2 Applications of Microcontrollers

Microcontrollers are widely used in various different devices such as –

- Light sensing and controlling devices like LED.
- Temperature sensing and controlling devices like microwave oven, chimneys.
- Fire detection and safety devices like Fire alarm.
- Measuring devices like Volt Meter.
- Washing machines,
- Smart Cars
- Aviation Control
- Smart doors and many more

1.5.3 Microcontroller Architecture

The fundamental and primary part of the microcontroller is the Central Processing Unit which is capable of processing a word of varying length ranging from 4-bit up to 64-bit. But in modern-day, with technological advancements, the word length has increased and accordingly the range. There is additionally a timer which is present in the microcontroller which acts as a watchdog. There are memory storages of different types that are present in the microcontroller. They act as storage devices for program as well as data.

The architecture of the microcontroller is the internal hardware design which is important to understand the applicability of its architecture for different reasons. The design is not too complex and is easy to understand. The architecture defines every section very clearly and distinctly. Fig.1.13 shows the general architecture of a microcontroller. It consists of the following basic components.

1. CPU (Central Processing Unit)

It comprises of an Arithmetic Logic Unit (ALU) and a Control Unit (CU) and some other components too which are important for its functioning. CPU co-ordinates the communication between the peripheral devices such as memory, Output, and Input. All the arithmetical and logical operations are performed by the Arithmetic Logic Unit (ALU). The timing to be maintained of the communication between the CPU and the different components in the device is controlled by the Control Unit (CU).

2. Program Memory

The instructions that are issued by the CPU are recorded and stored in the Program Memory. it is also termed as Read-Only Memory (ROM). It even stores the data whenever the device is not in functioning mode (silent) or is turned off so that there is a stored record of the functions and the implementation of the various actions of the device controls. Even on the possibility of a complete reset, there is no alteration of any data. Today we have alternative Program Memory such as, Electrically Erasable Programmable Read-Only Memory (EEPROM) which is also non-volatile memory.

3. Data Memory

This resides in the microcontroller and is totally responsible for the storage of temporary data and variables. It also stores intermediate results and some other data which are important for the proper functioning of the program. It is commonly called as Random-Access Memory (RAM) which is a volatile memory. It is commonly systematized as registers and it includes the Special Function Registers (SFRs) and also the memory locations accessible by the user.

4. Input and Output Ports

These are the ports that provide physical connection of the microcontroller with the outside world. There are sensors that are present in the ports and they assist in allowing the input of data from external sources into the microcontroller. The data which is received from the input ports is usually manipulated and that decide the data which will be available at the output port. Mostly, the ports present in the microcontroller function both as input and also as output ports. They can perform with dual functionality.

5. Clock Generator

The synchronization of data and the flow of the program need to be timely and ordered. The clock signal helps to maintain this important functioning of the microcontroller. Thereby the operations run smoothly. It is an integral and most important part of the microcontroller and its architecture. An additional timing circuit needs to be provided which is usually in the form of a crystal.

6. ADC and DAC

A/D and D/A converters are very useful to convert the output signal in the necessary form. For example, the data which is available in the form of analog signal can be converted into digital and vice-versa.

Apart from these, a microcontroller also includes interface for USB/ethernet, RS232 serial interface, PWM etc.

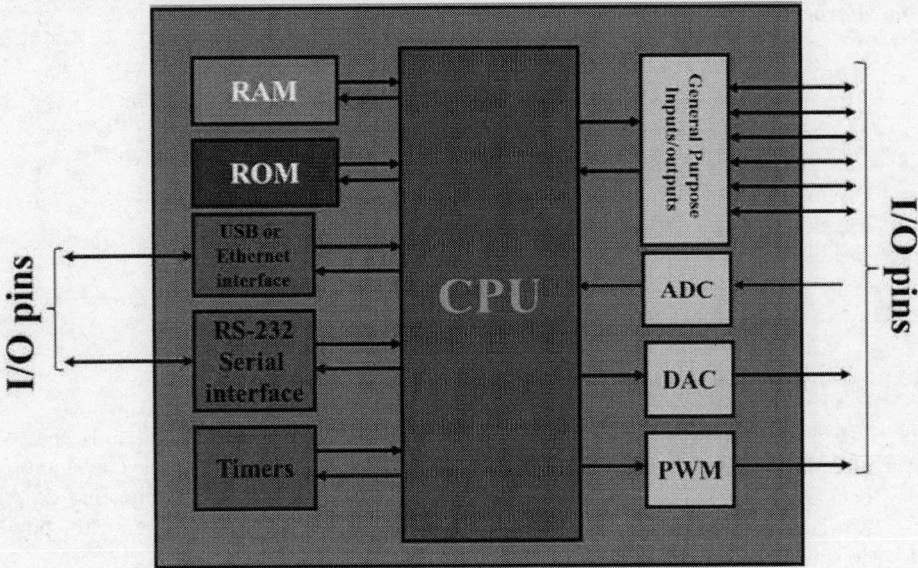

Fig. 1.18: Architectural Diagram of a Microcontroller

1.5.4 Comparison of 8-bit, 16-bit and 32-bit Microcontrollers

As already stated that microcontrollers can be of 8-bit, 16-bit or 32-bit depending upon the number of bits of data it processes. Certainly, they differ in terms of their execution time (speed), cost, efficiency, address space and storage capability. A brief comparison is given next.

8-bit Microcontroller

- Internal bus is 8-bit
- ALU performs operation on 8-bit data (1-byte)
- 8-bit microcontrollers are used in small systems
- Typically works on 4 MHZ clock
- Less cost
- Small RAM and ROM
- 8-bit microcontroller uses small memories that can be erased in-system
- Examples: AVR, PIC, HCS12, 8051 family
- Used in products like, miniature-washing machine, remote control toys, motor control etc.

16-bit Microcontroller

- Internal bus is 16 bit
- Typically works on 12-50MHz. clock
- ALU performs operation on 16-bit (2-bytes) data
- More precision compared to 8-bit microcontroller
- Typically has 16 to 32Kbyte of memory
- 16-bit microcontrollers use large memories that cannot be erased in-system
- Examples: Extended 8051 XA, Intel 8096, MC68HC12
- Used in micro-ovens, washing machines, video games etc.

32-bit Microcontroller

- Internal bus is 32-bit
- Usually have clocks more than 100MHZ
- ALU performs operations on 32-bit (4-byte) data
- Can address up to 4GB of memory (RAM)
- Even greater precision than 16-bit microcontroller
- Examples: PIC32, ARM, Intel 80960, Atmel 251 family
- Used in large embedded system

1.5.5 How to choose microcontrollers?

The criteria to choose a microcontroller are

- Whether the microcontroller meets the computing needs of the task efficiently and cost effectively. Factors affecting this are, speed, cost per unit, power consumption, packaging, amount of RAM and ROM in the chip, number of I/O pins and timers. Moreover, also depends on how easy to upgrade it to high performance or low power consumption version
- What are the software development tools available? For example, compilers, assemblers, debuggers, emulators etc. that is how easy to develop products around the chosen microcontroller.
- It must be readily available and there must be a wide availability of the reliable sources of microcontroller (manufacturer and supplier). At present the leading 8-bit microcontroller, the 8051 family has the largest number of multiple suppliers. For example, 8051 was originated by Intel but now several companies also produce 8051. These include, Intel, Atmel, AMD, Philips, Infineon, Dallas Semiconductor [Ref. 8].
-

1.6 Embedded Systems

Definition 1: Any computing system embedded within larger electronic devices, repeatedly carrying out a particular function, often going completely unrecognized by the user of the device is known as embedded system [Ref.9].

Definition 2: Nearly any device that runs on electricity, either already has or soon will have a computing system embedded within it-called an embedded system.

Alternatively, any computing system other than a desktop is also termed as embedded system.

1.6.1 Characteristics of Embedded Systems

- They are *single functioned*: Executes a specific task repeatedly. For example, a pager, a digital camera, washing machine, mobile phone etc. Whereas, desktop systems are general purpose and executes a variety of programs.
- *Tightly constrained*: They have stringent design constraints. Simultaneously, they need to be
    - Cheap
    - Small size and fit on a single chip
    - Fast enough for real-time
    - Consume extremely low power for long battery life
    - No cooling arrangement
- *Reactive and real-time*: They must respond to the environment very quickly. For example, braking system in cars (ABS), Cruise control, Aviation control.

1.6.2 Role of Microcontrollers in Embedded System Design

As it is clear from the definition of embedded systems that these are single-functioned. It means that embedded systems continue to perform a single task repeatedly throughout its life. For example, a washing machine will continue to perform the task of washing, rinsing and spinning throughout its life as and when asked to do so. Similarly, a digital camera will perform the task of capturing still and video images, internally process it and save, retrieve it as and when asked to do so. A printer will continue to do the task of printing only. Microcontrollers play a significant role in the design of embedded systems. As microcontroller is also designed for single functioned (usually a small program stored in on-chip ROM) and having low cost suitable for the design of embedded systems. Normally, for small, low cost embedded applications microcontrollers are mostly preferred. 8-bit and 16-bit microcontrollers are the most appropriate for applications such as in washing machine, microwave ovens, toys, video games. Although microcontrollers are most preferred for low-cost embedded applications there are situations where they are inadequate for the task. Therefore, in recent years, the manufacturer of general-purpose processors such as, Intel, Freescale Semiconductors Inc. (formerly Motorola), AMD (Advanced Micro Devices Inc.), Cyrix (a division of National Semiconductors Inc.), Apple Corporations have targeted their processors for high-end embedded applications. For example, 8086 processors, 68000 series processors, PowerPC and ARM processors are now quite often used for high-end embedded applications. Today, even 32-bit RISC processors are used for complex embedded applications such as mobile phones. Normally, for large embedded applications reconfigurable kind of processors such as Field Programmable Gate Arrays (FPGAs) are used. They are very much flexible. Consumers product can be upgraded even after shipment. FPGAs are most suitable for fast proto-typing also. However, the unit cost is very high compared to microprocessor and microcontroller-based design, so they are deployed only for large embedded systems.

Summary

In this chapter we have learnt the general structure of microprocessors and microcontrollers. We have also noticed the analogy between the human *brain versus computer.* History, growth and *evolution of computers* are also elucidated briefly. Progress in microprocessors and advances in semiconductor technology, *microcomputer systems* and the classification of computers are also illustrated. Then we introduced the readers on *machine language*, *assembly language* (abbreviated form of instruction or mnemonics) or *high-level languages* such as FORTRAN, BASIC, C, C++ or Java. The major component of the chapter is the overview of **8085** and **8086** microprocessors. We have covered the architecture, instruction set, addressing modes, interrupts, instruction cycles. We have also introduced readers about the fundamentals of microcontroller architecture beginning with 8-bit microcontroller such as **8051** and compared it with the other *microcontrollers* namely, 16-bit and 32-bit is also illustrated. Lastly, at the end of the chapter a brief introduction is given to *embedded systems* and its characteristics. Also, on how microcontrollers can be used to design an embedded system.

Review Questions and Exercise

Section 1.1 & 1.2

1. What are the components of a computer? List it.
2. What is a microprocessor? Compare between microprocessor and a CPU.
3. Find the differences between a microprocessor and a microcontroller.
4. Explain the terms: SSI, MSI and LSI.
5. Define bit, byte and instruction.
6. How many bytes are there in a word of 32 bits
7. Calculate the number of registers in a 64K memory chip.
8. Explain the difference between machine language and assembly language of 8085 microprocessor
9. What is an assembler?
10. What are low and high-level languages? State the relative benefits of high-level language over low-level language
11. Explain the difference between a compiler and an interpreter.

Section 1.3

12. Define opcode and operand. Specify the opcode and operand in the following instructions: (i) *MOV B, A* (ii) *MVI B, 4FH* (iii)*CMA*
13. Find the machine codes and number of bytes in the following instructions.
    a. MVI H, 47H
    b. ADI F5H
    c. SUB C
14. Write the corresponding HEX code for the following instruction set and number of bytes in each instruction.

```
MVI B, 4FH
MVI C, 78H
MOV A, C
ADD B
OUT 07H
HLT
```

15. If the starting address of the system memory is 2000H, what will be the address to enter the HEX code for OUT 07H in question 14.
16. Assemble the following program, starting at location 2000H.

```
START: IN F2H      //Read input switches at port F2H
       CMA         //set ON switches to logic 1
       ORA A       //set Z flag if no switch is ON
       JZ START    //Go back and read input port if all switches are off
```

17. Write an assembly language program to add the two Hex numbers, A2H and 18H. Keep the two numbers saved for future use and save the result in accumulator.
18. Two data bytes 28H and 97H are stored in register B and Accumulator respectively. What will be the contents of the register B, C and accumulator after execution of the following two instructions?

```
Mov A, B
Mov C, A
```

19. Draw the timing diagram, instruction cycle, machine cycle for the problem 18.

20. Find the contents of the registers A, B, C, D and flags S, Z, CY if the following instructions are executed.
    MVI A, 00H
    MVI B, F8H
    MOV C, A
    MOV D, B
    HLT
21. What will be instructions to load the hexadecimal numbers 62H in register C and 91H in accumulator A? Also display the number 62H in PORT0 and 91H in PORT1.
22. Draw the timing diagram of instruction cycle, machine cycle and T-states for the problem of 21.
23. Write instructions to read data at the input PORT 07H and PORT 08H. Also display the input data at PORT 07H to an output PORT 00H and store the input data from PORT 08H into register C.
24. Specify the output at PORT2 if the following program is executed.
    MOV B, 68H
    MOV A, B
    MOV C, A
    MVI D, 42H
    OUT PORT2
    HLT
25. Find the register contents and the status of flag registers when the following instructions are executed. Also indicate the output at PORT0.

Initial Status:	A	B	S	Z	CY
	00	9F	0	1	0

    MVI A, F2H
    MVI B, 7AH
    ADD B
    OUT PORT0
    HLT
26. Write a small program using ADI instruction to add two hexadecimal numbers 3AH and 48H and display the answer at an output port.
27. Draw the timing diagram for the instruction cycle, machine cycle for the program in problem 26.
28. Write a program to perform the following steps:
    a. Load 00H in to the accumulator
    b. Decrement accumulator
    c. Display the answer at the output port
29. Subtract two unsigned numbers F8H and 69H and specify the contents of A and the status registers S and CY. Explain the significance of sign flag if it set after the operation.
30. Find the content of the register and status flags (S, Z, CY) after the instruction ORA A is executed.
    MVI A, 48H
    MVI B, 58H
    ADD B
    ORA A
31. Load the data byte A7H in register C. Mask the higher-order bits (D7-D4), and display the lower-order bits (D3-D0) at an output port.

32. What will be the address of the output port? Explain the type of numbers that can be displayed at the output port.

```
            MVI A, BYTE1
            ORA A             //set flags
            JP OUTPRT         //Jump if byte is positive
            XRA A

OUTPRT:     OUT F2H

            HLT
```

If BYTE1 = 92H, what will be the output at port F2H?

33. In the following program if BYTE1=A7H, what will be displayed at port 01H?

```
            MVI A, BYTE1      //Get data byte
            ORA A             //Set flags
            JM OUTPRT
            OUT 01H
            HLT

OUTPRT:     CMA
            ADI 01H
            OUT 01H
            HLT
```

34. Specify the memory location and its content after the execution of the following instruction,

```
            MVI B, F7H
            MOV A, B
            STA XX75H
            HLT
```

35. Indicate the content of registers A, D and HL after the execution of the following instructions.

```
            LXI H, XX80H      //set up HL as memory pointer
            SUB A             //clear accumulator
            MVI D, 0FH        //set up register as a counter

      LOOP: MOV M, A          //clear memory
            INX H             //next memory location
            DCR D             //update counter
            JNZ LOOP
            HLT
```

36. How many times the following loop will executed? Explain

```
            LXI B, 0008H
      LOOP: DCX B
            MOV A, B
            ORA C
            JNZ LOOP
```

37. Indicate the content of the accumulator and status of CY flag when the following instructions are executed,

```
a.  MVI A, 8FH              b. MVI A, B7H
    ORA A                      ORA A
    RLC                        RAL
```

38. The following set of data bytes are stored in memory locations starting from 4050H. Check each data byte for bits D_7 and D_0. If D7 or D0 is 1, reject the data byte otherwise, store the data bytes in the memory locations starting at 4060H.
    Data(H): 80, 54, F8, 78, F1, 68, 35 and 62
39. Write a program to store the following set of data bytes in descending order.
    Data(H): 64, 40, 56, 68, 45, 5A, 4F, 4D, 56, 59

Section 1.4

40. What is the size of address and data bus in the 8086?
41. Draw the register organization of the 8086 and explain typical applications of each register.
42. How is the 20-bit physical memory address calculated in the 8086 processor?
43. Find the 20-bit physical address of an external memory location if the segment address is 1005H and offset address is 5555H.
44. What are the different memory segments used in the 8086 and explain their functions?
45. Write the function of the DF, IF and TF bits in the 8086.
46. The content of the different registers in the 8086 is CS = F000H, DS = 1000H, SS = 2000H and ES = 3000H. Find the base address of the different segments in the memory.
47. What is the difference between the minimum and maximum mode of operation of the 8086?
48. What is DMA operation? Which pins of the 8086 are used to perform the DMA operation in the minimum and maximum modes of the 8086?
49. Explain the function of different flags in the 8086.
50. Find the difference between maskable and non-maskable interrupts?
51. What is the difference between hardware and software interrupts?
52. Explain interrupt vector. What is the maximum number of interrupt vectors that can be stored in the IVT of the 8086?
53. Write a program to move a word string 200 bytes (i.e. 100 words) long from the offset address 1000H to the offset address 3000H in the segment 5000H.
54. Write a program to find the smallest word in an array of 100 words stored sequentially in the memory; starting at the offset address 1000H in the segment address 5000H. Store the result at the offset address 2000H in the same segment.
55. Write a program to add the two BCD data 29H and 98H and store the result in BCD form in the memory locations 2000H: 3000H and 2000H: 3001H.

Section 1.5 & 1.6

56. Write true or false. A Microcontroller is less expensive than a microprocessor.
57. Which of the following devices on chip, a microcontroller has?
    (a) RAM (b) ROM (c) I/O (d) All of the above
58. Which of the following devices a general-purpose microprocessor needs to be attached to?
    (a) RAM (b) ROM (c) I/O (d) All of them
59. An embedded system is also called a dedicated system. Why?
60. What does the term *embedded System* mean?
61. Why having multiple resources of a given product does matter?
62. What is an embedded system?
63. What are the characteristics of embedded system? Give examples.
64. What a role a microcontroller plays in designing an embedded system?

References

[1] Boyer, C.B. *A History of Mathematics*. 2nd ed. New York: Wiley 1989.

[2] Braun, E. and S. MacDonald. *Revolution in Miniature, The History and Impact of Semiconductor Electronics*. 2nd ed. Cambridge, England: Cambridge University Press, 1982.

[3] John P. Hayes. *Computer Architecture and Organization*. 3rd ed. Singapore: McGraw-Hill International Edition, 1998.

[4] R. R. Schaller, "Moore's law: past, present and future," in *IEEE Spectrum*, vol. 34, no. 6, pp. 52-59, June 1997, doi: 10.1109/6.591665.

[5] Siewiorek, D.P. , C.G. Bell, and A. Newell. *Computer Structures: Readings and Examples.* New York: McGraw-Hill, 1982.

[6] K.M. Bhurchandi and A.K. Ray, *ADVACNED MICROPROCESSORS AND PERIPHERALS,* 3rd ed. Tata McGraw-Hill, New Delhi, 2013.

[7] https://www.eeeguide.com/internal-architecture-of-8086/

[8] M. Ali Mazidi, J. Gillipsie Mazidi, Rolin D. McKinlay. The 8051Microcontrollers and Embedded System. 2nd ed. New Jersey, Pearson Prentice Hall, 2006.

[9] Santanu Chattopadhyay. *Embedded System Design*. 2nd ed. PHI Learning Private Ltd. New Delhi, 2016.

[10] https://www.vssut.ac.in/lecture_notes/lecture1423813120.pdf

Chapter 2

8051 Microcontroller

Key Features

- 8051 microcontroller and its essential features
- Internal architecture of 8051
- Various storage registers in 8051, SFRs
- Program and Data memory
- Stacks
- Clock and Reset circuit
- Timers
- I/O ports
- Assembly Language of 8051
- Instruction Set and Assembly Language Programs

Module-2 outcomes

Students should be

- able to understand the internal architecture of 8051
- able to explain the role of different registers, SFRs in 8051
- able to explain the functions of clock and reset circuit, timers and ports
- aware of the instruction set and tasks performed by instructions
- able to write assembly language programs

8051 is one of the most popular and low-cost microcontrollers also known as MCS-51. It was introduced in 1981 by Intel. It gained the popularity because Intel allowed other manufacturers to make and market variants of 8051(with variations in speed) which are code compatible with each other. It belongs to 8-bit microcontroller family. It has a built-in monitor program, built-in program memory, interrupts, analog I/O, serial I/O, facility to interface external memory, and a timer. It is called a system on chip because it has 128 bytes of RAM, 4K bytes of on-chip ROM, two timers, one serial port and 4 ports (8-bit wide), all on a single chip.

Other members of 8051 microcontroller family are 8052, 8031, Atmel AT89C51, Dallas DS89C4x0 and Philips 8051.

An 8051 microcontroller comes in bundle with the following features −

- 4KB bytes on-chip program memory (ROM)
- 128 bytes on-chip data memory (RAM)
- Four register banks
- 128 user defined software flags
- 8-bit bidirectional data bus

- 16-bit unidirectional address bus
- 32 general purpose registers each of 8-bit
- 16-bit Timers (usually 2, but may have more or less)
- Three internal and two external Interrupts
- Four 8-bit ports, (short models have two 8-bit ports)
- 16-bit program counter and data pointer
- 8051 may also have a number of special features such as UARTs, ADC, Op-amp, etc.

Like any other microprocessor-based systems, in 8051 microcontrollers, the system bus plays a key role to connect all the devices to the central processing unit. This bus includes a data bus-an 8-bit, an address bus-16-bit & bus control signals. Other devices can also be interfaced throughout the system bus like ports, memory, interrupt control, serial interface, the CPU, timers. 8051 microcontroller programming is usually done with *embedded C language* using Keil software. Although, it can be programmed to perform tasks using *assembly language*. It also has several other 8 bit and 16-bit registers. For internal functioning & processing of microcontroller, 8051 comes with integrated built-in RAM. This is the primary memory and is employed for storing temporary data. It is an unpredictable memory i.e. its data can be lost when the power supply to the microcontroller is switched OFF. This microcontroller is very simple to use, affordable, less computing power, has a simple architecture and instruction set.

2.1 **Architecture of 8051**

The architectural diagram of 8051 microcontroller is shown in Fig.2.1, whereas the detailed block diagram representation of it with internal registers, RAM, ROM, I/O ports and interconnections is shown in Fig.2.2.

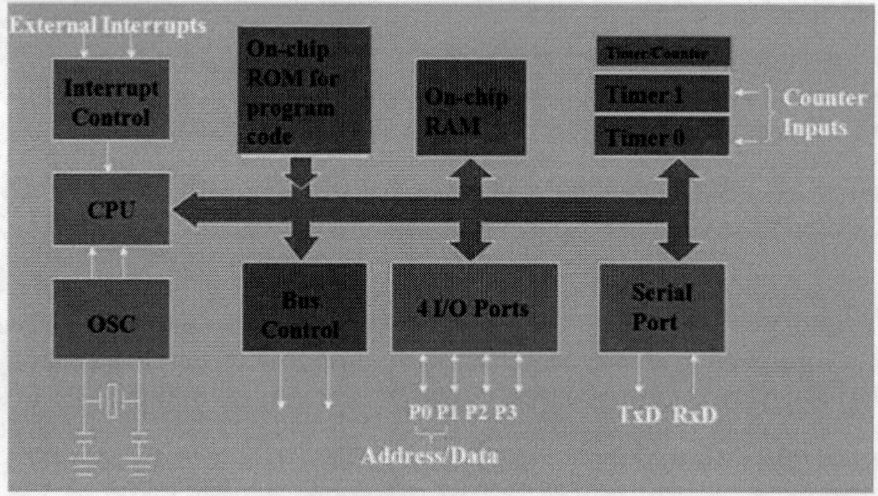

Fig.2.1: Architecture of 8051

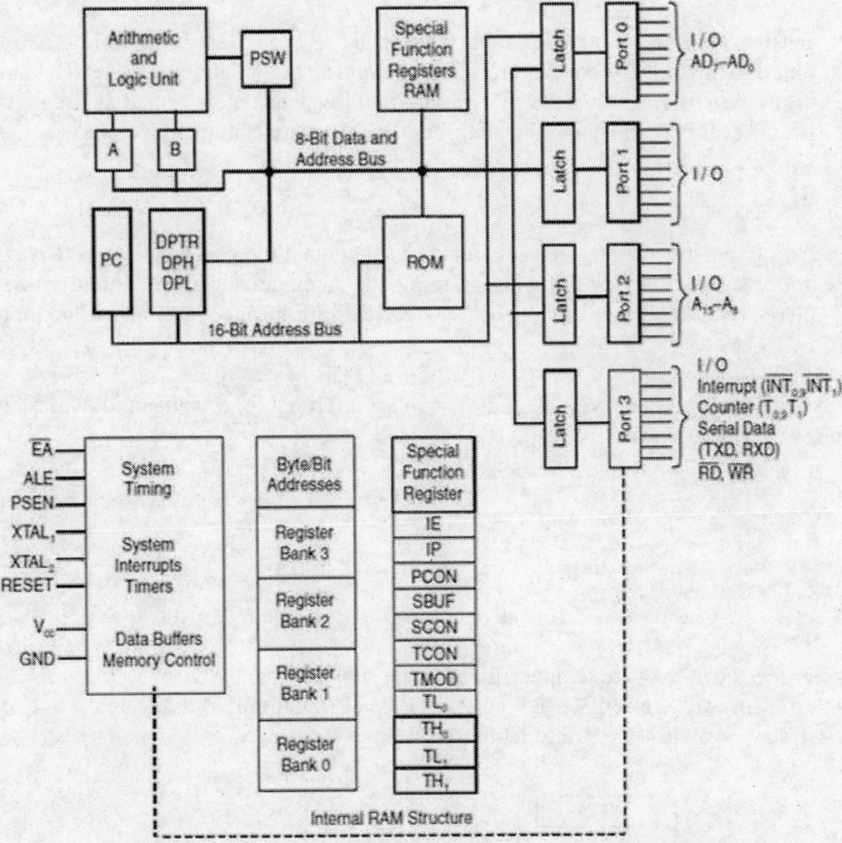

Fig.2.2: Detailed block diagram of 8051 microcontroller with internal registers

The flowing section explains various registers, internal logic units and other components in detail.

2.1.1 Storage Registers in 8051

We will discuss the following types of storage registers here –

- Accumulator
- R register
- B register
- Data Pointer (DPTR)
- Program Counter (PC)
- Stack Pointer (SP)

Accumulator

The accumulator, register A, is used for all arithmetic and logic operations. If the accumulator is not present, then every result of each calculation (addition, multiplication, shift, etc.) is to be stored into the main memory. Access to main memory is slower than access to a register like the accumulator because the technology used for the large main memory is slower (but cheaper) than the technology used for a register.

The "R" Registers

The "R" registers are a set of eight registers, namely, R0, R1 to R7 as shown in Fig. 2.3. These registers function as auxiliary or temporary storage registers in many operations. Consider an example of the sum of 10 and 20. Store a variable 10 in an accumulator and another variable 20 in, say, register R4. To carry out the addition, the following command is to be executed.

ADD A, R4

After executing this instruction, the accumulator will contain the value 30. Thus "R" registers are very important auxiliary or **helper registers**. The Accumulator alone would not be very useful if there were no "R" registers. The "R" registers are meant for temporarily storage of values.

Let us take another example. We will add the values in R1 and R2 together and then subtract the values of R3 and R4 from the result.

```
MOV A,R3    ;Move the value of R3 into the accumulator
ADD A,R4    ;Add the value of R4
MOV R5,A    ;Store the resulting value temporarily in R5
MOV A,R1    ;Move the value of R1 into the accumulator
ADD A,R2    ;Add the value of R2
SUBB A,R5   ;Subtract the value of R5 (which now contains R3 + R4)
```

As you can see, we used R5 to temporarily hold the sum of R3 and R4. Of course, this is not the most efficient way to calculate (R1 + R2) – (R3 + R4), but it does illustrate the use of the "R" registers as a way to store values temporarily.

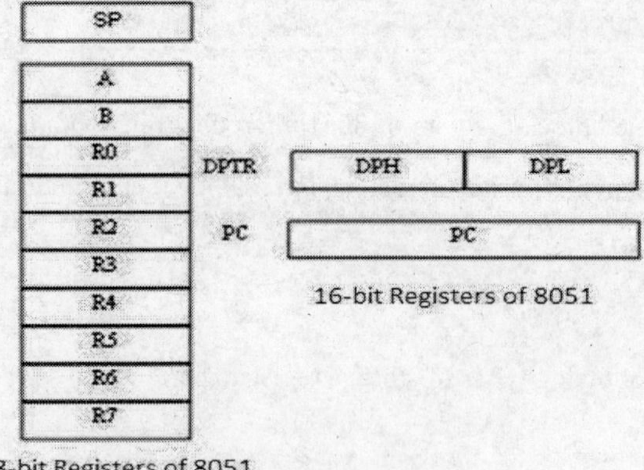

Fig.2.3: Various Storage Registers of 8051

The "B" Register

The "B" register is very similar to the Accumulator in the sense that it may hold an 8-bit (1-byte) value. The "B" register is used only by two 8051 instructions: **MUL AB** and **DIV AB**. To quickly and easily multiply or divide A by another number, you may store the other number in "B" and make use of these two instructions. Apart from using MUL and DIV instructions, the "B" register is often used as yet another temporary storage register, much like a ninth R register.

The Data Pointer

The Data Pointer (DPTR) is the 8051's only user-accessible 16-bit (2-byte) register. The Accumulator, R0–R7 registers and B register are 1-byte registers. DPTR is meant for pointing to data. It is used by the 8051 to access external memory using the address indicated by DPTR. DPTR is the only 16-bit register available and is often used to store 2-byte values.

2.1.2 Program Counter

The Program Counter (PC) is a register to store a 2-byte address which tells the 8051 where from the next instruction to be executed can be found (in the memory). PC starts at 0000h when the 8051 initializes and is incremented every time after an instruction is executed. PC is not always incremented by 1. Some instructions may require 2 or 3 bytes; in such cases, the PC will be incremented by 2 or 3.
Branch, jump, and **interrupt** operations load the Program Counter with an address other than the next sequential location. Activating a power-on reset will cause all values in the register to be lost. It means the value of the PC is 0 upon reset, forcing the CPU to fetch the first opcode from the ROM location 0000. It means we must place the first byte of opcode in ROM location 0000 because that is where the CPU expects to find the first instruction.

2.1.3 The Stack Pointer (SP)

Stack is implemented in RAM and a CPU register is used to access it called SP (Stack Pointer) register. The Stack Pointer, like all other registers except DPTR and PC, may hold an 8-bit (1-byte) value i.e. SP register is an 8-bit register and can address memory addresses of range 00H to FFH. When the content of a CPU register is stored in a stack, it is called a PUSH operation. When the content of a stack is stored in a CPU register, it is called a POP operation.

The Stack Pointer tells the location from where the next value is to be removed from the stack. When a value is pushed onto the stack, the value of SP is incremented and then the value is stored at the resulting memory location. When a value is popped off the stack, the value is returned from the memory location indicated by SP, and then the value of SP is decremented.

This order of operation is important. SP will be initialized to 07H when the 8051 is initialized. If a value is pushed onto the stack at the same time, the value will be stored in the internal RAM address 08H because the 8051 will first increment the value of SP (from 07H to 08H) and then will store the pushed value at that memory address (08H). SP is modified directly by the 8051 by six instructions: PUSH, POP, ACALL, LCALL, RET, and RETI.

2.1.4 Reset Vector

The significance of the reset vector is that it points the processor to the memory address which contains the firmware's first instruction. Without the Reset Vector, the processor would not know where to begin execution. Upon reset, the processor loads the Program Counter (PC) with the reset vector value from a predefined memory location. On CPU08 architecture, this is at location $FFFE to $FFFF.

When the reset vector is not necessary, developers normally take it for granted and don't program into the final image. As a result, the processor doesn't start up on the final product. It is a common mistake that takes place during the debug phase.

2.1.5 The SFR of 8051

A Special Function Register (or Special Purpose Register, or simply Special Register) is a register within a microprocessor that controls or monitors the various functions of a microprocessor. As the special registers are closely tied to some special function or status of the processor, they might not be directly writable by normal instructions (like add, move, etc.). Instead, some special registers in some processor architectures require special instructions to modify them.

In the 8051, register A, B, DPTR, and PSW are a part of the group of registers commonly referred to as SFR (special function registers). An SFR can be accessed by its name or by its address. The following table 2.1 shows a list of SFRs and their addresses.

Table 2.1: List of SFRs and their addresses

Byte Address				Bit Address					
FF									
F0	F7	F6	F5	F4	F3	F2	F1	F0	B
E0	E7	E6	E5	E4	E3	E2	E1	E0	ACC
D0	D7	D6	D5	D4	D3	D2	-	D0	PSW
B8	-	-	-	BC	BB	BA	B9	B8	IP
B0	B7	B6	B5	B4	B3	B2	B1	B0	P3
A2	AF	-	-	AC	AB	AA	A9	A8	IE
A0	A7	A6	A5	A4	A3	A2	A1	A0	P2
99				Not bit Addressable					SBUF
98	9F	9E	9D	9C	9B	9A	99	98	SCON
90	97	96	95	94	93	92	91	90	P1
8D				Not bit Addressable					TH1
8C				Not bit Addressable					TH0
8B				Not bit Addressable					TL1
8A				Not bit Addressable					TL0
89				Not bit Addressable					TMOD
88	8F	8E	8D	8C	8B	8A	89	88	TCON
87				Not bit Addressable					PCON
83				Not bit Addressable					DPH
82				Not bit Addressable					DPL
81				Not bit Addressable					SP
80	87	87	85	84	83	82	81	80	P0

The following two points are to be about the SFR addresses.

- A special function register can have an address between 80H to FFH. These addresses are above 80H, as the addresses from 00 to 7FH are the addresses of RAM memory inside the 8051.
- Not all the address space of 80 to FF are used by the SFR. Unused locations, 80H to FFH, are reserved and must not be used by the 8051 programmers.

Program Status Word (PSW)

The program status word (PSW) register is an 8-bit register, also known as **flag register**. It is of 8-bit wide but only 6-bit of it is used. The two unused bits are **user-defined flags**. Four of the flags are called **conditional flags**, which means that they indicate a condition which results after an instruction is executed. These four are **CY** (Carry), **AC** (auxiliary carry), **P** (parity), and **OV** (overflow). The bits RS0 and RS1 are used to change the bank registers. The following format shows the program status word register. The PSW Register contains that status bits (flags) that reflect the current status of the CPU is represented in 8-bit format as below.

7	6	5	4	3	2	1	0
CY	AC	F0	RS1	RS0	OV	–	P

CY	PSW.7	Carry Flag
AC	PSW.6	Auxiliary Carry Flag
F0	PSW.5	Flag 0 available to user for general purpose.
RS1	PSW.4	Register Bank selector bit 1
RS0	PSW.3	Register Bank selector bit 0
OV	PSW.2	Overflow Flag
-	PSW.1	User definable FLAG
P	PSW.0	Parity FLAG. Set/ cleared by hardware during instruction cycle to indicate even/odd number of 1 bit in accumulator.

We can select the corresponding Register Bank bit using RS0 and RS1 bits.

RS1	**RS0**	**Register Bank**	**Address**
0	0	0	00H-07H
0	1	1	08H-0FH
1	0	2	10H-17H
1	1	3	18H-1FH

- **CY, the carry flag** – This carry flag is set (1) whenever there is a carry out from the D7 bit. It is affected after an 8-bit addition or subtraction operation. It can also be reset to 1 or 0 directly by an instruction such as "SETB C" and "CLR C" where "SETB" stands for set bit carry and "CLR" stands for clear carry.

- **AC, auxiliary carry flag** – If there is a carry from D3 and D4 during an ADD or SUB operation, the AC bit is set; otherwise, it is cleared. It is used for the instruction to perform binary coded decimal arithmetic.
- **P, the parity flag** – The parity flag represents the number of 1's in the accumulator register only. If the A register contains odd number of 1's, then P = 1; and for even number of 1's, P = 0.
- **OV, the overflow flag** – This flag is set whenever the result of a signed number operation is too large causing the high-order bit to overflow into the sign bit. It is used only to detect errors in signed arithmetic operations.

Example 2.1

Show the status of CY, AC, and P flags after the addition of 9CH and 64H in the following instruction.

MOV A, #9CH

ADD A, # 64H

```
Solution: 9C     10011100
          +64    01100100
          100    00000000
```

CY = 1 since there is a carry beyond D7 bit
AC = 0 since there is a carry from D3 to D4
P = 0 because the accumulator has even number of 1's

2.1.6 Program Memory or ROM Space in 8051

Some family members of 8051 have only 4K bytes of on-chip ROM (e.g. 8751, AT8951); some have 8K ROM like, AT89C52 and there are few other family members with 32K bytes and 64K bytes of on-chip ROM such as Dallas Semiconductor [Ref. 1]. A point to be remembered is that no member of the 8051 family can access more than 64K bytes of opcode since the program counter in 8051 is a 16-bit register (0000 to FFFF address).

The first location of the program ROM inside the 8051 has the address of 0000H, whereas the last location can be different depending on the size of the ROM on the chip. Among the 8051 family members, AT8951 has 4k bytes of on-chip ROM having a memory address of 0000 (first location) to 0FFFH (last location) as shown in Fig.2.4.

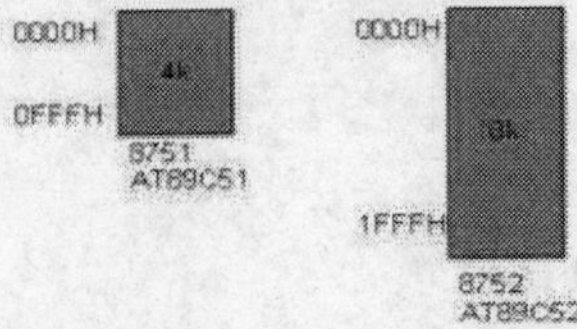

Fig. 2.4: Internal locations in ROM memory

Programming the ROM

To understand the role of program counter in fetching and executing a program memory, let us see the action of the program counter. Consider a simple program as shown below and see how the code is listed and placed in ROM of 8051 chip as in Table 2.2. For more details on 8051microcontrollers see the QR code.

Program

Mnemonics	Hex code
MOV R5, #25H	7D25
MOV R7, #34H	7F34
MOV A, #0	7400
ADD A, R5	2D
ADD A, R7	2F
ADD A, #12H	2412
HERE: SJMP HERE	80FE

As we can see from the table that opcode and operand for each instruction are listed on the left side of the list file. Once the program is burnt into a ROM of 8051 microcontroller family member (such as 8751, AT8951 or DS5000) the opcode and operand are placed in ROM locations starting at 0000 as shown in the list file in Table 2.2. The directives such as ORG and END does not create any object code, used only by the assembler for its own understanding. Thus, blank in the list file (no code). For a detail step-by-step procedure of action for executing a program the readers may refer section 2.4, program 2-1 in [2].

See micro controllers

Table 2.2: List File in ROM

1	0000		ORG 0H	//Start at location 0
2	0000	7D25	MOV R5, #25H	//Load 25H into R5
3	0002	7F34	MOV R7, #34H	//Load 34H into R7
4	0004	7400	MOV A, #0	//Load 0 into A
5	0006	2D	ADD A, R5	//Add contents of R5 to A, so A= A+R5
6	0007	2F	ADD A, R7	//Add contents of R7 to A, now A=A+R7
7	0008	2412	ADD A, #12H	//Add to A the value 12H, now A=A+12H
8	000A	80FE HERE:	SJMP HERE	//Stay in this loop
9	000C		END	//End of asm source file

2.1.7 Data Memory or RAM

The 8051 microcontroller has a total of 128 bytes of RAM. We will discuss about the allocation of these 128 bytes of RAM and examine their usage as stack and register.

RAM Memory Space Allocation in 8051

The 128 bytes of RAM inside the 8051 are assigned the address 00 to 7FH. They can be accessed directly as memory locations and are divided into three different groups as follows −

- 32 bytes from 00H to 1FH locations are set aside for register banks and the stack.
- 16 bytes from 20H to 2FH locations are set aside for bit-addressable read/write memory.
- 80 bytes from 30H to 7FH locations are used for read and write storage; it is called as **scratch pad**. These 80 locations RAM are widely used for the purpose of storing data and parameters by 8051 programmers.

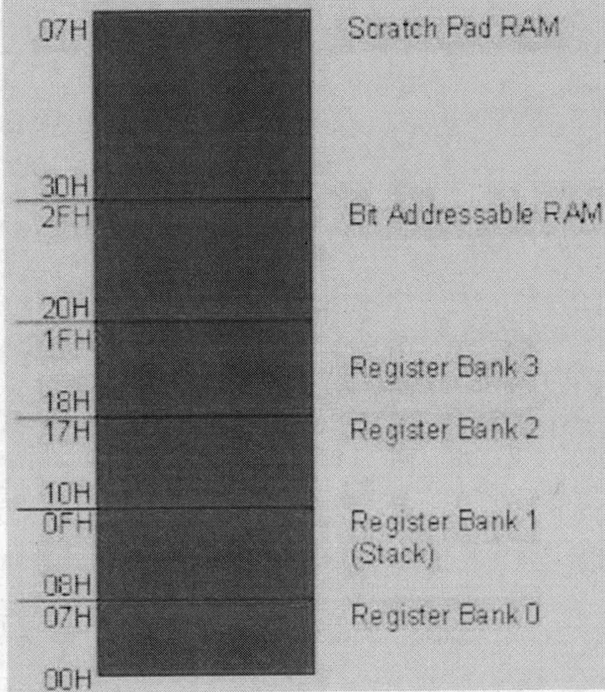

Fig. 2.5: RAM memory allocation in 8051

2.1.8 Register Banks in 8051

A total of 32 bytes of RAM are set aside for the register banks and the stack. These 32 bytes are divided into four register banks in which each bank has 8 registers, R0–R7. RAM locations from 0 to 7 are set aside for bank 0 of R0–R7 where R0 is RAM location 0, R1 is RAM location 1, R2 is location 2, and so on, until the memory location 7, which belongs to R7 of bank 0.

The second bank of registers R0–R7 starts at RAM location 08H and goes to locations OFH. The third bank of R0–R7 starts at memory location 10H and goes to location to 17H. Finally, RAM locations 18H to 1FH are set aside for the fourth bank of R0–R7. This is depicted in Fig.2.5.

Default Register Bank

If RAM locations 00–1F are set aside for the four registers banks, which register bank of R0–R7 do we have access to when the 8051 is powered up? The answer is register bank 0; that is, RAM locations from 0 to 7 are accessed with the names R0 to R7 when programming the 8051. Because it is much easier to refer these RAM locations by names such as R0 to R7, rather than by their memory locations.

How to Switch Register Banks

Register bank 0 is the default bank when the 8051 is powered up. We can switch to the other banks using PSW register. D4 and D3 bits of the PSW are used to select the desired register bank, since they can be accessed by the bit addressable instructions SETB and CLR. For example, "SETB PSW.3" will set PSW.3 = 1 and select the bank register 1.

RS1	RS0	Bank Selected
0	0	Bank0
0	1	Bank1
1	0	Bank2
1	1	Bank3

2.1.9 Stack in the 8051

The stack is a section of a RAM used by the CPU to store information such as data or memory address on temporary basis. The CPU needs this storage area considering limited number of registers.

How Stacks are Accessed

As the stack is a section of a RAM, there are registers inside the CPU to point to it. The register used to access the stack is known as the stack pointer register. The stack pointer in the 8051 is 8-bits wide, and it can take a value of 00 to FFH. When the 8051 is initialized, the SP register contains the value 07H. This means that the RAM location 08 is the first location used for the stack. The storing operation of a CPU register in the stack is known as a **PUSH**, and getting the contents from the stack back into a CPU register is called a **POP**.

Pushing into the Stack

In the 8051, the stack pointer (SP) points to the last used location of the stack. When data is pushed onto the stack, the stack pointer (SP) is incremented by 1. When PUSH is executed, the contents of the register are saved on the stack and SP is incremented by 1. To push the registers onto the stack, we must use their RAM addresses. For example, the instruction "PUSH 1" pushes register R1 onto the stack.

Popping from the Stack

Popping the contents of the stack back into a given register is the opposite to the process of pushing. With every pop operation, the top byte of the stack is copied to the register specified by the instruction and the stack pointer is decremented once.

The operation of the stack and SP is shown in Fig. 2.6. The stack pointer (SP) is set to 07H when 8051 is reset. But it can be changed to any internal RAM location by the programmer. The stack is limited in height to the size of internal RAM. Stack has the capability to overwrite the valuable data in register banks, bit addressable RAM and scratch pad areas of RAM. The stack is normally placed high in internal RAM, by an appropriate choice of the number placed in SP register to avoid any conflict with other registers, bit or scratch pad.

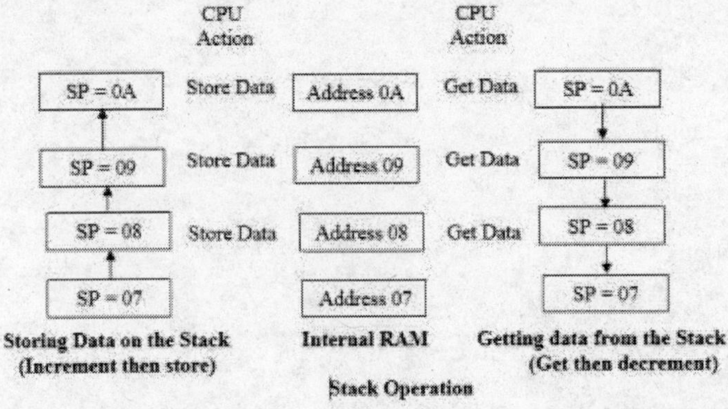

Fig. 2.6: Stack operation and Stack Pointer locations

2.1.10 Clock and Reset Circuit

The 8051 has on chip oscillator pins XTAL1 and XTAL2 which are provided for connecting a resonant network to from an oscillator crystal having a frequency range from 1 MHZ to 24 MHZ.

Ceramic resonators may be used as a low-cost alternative to crystal resonators but due to decrease in frequency stability and accuracy, ceramic resonators are not preferred for high-speed serial data communication with other system.

The oscillator is formed by the crystal, capacitors, and on chip inverter generates a pulse train at the frequency of the crystal as shown in Fig.2.7

The clock frequency establishes the smallest interval of time within the microcontroller, called the pulse, p, time. The smallest interval of time to accomplish any simple instruction, or part of a complex instruction, however, is the machine cycle. The machine cycle is made up of six states. A state is the basic time interval for discrete operations of the microcontroller such as, fetching on encoded byte, decoding encode, executing an encode, or writing a data byte. The oscillator pulses define each state.

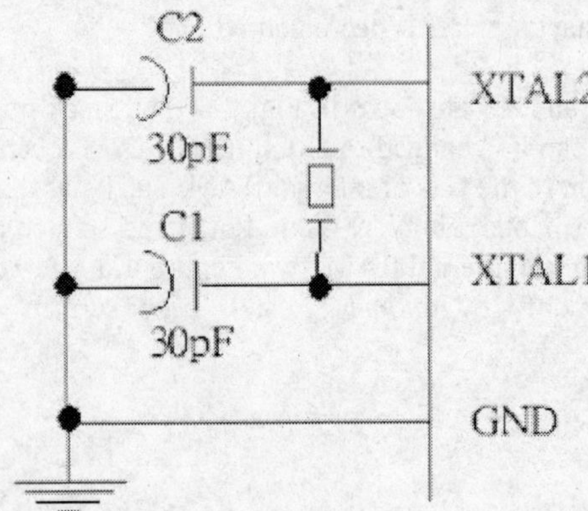

Fig. 2.7: Clocking Circuit (Crystal Oscillator) of 8051

We can calculate the time taken by any particular instruction to be executed as follows. The time to execute the instruction is found by multiplying the number of clock cycles required by the instruction (C) by 12 and then dividing the product by the crystal frequency.

$T_{(instruction)} = \quad C \times 12 / \text{Crystal frequency}$

A 12 MHZ crystal results in convenient time period of 1 microsecond per cycle. An 11.0592 MHZ crystal with a clock frequency of 921.6 KHz, can be divided evenly by the standard communication baud rates of 19200, 9600, 4800, 2400, 1200 and 300 HZ.

Reset

8051 can be reset in two ways 1) power-on reset – which resets the 8051 when power is turned ON and 2) manual reset – in which a reset happens only when a push button is pressed manually. When the rest circuit is power on, capacitor gradually charges and initially a high voltage appears across the resistor for some time. Till the voltage across the resistor is high 8051 remains in reset state for a few milliseconds time (usually within a time period of 2 machine cycles). By this time, all the transients in the circuit settles and then microcontroller starts working. Two different reset circuits are shown Fig.2.8 below. A reset doesn't affect contents of internal RAM

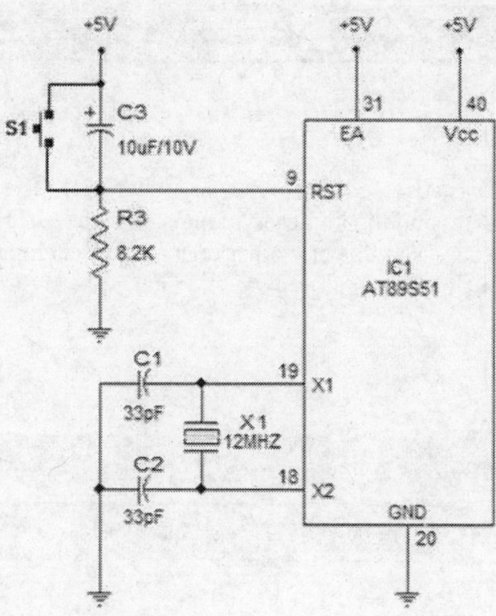

Fig. 2.8: Reset Circuit of 8051

2.1.11 Address, Data & Control Bus

The address bus in 8051 microcontrollers is consisting of **16-bit address lines** which carries the 16 bit addresses of memory locations. It is generally be used for transferring the data from Central Processing Unit to Memory. The 16-bit address bus can address a 64K (2^{16}) memory space and a separate 64K byte of data memory space. While the data bus in 8051 microcontrollers is consisting of 8 bits data lines which carries data between processor and other components. Data bus is bidirectional. The control bus manages the information flow between various components (ALU, registers, memory, I/O etc.) indicating whether the operation is a read or a write and ensuring that the operation happens at the right time.

2.1.12 Timers of 8051 and their Associated Registers

The 8051 has two timers, Timer 0 and Timer 1. They can be used as timers or as event counters. Both Timer 0 and Timer 1 are 16-bit wide. Since the 8051 follows an 8-bit architecture, each 16-bit is accessed as two separate registers of lower order byte and higher order byte.

Timer 0 Register

The 16-bit register of Timer 0 is accessed as lower-bye and higher-byte. The lower-byte register is called TL0 (Timer 0 low byte) and the higher-byte register is called TH0 (Timer 0 high byte). These registers can be accessed like any other register. For example, the instruction **MOV TL0, #4H** moves the value into the low-byte of Timer #0.

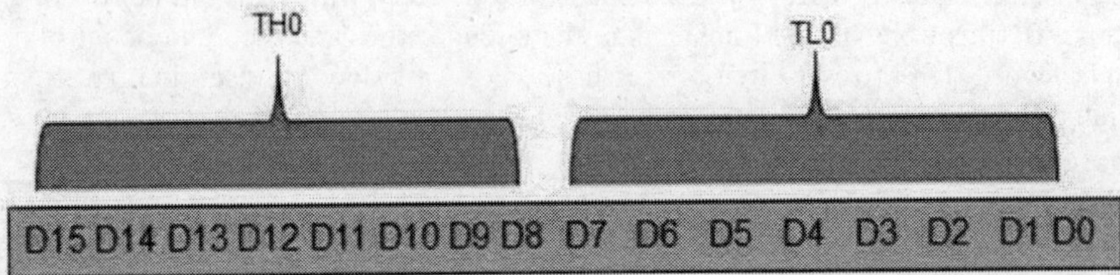

Timer 1 Register

The 16-bit register of Timer 1 is accessed as lower- and higher-byte. The lower-byte register is called TL1 (Timer 1 low byte) and the higher-byte register is called TH1 (Timer 1 high byte). These registers can be accessed like any other register. For example, the instruction **MOV TL1, #4H** moves the value into the low-byte of Timer 1.

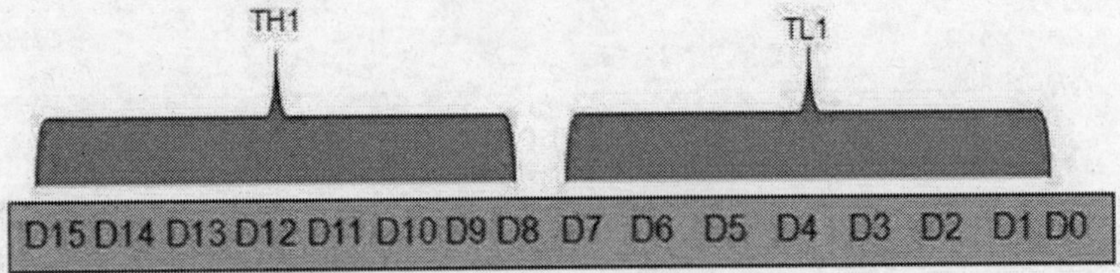

TMOD (Timer Mode) Register

Both Timer 0 and Timer 1 use the same register to set the various timer operation modes. It is an 8-bit register in which the lower 4 bits are set aside for Timer 0 and the upper four bits for Timers. In each case, the lower 2 bits are used to set the timer mode in advance and the upper 2 bits are used to specify the location.

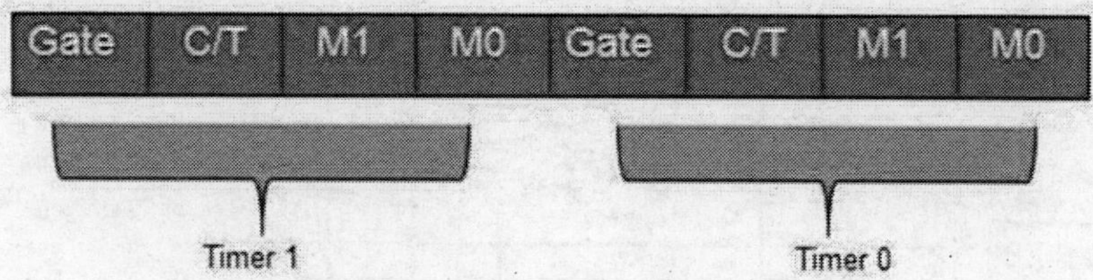

Gate – When set, the timer only runs while INT(0,1) is high.

C/T – Counter/Timer select bit.

M1 – Mode bit 1.

M0 – Mode bit 0.

GATE

Every timer has a means of starting and stopping. Some timers do this by software, some by hardware, and some have both software and hardware controls. 8051 timers have both software and hardware controls. The start and stop of a timer is controlled by software using the instruction **SETB TR1** and **CLR TR1** for timer 1, and **SETB TR0** and **CLR TR0** for timer 0.

The SETB instruction is used to start it and it is stopped by the CLR instruction. These instructions start and stop the timers as long as GATE = 0 in the TMOD register. Timers can be started and stopped by an external source by making GATE = 1 in the TMOD register.

2.1.13 I/O Ports and their Functions

The four ports P0, P1, P2, and P3, each use 8 pins, making them 8-bit ports. Upon RESET, all the ports are configured as inputs, ready to be used as input ports. When the first 0 is written into a port, it becomes an output. To reconfigure it as an input, a 1 must be sent to a port.

Port 0 (Pin No 32 – Pin No 39)

It has 8 pins (32 to 39). It can be used for input or output. Unlike P1, P2, and P3 ports, we normally connect P0 to 10K-ohm pull-up resistors to use it as an input or output port being an open drain. It is also designated as AD0-AD7, allowing it to be used as both address and data. In case of 8031 (i.e. ROM-less Chip), when we need to access the external ROM, then P0 will be used for both Address and Data Bus. ALE (Pin no 31) indicates if P0 has address or data. When ALE = 0, it provides data D0-D7, but when ALE = 1, it has address A0-A7. In case no external memory connection is available, P0 must be connected externally to a 10K-ohm pull-up resistor as shown in Fig. 2.9.

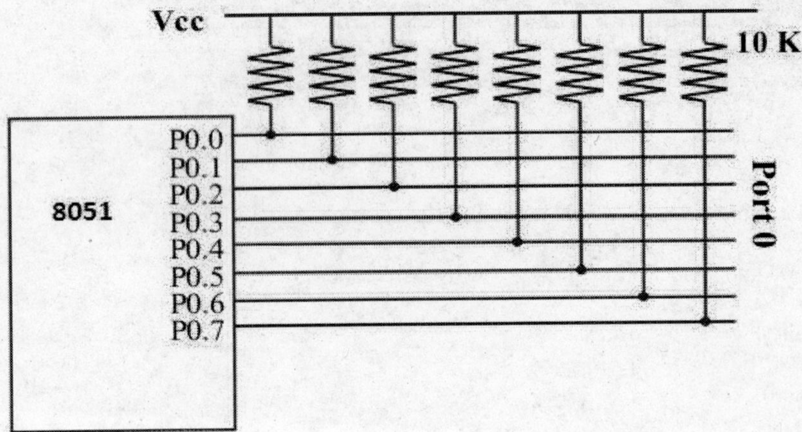

Fig. 2.9: Port 0 connectivity for external memory

```
MOV A, #0FFH //(comments: A=FFH(Hexadecimal  i.e. A=1111 1111)

MOV P0, A    //(Port0 have 1's on every pin so that it works as Input)
```

Port 1 (Pin 1 through 8)

It is an 8-bit port (pin 1 through 8) and can be used either as input or output. It doesn't require pull-up resistors because they are already connected internally. Upon reset, Port 1 is configured as an input port. The following code can be used to send alternating values of 55H and AAH to Port 1.

```
//Toggle all bits of continuously
MOV    A, #55
BACK:

MOV    P2, A
ACALL  DELAY
CPL    A    //complement(invert) reg. A
SJMP   BACK
```

If Port 1 is configured to be used as an output port, then to use it as an input port again, program it by writing 1 to all of its bits as in the following code.

```
//Toggle all bits of continuously

MOV    A, #0FFH   //A = FF hex
MOV    P1, A      //Make P1 an input port
MOV    A, P1      //get data from P1
MOV    R7, A      //save it in Reg R7
ACALL  DELAY      //wait

MOV    A, P1      //get another data from P1
MOV    R6, A      //save it in R6
ACALL  DELAY      //wait
```

```
MOV    A, P1      //get another data from P1
MOV    R5, A      //save it in R5
```

Port 2 (Pins 21 through 28)

Port 2 occupies a total of 8 pins (pins 21 through 28) and can be used for both input and output operations. Just as P1 (Port 1), P2 also doesn't require external Pull-up resistors because they are already connected internally. It must be used along with P0 to provide the 16-bit address for the external memory. So it is also designated as (A0–A7), as shown in the pin diagram. When the 8051 is connected to an external memory, it provides path for upper 8-bits of 16-bits address, and it cannot be used as I/O. Upon reset, Port 2 is configured as an input port. The following code can be used to send alternating values of 55H and AAH to port 2.

```
//Toggle all bits of continuously
MOV    A, #55
BACK:
MOV    P2, A
ACALL  DELAY
CPL    A       // complement(invert) reg. A
SJMP   BACK
```

If Port 2 is configured to be used as an output port, then to use it as an input port again, program it by writing 1 to all of its bits as in the following code.

```
//Get a byte from P2 and send it to P1
MOV   A, #0FFH   //A = FF hex
MOV   P2, A      //make P2 an input port
BACK:
MOV   A, P2      //get data from P2
MOV   P1, A      //send it to Port 1
SJMP  BACK       //keep doing that
```

Port 3 (Pins 10 through 17)

It is also of 8 bits and can be used as Input/Output. This port provides some extremely important signals. P3.0 and P3.1 are RxD (Receiver) and TxD (Transmitter) respectively and are collectively used for Serial Communication. P3.2 and P3.3 pins are used for external interrupts. P3.4 and P3.5 are used for timers T0 and T1 respectively. P3.6 and P3.7 are Write (WR) and Read (RD) pins. These are active low pins, means they will be active when 0 is given to them and these are used to provide Read and Write operations to External ROM in 8031 based systems.

P3 Bit	Function	Pin
P3.0	RxD	10
P3.1 <	TxD	11
P3.2 <	Complement of INT0	12
P3.3 <	INT1	13
P3.4 <	T0	14
P3.5 <	T1	15
P3.6 <	WR	16

P3.7 <	Complement of RD	17

2.2 Assembly Language of 8051

Assembly languages were developed to provide **mnemonics** or symbols for the machine level instructions. Assembly language programs consist of mnemonics and as such they should be translated into machine code. A program that is responsible for this conversion is known as **assembler**. Assembly language is often termed as a low-level language because it directly works with the internal structure of the CPU. To program in assembly language, a programmer must know all the registers of the CPU.

Different programming languages such as C, C++, Java and various other languages are called high-level languages because they do not deal with the internal details of a CPU. In contrast, an assembler is used to translate an assembly language program into machine code (sometimes also called **object code** or **opcode**). Similarly, a compiler translates a high-level language into machine code. For example, to write a program in C language, one must use a C compiler to translate the program into machine language.

2.2.1 Structure of Assembly Language

An assembly language program is a series of short-form English word or lines, which are either assembly language instructions such as ADD and MOV, or statements called **directives**.

An **instruction** tells the CPU what function it has to do, while a **directive** (also called **pseudo-instructions**) gives instruction to the assembler. For example, ADD and MOV instructions are commands which the CPU runs, while ORG and END are assembler directives. The assembler places the opcode to the memory location 0 when the ORG directive is used, while END indicates to the end of the source code. A program language instruction consists of the following four fields –

```
[ label: ]   mnemonics  [ operands ]   [;comment ]
```

A square bracket ([ ]) indicates that the field is optional.

- The **label field** allows the program to refer to a line of code by name. The label fields cannot exceed a certain number of characters.
- The **mnemonics** and **operands fields** together perform the actual task of the program and accomplish the specified tasks. Statements like ADD A , C & MOV C, #68 where ADD and MOV are the mnemonics, which are also known as opcodes, while "A, C" and "C, #68" are the operands. These two fields could contain directives. Directives do not generate machine code and are used only by the assembler, whereas instructions are translated into machine code for the CPU to execute.

```
0000             ORG  0H              //start (origin) at location 0
0000 7D25        MOV  R5,#25H         //load 25H into R5 register
0002 7F34        MOV  R7,#34H         //load 34H into R7 register
0004 7400        MOV  A,#0            //load 0 into accumulator A
0006 2D          ADD  A,R5            //add contents of R5 to A
0007 2F          ADD  A,R7            //add contents of R7 to A
0008 2412        ADD  A,#12H          //add to A value 12 H
000A 80FE  HERE: SJMP HERE            //stay in this loop
000C             END                  //end of asm. source file
```

- The **comment field** begins with a // which is an indicator of the comment.
- Any label in the program is specified by a label name such as, "HERE" in the program. Any label which refers to an instruction should be followed by a colon.

2.2.2 Assembling and Running an 8051 Program

Here we will discuss about the basic form of an assembly language. The steps to create and run an assembly language program are as follows:

- First, we use an editor to type in a program similar to the above program. Editors, like MS-DOS EDIT program that comes with all Microsoft operating systems can be used to create or edit a program. The Editor must be able to produce an ASCII file. The "asm" extension for the source file is used by an assembler in the next step.
- The "asm" source file contains the program code created in Step 1. It is fed to an 8051 assembler. The assembler then converts the assembly language instructions into machine code instructions and produces an **.obj file** (object file) and a **.lst file** (list file). It is also called as a **source file**, that's why some assemblers require that this file have the "src" extensions. The "lst" file is optional. It is very useful to the program because it lists all the opcodes and addresses as well as errors that the assemblers detected.
- Assemblers require a third step called **linking**. The link program takes one or more object files and produces an absolute object file with the extension "abs".
- Next, the "abs" file is fed to a program called "OH" (object to hex converter), which creates a file with the extension "hex" that is ready to burn in to the ROM. The complete set of steps are shown in the flowchart of Fig.2.10.

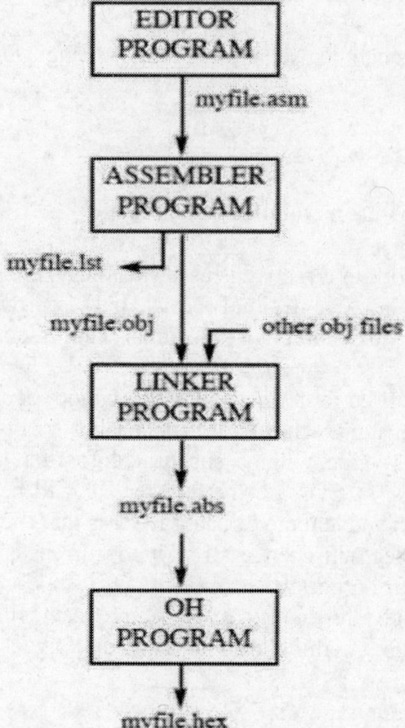

Fig. 2.10: Flow chart of steps to create a program

Data Type

The 8051 microcontroller contains a single data type of 8-bits, and each register is also of 8-bits size. The programmer has to break down data larger than 8-bits (00 to FFH, or to 255 in decimal) so that it can be processed by the CPU.

DB (Define Byte)

The DB directive is the most widely used data directive in the assembler. It is used to define the 8-bit data. It can also be used to define decimal, binary, hex, or ASCII formats data. For decimal, the "D" after the decimal number is optional, but it is required for "B" (binary) and "Hl" (hexadecimal).

To indicate ASCII, simply place the characters in quotation marks ('like this'). The assembler generates ASCII code for the numbers/characters automatically. The DB directive is the only directive that can be used to define ASCII strings larger than two characters; therefore, it should be used for all the ASCII data definitions. Some examples of DB are given below –

```
ORG 500H

DATA1: DB 28                  //DECIMAL (1C in hex)
DATA2: DB 00110101B           //BINARY (35 in hex)
DATA3: DB 39H            //HEX
ORG 510H
DATA4: DB "2591"         //ASCII NUMBERS
ORG 520H
DATA6: DA "MY NAME IS Michael"  //ASCII CHARACTERS
```

Either single or double quotes can be used around ASCII strings. DB is also used to allocate memory in byte sized chunks.

2.2.3 Assembler Directives

Some of the directives of 8051 are as follows –

- **ORG (origin)** – The origin directive is used to indicate the beginning of the address. It takes the numbers in hexa or decimal format. If H is provided after the number, the number is treated as hexa, otherwise decimal. The assembler converts the decimal number to hexa.
- **EQU (equate)** – It is used to define a constant without occupying a memory location. EQU associates a constant value with a data label so that the label appears in the program, its constant value will be substituted for the label. While executing the instruction "MOV R3, #COUNT", the register R3 will be loaded with the value 25 (notice the # sign). The advantage of using EQU is that the programmer can change it once and the assembler will change all of its occurrences; the programmer does not have to search the entire program.
- **END directive** – It indicates the end of the source (asm) file. The END directive is the last line of the program; anything after the END directive is ignored by the assembler.

2.2.4 Labels in Assembly Language

All the labels in assembly language must follow the rules given below –

- Each label name must be unique. The names used for labels in assembly language programming consist of alphabetic letters in both uppercase and lowercase, number 0 through 9, and special characters such as question mark (?), period (.), at the rate @, underscore (_), and dollar ($).
- The first character should be in alphabetical character; it cannot be a number.
- Reserved words cannot be used as a label in the program. For example, ADD and MOV words are the reserved words, since they are instruction mnemonics.
- In addition to these there may be some other revered words specific to a particular assembler.

2.3 Instruction Set of 8051

To perform any task by a microprocessor or a microcontroller it is to be programmed using specific instructions from its set. Writing a program for any microcontroller is nothing but giving a set of commands to the microcontroller in a particular order in which they must be executed in order to perform a specific task. These commands to the microcontroller are known as its instructions. An instruction set is unique to a family of computer or microcontroller. 8051 microcontrollers instruction set is also known as MCS-51 instruction set. As the family of 8051 microcontrollers use 8-bit processors, so its instruction set is optimized for 8-bit control applications. As a typical 8-bit processor, the 8051 microcontroller instructions have 8-bit opcodes. Thus, 8051 microcontroller's instruction set can be up to $2^8 = 256$ instructions. However, depending upon the types of instructions (groups) and addressing modes there 49 instruction Mnemonics in the 8051 Microcontroller. These 49 Mnemonics are divided into five groups as shown in the following table (Table 2.1).

Table 2.3: Instruction set of 8051 and Types

DATA TRANSFER	***ARITHMETIC***	***LOGICAL***	***BOOLEAN***	***PROGRAM BRANCHING***
MOV	ADD	ANL	CLR	LJMP
MOVC	ADDC	ORL	SETB	AJMP
MOVX	SUBB	XRL	MOV	SJMP
PUSH	INC	CLR	JC	JZ
POP	DEC	CPL	JNC	JNZ
XCH	MUL	RL	JB	CJNE
XCHD	DIV	RLC	JNB	DJNZ
	DA A	RR	JBC	NOP
		RRC	ANL	LCALL
		SWAP	ORL	ACALL
			CPL	RET
				RETI
				JMP

As we can see from the table that there are basically five groups of instructions. These are *data transfer, arithmetic, logical, Boolean or bit manipulation* and *program control* or *branch* instructions. A brief explanation of each type of instruction Mnemonics is given below. The detail of these instructions will be explained with appropriate examples in the next Chapter.

However, before proceeding further on the types of instructions, let us see the structure of the 8051 microcontroller instructions. An 8051 instruction consists of an Opcode (or Operation –

Code) followed by Operand(s) of size Zero Byte, One Byte or Two Bytes. While opcode specifies the operation to be performed, the operand part of instruction indicates the data being processed by the instruction. The operand can be in any of the following forms-

- No Operand
- Data value
- I/O Port
- Memory Location
- CPU register

There can be multiple operands also in an instruction. Accordingly, the format for an instruction can be written as,

MNEMONIC OPERAND1, OPERAND2

Where, OPERAND1 is the destination operand and OPERAND2 is the source operand. A simple instruction may have only opcode. Other instructions may include one or more operands. One operand instruction is essentially a 2-byte instruction whereas two operand instruction is a 3-byte instruction.

2.3.1 Data Transfer Instructions

Data transfer instructions are associated with the transfer of data between registers or external program memory or external data memory. The Mnemonics associated with Data Transfer are given below.

- *MOV* *// Move data*
- *MOVC* *//Move code*
- *MOVX* *// Move external data*
- *PUSH* *// Move data to stack*
- *POP* *// Copy data from stack*
- *XCH* *//Exchange data between two registers*
- *XCHD* *//Exchange lower order data between two registers*

2.3.2 Arithmetic Instructions

Arithmetic instructions are meant to perform addition, subtraction, multiplication and division. The arithmetic instructions also include increment or decrement by one, and a special instruction called Decimal Adjust Accumulator.

The Mnemonics associated with the arithmetic instructions of the 8051 Microcontroller instruction set are:

- *ADD* *// Addition without a carry*
- *ADDC* *// Addition with carry*
- *SUBB* *// Subtract with carry*
- *INC* *// Increment by 1*
- *DEC* *// Decrement by 1*
- *MUL* *// Multiply*
- *DIV* *// Divide*
- *DAA* *// Decimal Adjust the Accumulator (register A)*

2.3.3 Logical Instructions

The next group of instructions are the Logical Instructions, which perform logical operations like AND, OR, XOR, NOT, Rotate, Clear and Swap. Logical Instruction are performed on Bytes of data on a bit-by-bit basis.

Mnemonics associated with Logical Instructions are as follows:

- *ANL* *// Logical AND operation*
- *ORL* *// Logical OR operation*
- *XRL* *// Logical EX-OR operation*
- *CLR* *// Clear register content*
- *CPL* *// Complement the register content*
- *RL* *//Rotate a byte left*
- *RLC* *// Rotate a byte and carry bit to left*
- *RR* *// Rotate a byte to right*
- *RRC* *// Rotate a byte and carry bit to right*
- *SWAP* *// Swap lower and higher nibble in a byte*

2.3.4 Boolean or Bit Manipulation Instructions

Boolean or Bit Manipulation Instructions deal with bit variables. In 8051 microcontrollers, there is a special bit-addressable area in the RAM, so also, some of the Special Function Registers (SFRs) are bit addressable.

The Mnemonics corresponding to the Boolean or Bit Manipulation instructions are:

- *CLR* *// Clear a bit (reset to 0)*
- *SETB* *// Set a bit (set to 1)*
- *MOV* *// Move a bit*
- *JC* *// Jump if the carry flag is set (i.e. if C=1)*
- *JNC* *// Jump if the carry flag is not set (i.e. if C=0)*
- *JB* *// Jump if the specified bit is set*
- *JNB* *// Jump if the specified bit is not set*
- *JBC* *// Jump if the specified bit set and also clear the bit*
- *ANL* *// Bitwise logical AND operation*
- *ORL* *// Bitwise logical OR operation*
- *CPL* *// Complement the bit*

2.3.5 Program Control or Branching Instructions

The last group of instructions in the 8051 Microcontroller instruction set are the program control or branching instructions. These instructions control the flow of program logic. The mnemonics of this set are as follows.

- *LJMP* // Long Jump (Unconditional)
- *AJMP* // Absolute Jump (Unconditional)
- *SJMP* // Short Jump (Unconditional)
- *JZ* *// Jump if accumulator A = 0*
- *JNZ* *// Jump if accumulator A is not 0*
- *CJNE* // Compare and jump if not equal
- *DJNZ* // Decrement and Jump if not 0

- *NOP* *// No operation*
- *LCALL// Long Call to subroutine, can have target address anywhere within*

  // 64K-bytes address space (ROM) of 8051

- *ACALL* // Absolute Call to Subroutine (Unconditional), must have target

  //address within 2K-bytes of ROM space

- *RET* *// Return from subroutine*
- *RETI* *// Return from interrupt*
- *JMP* *// Jump to an address unconditionally*

Each of these 05 groups of instructions will be discussed in details in Chapter 3 with examples. Moreover, some problems will be solved and illustrated next in section 2. for further clarification of the underlying concepts and utility of the instruction set.

2.4 Timing and Machine Cycle for 8051

Just like a general-purpose processor such as 8085, the tasks carried out by a microcontroller are also measured in terms of systems clock or clock cycles. However, in contrast to 8085, CPU of a microcontroller takes certain number of clock cycles to execute an instruction. In 8051 family, these clock cycles are referred to as the *machine cycles.* As for example, MOV, DEC, NOP instructions take just 1 machine cycle, whereas, LJMP, DJNZ, RET etc. takes 2 machine cycles to execute. Again, a MUL instruction takes 4 machine cycles. To calculate the time delay associated with these instructions it is necessary to know the clock frequency of the crystal oscillator connected to 8051 family of microcontrollers. In 8051, one machine cycle lasts for 12 oscillator periods. So, to calculate the machine cycle for the 8051, we take 1/12 of the crystal frequency. For a crystal with 16 MHz clock, the *clock frequency* will be 16MHz/12 = 1.333 Mhz. and the *machine cycle* =1/1.333MHz = 0.75 micro-sec.

2.5 Assembly Language Programming of 8051

Although 8051 programming is emphasised in Chapter 3, we will see some assembly language programs in this section through a few examples. Solutions to each of the examples and necessary explanations are given through comments written side by side to the assembly language instructions.

Example 2.2

Suppose the RAM locations 40-44 have the following numbers. Write a program to find the sum of the numbers. At the end of the program, register A should contain lower order byte and R7 should higher order byte. All values are in hex.

40 = (7D)
41 = (EB)
42 = (C5)
43 = (5B)
44 = (30)

Solution:

```
        MOV  R0, #40H        //load pointer
        MOV  R2, #5          //load counter
        CLR  A               //A=0
        MOV  R7, A           //Clear R7
AGAIN:  ADD  A, @RO      //add the byte pointed by R0 with the accumulator
```

```
            JNC   NEXT          //If CY=0, do not accumulate carry
            INC   R7            //keep on adding carry
NEXT:       INC   R0            //increment pointer
            DJNZ  R2, AGAIN     //repeat until R2=0
```

Example 2.3

The marks obtained by a student (out of 25) for the six courses in a semester are stored in a RAM locations 47H onwards. Find the average of marks and output it in port 1.

Solution:

```
            MOV   R1, #06       //R1 stores the number of courses which is 6
            MOV   R0, #47H      //R0 acts as a pointer to the data in ROM
            MOV   B, #06        //only B can be used as divisor register
            MOV   A, #0         //clear accumulator, A=0
REPEAT:     ADD   A, @R0        //add the data pointed by R0 to A
                                //since each number is less than 25, CY=0
            INC   R0            //increment the pointer
            DJNZ  R1, REPEAT    //repeat the addition until R1=0
            DIV   AB            //divide the sum in A by 6 in B to get average
                                //keep quotient in A and remainder in B
            MOV   P1, A         //output average in Port 1, ignoring remainder
```

Example 2.4

Daily temperatures of five days are stored in ROM locations 40H-44H as shown below. Check if any of the values equals 65. If the value 65 exists in the table then store it to R4, else make R4=0.

40H = (75)   41H= (79)   42H=(69)   43H= (65)   44H= (62)

Solution:

```
            MOV   R4, #0        //R4=0
            MOV   R0, #40H      //load pointer with initial ROM location
            MOV   R2, #05       //load counter
            MOV   A, #65        //load A with 65 to be verified in the list
BACK:       CJNE  A, @R0, NEXT  //compare RAM data with 65
            MOV   R4, R0        //if 65 then save to R4
            SJMP  EXIT          //and exit
NEXT:       INC R0              //otherwise increment pointer
            DJNZ R2, BACK       //keep on checking all the values until count=0
EXIT        .....
```

Example 2.5

Write a program that will toggle all the bits of Port 1 continuously after a time delay. The value that will be sent to port 1 is 55H.

Solution:

```
            ORG       0
            MOV       A, #55H   //load A with 55H
BACK:       MOV       P1, A     //send the value of reg A in port 1
            ACALL     DELAY     //a subroutine call for time delay
            CPL       A         //complement content of reg A
            SJMP      BACK      //keep doing it indefinitely
//DELAY subroutine starts here
DELAY:
```

```
         MOV      R5, #0FFH      //load R5 with FFH (counter with delay of 255)
REPEAT:  DJNZ     R5, REPEAT     //stay here until content of R5 becomes 0
         RET                     //return to calling program
END                              //end of asm file
```

SUMMARY

This chapter introduces readers about the important features of 8051 microcontrollers and different other manufactures of 8051 family of microcontrollers. Next, the architecture and internal details of 8051 are explained in detail. All the major registers of 8051 including A, B, R0, R1, R2, R3, R4, R5, R6, R7, DPTR and PC along with SFRs are described next. Then we talk about program memory or ROM space allocation in 8051 and how to burn a program in ROM is illustrated with examples. Programmers must be aware of where programs are placed in ROM and how much memory is available. We then describe the register banks, RAM space allocation for data and the default register bank. Next, a detailed pictorial representation of stack operations and manipulation of stack and SP via PUSH and POP operation is elucidated. The process of creating an assembly language program is also described starting from a source file, to assembling it, linking and executing the program. Assembly language programs consist of sequence of statements called instructions. Some of them are pseudo-instructions which are also known as *directives.* Instructions are translated by assembler into machine codes. Pseudo-instructions are not translated into machine code. They direct the assembler, how to translate instructions into machine codes. Program status word (PSW) is indicated with flags. Flags are useful to programmers as they indicate the status after the execution of an instruction. For example, whether it has resulted in a carry or overflow. We have also described the clock generation in 8051 with crystal oscillator circuit and followed by reset circuit in detail. Timers and their associated registers are explained next. Additionally, I/O ports of 8051 are defined along with their configuration and connectivity. Instruction set of 8051 microcontroller consists of 49 distinct instruction divided into five groups which are also explained briefly. Lastly, this chapter illustrates on some assembly language programs.

Review Questions and Exercise

Section 2.1: Architecture of 8051

1. The program counter of 8051 is 8-bit/16-bit/32-bit wide. Pick the correct answer.
2. Accumulator A and reg B are 8-bit/16-bit/32-bit wide registers. Pick the correct one.
3. Name a 16-bit register in the 8051 microcontrollers.
4. What is the size of the registers R0-R7?
5. Check the following program segment and find the result. Also mention the location of result.

```
MOV  A, #25H
MOV R2, #14H
ADD  A, R2
```

6. Which of the following instructions are illegal?

a. MOV R3, #500
b. MOV R1, #50
c. MOV A, #255H
d. MOV A, #F5H
e. MOV R9, #50H
f. MOV R7, #00
g. ADD A, R5
h. ADD A, #50H
i. ADD R3, A

7. If the contents of R0 and A are 25H and 55H respectively, then what be will be content of destination registers after the execution of each line of the following instructions?

```
ADD  A, R0
MOV  R0, A
ADD  A, R0
ADD  R0, #07
```

Section 2.2 Introduction to Assembly Language Programming

8. Which program produces "obj' file?
9. Answer True or False.
   a. Source file has an extension "src" or "asm".
   b. Source code file can be a non-ASCII file.
   c. Every source file must have ORG and END directives.
   d. ORG and END directive appear in ".lst" file.
10. Is there any difference between instruction and directive?

Section 2.3: Program Counter and ROM space in 8051

11. Why do we write the programs always with ORG 0000 at the starting?
12. Find the number of bytes in each of the following instructions?
    a. MOV A, #55H
    b. MOV R3, #5
    c. ADD A, #0
    d. MOV A, R1
    e. INC R2
    f. MOV R3, A
13. If the following program is burnt into ROM, what will be the content of each ROM locations?

```
ORG     0000H
MOV     R0, #26H
MOV     R1, #36H
MOV     A, #0
ADD     A, R0
MOV     R2, A
```

Section 2.4: Instruction Set and Machine Cycle

14. What the mnemonics SJMP stands for? What is its length in bytes?
15. In which way SJMP and LJMP differ?
16. If the current PC value is 0100H, calculate the target address in the instruction

SJMP HERE, where HERE corresponds to 003FH.

17. Write True or False. All 8051 jumps are short jumps?
18. Which of the following instructions is/are not a short jump?
    a. JZ b. JNC c. LJMP d. DJNZ
19. Write true or false. All conditional jumps are short jumps.
20. Write a program to add 2 to the accumulator four times.
21. Analyse the following program:

```
       CLR  C
       MOV  A, #4CH          //load A with 4CH
       SUBB A, #6EH          //subtract 6EH from A
       JNC  NEXT             //if CY=0, jump to NEXT
       CPL  A                //if CY=1 then take 1's complement
       INC  A                //and increment to get 2's complement
NEXT:  MOV  R1, A            // save content of A in R1
```

22. For an AT8051microcontroller system with crystal frequency of 11.0592MHz, what will be the time taken to execute each of the following instructions:
    a. MOV R3, #55 b. LJMP c. MUL AB d. DEC R3
    e. NOP f. DJMP R2, target

References

1. Dallas Semiconductors: www.maxim-ic.com
2. M. Ali Mazidi, J. Gillipsie Mazidi, Rolin D. McKinlay. The 8051Microcontrollers and Embedded System. 2nd ed. New Jersey, Pearson Prentice Hall, 2006.
3. Kenneth J. Ayala. The 8051 Microcontroller. St. Paul, MN, WEST PUBLISHING COMPANY, 1991
4. http://techknowlearn.blogspot.com/2013/07/reset-oscillator-circuit-of-8051-micro.html
5. https://codembedded.wordpress.com/2017/03/27/architecture-of-8051-microcontroller

Chapter 3

Instruction Set and Programming

Key features of Module – 3

- Different types of addressing modes in 8051 microcontrollers
- Detailed instruction sets of 8051 microcontrollers
- Fundamental programs in C language
- Different assemblers and compilers

Pre-requisites

- Fundamentals C programming
- Basics of Computers

Module – 3 Outcomes

- Students should be able to understand the different addressing modes of 8051 microcontrollers and their implications
- Students should be able to write the proper syntax of instructions in 8051 microcontrollers
- Students should be able to write programs in assembly language and C language

This chapter gives an overview of the addressing modes of 8051 microcontrollers. The understanding of how to address a source data is discussed. There are different types of addressing like Register Addressing, Direct Addressing, Indirect Addressing, Relative Addressing, Indexed Addressing, Bit Inherent Addressing, bit Direct Addressing. These are the modes how a data can be represented through instruction depending on the location of the data. The syntax of writing any instruction is shown in the chapter along with some fundamental programs of 8051 microcontrollers.

3.1 Addressing Mode

Addressing mode is a way to address an operand. Operand means the data we are operating upon (source data). It can be a direct address of memory, it can be register names, it can be any numerical data etc. depending on the programming situation. The classification of the addressing mode is not very significant, except that it provides some clues in understanding mnemonics.

The CPU can access data in various ways, which are called addressing modes

- Immediate
- Register
- Direct

- Register indirect
- Indexed

Direct, register indirect and indexed are accessing memories. The addressing modes are discussed later in the chapter.

3.2 Instruction Syntax

There are 49 Instruction Mnemonics in the 8051 Microcontroller Instruction Set and these 49 Mnemonics are divided into five groups.

Table 3. 1. Types of instructions

DATA TRANSFER	ARITHMETIC	LOGICAL	BOOLEAN	PROGRAM BRANCHING
MOV	ADD	ANL	CLR	LJMP
MOVC	ADDC	ORL	SETB	AJMP
MOVX	SUBB	XRL	MOV	SJMP
PUSH	INC	CLR	JC	JZ
POP	DEC	CPL	JNC	JNZ
XCH	MUL	RL	JB	CJNE
XCHD	DIV	RLC	JNB	DJNZ
	DA A	RR	JBC	NOP
		RRC	ANL	LCALL
		SWAP	ORL	ACALL
			CPL	RET
				RETI
				JMP

The 8051 microcontroller instructions set includes 110 instructions, 49 of which are single byte instructions, 45 are two bytes instructions and 17 are three bytes instructions. The instructions format consists of a function mnemonic followed by destination and source field. Data transfer group. Arithmetic group. The syntax of 8051 microcontroller is given as

<Memory address> <Mnemonics>;

For example, to add two numbers, first one number has to be in accumulator, then we add the other number with the number in the accumulator.

2001 ADD A, Rn

The program illustrates how to assemble and run an 8051 program

```
0000 ORG 0H; start (origin) at 0
0000 7D25 MOV R5, #25H; load 25H into R5
0002 7F34 MOV R7, #34H; load 34H into R7
0004 7400 MOV A, #0; load 0 into A
0006 2D ADD A, R5; add contents of R5 to A; now A = A + R5
0007 2F ADD A, R7; add contents of R7 to A; now A = A + R7
0008 2412 ADD A, #12H; add to A value 12H; now A = A + 12H
000A 80EF HERE: SJMP HERE; stay in this loop
000C END; end of asm source file
```

3.3 Data types and directives

A good understanding of C data types for 8051 can help programmers to create smaller hex files

- Signed char
- Unsigned int
- Signed int
- Sbit (single bit)
- Bit and sfr

3.3.1 Unsigned char

The character data type is the most natural choice

- 8051 is an 8-bit microcontroller

Unsigned char is an 8-bit data type in the range of 0 – 255 (00 – FFH)

- One of the most widely used data types for the 8051 *f*
    i. Counter value *f*
    ii. ASCII characters

C compilers use the signed char as the default if we do not put the keyword unsigned.

1. *Write an 8051 C program to send values 00 – FF to port P1.*
   Solution:

```
#include <reg51.h>
void main(void)
{
unsigned char z;
for (z=0;z<=255;z++)
P1=z;
}
```

2. *Write an 8051 C program to send hex values for ASCII characters of 0, 1, 2, 3, 4, 5, A, B, C, and D to port P1.*
   Solution:

```
#include <reg51.h>
void main(void)
{
unsigned char mynum[]="012345ABCD";
unsigned char z;
for (z=0;z<=10;z++)
P1=mynum[z];
}
```

3. *Write an 8051 C program to toggle all the bits of P1 continuously.*

Solution:

```
//Toggle P1 forever
```

```
#include <reg51.h>
void main(void)
{
for (;;)
{
p1=0x55; p1=0xAA;
}
}
```

3.3.2 Signed char

The signed char is an 8-bit data type

- Use the MSB D7 to represent – or +
- Give us values from –128 to +127 ‰

We should stick with the unsigned char unless the data needs to be represented as signed numbers.

4. *Write an 8051 C program to send values of –4 to +4 to port P1.*

Solution:

```
//Singed numbers
#include <reg51.h>
void main(void)
{
char mynum[]={+1,-1,+2,-2,+3,-3,+4,-4};
unsigned char z;
for (z=0;z<=8;z++)
P1=mynum[z];
}
```

3.3.3 Unsigned and Signed int

The unsigned int is a 16-bit data type

- Takes a value in the range of 0 to 65535 (0000 – FFFFH)
- Define 16-bit variables such as memory addresses
- Set counter values of more than 256
- Since registers and memory accesses are in 8-bit chunks, the misuse of int variables will result in a larger hex file.

Signed int is a 16-bit data type

- Use the MSB D15 to represent – or +
- We have 15 bits for the magnitude of the number from –32768 to +32767

3.3.4 Single Bit

5. *Write an 8051 C program to toggle bit D0 of the port P1 (P1.0) 50,000 times.*

Solution:

```
#include <reg51.h>
sbit MYBIT=P1^0;
void main(void)
{
unsigned int z;
for (z=0;z<=50000;z++)
{
MYBIT=0; MYBIT=1;
}
}
```

3.3.5 Bit and sfr

The bit data type allows access to single bits of bit-addressable memory spaces 20 – 2FH. To access the byte-size SFR registers, we use the sfr data type

Table 3.2. Data types, number of bits, bytes and range of values

Data type	Bits	Bytes	Value range
bit	1		0 to 1
signed char	8	1	-128 to +127
unsigned char	8	1	0 to 255
enum	8 or 16	1 or 2	-128 to +127 or -32768 to +32767
signed short	16	2	-32768 to +32767
unsigned short	16	2	0 to 65535
signed int	16	2	-32768 to +32767
unsigned int	16	2	0 to 65535
signed long	32	4	-2147483648 to 2147483647
unsigned long	32	4	0 to 4294967295
float	32	4	±1.175494E-38 to ±3.402823E+38
sbit	1		0 to 1
sfr	8	4	0 to 255
sfr16	16	2	0 to 65535

The following are some more widely used directives of the 8051.

<u>ORG (origin)</u>

The ORG directive is used to indicate the beginning of the address. The number that comes after ORG can be either in hex or in decimal. If the number is not followed by H, it is decimal and the assembler will convert it to hex. Some assemblers use ". ORG" (notice the dot) instead of "ORG" for the origin directive. Check your assembler.

<u>EQU (equate)</u>

This is used to define a constant without occupying a memory location. The EQU directive does not set aside storage for a data item but associates a constant value with a data label so that when the label appears in the program, its constant value will be substituted for the label. The following uses EQU for the counter constant and then the constant is used to load the R3 register.

```
COUNT      EQU 25
........   ........
MOV        R3, #COUNT
```

When executing the instruction "MOV R3, #COUNT", the register R3 will be loaded with the value 25 (notice the # sign). What is the advantage of using EQU? Assume that there is a constant (a fixed value) used in many different places in the program, and the programmer wants to change its value throughout. By the use of EQU, the programmer can change it once and the assembler will change all of its occurrences, rather than search the entire program trying to find every occurrence.

END directive

Another important pseudocode is the END directive. This indicates to the assembler the end of the source (asm) file. The END directive is the last line of an 8051 program, meaning that in the source code anything after the END directive is ignored by the assembler. Some assemblers use ". END" (notice the dot) instead
of "END".

3.4 Subroutines

The CPU also uses the stack to save the address of the instruction just below the CALL instruction. This is how the CPU knows where to resume when it returns from the called subroutine. Subroutines are a set of instructions that perform specific function, which is written in some other memory location other than the main program. Call instruction is used to call subroutine

- Subroutines are often used to perform tasks that need to be performed frequently
- This makes a program more structured in addition to saving memory space

LCALL (long call)
3-byte instruction *f*

- First byte is the opcode *f*
- Second and third bytes are used for address of target subroutine

Subroutine is located anywhere within 64K byte address space

ACALL (absolute call)
2-byte instruction

- *f* 11 bits are used for address within 2K-byte range

When a subroutine is called, control is transferred to that subroutine, the processor

- Saves on the stack the the address of the instruction immediately below the LCALL
- Begins to fetch instructions form the new location ‰

After finishing execution of the subroutine
The instruction RET transfers control back to the caller *f*

- Every subroutine needs RET as the last instruction

6. *Write an example of LCALL*

```
ORG 0
```

```
BACK: MOV A, #55H; load A with 55H
 MOV P1, A; send 55H to port 1
LCALL DELAY; time delay
MOV A, #0AAH; load A with AA (in hex)
MOV P1, A; send AAH to port 1
 LCALL DELAY
SJMP BACK; keep doing this indefinitely;
---------- this is delay subroutine ------------
ORG 300H; put DELAY at address 300H
DELAY: MOV R5, #0FFH; R5=255 (FF in hex), counter
AGAIN: DJNZ R5, AGAIN; stay here until R5 become 0
RET; return to caller (when R5 =0)
END
```

3.4.2 Calling Subroutines

It is common to have one main program and many subroutines that are called from the main program.

```
;MAIN program calling subroutines
ORG 0
MAIN: LCALL SUBR_1
LCALL SUBR_2
 LCALL SUBR_3
HERE: SJMP HERE
 ;-----------end of MAIN
SUBR_1: ...
 ...
RET
 ;-----------end of subroutine1
SUBR_2: ...
 ...
RET
 ;-----------end of subroutine2
SUBR_3: ...
 ...
RET
 ;-----------end of subroutine3
END ;end of the asm file
```

This allows you to make each subroutine into a separate module
- Each module can be tested separately and then brought together with main program
- In a large program, the module can be assigned to different programmers.

ACALL

The only difference between ACALL and LCALL is

- The target address for LCALL can be anywhere within the 64K byte address
- The target address of ACALL must be within a 2K-byte range ‰

The use of ACALL instead of LCALL can save a number of bytes of program ROM space

```
ORG 0
BACK: MOV A,#55H ;load A with 55H
MOV P1,A ;send 55H to port 1
 LCALL DELAY ;time delay
MOV A,#0AAH ;load A with AA (in hex)
MOV P1,A ;send AAH to port 1
 LCALL DELAY
SJMP BACK ;keep doing this indefinitely
...
END ;end of asm file
```

- A rewritten program which is more efficient

```
ORG 0
MOV A,#55H ;load A with 55H
BACK: MOV P1,A ;send 55H to port 1
ACALL DELAY ;time delay
CPL A ;complement reg A
SJMP BACK ;keep doing this indefinitely
...
END ;end of asm file
```

3.5 Addressing Modes

The CPU can access data in various ways, which are called addressing modes

- Immediate
- Register
- Direct
- Register indirect
- Indexed

Direct, register indirect and indexed are accessing memories.

3.5.1 Immediate Addressing Mode

The source operand is a constant

- The immediate data must be preceded by the pound sign, "#"
- Can load information into any registers, including 16-bit DPTR register *f*

DPTR can also be accessed as two 8-bit registers, the high byte DPH and low byte DPL

```
MOV A,#25H ;load 25H into A
MOV R4,#62 ;load 62 into R4
MOV B,#40H ;load 40H into B
MOV DPTR,#4521H ;DPTR=4512H
MOV DPL,#21H ;This is the same
MOV DPH,#45H
;as above ;illegal!! Value > 65535 (FFFFH)
MOV DPTR,#68975
```

- We can use EQU directive to access immediate data

```
Count EQU 30
... ...
MOV R4,#COUNT ;R4=1EH
MOV DPTR,#MYDATA ;DPTR=200H
ORG 200H
MYDATA: DB "America"
```

- We can also use immediate addressing mode to send data to 8051 ports

MOV P1,#55H

3.5.2 Register Addressing Mode

Use registers to hold the data to be manipulated

```
MOV A,R0 ;copy contents of R0 into A
MOV R2,A ;copy contents of A into R2
ADD A,R5 ;add contents of R5 to A
ADD A,R7 ;add contents of R7 to A
MOV R6,A ;save accumulator in R6
```

The source and destination registers must match in size

- MOV DPTR,A will give an error

```
MOV DPTR,#25F5H
MOV R7,DPL
MOV R6,DPH
```

The movement of data between Rn registers is not allowed
MOV R4,R7 is invalid

3.5.3 Direct Addressing Mode

It is most often used the direct addressing mode to access RAM locations 30 – 7FH

- The entire 128 bytes of RAM can be accessed
- The register bank locations are accessed by the register names

```
MOV A,4 ;is same as
MOV A,R4 ;which means copy R4 into A
```

Contrast this with immediate addressing mode

- There is no "#" sign in the operand

```
MOV R0,40H ;save content of 40H in R0
MOV 56H,A ;save content of A in 56H
```

7. *Write code to send 55H to ports P1 and P2, using (a) their names (b) their addresses*

Solution :

```
(a) MOV A,#55H ;A=55H
    MOV P1,A ;P1=55H
    MOV P2,A ;P2=55H
(b) From Table 5-1, P1 address=80H; P2 address=A0H
    MOV A,#55H ;A=55H
    MOV 80H,A ;P1=55H
    MOV 0A0H,A ;P2=55H
```

3.5.4 Stack and Direct Addressing Mode

Only direct addressing mode is allowed for pushing or popping the stack

- PUSH A is invalid
- Pushing the accumulator onto the stack must be coded as PUSH 0E0H

8. *Show the code to push R5 and A onto the stack and then pop them back them into R2 and B, where B = A and R2 = R5*

Solution:

```
PUSH 05 ;push R5 onto stack
PUSH 0E0H ;push register A onto stack
POP 0F0H ;pop top of stack into B ;now register B = register A
POP 02 ;pop top of stack into R2 ;now R2=R6
```

3.5.5 Indirect Addressing Mode

A register is used as a pointer to the data

- Only register R0 and R1 are used for this purpose
- R2 – R7 cannot be used to hold the address of an operand located in RAM

When R0 and R1 hold the addresses of RAM locations, they must be preceded by the "@" sign

```
MOV A,@R0 ;move contents of RAM whose ;address is held by R0 into A
MOV @R1,B ;move contents of B into RAM ;whose address is held by R1
```

9. *Write a program to copy the value 55H into RAM memory locations 40H to 41H using (a) direct addressing mode, (b) register indirect addressing mode without a loop, and (c) with a loop*

Solution:

```
(a) MOV A,#55H ;load A with value 55H
```

```
MOV 40H,A ;copy A to RAM location 40H
MOV 41H.A ;copy A to RAM location 41H

(b) MOV A,#55H ;load A with value 55H
MOV R0,#40H ;load the pointer. R0=40H
MOV @R0,A ;copy A to RAM R0 points to
INC R0 ;increment pointer. Now R0=41h
MOV @R0,A ;copy A to RAM R0 points to

(c)MOV A,#55H ;A=55H
MOV R0,#40H ;load pointer.R0=40H,
MOV R2,#02 ;load counter, R2=3
AGAIN: MOV @R0,A ;copy 55 to RAM R0 points to
INC R0 ;increment R0 pointer
DJNZ R2,AGAIN ;loop until counter = zero
```

The advantage is that it makes accessing data dynamic rather than static as in direct addressing mode

- Looping is not possible in direct addressing mode

10. Write a program to clear 16 RAM locations starting at RAM address 60H

Solution:

```
CLR A ;A=0
MOV R1,#60H ;load pointer. R1=60H
MOV R7,#16 ;load counter, R7=16
AGAIN: MOV @R1,A ;clear RAM R1 points to
INC R1 ;increment R1 pointer
DJNZ R7,AGAIN ;loop until counter=zero
```

11. Write a program to copy a block of 10 bytes of data from 35H to 60H

Solution:

```
MOV R0,#35H ;source pointer
MOV R1,#60H ;destination pointer
MOV R3,#10 ;counter BACK:
MOV A,@R0 ;get a byte from source
MOV @R1,A ;copy it to destination
INC R0 ;increment source pointer
INC R1 ;increment destination pointer
DJNZ R3,BACK ;keep doing for ten bytes
```

- R0 and R1 are the only registers that can be used for pointers in register indirect addressing mode.
- Since R0 and R1 are 8 bits wide, their use is limited to access any information in the internal RAM

- Whether accessing externally connected RAM or on-chip ROM, we need 16-bit pointer In such case, the DPTR register is used
- Indexed addressing mode is widely used in accessing data elements of look-up table entries located in the program ROM ‰
- The instruction used for this purpose is MOVC A,@A+DPTR
    - ➤ Use instruction MOVC, "C" means code
    - ➤ The contents of A are added to the 16-bit register DPTR to form the 16-bit address of the needed data

3.5.6 Indexed Addressing Mode and Onchip ROM Access

12. In this program, assume that the word "USA" is burned into ROM locations starting at 200H. And that the program is burned into ROM locations starting at 0. Analyze how the program works and state where "USA" is stored after this program is run.

Solution:

```
ORG 0000H ;burn into ROM starting at 0
MOV DPTR,#200H ;DPTR=200H look-up table addr
CLR A ;clear A(A=0)
MOVC A,@A+DPTR ;get the char from code space
MOV R0,A ;save it in R0
INC DPTR ;DPTR=201 point to next char
CLR A ;clear A(A=0)
 MOVC A,@A+DPTR ;get the next char
MOV R1,A ;save it in R1
INC DPTR ;DPTR=202 point to next char
CLR A ;clear A(A=0)
MOVC A,@A+DPTR ;get the next char
MOV R2,A ;save it in R2
Here: SJMP HERE ;stay here ;Data is burned into code space
starting at 200H
ORG 200H
MYDATA:DB "USA"
 END ;end of program
```

The look-up table allows access to elements of a frequently used table with minimum operations

13. Write a program to get the x value from P1 and send x2 to P2, continuously

Solution:

```
ORG 0
MOV DPTR,#300H ;LOAD TABLE ADDRESS
MOV A,#0FFH ;A=FF
MOV P1,A ;CONFIGURE P1 INPUT PORT
BACK:MOV A,P1 ;GET X
MOV A,@A+DPTR ;GET X SQAURE FROM TABLE
MOV P2,A ;ISSUE IT TO P2
SJMP BACK ;KEEP DOING IT
```

```
ORG 300H
 XSQR_TABLE:
DB 0,1,4,9,16,25,36,49,64,81
 END
```

3.5.6.1 Indexed Addressing Mode and MOVX

In many applications, the size of program code does not leave any room to share the 64K-byte code space with data

- The 8051 has another 64K bytes of memory space set aside exclusively for data storage

This data memory space is referred to as external memory and it is accessed only by the MOVX instruction

The 8051 has a total of 128K bytes of memory space

- 64K bytes of code and 64K bytes of data
- The data space cannot be shared between code and data

In many applications we use RAM locations 30 – 7FH as scratch pad

- We use R0 – R7 of bank 0
- Leave addresses 8 – 1FH for stack usage
- If we need more registers, we simply use RAM locations 30 – 7FH

14. *Write a program to toggle P1 a total of 200 times. Use RAM location 32H to hold your counter value instead of registers R0 – R7*

Solution:

```
MOV P1,#55H ;P1=55H
MOV 32H,#200 ;load counter value ;into RAM loc 32H
LOP1: CPL P1 ;toggle P1
ACALL DELAY
DJNZ 32H,LOP1 ;repeat 200 times
```

3.5.7 Bit Inherent Addressing

Many microprocessors allow program to access registers and I/O ports in byte size only. However, in many applications we need to check a single bit. One unique and powerful feature of the 8051 is single-bit operation single-bit instructions allow the programmer to set, clear, move, and complement individual bits of a port, memory, or register. It is registers, RAM, and I/O ports that need to be bit-addressable. ROM, holding program code for execution, is not bit-addressable.

3.5.8 Bit Addressable RAM

The bit-addressable RAM location are 20H to 2FH

These 16 bytes provide 128 bits of RAM bit-addressability, since $16 \times 8 = 128$

0 to 127 (in decimal) or 00 to 7FH

- The first byte of internal RAM location 20H has bit address 0 to 7H
- The last byte of 2FH has bit address 78H to 7FH ‰ Internal RAM locations 20-2FH are both byte-addressable and bit- addressable
- Bit address 00-7FH belong to RAM byte addresses 20-2FH
- Bit address 80-F7H belong to SFR P0, P1, …

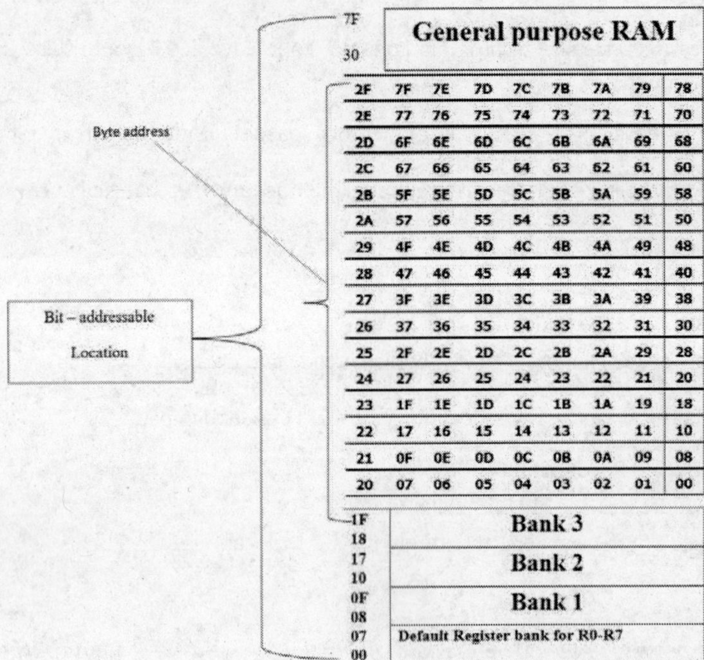

Fig.3.3: Bit Addressable RAM

15. *Find out to which by each of the following bits belongs. Give the address of the RAM byte in hex (a) SETB 42H, (b) CLR 67H, (c) CLR 0FH (d) SETB 28H, (e) CLR 12, (f) SETB 05*

Solution:

(a) D2 of RAM location 28H

(b) D7 of RAM location 2CH

(c) D7 of RAM location 21H

(d) D0 of RAM location 25H

(e) D4 of RAM location 21H

(f) D5 of RAM location 20H

	D7	D6	D5	D4	D3	D2	D1	D0
2F	7F	7E	7D	7C	7B	7A	79	78
2E	77	76	75	74	73	72	71	70
2D	6F	6E	6D	6C	6B	6A	69	68
2C	67	66	65	64	63	62	61	60
2B	5F	5E	5D	5C	5B	5A	59	58
2A	57	56	55	54	53	52	51	50
29	4F	4E	4D	4C	4B	4A	49	48
28	47	46	45	44	43	42	41	40
27	3F	3E	3D	3C	3B	3A	39	38
26	37	36	35	34	33	32	31	30
25	2F	2E	2D	2C	2B	2A	29	28
24	27	26	25	24	23	22	21	20
23	1F	1E	1D	1C	1B	1A	19	18
22	17	16	15	14	13	12	11	10
21	0F	0E	0D	0C	0B	0A	09	08
20	07	06	05	04	03	02	01	00

To avoid confusion regarding the addresses 00 – 7FH

- The 128 bytes of RAM have the byte addresses of 00 – 7FH can be accessed in byte size using various addressing modes

Direct and register-indirect

- The 16 bytes of RAM locations 20 – 2FH have bit address of 00 – 7FH

We can use only the single-bit instructions and these instructions use only direct addressing mode

Table 3.3. Instructions that are used for signal-bit operations

Instruction		Function
SETB bit		Set the bit (bit = 1)
CLR	bit	Clear the bit (bit = 0)
CPL	bit	Complement the bit (bit = NOT bit)
JB	bit, target	Jump to target if bit = 1 (jump if bit)
JNB	bit, target	Jump to target if bit = 0 (jump if no bit)
JBC	bit, target	Jump to target if bit = 1, clear bit (jump if bit, then clear)

3.5.9 Registers Bit Addressability

Only registers A, B, PSW, IP, IE, ACC, SCON, and TCON are bit-addressable

- While all I/O ports are bit-addressable

In PSW register, two bits are set aside for the selection of the register banks

- Upon RESET, bank 0 is selected
- We can select any other banks using the bit-addressability of the PSW

CY	AC	--	RS1	RS0	OV	--	P

Table 3.4. Register Bits and addresses

RS1	RS0	Register Bank	Address
0	0	0	00H - 07H
0	1	1	08H - 0FH
1	0	2	10H - 17H
1	1	3	18H - 1FH

16. *Write a program to save the accumulator in R7 of bank 2.*

Solution:

CLR PSW.3 SETB PSW.4 MOV R7,A

17. *While there are instructions such as JNC and JC to check the carry flag bit (CY), there are no such instructions for the overflow flag bit (OV). How would you write code to check OV?*

Solution:

JB PSW.2, TARGET; jump if OV=1

CY	AC	--	RS1	RS0	OV	--	P

18. *While a program to save the status of bit P1.7 on RAM address bit 05.*

Solution: MOV C,P1.7 MOV 05,C

19. *Write a program to see if the RAM location 37H contains an even value. If so, send it to P2. If not, make it even and then send it to P2.*

Solution: MOV A,37H ;load RAM 37H into ACC JNB ACC.0,YES ;if D0 of ACC 0? If so jump INC A ;it's odd, make it even YES: MOV P2,A ;send it to P2

20. *The status of bits P1.2 and P1.3 of I/O port P1 must be saved before they are changed. Write a program to save the status of P1.2 in bit location 06 and the status of P1.3 in bit location 07*

Solution: CLR 06 ;clear bit addr. 06 CLR 07 ;clear bit addr. 07 JNB P1.2,OVER ;check P1.2, if 0 then jump SETB 06 ;if P1.2=1,set bit 06 to 1 OVER: JNB P1.3,NEXT ;check P1.3, if 0 then jump SETB 07 ;if P1.3=1,set bit 07 to 1 NEXT: ...

Using BIT

The BIT directive is a widely used directive to assign the bit-addressable I/O and RAM locations

- Allow a program to assign the I/O or RAM bit at the beginning of the program, making it easier to modify them

21. *A switch is connected to pin P1.7 and an LED to pin P2.0. Write a program to get the status of the switch and send it to the LED.*

Solution: LED BIT P1.7 ;assign bit SW BIT P2.0 ;assign bit HERE: MOV C,SW ;get the bit from the port MOV LED,C ;send the bit to the port SJMP HERE ;repeat forever

22. *Assume that bit P2.3 is an input and represents the condition of an oven. If it goes high, it means that the oven is hot. Monitor the bit continuously. Whenever it goes high, send a high-to-low pulse to port P1.5 to turn on a buzzer.*

Solution: OVEN_HOT BIT P2.3 BUZZER BIT P1.5 HERE: JNB OVEN_HOT, HERE; keep monitoring ACALL DELAY CPL BUZZER; sound the buzzer ACALL DELAY SJMP HERE

Using EQU

Use the EQU to assign addresses

- Defined by names, like P1.7 or P2
- Defined by addresses, like 97H or 0A0H

3.6 8051 Instruction Set

A simple instruction consists of just the opcode. Other instructions may include one or more operands. Instruction can be one-byte instruction, which contains only opcode, or two-byte instructions, where the second byte is the operand or three-byte instructions, where the operand makes up the second and third byte.

Based on the operation they perform, all the instructions in the 8051 Microcontroller Instruction Set are divided into five groups. They are:

- Data Transfer Instructions
- Arithmetic Instructions
- Logical Instructions
- Boolean or Bit Manipulation Instructions
- Program Branching Instructions

3.6.1 Data Transfer Instructions

The Data Transfer Instructions are associated with transfer of data between registers or external program memory or external data memory. The Mnemonics associated with Data Transfer are given below.

- *MOV*
- *MOVC*
- *MOVX*
- *PUSH*
- *POP*
- *XCH*
- *XCHD*

Table 3.5. Data transfer mnemonics and its function

Mnemonic	Description
MOV	Move Data
MOVC	Move Code
MOCX	Move External Data
PUSH	Move Data to Stack
POP	Copy Data from Stack
XCH	Exchange Data between two Registers
XCHD	Exchange Lower Order Data between two Registers

The following table lists out all the possible data transfer instructions along with other details like addressing mode, size occupied and number machine cycles it takes.

Table 3.6 Data transfer instructions with details

Mnemonic	Instruction	Description	Addressing Mode	No. of Bytes	No. of Cycles
MOV	A, #Data	A ← Data	Immediate	2	1
	A,Rn	A ← Rn	Register	1	1
	A, Direct	A ← (Direct)	Direct	2	1
	A,@Ri	A← @Ri	Indirect	1	1
	Rn,#Data	Rn ← data	Immediate	2	1
	Rn,A	Rn← A	Register	1	1
	Rn,Direct	Rn ← (Direct)	Direct	2	2
	Direct, A	(Direct) ← A	Direct	2	1
	Direct,Rn	(Direct) ← Rn	Direct	2	2
	Direct1, Direct2	(Direct1) ← (Direct2)	Direct	3	2
	Direct, @Ri	(Direct) ← @Ri	Indirect	2	2
	Direct, #Data	(Direct) ← #Data	Direct	3	2
	@Ri,A	@Ri ← A	Indirect	1	1
	@Ri,Direct	@Ri ← Direct	Indirect	2	2
	@Ri,#Data	@Ri ← #Data	Indirect	2	1

	DPTR,#Data16	DPTR ← #Data16	Immediate	3	2
MOVC	A,@A+DPTR	A← Code pointed by A+DPTR	Indexed	1	2
	A,@A+PC	A← Code pointed by A+PC	Indexed	1	2
	A,@Ri	A ← Code pointed by Ri (8-bit Address)	Indirect	1	2
MOVX	A,@DPTR	A← External Data pointed by DPTR	Indirect	1	2
	@Ri,A	@Ri ← A (External Data 8-bit Addr)	Indirect	1	2
	@DPTR,A	@DPTR← A (External Data 16- bit Addr)	Indirect	1	2
PUSH	Direct	Stack Pointer SP ← (Direct)	Direct	2	2
POP	Direct	(Direct) ← Stack Pointer SP	Direct	2	2
XCH	Rn	Exchange ACC with Rn	Register	1	1
	Direct	Exchange ACC with Direct Byte	Direct	2	1
	@Ri	Exchange ACC with Indirect RAM	Indirect	1	1
XCHD	A,@Ri	Exchange ACC with Lower Order Indirect RAM	Indirect	1	1

3.6.2 Arithmetic Instructions

Using Arithmetic Instructions, you can perform addition, subtraction, multiplication and division. The arithmetic instructions also include increment by one, decrement by one and a special instruction called Decimal Adjust Accumulator.

The Mnemonics associated with the Arithmetic Instructions of the 8051 Microcontroller Instruction Set are:

- *ADD*
- *ADDC*
- *SUBB*
- *INC*
- *DEC*
- *MUL*
- *DIV*
- *DA A*

Table 3.7. Arithmatic mnemonics and its function

Mnemonic	**Description**
ADD	Addition without Carry
ADDC	Addition with Carry
SUBB	Subtract with Carry
INC	Increment by 1
DEC	Decrement by 1

MUL	Multiply
DIV	Divide
DA A	Decimal Adjust the Accumulator (A Register)

The arithmetic instructions have no knowledge about the data format i.e., signed, unsigned, ASCII, BCD, etc. Also, the operations performed by the arithmetic instructions affect flags like carry, overflow, zero, etc. in the PSW Register.

All the possible Mnemonics associated with Arithmetic Instructions are mentioned in the following table.

Table 3.8. Arithmetic instructions with details

Mnemonic	Instruction	Description	Addressing Mode	# of Bytes	# of Cycles
ADD	A, #Data	A ← A +Data	Immediate	2	1
	A,Rn	A ←A+ Rn	Register	1	1
	A, Direct	A ←A+ (Direct)	Direct	2	1
	A,@Ri	A← A+ @Ri	Indirect	1	1
ADDC	A, #Data	A ←A + Data +C	Immediate	2	1
	A,Rn	A ←A+ Rn +C	Register	1	1
	A, Direct	A ←A +(Direct) + C	Direct	2	1
	A,@Ri	A← A+ @Ri + C	Indirect	1	1
SUBB	A, #Data	A ←A- Data - C	Immediate	2	2
	A,Rn	A ←A – Rn - C	Register	3	2
	A, Direct	A← A - (Direct) - C	Direct	1	1
	A,@Ri	A ←A - @Ri - C	Indirect	2	2
MUL	AB	Multiply A with B (A ← Lower Byte of A*B and B ←Higher Byte of A*B)	—	1	4
DIV	AB	Divide A by B (A ← Quotient and B ← Remainder	—	1	4
DEC	A	A← A - 1	Register	1	1
		Rn← Rn - 1	Register	1	1
		(Direct)← (Direct) - 1	Direct	2	1
		@Ri← @Ri - 1	Indirect	1	1
INC	A	A← A+1	Register	1	1

	A,Rn	Rn← Rn +1	Register	1	1
	Direct	(Direct)← (Direct) +1	Direct	2	1
	@Ri	@Ri← @Ri +1	Indirect	1	1
	DPTR	DPTR← DPTR +1	Register	1	2
DA	A	Decimal Adjust Accumulator	—	1	1

3.6.3 Logical Instructions

The next group of instructions are the Logical Instructions, which perform logical operations like AND, OR, XOR, NOT, Rotate, Clear and Swap. Logical Instruction are performed on Bytes of data on a bit-by-bit basis.

Mnemonics associated with Logical Instructions are as follows:

- *ANL*
- *ORL*
- *XRL*
- *CLR*
- *CPL*
- *RL*
- *RLC*
- *RR*
- *RRC*
- *SWAP*

Table 3.9. Logical instructions with details

Mnemonic	Description
ANL	Logical AND
ORL	Logical OR
XRL	Ex-OR
CLR	Clear Register
CPL	Complement the Register
RL	Rotate a Byte to Left
RLC	Rotate a Byte and Carry Bit to Left
RR	Rotate a Byte to Right
RRC	Rotate a Byte and Carry Bit to Right
SWAP	Exchange lower and higher nibbles in a Byte

Table 3.10. Mnemonics of the Logical Instructions.

Mnemonic	instruction	Description	Addressing Mode	# of Bytes	# of Cycles
ANL	A, #Data	A ← A AND Data	Immediate	2	1

	A,Rn	A ←A AND Rn	Register	1	1
	A,Direct	A ←A AND (Direct)	Direct	2	1
	A,@Ri	A ←A AND @Ri	Indirect	1	1
	Direct, A	(Direct) ←(Direct) AND A	Direct	2	1
	Direct, #Data	(Direct) ←(Direct) AND # Data	Direct	3	2
ORL	A, #Data	A ←A OR Data	Immediate	2	1
	A,Rn	A ← A OR Rn	Register	1	1
	A,Direct	A ←A OR (Direct)	Direct	2	1
	A,@Ri	A ←A+ @Ri	Indirect	1	1
	Direct, A	(Direct) ← (Direct) OR A	Direct	2	1
	Direct, #Data	(Direct) ←(Direct) OR # Data	Direct	3	2
XRL	A, #Data	A ←A XRL Data	Immediate	2	1
	A,Rn	A ←A XRL Rn	Register	1	1
	A,Direct	A ←A XRL (Direct)	Direct	2	1
	A,@Ri	A ←A XRL @Ri	Indirect	1	1
	Direct, A	(Direct) ←(Direct) XRL A	Direct	2	1
	Direct, #Data	(Direct) ←(Direct) XRL # Data	Direct	3	2
CLR	A	A ←00H	—	1	1
CPL	A	A← A	—	1	1
RL	A	Rotate ACC Left	—	1	1
				1	1
RLC	A	Rotate ACC Left through Carry	—	2	1
				1	1
RR	A	Rotate ACC Right	—		
				1	1
RRC	A	Rotate ACC Right through Carry	—	1	1
SWAP	A	Swap Nibble within ACC	—	1	1

3.6.4 Boolean or Bit Manipulation Instructions

As the name suggests, Boolean or Bit Manipulation Instructions deal with bit variables. We know that there is a special bit-addressable area in the RAM and some of the Special Function Registers (SFRs) are also bit addressable.

The Mnemonics corresponding to the Boolean or Bit Manipulation instructions are:

- *CLR*
- *SETB*
- *MOV*
- *JC*
- *JNC*
- *JB*
- *JNB*
- *JBC*
- *ANL*
- *ORL*
- *CPL*

Table 3.11. Bit Manipulation instructions with details

Mnemonic	Description
CLR	Clear a Bit (Reset to 0)
SETB	Set a Bit (Set to 1)
MOV	Move a Bit
JC	Jump if Carry Flag is Set
JNC	Jump if Carry Flag is Not Set
JB	Jump if specified Bit is Set
JNB	Jump if specified Bit is Not Set
JBC	Jump if specified Bit is Set and also clear the Bit
ANL	Bitwise AND
ORL	Bitwise OR
CPL	Complement the Bit

These instructions can perform set, clear, and, or, complement etc. at bit level. All the possible mnemonics of the Boolean Instructions are specified in the following table.

Table 3.12. Mnemonics of the Bit Manipulation instructions

Mnemonic	instruction	Description	# of Bytes	# of Cycles
CLR	C	C← 0 (C = Carry Bit)	1	1
	Bit	Bit ←0 (Bit = Direct Bit)	2	1
SET	C	C← 1	1	1
	Bit	Bit ←1	2	1
CPL	C	C ←C —	1	1
	Bit	Bit Bit	2	1
ANL	C, /Bit	C ←C. Bit ($\overline{\text{AND}}$)	2	1
	C, Bit	C← C. Bit (AND)	2	1

ORL	C, /Bit	C ←C+ Bit ($\overline{\text{AND}}$)	2	1
	C, Bit	C ←C+ Bit (AND)	2	1
MOV	C, Bit	C← Bit	2	1
	Bit, C	Bit← C	2	2
JC	rel	Jump is carry (C) is Set	2	2
JNC	rel	Jump is carry (C) is Not Set	2	2
JB	Bit,rel	Jump is Direct Bit is Set	3	2
JNB	Bit,rel	Jump is Direct Bit is Not Set	3	2
JBC	Bit,rel	Jump is Direct Bit is Set and Clear Bit	3	2

3.6.5 Program Branching Instructions

The last group of instructions in the 8051 Microcontroller Instruction Set are the Program Branching Instructions. These instructions control the flow of program logic. The mnemonics of the Program Branching Instructions are as follows.

- *LJMP*
- *AJMP*
- *SJMP*
- *JZ*
- *JNZ*
- *CJNE*
- *DJNZ*
- *NOP*
- *LCALL*
- *ACALL*
- *RET*
- *RETI*
- *JMP*

Table 3.13. Program Branching instructions with details

Mnemonic	**Description**
LJMP	Long Jump (Unconditional)
AJMP	Absolute Jump (Unconditional)
SJMP	Short Jump (Unconditional)
JZ	Jump if A is equal to 0
JNZ	Jump if A is not equal to 0
CJNE	Compare and Jump if Not Equal
DJNZ	Decrement and Jump if Not Zero
NOP	No Operation

LCALL	Long Call to Subroutine
ACALL	Absolute Call to Subroutine (Unconditional)
RET	Return from Subroutine
RETI	Return from Interrupt
JMP	Jump to an Address (Unconditional)

All these instructions, except the NOP (No Operation) affect the Program Counter (PC) in one way or other. Some of these instructions has decision making capability before transferring control to other part of the program.

The following table shows all the mnemonics with respect to the program branching instructions.

Table 3.14. Mnemonics of the Program Branching instructions

Mnemonic	instruction	Description	# of Bytes	# of Cycles
ACALL	ADDR11	Absolute Subroutine Call PC+2 → (SP); ADDR16 → PC	2	2
LCALL	ADDR16	Long Subroutine call PC+3 → (SP); ADDR16 → PC	3	2
RET	-	Return from subroutine (SP) → PC	1	2
RETI	-	Return from Interrupt	1	2
AJMP	ADDR11	Absolute Jump ADDR16 → PC	2	2
LJMP	ADDR16	Long Jump ADDR16 → PC	3	2
SJMP	rel	Short Jump PC+2+rel→PC	2	2
JMP	@A+DPTR	A+DPTR→PC	1	2
JZ	rel	If A=0 , Jump to PC +rel	2	2
JNZ	rel	If A ≠0 , Jump to PC +rel		2
CJNE	A, Direct, rel,	Compare (Direct) with A, Jump to PC +rel if not equal	3	2
	A, Data, rel	Compare # Data with A, Jump to PC +rel if not equal	3	2
	A, Data, rel	Compare #Data with Rn, Jump to PC +rel if not equal	3	2
	A, Data, rel	Compare #Data with @Ri, Jump to PC +rel if not equal	3	2
DJNZ	Rn ,rel	Department Rn , Jump to PC + rel if not Zero	2	2
	Direct, rel	Department (Direct) , Jump to PC + rel if not Zero	3	2
NOP		No Operation	1	1

In this chapter, we have seen the introduction to the 8051 Microcontroller Instruction Set, Addressing Modes in 8051 Microcontroller and different types of instructions in the Instruction Set of the 8051 Microcontroller.

3.7 Instructions and Programs

3.7.1 Arithmetic Instructions

Addition of Unsigned Numbers

ADD A, source ;   A = A + source

- The instruction ADD is used to add two operands
  - Destination operand is always in register A
  - Source operand can be a register, immediate data, or in memory
  - Memory-to-memory arithmetic operations are never allowed in 8051 Assembly language

23. *Show how the flag register is affected by the following instruction*

```
MOV A,#0F5H ;A=F5 hex
ADD A,#0BH  ;A=F5+0B=0
```

Solution:

```
     F5H          1111  0101
+    0BH     +    0000  1011
    ----         -----------
    100H          0000  0000
```

Addition of Individual Bytes

24. *Assume that RAM locations 40 – 44H have the following values. Write a program to find the sum of the values. At the end of the program, register A should contain the low byte and R7 the high byte*

    Solution:

    40 = (7D)
    41 = (EB)
    42 = (C5)
    43 = (5B)
    44 = (30)

```
        MOV   R0,#40HR2,#5     ;load pointer
        MOV   A                ;load counter
        CLR                    ;A=0

        MOV   R7,A             ;clear R7

AGAIN:  ADD   A,@R0            ;add the byte ptr to by R0
        JNC   NEXT             ;if CY=0 don't add carry
        INC   R7               ;keep track of carry
```

```
NEXT:     INC     R0              ;increment pointer
          DJNZ R2, AGAIN; repeat until R2 is zero
```

ADDC and Addition of 16- Bit Numbers

- When adding two 16-bit data operands, the propagation of a carry from lower byte to higher byte is concerned

```
      1  <------------
      3C  E7
  +   3B  8D
      ------
      78  74
```

When the first byte is added (E7+8D=74, CY=1). The carry is propagated to the higher byte, which result in 3C + 3B + 1 =78 (all in hex)

3.7.2 BCD Number System

- The binary representation of the digits 0 to 9 is called BCD (Binary Coded Decimal)
  - Unpacked BCD
    - In unpacked BCD, the lower 4 bits of the number represent the BCD number, and the rest of the bits are 0
    - Ex. 00001001 and 00000101 are unpacked BCD for 9 and 5
  - Packed BCD
    - In packed BCD, a single byte has two BCD number in it, one in the lower 4 bits, and one in the upper 4 bits
    - Ex. 0101 1001 is packed BCD for 59H

Digit	BCD
0	0000
1	0001
2	0010
3	0011
4	0100
5	0101
6	0110
7	0111
8	1000
9	1001

Unpacked and Packed BCD

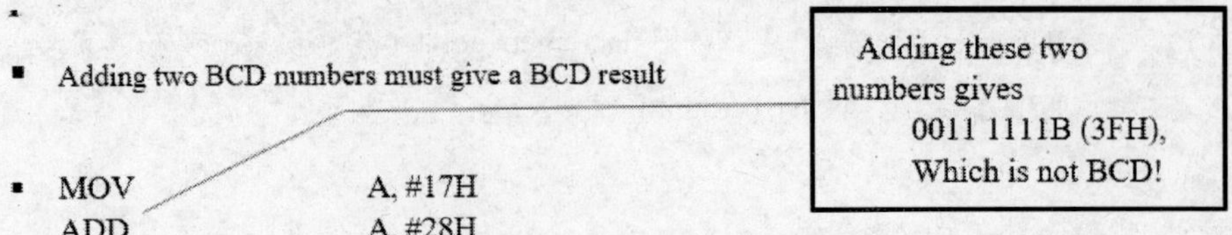

- The result above should have been 17 + 28 = 45 (0100 0101).To correct this problem, the programmer must add 6 (0110) to thelow digit: 3F + 06 = 45H.

3.7.3 DA Instruction

DA A; decimal adjust for addition

- The DA instruction is provided to correct the aforementioned problem associated with BCD addition
  - The DA instruction will add 6 to the lower nibble or higher nibble if need

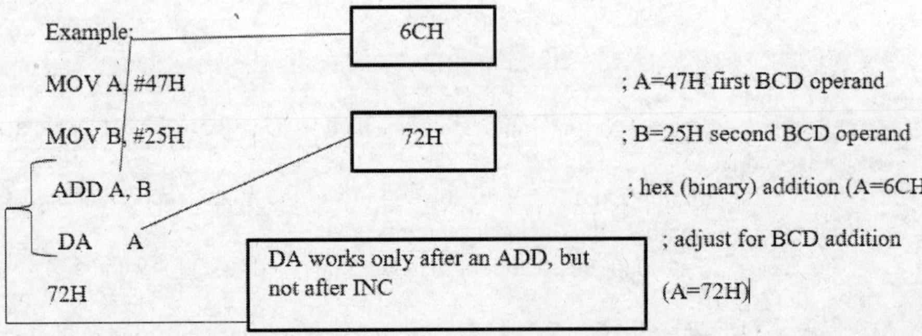

The "DA" instruction works only on A. In other word, while the source can be an operand of any addressing mode, the destination must be in register A in order for DA to work.

- Summary of DA instruction
  - After an ADD or ADDC instruction

    1. If the lower nibble (4 bits) is greater than 9, or if AC=1, add 0110 to the lower 4 bits

    2. If the upper nibble is greater than 9, or if CY=1, add 0110 to the upper 4 bits

	HEX		BCD	
	29		0010 1001	
+	18	+	0001 1000	
	41		0100 0001	AC=1
+	6	+	0110	
	47		0100 0111	

Since AC=1 after the addition, "DA A" will add 6 to thelower nibble.

The final result is in BCD format.

25. *Assume that 5 BCD data items are stored in RAM locations startingat 40H, as shown below. Write a program to find the sum of all thenumbers. The result must be in BCD.*

40= (71)
41= (11)
42= (65)
43= (59)
44= (37)

Solution:

```
       MOV R0, #40H        ; Load pointer
       MOV  R2, #5         ; Load counter
       CLR A               ; A=0
       MOV  R7, A          ; Clear R7
AGAIN: ADD  A,@R0          ; add the byte pointer; to by R0
       JNC NEXT            ; if CY=0 don't; add carry
       INC     R7          ; keep track of carries
NEXT:  INC     R0          ; increment pointer
       DJNZ R2, AGAIN      ; repeat until R2 is 0
```

Subtraction of Unsigned Numbers

- In many microprocessors there are two different instructions for subtraction: SUB and SUBB (subtract with borrow)
  - In the 8051 we have only SUBB
  - The 8051 uses adder circuitry to perform the subtraction

SUBB A, source; A = A – source – CY

- To make SUB out of SUBB, we have to make CY=0 prior to the execution of the instruction
    - Notice that we use the CY flag for the borrow
- SUBB when CY = 0
    1. Take the 2's complement of the subtrahend (source operand)
    2. Add it to the minuend (A)
    3. Invert the carry

```
        CLR     C
        MOV     A, #4C          ;load A with value 4CH
        SUBB    A, #6EH         ;subtract 6E from A
        JNC     NEXT            ;if CY=0 jump to NEXT
        CPL     A; if CY=1, take 1's complement
        INC     A   ;and increment to get 2's comp
NEXT:   MOV     R1,A            ;save A in R1
```

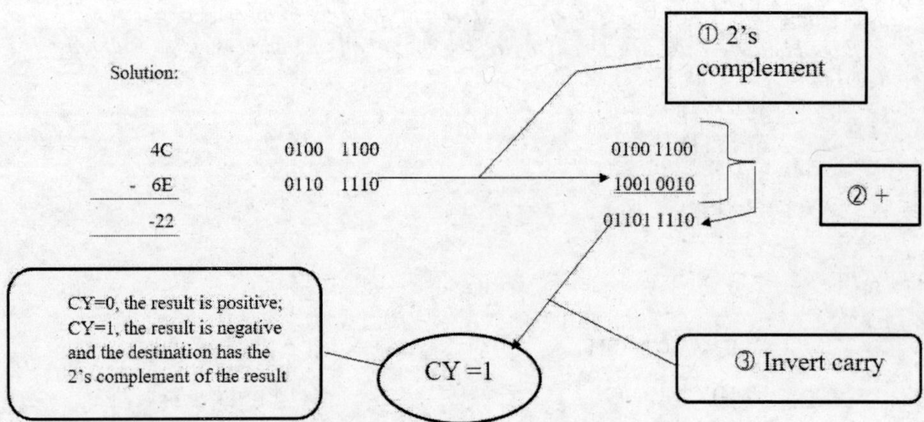

- SUBB when CY = 1
    - This instruction is used for multi-byte numbers and will take care of the borrow of the lower operand

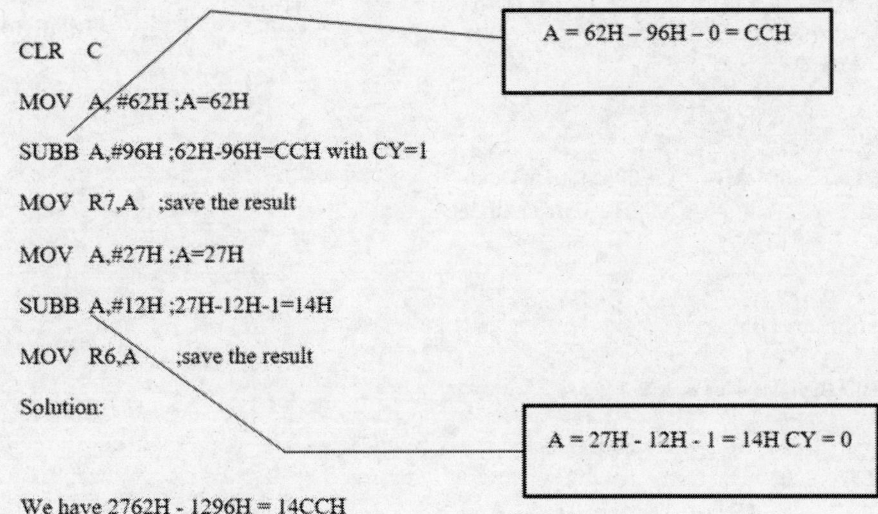

We have 2762H - 1296H = 14CCH

3.7.4 Unsigned Multiplication

- The 8051 supports byte by byte multiplication only
  - The byte are assumed to be unsigned data
    MUL AB ;AxB, 16-bit result in B, A

```
MOV     A,#25H     ;load 25H to reg. A

MOV     B,#65H     ;load 65H to reg. B

MUL     AB         ;25H * 65H = E99 where
                   ;B = OEH and A = 99H
```

Unsigned Multiplication Summary (MUL AB)			
Multiplication	Operand1	Operand2	Result
Byte x byte	A	B	B = high byte A = low byte

3.7.5 Unsigned Division

- The 8051 supports byte over byte division only
  - The byte are assumed to be unsigned data

```
MOV   A,#95      ;load 95 to          reg.    A
```

```
MOV   B,#10        ;load 10 to          reg.    B        DIV
                                                         AB; divide
A by B, A/B

MUL         AB  ; A = 09(quotient) and
                ; B = 05(remainder)
```

Application for DIV

DIV AB; divide A by B, A/B

```
MOV    A,#95        ;load 95 to        reg.    A
MOV    B,#10        ;load 10 to        reg.    B
MUL        AB ; A = 09(quotient) and
              ; B = 05(remainder)
```

Unsigned Division Summary (DIV AB)

Division	Numerator	Denominator	Quotient	Remainder
Byte / byte	A	B	A	B

CY is always 0
If B ≠ 0, OV =0

If B = 0, OV = 1 indicates error

(a) Write a program to get hex data in the range of 00 – FFH fromport 1 and convert it to decimal. Save it in R7, R6 and R5.

(b) Assuming that P1 has a value of FDH for data, analyse program.

Solution:

(a)

```
MOV    A,#0FFH

MOV    P1,A             ;make  P1 an input port
MOV    A,P1             ;read  data from P1
MOV    B,#10            ;B=0A  hex
DIV    AB               ;divide by 10
MOV    R7,B             ;save lower digit
MOV    B,#10
DIV    AB               ;divide by 10 once more
MOV    R6,B             ;save the next digit
MOV    R5,A             ;save the last digit
```

(b) To convert a binary (hex) value to decimal, we divide it by 10 repeatedly until the quotient is less than 10. After each division the remainder is saves

	Q	R
FD/0A =	19	3 (low digit)
19/0A =	2	5 (middle digit)

2 (high digit)
Therefore, we have FDH=253.

3.8 Signed Arithmetic Instructions

3.8.1 Signed 8-bit Operands

- D7 (MSB) is the sign and D0 to D6 are the magnitude of the number
    - If D7=0, the operand is positive, and if D7=1, it is negative

D7	D6	D5	D4	D3	D2	D1	D0
Sign	**Magnitude**						

- Positive numbers are 0 to +127
- Negative number representation (2's complement)
  1. Write the magnitude of the number in 8-bit binary (no sign)
  2. Invert each bit
  3. Add 1 to it

26. Show how the 8051 would represent -34H

Solution:

1.	0011 0100	34H given in binary
2.	1100 1011	invert each bit
3.	1100 1100	add 1 (which is CC in hex)

Signed number representation of -34 in 2's complement is CCH

Decimal	Binary	Hex
-128	1000 0000	80
-127	1000 0001	81
-126	1000 0010	82
...	... ...	...

-2	1111 1110	FE
-1	1111 1111	FF
0	0000 0000	00
+1	0000 0001	01
+2	0000 0010	02
...	... ...	...
+127	0111 1111	7F

3.8.2 Overflow Problem

- If the result of an operation on signed numbers is too large for the register
  - An overflow has occurred and the programmer must be noticed

27. Examine the following code and analyze the result.

```
MOV     A,#+96      ;A=0110 0000 (A=60H)
MOV     R1,#+70     ;R1=0100 0110(R1=46H)
ADD     A,R1        ;A=1010  0110
                    ;A=A6H=-90,INVALID
```

Solution:

```
      +96     0110     0000
  +   +70     0100     0110
     -----    -------------
  +   166     1010     0110   and OV =1
```

According to the CPU, the result is -90, which is wrong. The CPUsets OV=1 to indicate the overflow

3.8.3 OV Flag

- In 8-bit signed number operations, OV is set to 1 if either occurs:
  1. There is a carry from D6 to D7, but no carry out of D7 (CY=0)
  2. There is a carry from D7 out (CY=1), but no carry from D6 to D7

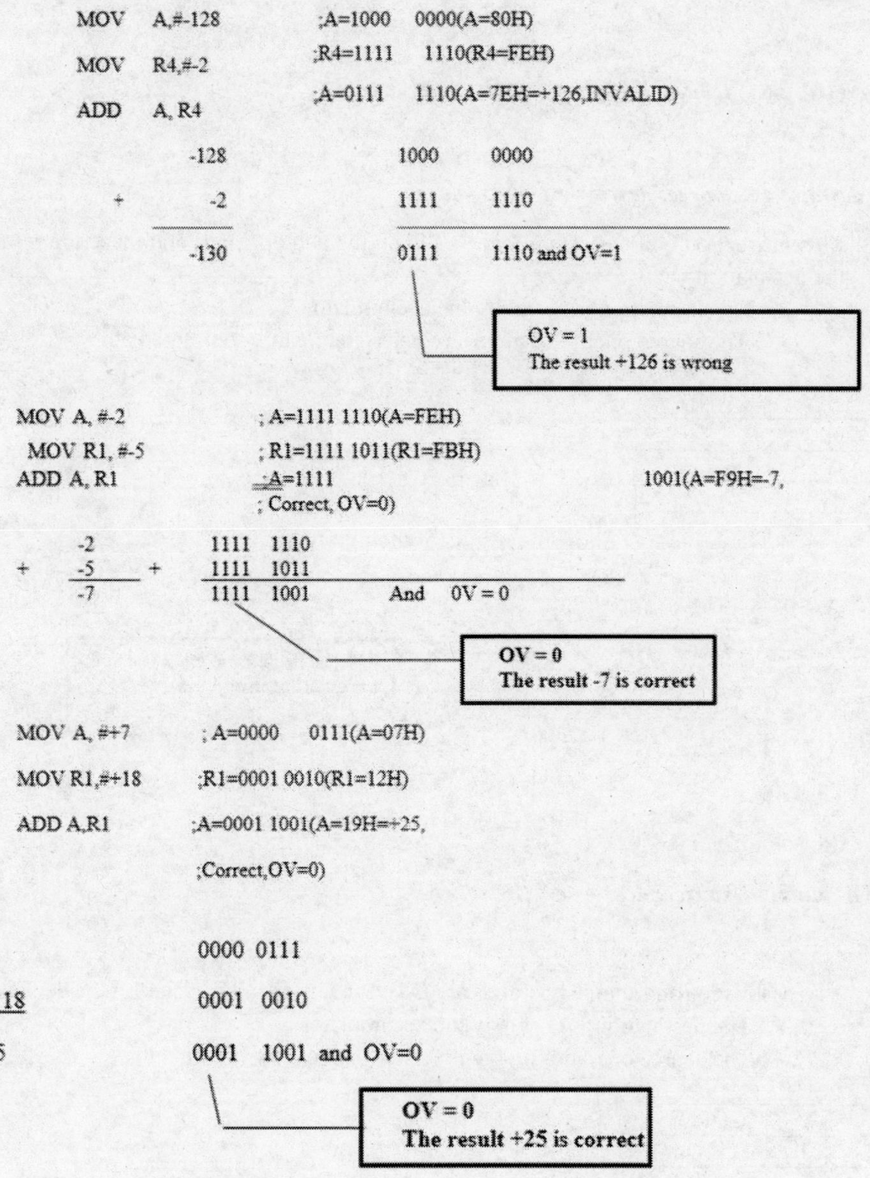

```
MOV    A,#-128        ;A=1000    0000(A=80H)
MOV    R4,#-2         ;R4=1111    1110(R4=FEH)
ADD    A, R4          ;A=0111    1110(A=7EH=+126,INVALID)

       -128           1000      0000
   +     -2           1111      1110
       ----           -------------------
       -130           0111      1110 and OV=1
```

OV = 1
The result +126 is wrong

```
MOV A, #-2            ; A=1111 1110(A=FEH)
 MOV R1, #-5          ; R1=1111 1011(R1=FBH)
ADD A, R1             ;A=1111                    1001(A=F9H=-7,
                      ; Correct, OV=0)

    -2          1111  1110
+   -5    +     1111  1011
    -7          1111  1001        And   0V = 0
```

OV = 0
The result -7 is correct

```
MOV A, #+7        ; A=0000    0111(A=07H)

MOV R1,#+18       ;R1=0001 0010(R1=12H)

ADD A,R1          ;A=0001 1001(A=19H=+25,

                  ;Correct,OV=0)

7                 0000  0111

+ 18              0001  0010

25                0001   1001  and  OV=0
```

OV = 0
The result +25 is correct

- In unsigned number addition, we must monitor the status of CY (carry)
  - Use JNC or JC instructions
- In signed number addition, the OV (overflow) flag must be monitored by the programmer
  - JB PSW.2 **or** JNB PSW.2

2's Complement

- To make the 2's complement of a number

```
CPL        A              ;1's complement (invert)
```

```
ADD     A, #1          ; add 1 to make 2's comp.
```

3.9 LOGIC AND COMPARE INSTRUCTIONS

3.9.1 AND

ANL destination, source; dest = dest AND source

- This instruction will perform a logic AND on the two operands and place the result in the destination
  - The destination is normally the accumulator
  - The source operand can be a register, in memory, or immediate

X	Y	X AND Y
0	0	0
0	1	0
1	0	0
1	1	1

Show the results of the following.

MOV A,#35H ;A = 35H

ANL A,#0FH ;A = A AND 0FH

35H	0	0	1	1	0	1	0	1
0FH	0	0	0	0	1	1	1	1
05H	0	0	0	0	0	1	0	1

ANL is often used to mask (set to 0) certainbits of an operand

3.9.2 OR

ORL destination, source; dest = dest OR source

- The destination and source operands are ORed and the result is placed in the destination
  - The destination is normally the accumulator
  - The source operand can be a register, in memory, or immediate

X	Y	X OR Y
0	0	0
0	1	1
1	0	1
1	1	1

28. *Show the results of the following.*

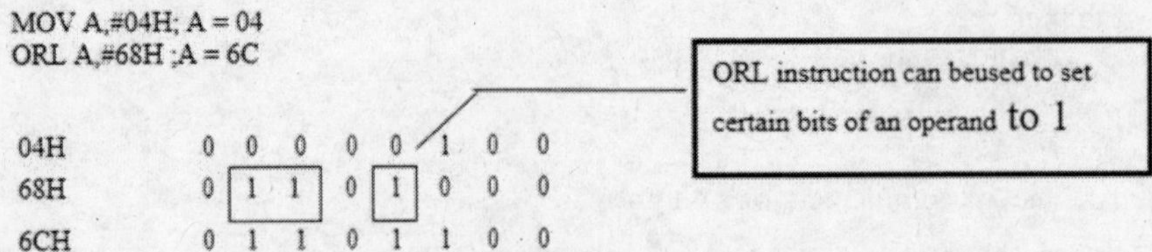

3.9.3 XOR

XRL destination, source; dest = dest XOR source

- This instruction will perform XOR operation on the two operands and place the result in the destination
  - The destination is normally the accumulator
  - The source operand can be a register, in memory, or immediate

X	Y	X XOR Y
0	0	0
0	1	1
1	0	1
1	1	0

29. *Show the results of the following.*

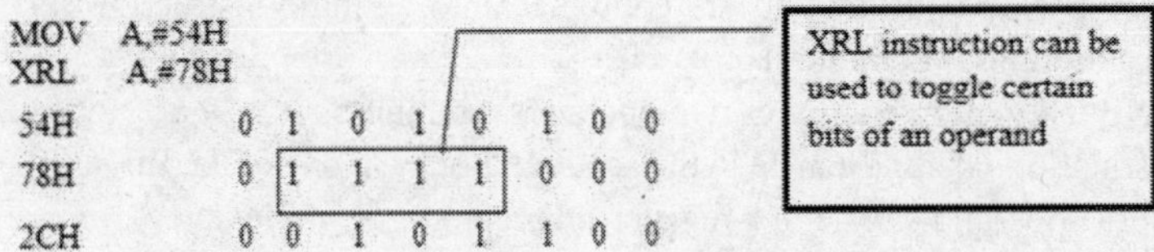

30. *The XRL instruction can be used to clear the contents of a register by XORing it with itself. Show how XRL A, A clears A, assuming that AH = 45H.*

```
45H        0 1   0 0   0 1   0 1
45H        0 1   0 0   0 1   0 1
----       -----------------------
00H        0 0   0 0   0 0   0 0
```

Read and test P1 to see whether it has the value 45H. If it does, send 99H to P2 otherwise, it stays cleared

Solution:

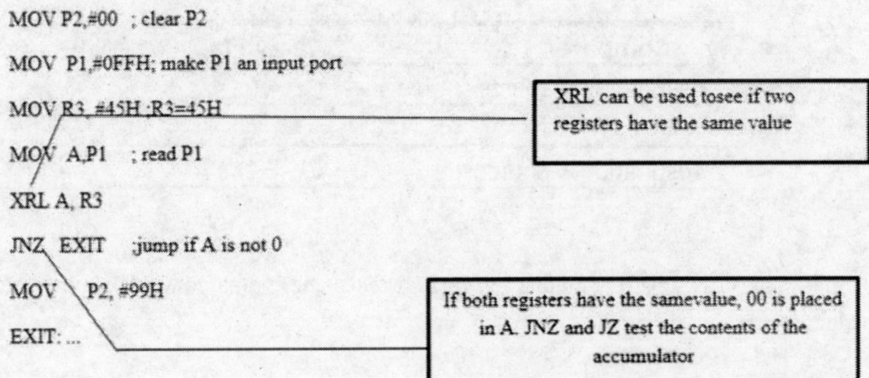

3.9.4 Complement Accumulator

CPL A ;complements the register A

- This is called 1's complement
  MOV A #55H
  CPL A

;now A=AAH

;0101 0101(55H)

;becomes 1010 1010(AAH)

- To get the 2's complement, all we have to do is to to add 1 to the 1's complement

3.9.5 Compare Instruction

CJNE destination, source,rel. addr.

- The actions of comparing and jumping are combined into a single instruction called ***CJNE*** (compare and jump if not equal)
  - The CJNE instruction compares two operands, and jumps if they are not equal
  - The destination operand can be in the accumulator or in one of the Rn registers
  - The source operand can be in a register, in memory, or immediate
- The operands themselves remain unchanged
  - It changes the CY flag to indicate if the destination operand is larger or small.
  -

```
CJNE R5, #80, NOT_EQUAL; check R5 for 80
...                     ; R5 = 80
NOT_EQUAL:
            JNC    NEXT      ; jump if
R5 > 80
  ...                     ; R5 < 80
NEXT:
```

CY flag always checked for cases of greater or less than but only after it is determined that they are not equal

Compare	Carry Flag
destination ≥ source	CY = 0
destination < source	CY = 1

- Notice in the CJNE instruction that any Rn register can be compared with an immediate value.
  - There is no need for register A to be involved

- The compare instruction is really a subtraction, except that the operands remain unchanged
  - Flags are changed according to the execution of the SUBB instruction

31. Write a program to read the temperature and test it for the value 75. According to the test results, place the temperature value into the registers indicated by the following.

If T = 75 then A = 75

If T < 75 then R1 = T

If T > 75 then R2 = T

Solution:

```
MOV P1,#0FFH        ;make P1 an input port
MOV A,P1            ;read P1 port
CJNE A,#75,OVER     ;jump if A is not 75
SJMP EXIT           ;A=75, exit
OVER: JNC NEXT      ;if CY=0 then A>75
MOV R1,A            ;CY=1, A<75, save in R1
SJMP EXIT           ; and exit
NEXT: MOV R2,A      ;A>75, save it in R2
EXIT: .....
```

3.10 Rotate Instruction and Data Serialization

3.10.1 Rotating Right and Left

RR A ; rotate right A

- In rotate right
  - The 8 bits of the accumulator are rotated right one bit, and
  - Bit D0 exits from the LSB and enters into MSB, D7

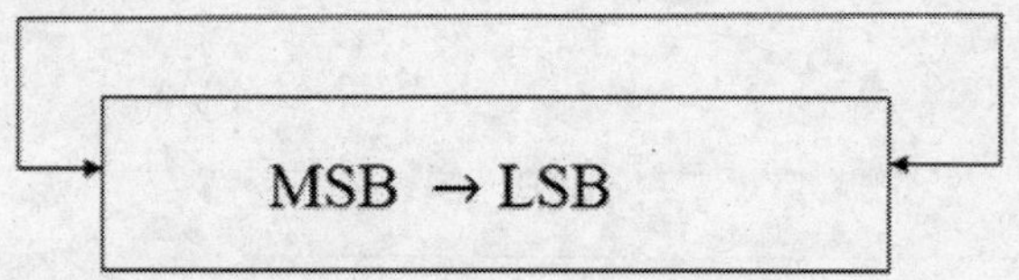


```
MOV   A,#36H        ;A   =   0011   0110
RR    A             ;A   =   0001   1011
RR    A             ;A   =   1000   1101
```

```
RR    A          ;A  =  1100  0110
RR    A          ;A  =  0110  0011
```

RL A ;rotate left A

- In rotate left
  - The 8 bits of the accumulator are rotated left one bit, and
  - Bit D7 exits from the MSB and enters into LSB, D0

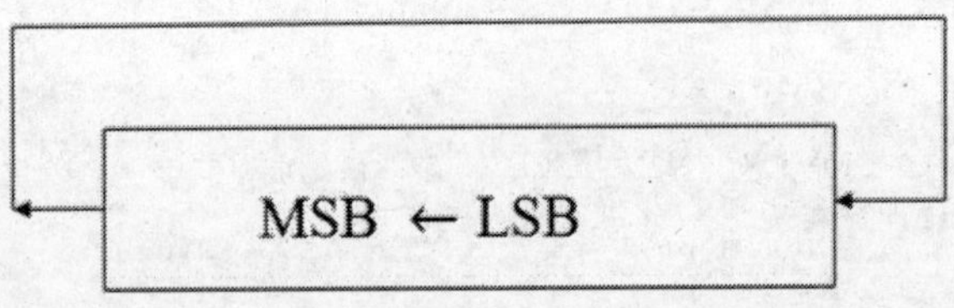

Rotating through Carry

RRC A ;rotate right through carry

```
MOV   A,#72H     ;A  =  0111  0010
RL    A          ;A  =  1110  0100
RL    A          ;A  =  1100  1001
```

- In RRC A
  - Bits are rotated from left to right
  - They exit the LSB to the carry flag, and the carry flag enters the MSB

```
CLR C            ; make CY = 0
MOV   A,#26H     ;A  =  0010  0110
```

```
RRC  A   ;A = 0001 0011   CY = 0
RRC  A   ;A = 0000 1001   CY = 1
RRC  A   ;A = 1000 0100   CY = 1
```

RLC A ;rotate left through carry

- In RLC A
    - Bits are shifted from right to left
    - They exit the MSB and enter the carry flag, and the carry flag enters the LSB

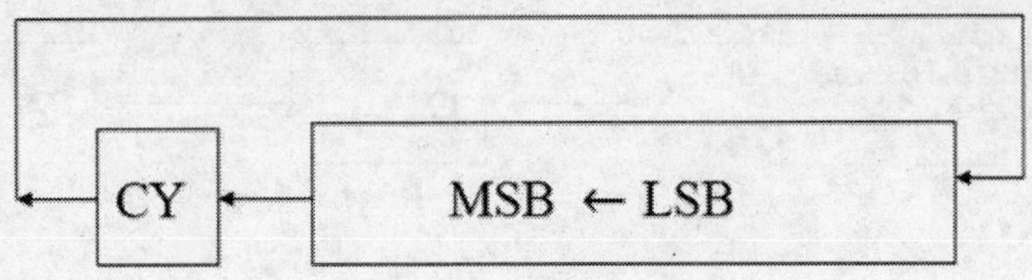

32. Write a program that finds the number of 1s in a given byte

```
MOV  R1,#0
MOV  R7,#8  ;count=08
MOV  A,#97H
AGAIN: RLC A
JNC  NEXT ;check for CY
INC  R1   ;if CY=1 add to count
NEXT: DJNZ R7,AGAIN
```

3.11 Serializing Data

- Serializing data is a way of sending a byte of data one bit at a time through a single pin of microcontroller
    - Using the serial port, discussed in Chapter 10
    - To transfer data one bit at a time and control the sequence of data and spaces in between them
- Transfer a byte of data serially by
    - Moving CY to any pin of ports P0 – P3
    - Using rotate instruction

33. Write a program to transfer value 41H serially (one bit at a time) via pin P2.1. Put two highs at the start and end of the data. Send the byte LSB first.

Solution:

```
MOV  A, #41H
```

```
SETB P2.1   ; high
SETB P2.1   ; high MOV   R5, #8
AGAIN: RRC  A
MOV  P2.1, C; send CY to P2.1
 DJNZ R5, HERE
SETB P2.1   ; high
SETB P2.1   ; high
```

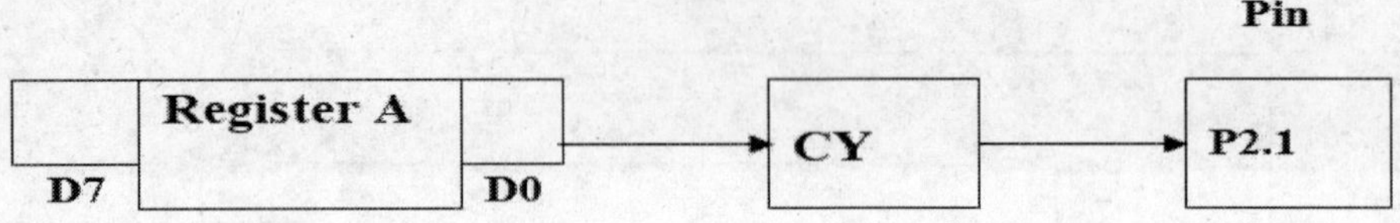

34. *Write a program to bring in a byte of data serially one bit at a time via pin P2.7 and save it in register R2. The byte comes in with the LSB first.*

```
MOV  R5, #8
AGAIN: MOV         C, P2.7; bring in bit
 RRC  A
DJNZ  R5, HERE
MOV  R2, A  ; save it
```

Pin

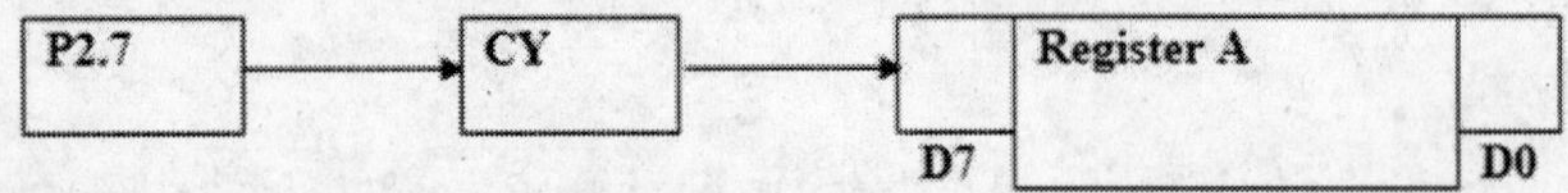

Single-bit Operations with CY

- There are several instructions by which the CY flag can be manipulated directly

Instruction	Function
SETB C	Make CY = 1
CLR C	Clear carry bit (CY = 0)
CPL C	Complement carry bit
MOV b,C	Copy carry status to bit location (CY = b)
MOV C,b	Copy bit location status to carry (b = CY)
JNC target	Jump to target if CY = 0
JC target	Jump to target if CY = 1

ANL C,bit	AND CY with bit and save it on CY
ANL C,/bit	AND CY with inverted bit and save it on CY
ORL C,bit	OR CY with bit and save it on CY
ORL C,/bit	OR CY with inverted bit and save it on CY

35. Assume that bit P2.2 is used to control an outdoor light and bit P2.5 a light inside a building. Show how to turn on the outside light and turn off the inside one.

Solution:

```
SETB    C           ;CY =      1
ORL     C,P2.2      ;CY =      P2.2 ORed w/ CY
MOV     P2.2,C      ;turn      it on if not on
CLR     C           ;CY =      0
ANL     C,P2.5      ;CY =      P2.5 ANDed w/ CY
MOV     P2.5, C; turn it off if not off
```

36. Write a program that finds the number of 1s in a given byte.

```
MOV     R1, #0              ; R1 keeps number of 1s
MOV     R7, #8              ; counter, rotate 8 times
MOV     A, #97H             ; find number of 1s in 97H
AGAIN:  RLC     A           ; rotate it thru CY
        JNC     R1          ; check CY
NEXT:   DJNZ    R7, AGAIN   ; if CY=1, Inc count
                            ; go thru 8 times
```

3.12 SWAP

SWAP A

- It swaps the lower nibble and the higher nibble
  - In other words, the lower 4 bits are put into the higher 4 bits and the higher 4 bits are put into the lower 4 bits
- SWAP works only on the accumulator (A)

Before:	D7-D4	D3-D0
After:	D3-D0	D7-D4

37. (a) Find the contents of register A in the following code.

(b) In the absence of a SWAP instruction, how would you exchange the nibbles? Write a simple program to show the process

Solution:

(a)

```
MOV     A,#72H      ;A  =  72H
SWAP    A           ;A  =  27H
```

(b)

```
MOV     A,#72H      ;A  =  0111  0010
RL      A           ;A  =  0111  0010
RL      A           ;A  =  0111  0010
RL      A           ;A  =  0111  0010
RL      A           ;A  =  0111  0010
```

3.13 BCD AND ASCII APPLICATION PROGRAMS

ASCII code and BCD for digits 0 - 9

Key	ASCII (hex)	Binary	BCD (unpacked)
0	30	011 0000	0000 0000
1	31	011 0001	0000 0001
2	32	011 0010	0000 0010
3	33	011 0011	0000 0011
4	34	011 0100	0000 0100
5	35	011 0101	0000 0101
6	36	011 0110	0000 0110
7	37	011 0111	0000 0111
8	38	011 1000	0000 1000
9	39	011 1001	0000 1001

3.13.1 Packed BCD to ACSII Conversion

- The DS5000T microcontrollers have a real-time clock (RTC)
  - The RTC provides the time of day (hour, minute, second) and the date (year, month, day) continuously, regardless of whether the power is on or off
- However, this data is provided in packed BCD

- To be displayed on an LCD or printed by the printer, it must be in ACSII format

3.13.2 ASCII to Packed BCD Conversion

- To convert ASCII to packed BCD
  - It is first converted to unpacked BCD (to get rid of the 3)
  - Combined to make packed BCD

Key	ASCII	Unpacked BCD	Packed BCD
4	34	0000 0100	
7	37	0000 0111	0100 0111 or 47H

```
MOV    A, #'4'     ;A=34H, hex    for '4'
MOV    R1,#'7'     ;R1=37H,hex    for '7'

ANL    A, #0FH     ;mask upper  nibble (A=04)
ANL    R1,#0FH     ;mask upper  nibble (R1=07)
SWAP   A           ;A=40H
ORL    A, R1       ;A=47H, packed BCD
```

37. *Assume that register A has packed BCD, write a program to convert packed BCD to two ASCII numbers and place them in R2 and R6.*

```
MOV A, #29H; A=29H, packed BCD
MOV R2, A   ; keep a copy of BCD data
ANL A, #0FH; mask the upper nibble (A=09)
ORL A, #30H; make it an ASCII, A=39H ('9')
MOV R6, A   ; save it
MOV A, R2   ; A=29H, get the original
Data
ANL A, #0F0H; mask the lower nibble
RR   A ; rotate right
RR  A   ; rotate right
```

```
RR  A   ; rotate right                SWAP A
RR   A   ; rotate right
ORL A, #30H    ; A=32H, ASCII char. '2'
MOV R2, A      ; save ASCII char in R2
```

3.13.3 Using a Look-up Table for ASCII

38. Assume that the lower three bits of P1 are connected to three switches. Write a program to send the following ASCII characters to P2 based on the status of the switches.

000 '0'
001 '1'
010 '2'
011 '3'
100 '4'
101 '5'
110 '6'
111 '7'
MOV DPTR,#MYTABLE

Solution:

```
MOV  A,P1   ;get SW status
ANL  A,#07H          ;mask all but lower 3
MOVC       A,@A+DPTR ;get data from table
MOV P2,A   ;display value
SJMP  $      ;stay here
;------------------
ORG  400H
MYTABLE DB       '0','1','2','3','4','5','6','7'
END
```

3.13.4 Checksum Byte in ROM

- To ensure the integrity of the ROM contents, every system must perform the checksum calculation
  - The process of checksum will detect any corruption of the contents of ROM
  - The checksum process uses what is called a checksum byte
- The checksum byte is an extra byte that is tagged to the end of series of bytes of data
- To calculate the checksum byte of a series of bytes of data
  - Add the bytes together and drop the carries
  - Take the 2's complement of the total sum, and it becomes the last byte of the series
- To perform the checksum operation, add all the bytes, including the checksum byte
  - The result must be zero

- If it is not zero, one or more bytes of data have been changed

39. *Assume that we have 4 bytes of hexadecimal data: 25H, 62H, 3FH, and 52H.(a) Find the checksum byte, (b) perform the checksum operation to ensure data integrity, and (c) if the second byte 62H has been changed to 22H, show how checksum detects the error.*

Solution:

(a) Find the checksum byte.

```
     25H   The checksum is calculated by first adding the
+    62H   bytes. The sum is 118H, and dropping the carry,
+    3FH   we get 18H. The checksum byte is the 2's
+    52H   complement of 18H, which is E8H
---------
     118H
```

(b) Perform the checksum operation to ensure data integrity.

```
     25H
+    62H   adding the series of bytes including the checksum
+    3FH   byte must result in zero. This indicates that all the
+    52H   bytes are unchanged and no byte is corrupted.
+    E8H
---------
     200H (dropping the carries)
```

(c) If the second byte 62H has been changed to 22H, show how checksum detects the error.

```
     25H
+    22H   Adding the series of bytes including the checksum
+    3FH   byte shows that the result is not zero, which indicates
+    52H   that one or more bytes have been corrupted.
+    E8H
---------
     1C0H (dropping the carry, we get C0H)
```

3.13.5 Binary (Hex) to ASCII Conversion

- Many ADC (analog-to-digital converter) chips provide output data in binary (hex)
  - To display the data on an LCD or PC screen, we need to convert it to ASCII
    - Convert 8-bit binary (hex) data to decimal digits, 000 – 255
    - Convert the decimal digits to ASCII digits, 30H – 39H

3.14 Assembly language Programs

8051 PROGRAMMING IN C

Why Program 8051 In C

- Compilers produce hex files that is downloaded to ROM of microcontroller
    - ➢ The size of hex file is the main concern
- Microcontrollers have limited on-chip ROM
- Code space for 8051 is limited to 64K bytes
- C programming is less time consuming, but has larger hex file size
- The reasons for writing programs in C
    - ➢ It is easier and less time consuming to write in C than Assembly
    - ➢ C is easier to modify and update
    - ➢ You can use code available in function libraries
    - ➢ C code is portable to other microcontroller with little of no modification

For more examples of 8051 assembly language programs, see the QR code.

3.14.1 DATA TYPES

- A good understanding of C data types for 8051 can help programmers to create smaller hex files
    - ➢ Unsigned char
    - ➢ Signed char
    - ➢ Unsigned int
    - ➢ Signed int
    - ➢ Sbit (single bit)
    - ➢ Bit and sfr

3.14.2 Unsigned char

- The character data type is the most natural choice
    - ➢ 8051 is an 8-bit microcontroller
- Unsigned char is an 8-bit data type in the range of 0 – 255 (00 – FFH)
    - ➢ One of the most widely used data types for the 8051
        - Counter value
        - ASCII characters
- C compilers use the signed char as the default if we do not put the keyword unsigned

40. Write an 8051 C program to send values 00 – FF to port P1.

Solution:

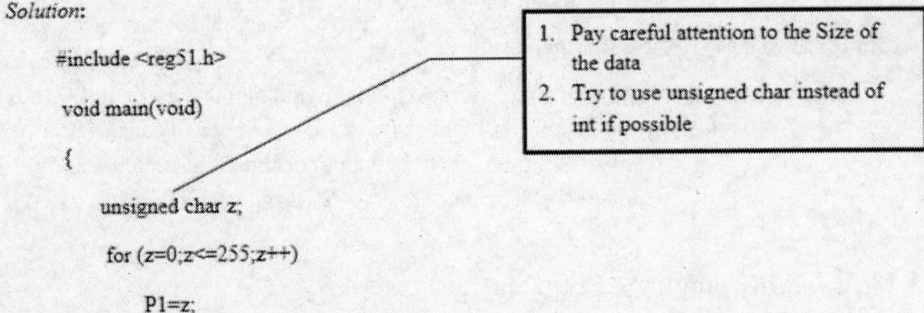

```
#include <reg51.h>
void main(void)
{
    unsigned char z;
    for (z=0;z<=255;z++)
        P1=z;
```


41. Write an 8051 C program to send hex values for ASCII characters of 0, 1, 2, 3, 4, 5, A, B, C, and D to port P1.

Solution

```
#include <reg51.h>
void main(void)
{
unsigned char mynum[]="012345ABCD";
unsigned char z;
for (z=0;z<=10;z++)
 P1=mynum[z];
}
```

42. Write an 8051 C program to toggle all the bits of P1 continuously.

Solution:

```
//Toggle P1 forever #include <reg51.h>
void main(void)
{
for (;;)
  {
  p1=0x55;
  p1=0xAA;
    }
}
```

3.14.3 Signed Char

- The signed char is an 8-bit data type
  - Use the MSB D7 to represent – or +
  - Give us values from –128 to +127 ‰ We should stick with the unsigned char unless the data needs to be represented as signed numbers
  - Temperature

43. Write an 8051 C program to send values of –4 to +4 to port P1.

Solution:

```
//Singed numbers
#include <reg51.h>
void main(void)
{
char mynum[ ]={+1,-1,+2,-2,+3,-3,+4,-4};
unsigned char z; for (z=0;z<=8;z++)
```

```
P1=mynum[z];
}
```

3.14.4 Unsigned and Signed int

- The unsigned int is a 16-bit data type
  - Takes a value in the range of 0 to 65535 (0000 – FFFFH)
  - Define 16-bit variables such as memory addresses
  - Set counter values of more than 256
  - Since registers and memory accesses are in 8-bit chunks, the misuse of int variables will result in a larger hex file
- Signed int is a 16-bit data type
  - Use the MSB D15 to represent – or +
  - We have 15 bits for the magnitude of the number from –32768 to +32767

44. Write an 8051 C program to toggle bit D0 of the port P1 (P1.0) 50,000 times.

Solution:

```
#include <reg51.h>
sbit MYBIT=P1^0;

void main(void)
{
    unsigned int z;
    for (z=0;z<=50000;z++)
    {
      MYBIT=0;
      MYBIT=1;
    }
}
```

Sbit keyword allows access to the single bits of the SFR registers

3.14.5 Bit and sfr

- The bit data type allows access to single bits of bit-addressable memory spaces 20 – 2FH
- To access the byte-size SFR registers, we use the sfr data type

Data Type	Size in Bits	Data Range/Usage
unsigned char	8-bit	0 to 255

(signed) char	8-bit	-128 to +127
unsigned int	16-bit	0 to 65535
(signed) int	16-bit	-32768 to +32767
sbit	1-bit	SFR bit-addressable only
bit	1-bit	RAM bit-addressable only
sfr	8-bit	RAM addresses 80 – FFH only

Review Questions and Exercise

1.

a. Explain briefly the five addressing model of 8051 with example foe each.

b. After reset , the contents of internal memory of 8051 with address 0AH and 0BH contains data 22H and 33H , respectively . Sketch the contents of internal memory from address 07H to 0BH and the value of register SP , after executing the following code:

```
PUSH  0AH
:
MOV 81H,#0BH
POP 09H
```

c. Write a subroutine which checks the content of 20H . If it is a positive number , the subroutine find its two's complement and store it in same location and returns.

2.

a. What are assembler directives ? Explain any four of them.

b. If the XTAL frequwncy of 8051 is 8 MHz , find the time taken to execute the following program:

```
        MOV R2,#04
        MOV R1,#06
WAIT:   DJNZ R2, WAIT.
```

c. Write 8051 ALP which checks whether the ten numbers stored from external RAM memory address , 2000H are odd/even . The programs should store accordingly 00H/FFH from internal location 30H onwards.

3.

a. Interface ADC0809 to 8051 and write ALP to convert the analog voltage connected to second channel . Display the digital value on LEDs connected to Port-0.

b. Interface 8051 to stepper motor and write an ALP to rotate the motor first +4 steps and then -6 steps.

4.

a. What is the difference between timer and counter operation of8051 ? How to start/stop the timer/counter o 8051 when
   i. GATE control is not used
   ii. GATE control is used
b. Explain briefly the interrupts of 8051 , indicate their vector addresses.
c. Weite an ALP in 8051 which generates a square wave of frequency 10 kHz on pin P1.2 , using time-1 . Assume XTAL frequency as 11.0592 MHz .
   What is the minimum frequency that can be generated ?

5.

a. Explain the function of the pins of 9-pin RS-232 connector .
b. Explain how 8051 transmit the character and receives a character serially using UART .
c. Write 8051 C program to transmit serially the message 'SWITCH' or 'SWITCH OFF' depending on the status of the simple switch connected to pin P1.2 . use 2400 baud rate . 1 stop bit , 8 data bits format and assume XTAL frequency as 11.0592 Mhz.

6.

a. Interface an LCD display to 8051 write an ALP display the message 'VERY GOOD' .
b. With a block schematic explain the features 8255 PPI chip and its MODE-0 operation.
c. If the internal memory 20H contains AAH and 07H contains 55H . What is the content of register A and status of carry bit after executing the following code:

```
MOV C,07H
MOV A,#20H
ADDC A,07
```

References

[1] M. Ali Mazidi, J. Gillipsie Mazidi, Rolin D. McKinlay. The 8051Microcontrollers and Embedded System. 2nd ed. New Jersey, Pearson Prentice Hall, 2006.

[2] Santanu Chattopadhyay. *Embedded System Design.* 2nd ed. PHI Learning Private Ltd. New Delhi, 2016.

[3] Manish Patel "Question Paper with Solution the 8051 Microcontroller Based Embedded…." Question Paper with Solution the 8051 Microcontroller Based Embedded…, www.slideshare.net, 1 Mar. 2001, https://www.slideshare.net/manishpatel_79/question-paper-with-solution-the-8051-microcontroller-based-embedded-systems-junejuly-2013-vtu

Chapter 4

Memory and I/O Interfacing

Key features of Module – 4

- Memory and I/O Expansion Buses
- Control Signals, Memory Wait States
- External Memory
- Memory Interfacing
- Direct Memory Access
- interfacing of Peripheral Devices

Pre-requisites

- Fundamentals C programming
- Basics of Computers

Module – 4 Outcomes

- Students should be able to know about the different types of Memory and buses of 8051 microcontrollers
- Students should be able to know about the control signal and Memory Wait Status in 8051 microcontrollers
- Students should be able to write programs to interfacing the memory and Peripheral devices

This chapter gives an overview of the interfacing of the memory and peripheral devices of 8051 microcontrollers. The understanding of how to applied the control signal at microcontrollers is discussed. There are three types of control signals like RD, WR & ALE. And discussed about the interfacing of the external memory, memory interfacing and peripherals devices such as LEDS, LCD, Hex Keyboard, 7- Segment Multiplexed Display, Timers, Counters, ADC, DAC, DC Motor, Stepper Motor The syntax of writing any instruction is shown in the chapter along with some fundamental programs of 8051 microcontrollers.

4.1 Memory and I/O Expansion Buses

There are two main types of buses: system bus and I/O bus. The system bus, also called the memory bus, makes a connection between the CPU and the main memory of the computer that resides on the motherboard. Input/output (I/O) or expansion buses are responsible for connecting the peripheral devices (mouse, keyboard, flash drives) to the Central Processing Unit (CPU). The system bus and I/O buses are connected through a bridge that is implemented in the chipset of the processor.

4.2 Control and status signals

Three control signals are RD, WR & ALE.

RD – This signal indicates that the selected IO or memory device is to be read and is ready for accepting data available on the data bus.

WR – this signal indicates that the data on the data bus is to be written into a selected memory or IO location.

ALE – It is a positive going pulse generated when a new operation is started by the microprocessor. When the pulse goes high, it indicates address. When the pulse goes down it indicates data.

4.2.1 Three status signals- IO/$\overline{M}$, *S0 & S1*

IO/$\overline{M}$–This signal is used to differentiate between IO and Memory operations, i.e. when it is high indicates IO operation and when it is low then it indicates memory operation.

S1 & S0 –These signals are used to identify the type of current operation.

Power supply – There are 2 power supply signals – VCC & VSS.
VCC indicates +5v power supply and VSS indicates ground signal.

- Clock signals

There are 3 clock signals, i.e. X1, X2, CLK OUT.

X1, X2 – A crystal (RC, LC N/W) is connected at these two pins and is used to set frequency of the internal clock generator. This frequency is internally divided by 2.

CLK OUT – this signal is used as the system clock for devices connected with the microprocessor.

4.2.2 Interrupts & externally initiated signals

Interrupts are the signals generated by external devices to request the microprocessor to perform a task. There are 5 interrupt signals, i.e. TRAP, RST 7.5, RST 6.5, RST 5.5, and INTR. We will discuss interrupts in detail in interrupts section.

INTA – It is an interrupt acknowledgment signal.

RESET IN – this signal is used to reset the microprocessor by setting the program counter to zero.

RESET OUT – this signal is used to reset all the connected devices when the microprocessor is reset.

READY – this signal indicates that the device is ready to send or receive data. If READY is low, then the CPU has to wait for READY to go high.

HOLD – this signal indicates that another master is requesting the use of the address and data buses.

HLDA (HOLD Acknowledge) – It indicates that the CPU has received the HOLD request and it will relinquish the bus in the next clock cycle. HLDA is set to low after the HOLD signal is removed.

4.2.3 Serial I/O signals

There are 2 serial signals, i.e. SID and SOD and these signals are used for serial communication.

SOD (Serial output data line) – the output SOD is set/reset as specified by the SIM instruction.

SID (Serial input data line) – the data on this line is loaded into accumulator whenever a RIM instruction is executed.

4.3 Memory Wait States

A wait state is a delay experienced by a computer processor when accessing external memory or another device that is slow to respond. A program or process in a wait state is inactive for the duration of the wait state.

For example, an application program that communicated with one other program might send that program a message and then go into a wait state until it was "reawakened" by a message back from the other program.
When a computer processor works at a faster clock speed (expressed in MHz or millions of cycles per second) than the random access memory (RAM) that sends it instructions, it is set to go into a wait state for one or more clock cycles so that it is synchronized with RAM speed. In general, the more time a processor spends in wait states, the slower the performance of that processor.

4.3.1 External Memory Interfacing

Memory Capacity

The number of bits that a semiconductor memory chip can store is called chip capacity. It can be in units of Kbits (kilobits), Mbits (megabits), and so on. This must be distinguished from the storage capacity of computer systems. While the memory capacity of a memory IC chip is always given bits, the memory capacity of a computer system is given in bytes

- 16M memory chip – 16 megabits
  - A computer comes with 16M memory – 16 megabytes

Memory Organization

- Memory chips are organized into a number of locations within the IC
  - Each location can hold 1 bit, 4 bits, 8 bits, or even 16 bits, depending on how it is designed internally
- The number of locations within a memory IC depends on the address pins
- The number of bits that each location can hold is always equal to the number of data pins

- To summarize
  - A memory chip contains 2^x (2 raised to power of x) location, where x is the number of address pins
  - Each location contains y bits, where y is the number of data pins on the chip
  - The entire chip will contain 2^x × y bits.

Speed

- One of the most important characteristics of a memory chip is the speed at which its data can be accessed
- To access the data, the address is presented to the address pins, the READ pin is activated, and after a certain amount of time has elapsed, the data shows up at the data pins
- The shorter this elapsed time, the better, and consequently, the more expensive the memory chip
- The speed of the memory chip is commonly referred to as its access time

Example

1. *A given memory chip has 12 address pins and 4 data pins. Find: (a) The organization, and (b) the capacity.*

Solution:

(a) This memory chip has 4096 locations ($2^{12} = 4096$), and each location can hold bits of data. This gives an organization of 4096 × 4, often represented as 4K× 4.

(b) The capacity is equal to 16K bits since there is a total of 4K locations and each location can hold 4 bits of data.

2. *A 512K memory chip has 8 pins for data. Find: (a) The organization, and (b) the number of address pins for this memory chip.*

Solution:

(a) A memory chip with 8 data pins means that each location within the chip can hold 8 bits of data. To find the number of locations within this memory chip, divide the capacity by the number of data pins. 512K/8 = 64K; therefore, the organization for this memory chip is 64K × 8

(b) The chip has 16 address lines since 2^{16} = 64K

4.3.2 Interfacing External ROM

- The 8031 chip is a ROM less version of the 8051

- It is exactly like any member of the 8051 family as far as executing the instructions and features are concerned, but it has no on-chip ROM
- To make the 8031 execute 8051 code, it must be connected to external ROM memory containing the program code
- 8031 is ideal for many systems where the on-chip ROM of 8051 is not sufficient, since it allows the program size to be as large as 64K bytes

- For 8751/89C51/DS5000-based system, we connected the EA pin to Vcc to indicate that the program code is stored in the microcontroller's on-chip ROM
- To indicate that the program code is stored in external ROM, this pin must be connected to GND

P0 and P2 in Providing Address

- Since the PC (program counter) of the 8031/51 is 16-bit, it is capable of Accessing up to 64K bytes of program code
- In the 8031/51, port 0 and port 2 provide the 16-bit address to access external Memory
  - P0 provides the lower 8-bit address A0 – A7, and P2 provides the upper 8-bit address A8 – A15
  - P0 is also used to provide the 8-bit data bus D0 – D7
- P0.0 – P0.7 are used for both the address and data paths
  - address/data multiplexing

- ALE (address latch enable) pin is an output pin for 8031/51
- ALE = 0, P0 is used for data path
- ALE = 1, P0 is used for address path
- To extract the address from the P0 pins we connect P0 to a 74LS373 and use the ALE pin to latch the address
- Normally ALE = 0, and P0 is used as a data bus, sending data out or bringing data in

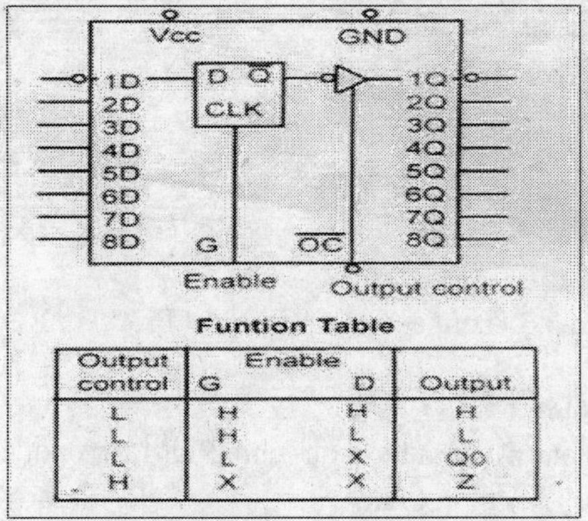

Output control	Enable G	D	Output
L	H	H	H
L	H	L	L
L	L	X	Q0
H	X	X	Z

74LS373 D Latch

Fig.4.1: 74LS373 D Latch

- Whenever the 8031/51 wants to use P0 as an address bus, it puts the addresses A0 – A7 on the P0 pins and activates ALE = 1

4.3.3 Address/Data Multiplexing

- PSEN (program store enables) signal is an output signal for the 8031/51 microcontroller and must be connected to the OE pin of a ROM containing the program code
- It is important to emphasize the role of EA and PSEN when connecting the 8031/51 to external ROM
  - When the EA pin is connected to GND, the 8031/51 fetches opcode from external ROM (8031)2—PSEN by using PSEN

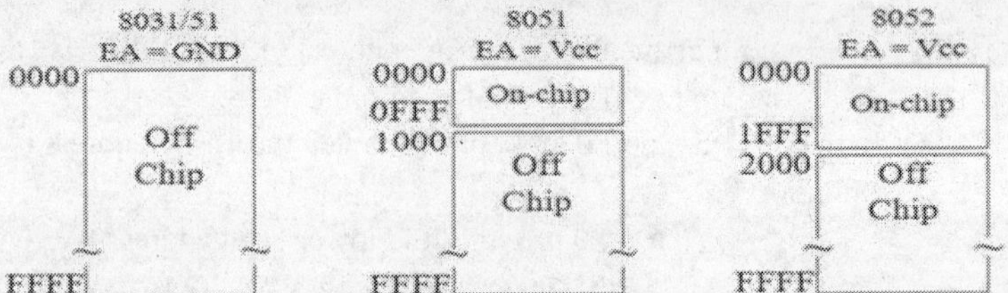

Fig.4.2: Circuit diagram to interface external ROM with 8051

- The connection of the PSEN pin to the OE pin of ROM
  - In systems based on the 8751/89C51/ DS5000 where EA is connected to Vcc, these chips do not activate the PSEN pin
  - This indicates that the on-chip ROM contains program code

4.3.4 Connection to External Program ROM

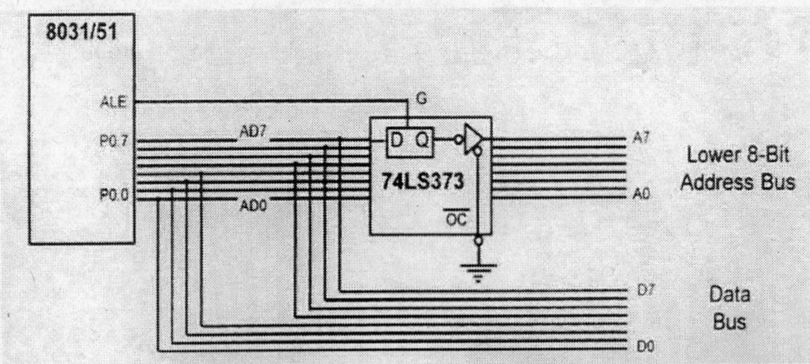

Fig.4.3. Connection to External Program ROM

4.3.5 On-Chip and Off-Chip Code ROM

- In an 8751 system we could use on- chip ROM for boot code and an external ROM will contain the user's program
  - We still have EA = Vcc,
    - Upon reset 8051 executes the on-chip program first, the
    - When it reaches the end of the on-chip ROM, it switches to external ROM for rest of program

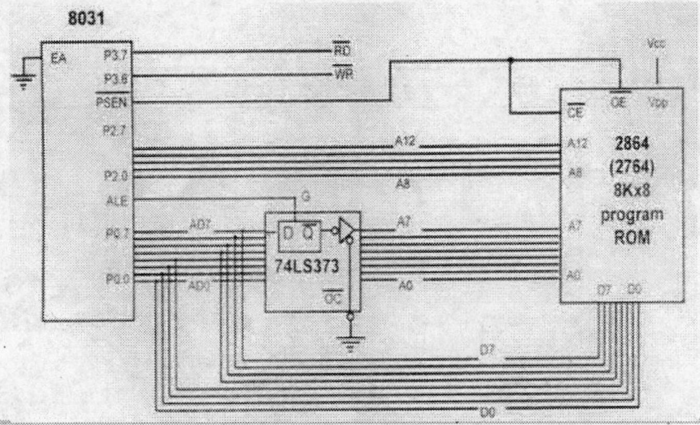

Fig.4.4. Off-chip Program Code Access

3. *Discuss the program ROM space allocation for each of the following cases.*

(a) EA = 0 for the 8751 (89C51) chip.

(b) EA = Vcc with both on-chip and off-chip ROM for the 8751.

(c) EA = Vcc with both on-chip and off-chip ROM for the 8752.

Solution:

(a) When EA = 0, the EA pin is strapped to GND, and all program fetches are directed to external memory regardless of whether or not the 8751 has some on-chip ROM for program code. This external ROM can be as high as 64K bytes with address space of 0000 – FFFFH. In this case an 8751(89C51) is the same as the 8031 system.

(b) With the 8751 (89C51) system where EA=Vcc, it fetches the program code of address 0000 – 0FFFH from on-chip ROM since it has 4K bytes of on-chip program ROM and any fetches from addresses 1000H – FFFFH are directed to external ROM.

(c) With the 8752 (89C52) system where EA=Vcc, it fetches the program code of addresses 0000 – 1FFFH from on-chip ROM since it has 8K bytes of on-chip program ROM and any fetches from addresses 2000H – FFFFH are directed to external ROM

4.4 Interfacing to Large External Memory

- In some applications we need a large amount of memory to store data
  - The 8051 can support only 64K bytes of external data memory since DPTR is 16-bit
  - To solve this problem, we connect A0 – A15 of the 8051 directly to the external memory's A0 – A15 pins, and use some of the P1 pins to access the 64K bytes blocks inside the single 256K ×8 memory chip

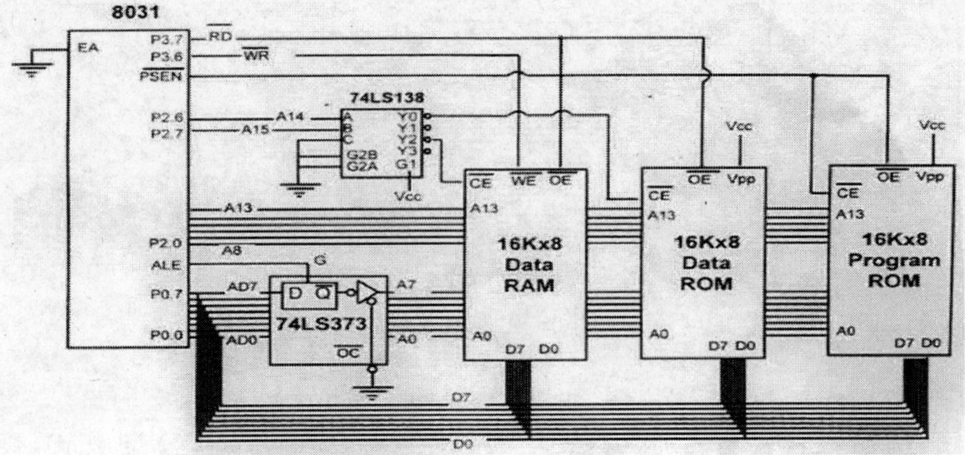

Fig.4.5. 8051 Accessing 256K*8 External NV-RAM

4. *In a certain application, we need 256K bytes of NV-RAM to store data collected by 8051 microcontrollers. (a) Show the connection of an 8051 to a single 256K ×8 NV-RAM chip. (b) Show how various blocks of this single chip are accessed*

Solution:

(a) The 256K ×8 NV-RAM has 18 address pins (A0 – A17) and 8 data Lines. As shown in Fig.5, A0 – A15 go directly to the memory chip while A16 and A17 are controlled by P1.0 and P1.1, respectively. Also notice that chip select of external RAM is connected to P1.2 of the 8051.

(b)The 256K bytes of memory are divided into four blocks, and each block is accessed as follows:

Chip select	**A17**	**A16**	
P1.2	**P1.1**	**P1.0**	**Block address space**
0	0	0	00000H - 0FFFFH
0	0	1	10000H - 1FFFFH
0	1	0	20000H - 2FFFFH
0	1	1	30000H - 3FFFFH
1	X	X	External RAM disabled

For example, to access the 20000H – 2FFFFH address space we need the following

```
CLR     P1.2 DPTR,   ; enable external RAM
MOV     #0           ; start of 64K memory block
CLR     P1.0         ; A16 = 0

SETB    P1.1         ; A17 = 1 for 20000H block
MOV     A, SBUF      ;get data from serial port
MOVX    @DPTR, A
INC     DPTR         ; next location
```

4.5 Interfacing of Peripheral Devices

Table 4.1. Pin Descriptions for LCD

Pin	Symbol	I/O	Descriptions
1	VSS	--	Ground
2	VCC	--	+5V power supply
3	VEE	--	Power supply to control contrast
4	RS	I	RS=0 to select command register, RS=1 to select data register
5	R/W	I	R/W=0 for write, R/W=1 for read
6	E	I/O	Used by the LCD to latch
7	DBO	I/O	
8	DB1	I/O	the 8- bit data bus
9	DB2	I/O	the 8- bit data bus
10	DB3	I/O	the 8- bit data bus
11	DB4	I/O	the 8- bit data bus
12	DB5	I/O	the 8- bit data bus
13	DB6	I/O	the 8- bit data bus
14	DB7	I/O	the 8- bit data bus

Send displayed information or instruction command codes to the LCD
Read the contents of the LCD's internal registers

Used by the LCD to latch
The 8-bit data bus information

- LCD is finding widespread use replacing LEDs
- The declining prices of LCD
- The ability to display numbers, characters, and graphics
- Incorporation of a refreshing controller into the LCD, thereby relieving the CPU of the task of refreshing the LCD
- Ease of programming for characters and graphics

Table 4.2. LCD Command Codes

Code (Hex)	Command to LCD Instruction Register
1	Clear display screen
2	Return home
4	Decrement cursor (shift cursor to left)
6	Increment cursor (shift cursor to right)
5	Shift display right
7	Shift display left
8	Display off, cursor off
A	Display off, cursor on
C	Display on, cursor off
E	Display on, cursor blinking
F	Display on, cursor blinking
10	Shift cursor position to left
14	Shift cursor position to right
18	Shift the entire display to the left
1C	Shift the entire display to the right
80	Force cursor to beginning to 1st line
C0	Force cursor to beginning to 2nd line
38	2 lines and 5x7 matrix

4.5.1 Interfacing LCD to 8051

4.To send any of the commands to the LCD, make pin RS=0. For data, make RS=1. Then send a high-to-low pulse to the E pin to enable the internal latch of the LCD. This is shown in the code below.

```
;calls a time delay before sending next data/command
;P1.0-P1.7 are connected to LCD data pins D0-D7
;P2.0 is connected to RS pin of LCD
;P2.1 is connected to R/W pin of LCD
;P2.2 is connected to E pin of LCD
ORG

MOV  A, #38H; INIT. LCD 2 LINES, 5X7 MATRIX

ACALL COMNWRT; call command subroutine

ACALL DELAY       ;give LCD some time

MOV  A,#0EH ;display on, cursor on

ACALL COMNWRT ;call command subroutine

ACALL DELAY       ;give LCD some time
```

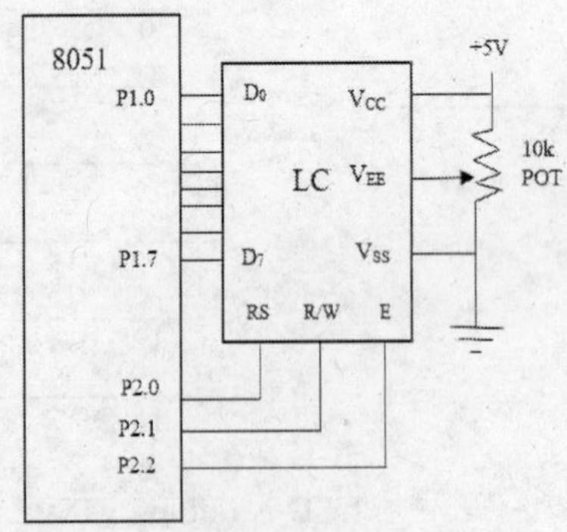

Fig.4.6. Interfacing LCD to 8051

```
MOV  A,#01  ;clear LCD
ACALL COMNWRT ;call command subroutine
ACALL DELAY       ;give LCD some time
MOV  A,#06H ;shift cursor right
ACALL COMNWRT ;call command subroutine ACALL DELAY  ;give LCD some time
MOV  A,#84H ;cursor at line 1, pos. 4
ACALL COMNWRT ;call command subroutine
ACALL DELAY       ;give LCD some time
MOV  A,#'N' ;display letter N
ACALL        DATAWRT    ; call display subroutine
ACALL        DELAY; give LCD some time
MOV  A, #'O'; display letter O
ACALL   DATAWRT          ; call display subroutine
AGAIN:       SJMP AGAIN; stay here
MOV  P1, A  ; stay here
COMNWRT:
MOV  P1, A  ; copy reg A to port 1
CLR   P2.0  ; RS=0 for command
CLR   P2.1  ; R/W=0 for write
SETB  P2.2  ; E=1 for high pulse
ACALL        DELAY        ; give LCD some time
CLR   P2.2  ; E=0 for H-to-L pulse
RET
DATAWRT:           ; write data to LCD
MOV  P1, A  ; copy reg A to port 1
SETB  P2.0  ; RS=1 for data
CLR   P2.1  ; R/W=0 for write
SETB  P2.2  ; E=1 for high pulse
ACALL        DELAY        ; give LCD some time
CLR   P2.2  ; E=0 for H-to-L pulse
RET
DELAY:       MOV  R3, #50          ;50 or higher for fast CPUs
```

```
HERE2:        MOV  R4, #255        ; R4 = 255
HERE: DJNZ  R4, HERE; stay until R4 becomes 0
DJNZ  R3, HERE2
RET
END
;Check busy flag before sending data, command to LCD
;p1=data pin
;P2.0 connected to RS pin
;P2.1 connected to R/W pin
;P2.2 connected to E pin
ORG   0H
MOV  A,#38H          ;init. LCD 2 lines ,5x7 matrix
ACALL COMMAND;issue command
MOV  A,#0EH          ;LCD on, cursor on
ACALL COMMAND;issue command
MOV  A,#01H          ;clear LCD command
ACALL COMMAND;issue command
MOV  A,#06H          ;shift cursor right
ACALL COMMAND;issue command
MOV  A,#86H          ;cursor: line 1, pos. 6
 ACALL COMMAND           ;command subroutine
MOV  A,#'N' ;display letter N
ACALL DATA_DISPLAY
MOV  A,#'O' ;display letter O
 ACALL DATA_DISPLAY
HERE: SJMP HERE  ; STAY HERE
COMMAND:
ACALL READY        ;is LCD ready?
MOV  P1,A  ;issue command code
CLR   P2.0   ;RS=0 for command
CLR   P2.1   ;R/W=0 to write to LCD
SETB  P2.2   ;E=1 for H-to-L pulse
```

```
CLR   P2.2    ;E=0,latch in
RET
DATA_DISPLAY:
ACALL READY        ; is LCD ready?
MOV  P1, A  ; issue data
SETB P2.0            ; RS=1 for data
CLR   P2.1   ; R/W =0 to write to LCD
SETB P2.2     ; E=1 for H-to-L pulse
RET
READY
SETB P1.7   ; make P1.7 input port
CLR P2.0    ; RS=0 access command reg
SETB P2.1     ; R/W=1 read command reg
; read command reg and check busy flag
BACK: SETB P2.2    ; E=1 for H-to-L pulse
CLR   P2.2   ; E=0 H-to-L pulse
JB     P1.7, BACK   ; stay until busy flag=0
RET
END
```

To read the command register, we make R/W=1, RS=0, and a H-to-L pulse for the E pin

If bit 7 (busy flag) is high, the LCD is busy and no information Should be issued to it

- One can put data at any location in the LCD and the following shows address locations and how they are accessed

RS	R/W	DB7	DB6	DB5	DB4	DB3	DB2	DB1	DB0
0	0	1	A	A	A	A	A	A	A

- AAAAAAA=000_0000 to 010_0111 for line1
- AAAAAAA=100_0000 to 110_0111 for line2

LCD Timing

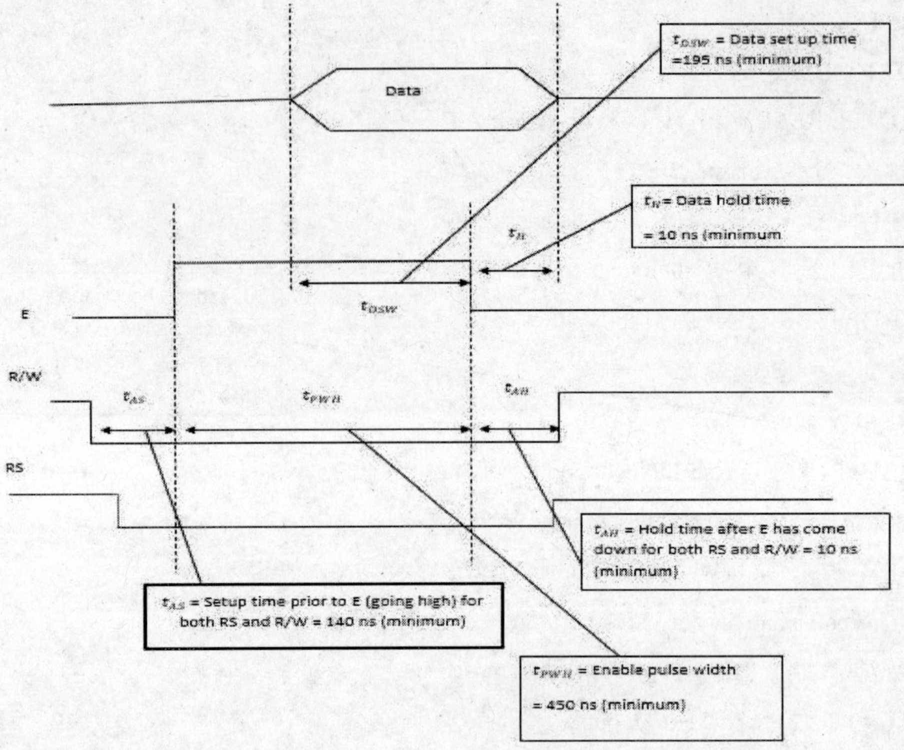

Fig.4.7. LCD Timing Diagram

4.5.2 Interfacing to ADC and Sensors

4.5.2.1 ADC Devices

- ADCs (analog-to-digital converters) are among the most widely used devices for data acquisition
- A physical quantity, like temperature, pressure, humidity, and velocity, etc., is converted to electrical (voltage, current) signals using a device called a transducer, or sensor.

Table 4.3. LCD Addressing for the LCD of 40 × 2 Size

LCD Addressing for the LCDs of 40 ×2 size

The upper address range can go as high as 0100111

For the 40- character-wide LCD, which corresponds to locations 0 to 39

	DB7	DB6	DB5	DB4	DB3	DB2	DB1	DB0
Line1 (min)	1	0	0	0	0	0	0	0
Line1 (max)	1	0	1	0	0	1	1	1
Line2 (min)	1	1	0	0	0	0	0	0
Line2 (max)	1	1	1	0	0	1	1	1

- We need an analog-to-digital converter to translate the analog signals to digital numbers, so microcontroller can read them

4.5.2.2 ADC804 Chip

- ADC804 IC is an analog-to-digital converter
  - It works with +5 volts and has a resolution of 8 bits
  - Conversion time is another major factor in judging an ADC
    - Conversion time is defined as the time it takes the ADC to convert the analog input to a digital (binary) number
    - In ADC804 conversion time varies depending on the clocking signals applied to CLK R and CLK IN pins, but it cannot be faster than 110 ns

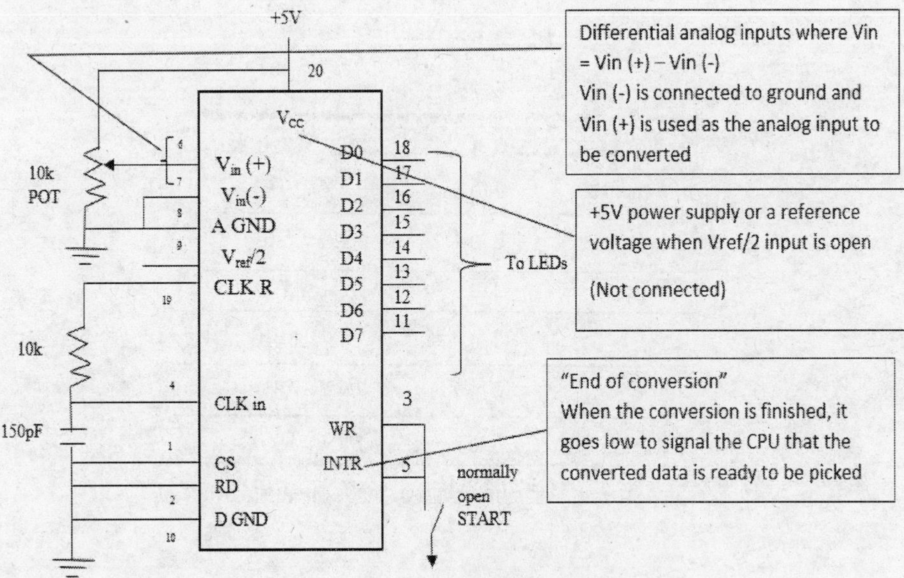

Fig.4.8. ADC804 Chip

- WR = "start conversion" When WR makes a low-to- high transition, ADC804 starts converting the analog input value of Vin to an 8-bit digital number
- CS= CS is an active low input used to activate ADC804
- RD= "output enable" a high-to-low RD pulse is used to get the 8-bit converted data out of ADC804

- CLK IN and CLK R
  - CLK IN is an input pin connected to an external clock source
  - To use the internal clock generator (also called self-clocking), CLK IN and CLK R pins are connected to a capacitor and a resistor, and the clock frequency is determined by

$$F = \frac{1}{1.1\,RC}$$

- Typical values are R = 10K ohms and C =150 pF
- We get f = 606 kHz and the conversion time is 110 ns

4.5.2.3 Vref/2

- It is used for the reference voltage
  - ➢ If this pin is open (not connected), the analog input voltage is in the range of 0 to 5 volts (the same as the Vcc pin)
  - ➢ If the analog input range needs to be 0 to 4 volts, Vref/2 is connected to 2 volts

4.5.2.4 Vref/2 Relation to Vin Range

- **D0-D7**
- ➢ The digital data output pins
- ➢ These are tri-state buffered
- The converted data is accessed only when CS = 0 and RD is forced low
- ➢ To calculate the output voltage, use the following formula

$$D_{out} = \frac{V_{in}}{Step\ Size}$$

$V_{ref}/2$(v)	V_{in}(V)	Step Size (mV)
Not connected*	0 to 5	5/256=19.53
2.0	0 to 4	4/255=15.62
1.5	0 to 3	3/256=11.71
1.28	0 to 2.56	2.56/256=10
1.0	0 to 2	2/256=7.81
0.5	0 to 1	1/256=3.90

Step size is the smallest change can be discerned by an ADC

Table 4.4. Vref/2 Relation to Vin Range

- Dout = digital data output (in decimal),
- Vin = analog voltage, and
- step size (resolution) is the smallest change
- Analog ground and digital ground
- ➢ Analog ground is connected to the ground of the analog Vin
- ➢ Digital ground is connected to the ground of the Vcc pin

- To isolate the analog Vin signal from transient voltages caused by digital switching of the output D0 – D7
  - ➢ This contributes to the accuracy of the digital data output.

- The following steps must be followed for data conversion by the ADC804 chip
    - Make CS = 0 and send a low-to-high pulse to pin WR to start conversion
    - Keep monitoring the INTR pin
- If INTR is low, the conversion is finished
- If the INTR is high, keep polling until it goes low
- After the INTR has become low, we make CS = 0 and send a high-to-low pulse to the RD pin to get the data out of the ADC804

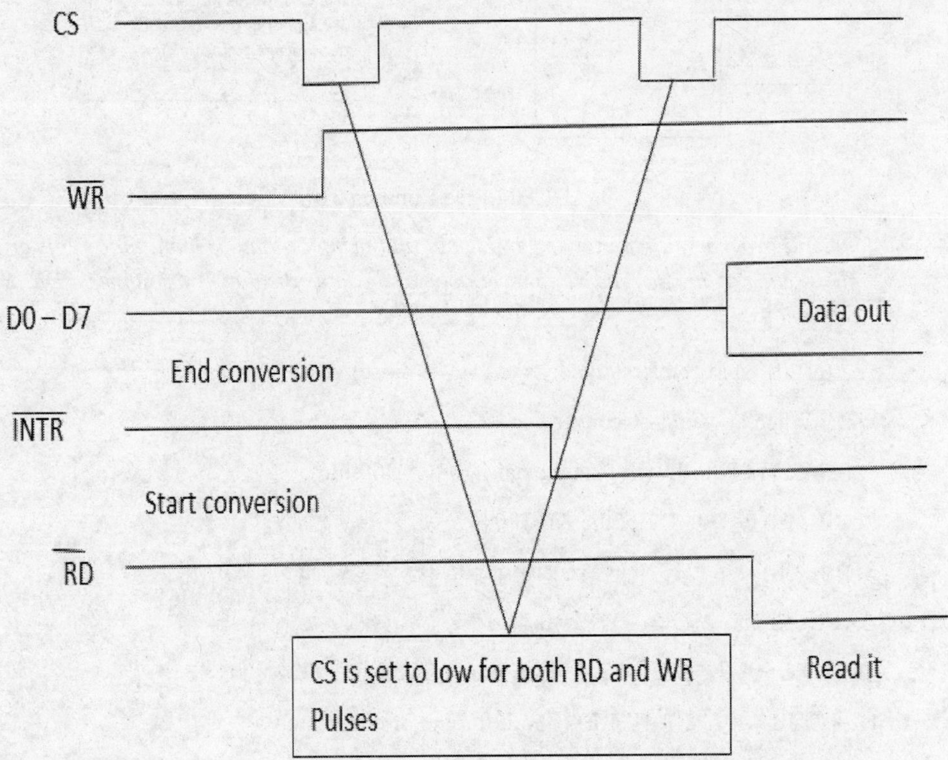

Fig.4.9. Data conversion by the ADC804 chip

4.5.2.5 ADC804 Free Running Test Mode

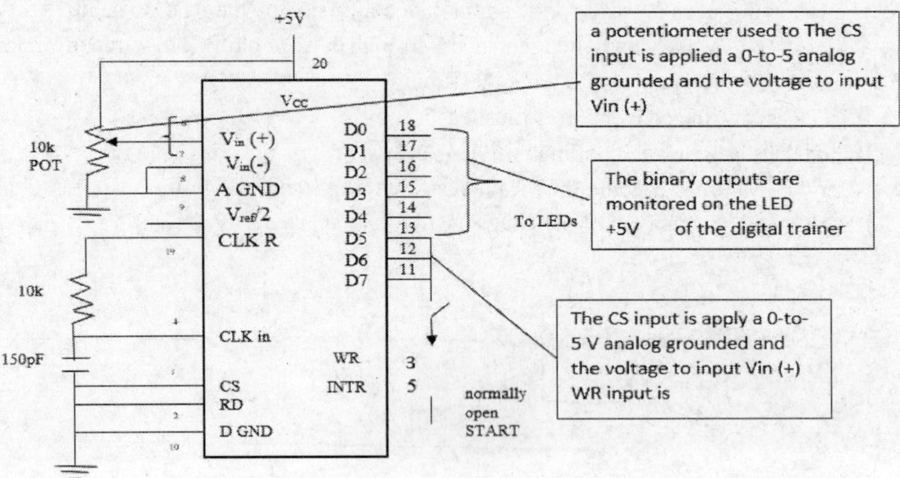

Fig.4.10. ADC804 Free Running Test Mode

5. *Write a program to monitor the INTR pin and bring an analog input into register A. Then call a hex-to ACSII conversion and data display subroutines. Do this continuously.*

```
; p2.6=WR (start conversion needs to L-to-H pulse)
; p2.7 When low, end-of-conversion)
; p2.5=RD (a H-to-L will read the data from ADC chip)
; p1.0 – P1.7= D0 - D7 of the ADC804
MOV   P1, #0FFH      ; make P1 = input
BACK: CLR    P2.6    ; WR = 0
SETB P2.6            ; WR = 1 L-to-H to start conversion
HERE: JB       P2.7, HERE    ; wait for end of conversion
CLR    P2.5   ; conversion finished, enable RD
MOV    A, P1  ; read the data
ACALL CONVERSION; hex-to-ASCII conversion
ACALL DATA_DISPLAY; display the data
SETB p2.5        ; make RD=1 for next round
SJMP BACK
```

4.6 LCD Interfacing

- One can put data at any location in the LCD and the following shows address locations and how they are accessed

Table 4.5. LCD Addressing for the LCDs of 40 ×2 size

R/W	DB7	DB6	DB5	DB4	DB3	DB2	DB1	DB0
0	1	A	A	A	A	A	A	A

- AAAAAAA=000_0000 to 010_0111 for line1
- AAAAAAA=100_0000 to 110_0111 for line2

The upper address range can go as high as 0100111

For the 40- character-wide LCD, which corresponds to locations 0 to 39

	DB7	DB6	DB5	DB4	DB3	DB2	DB1	DB0
Line1 (min)	1	0	0	0	0	0	0	0
Line1 (max)	1	0	1	0	0	1	1	1
Line2 (min)	1	1	0	0	0	0	0	0
Line2 (max)	1	1	1	0	0	1	1	1

4.6.1 Sending Information to LCD Using MOVC Instruction

```
; Call a time delay before sending next data/command

; P1.0-P1.7=D0-D7, P2.0=RS, P2.1=R/W, P2.2=E

ORG  0

MOV DPTR, #MYCOM

C1: CLR A

MOVC    A,@A+DPTR

ACALL COMNWRT              ; call command subroutine

ACALL DELAY                ; give LCD some time

INC   DPTR

JZ SEND_DAT

SJMP   C1

SEND_DAT:

MOV   DPTR, #MYDATA

D1: CLR  A
```

```
MOVC    A,@A+DPTR
ACALL DATAWRT           ; call command subroutine
ACALL DELAY             ; give LCD some time
INC   DPTR
JZ   AGAIN
SJMP   D1
AGAIN:   SJMP   AGAIN   ; stay here
COMNWRT:                ;send   command   to   LCD
MOV P1, A               ;copy reg A to P1 CLR  P2.0
                        ;RS=0 for command CLR  P2.1
                        ;R/W=0 for write SETB   P2.2
                        ;E=1 for high pulse ACALL DELAY
                        ;give LCD some time
CLR P2.2                ; E=0 for H-to-L pulseRET
DATAWRT:                 write   data   to   LCD
MOV P1, A               ; copy reg A to port 1
SETB   P2.0             ; RS=1 for data
CLR P2.1                ; R/W=0 for write SETB
P2.2; E=1               for high pulse
ACALL DELAY             ; give LCD some time
CLR P2.2                ; E=0 for H-to-L pulseRET
DELAY:   MOV R3, #250   ; 50 or higher for fast CPUs
HERE2:   MOV            R4, #255; R4 = 255
HERE: DJNZ R4, HERE     ; stay until R4 becomes 0
DJNZ R3, HERE2
RET
ORG 300H
MYCOM:   DB 38H, 0EH, 01, 06, 84H, 0      ; commands and null
MYDATA: DB   "HELLO", 0
END
```

6. *Write an 8051 C program to send letters 'M', 'D', and 'E' to the LCD using the busy flag method.*

Solution:

```
#include <reg51.h>
```

```
sfr ldata = 0x90; //P1=LCD data pins

sbit rs = P2^0;

sbit rw = P2^1;

sbit en = P2^2;

sbit busy = P1^7;

Void main ()

{

lcdcmd(0x38);

lcdcmd(0x0E);

lcdcmd(0x01);

lcdcmd(0x06);

lcdcmd(0x86);  //line 1, position 6

lcdcmd('M');

lcdcmd('D');

lcdcmd('E');

}

Void lcdcmd (unsigned char value)

{

lcdready();          //check the LCD busy flag

Ldata = value;  //put the value on the pins

rs = 0;

rw = 0;

en = 1;  //strobe the enable pin

 MSDelay(1);

en = 0;

Return;

}

Void lcddata (unsigned char value) {

lcdready();          //check the LCD busy flag
```

```
Ldata = value;   //put the value on the pins

rs = 1;

rw = 0;

en = 1;   //strobe the enable pin

 MSDelay(1);

en = 0; return;


}

Void lcdready ( )

{

Busy = 1;          //make the busy pin at input

 rs = 0;

rw = 1;

While (busy==1) {     //wait here for busy flag

en = 0;                        //strobe the enable pin
 MSDelay(1);

en = 1;

}

Void lcddata (unsigned int itime)

{

Unsigned int i, j; for (i=0; i<itime; i++)

For (j=0;j<1275;j++);

}
```

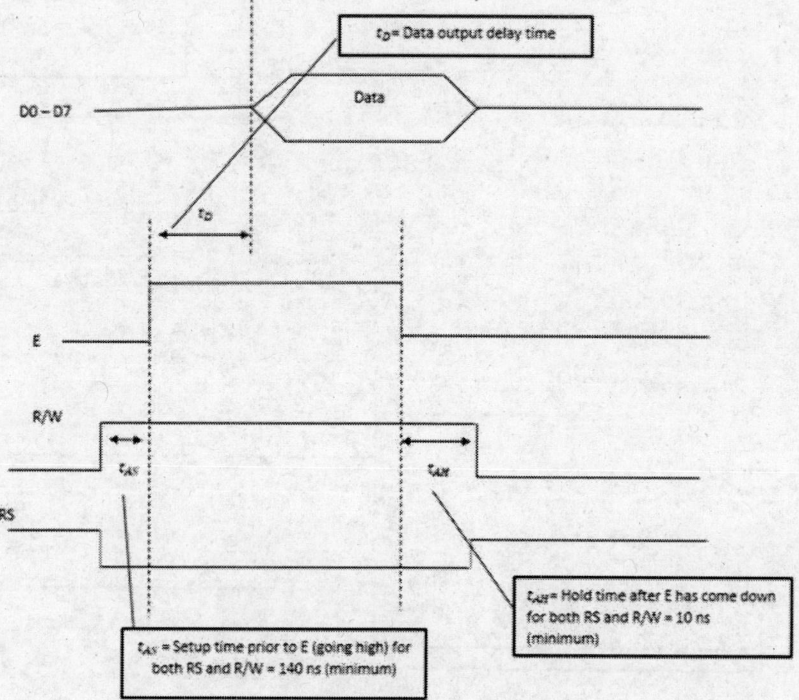

Fig.4.11. LCD Timing diagram for Read

Note: Read requires an L-to-H pulse for the E pin

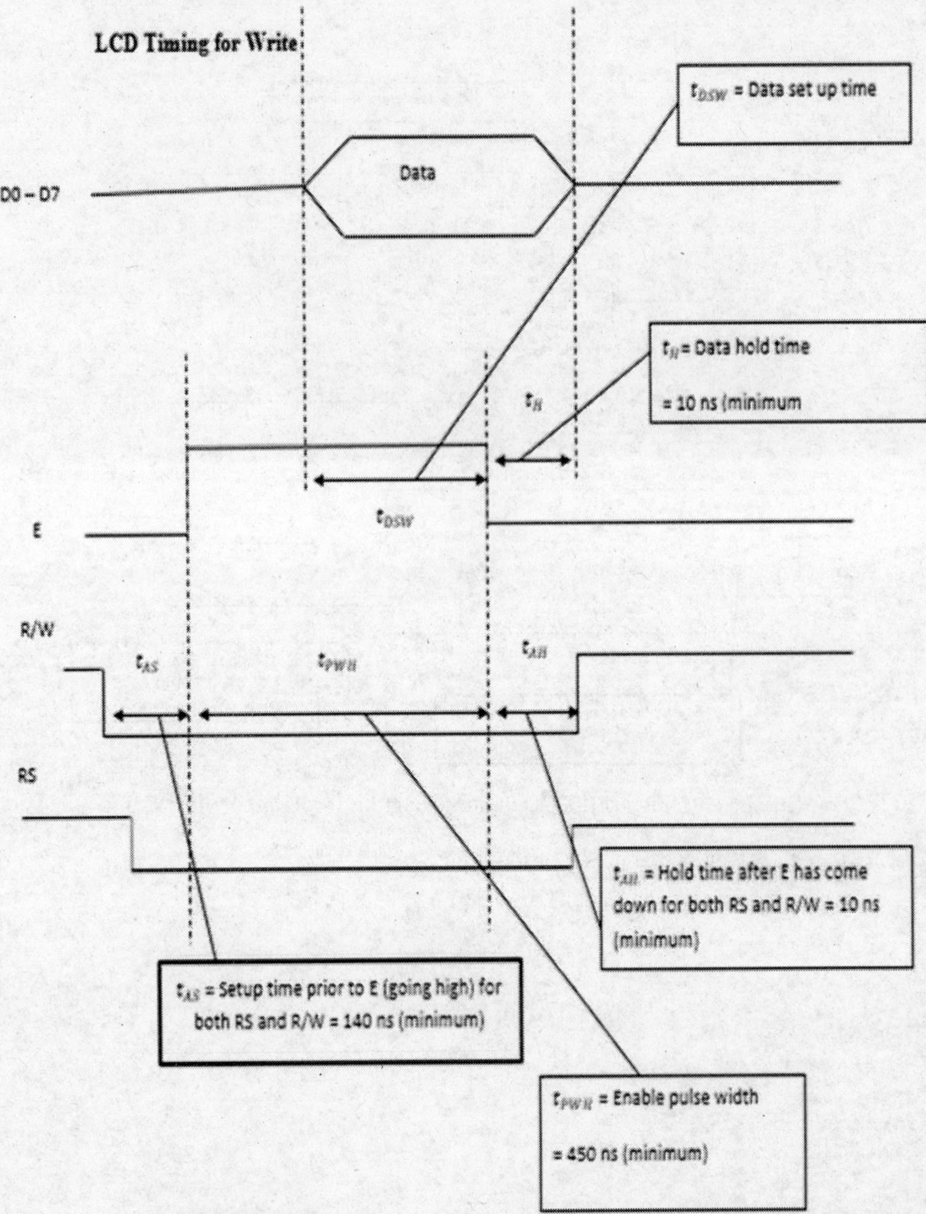

Fig.4.12. LCD Timing Diagram For write

4.7. Keyboard Interfacing

- Keyboards are organized in a matrix of rows and columns
- The CPU accesses both rows and columns through ports
    - Therefore, with two 8-bit ports, an 8 x 8 matrix of keys can be connected to a microprocessor
- When a key is pressed, a row and a column make a contact
    - Otherwise, there is no connection between rows and columns

- In IBM PC keyboards, a single microcontroller takes care of hardware and software interfacing
- A 4x4 matrix connected to two ports
  - The rows are connected to an output port and the columns are connected to an input port

4.7.1. Matrix Keyboard Connection to ports

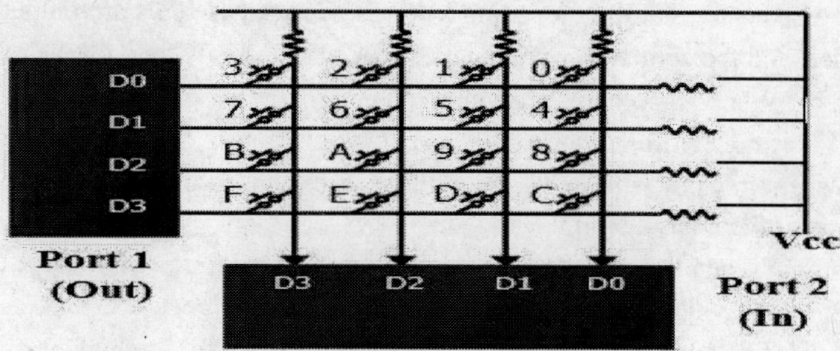

Fig.4.13. Matrix Keyboard Connection to ports

- It is the function of the microcontroller to scan the keyboard continuously to detect and identify the key pressed
- To detect a pressed key, the microcontroller grounds all rows by providing 0 to the output latch, then it reads the columns
  - If the data read from columns is D3 – D0 = 1111, no key has been pressed and the process continues till key press is detected
  - If one of the column bits has a zero, this means that a key press has occurred
- For example, if D3 – D0 = 1101, this means that a key in the D1 column has been pressed
- After detecting a key press, microcontroller will go through the process of identifying the key
- Starting with the top row, the microcontroller grounds it by providing a low to row D0 only
  - It reads the columns, if the data read is all 1s, no key in that row is activated and the process is moved to the next row
- It grounds the next row, reads the columns, and checks for any zero
  - This process continues until the row is identified
- After identification of the row in which the key has been pressed
  - Find out which column the pressed key belongs to

7. *From given Figure identify the row and column of the pressed key for each of the following.*

(a) D3 – D0 = 1110 for the row, D3 – D0 = 1011 for the column

(b) D3 – D0 = 1101 for the row, D3 – D0 = 0111 for the column

Solution:

From Fig.13 the row and column can be used to identify the key.

(a) The row belongs to D0 and the column belongs to D2; therefore, key number 2 was pressed.

(b) The row belongs to D1 and the column belongs to D3; therefore, key number 7 was pressed.

❖ Program 12-4 for detection and identification of key activation goes through the following stages:

1. To make sure that the preceding key has been released, 0s are output to all rows at once, and the columns are read and checked repeatedly until all the columns are high
   - When all columns are found to be high, the program waits for a short amount of time before it goes to the next stage of waiting for a key to be pressed
2. To see if any key is pressed, the columns are scanned over and over in an infinite loop until one of them has a 0 on it
   - Remember that the output latches connected to rows still have their initial zeros (provided in stage 1), making them grounded
   - After the key press detection, it waits 20 ms for the bounce and then scans the columns again

   (a) it ensures that the first key press detection was not an erroneous one due a spike noise

   (b) The key press. If after the 20-ms delay the key is still pressed, it goes back into the loop to detect a real key press

3. To detect which row key press belongs to, it grounds one row at a time, reading the columns each time
   - If it finds that all columns are high, this means that the key press cannot belong to that row

– Therefore, it grounds the next row and continues until it finds the row the key press belongs to

- Upon finding the row that the key press belongs to, it sets up the starting address for the look-up table holding the scan codes (or ASCII) for that row

4. To identify the key press, it rotates the column bits, one bit at a time, into the carry flag and checks to see if it is low
   - Upon finding the zero, it pulls out the ASCII code for that key from the look-up table
   - otherwise, it increments the pointer to point to the next element of the look-up table

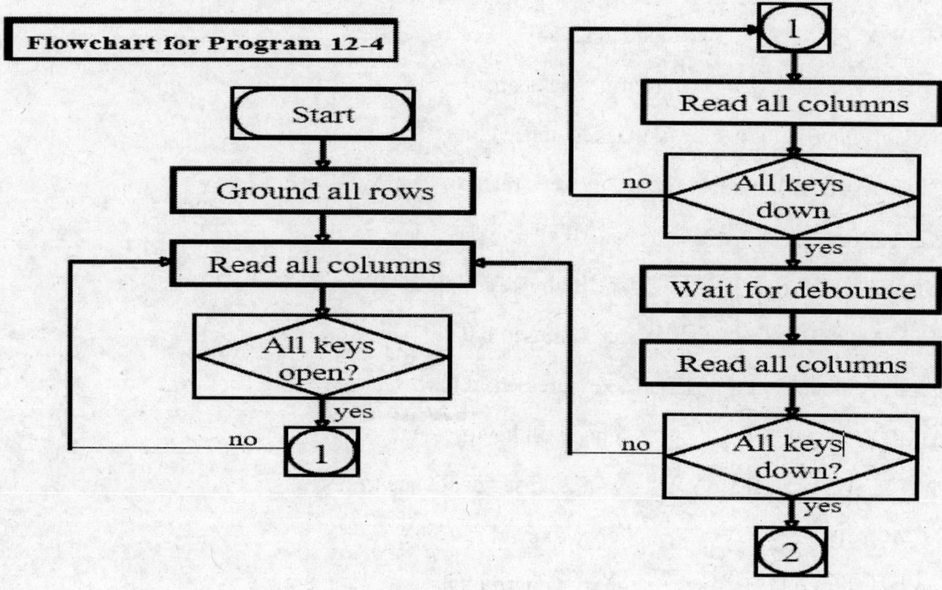

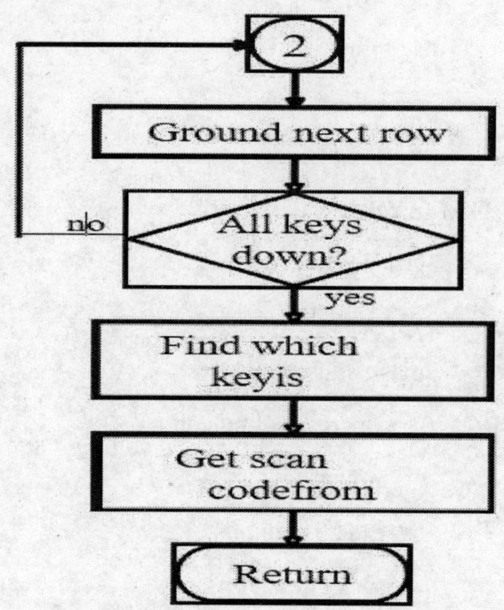

Fig.4.14. Flow chart for the program 12-4

8. *Program 12-4: Keyboard Program*

; Keyboard subroutine. This program sends the ASCII; Code for pressed key to P0.1; P1.0-P1.3 connected to rows, P2.0-P2.3 to column

```
MOV P2, #0FFH              ; make P2 an input port
```

```
K1:MOV P1, #0               ; ground all rows at once
MOV A, P2                   ; read all col
                            ;( ensure keys open)
ANL A, 00001111B            ; masked unused bits
CJNE A, #00001111B, K1      ; till all keys release
K2:     ACALL DELAY         ; call 20 msec delay
MOV A, P2                   ; see if any key is pressed
ANL A,00001111B             ;mask unused bits
CJNE A, #00001111B, OVER ; key pressed, find row
SJMP K2                     ; check till key pressed
OVER: ACALL DELAY           ; wait 20 msec debounce time
MOV A, P2                   ; check key closure
ANL A, 00001111B            ; mask unused bits
CJNE A, #00001111B, OVER1; key pressed, find row
SJMP K2                     ; if none, keep polling
OVER1: MOV P1, #11111110B ; ground row 0
MOV A, P2                   ; read all columns
ANL A, #00001111B           ; mask unused bits
CJNE A, #00001111B, ROW_0; key row 0, find col.
MOV P1, #11111101B          ; ground row 1
MOV A, P2                   ; read all columns
ANL A, #00001111B           ; mask unused bits
CJNE A, #00001111B, ROW_1 ; key row 1, find col.
MOV P1, #11111011B          ; ground row 2
MOV A, P2                   ; read all columns
ANL A, #00001111B           ; mask unused bits
CJNE A, #00001111B, ROW_2 ; key row 2, find col.
MOV P1,#11110111B           ;ground row 3
MOV A, P2                   ; read all columns
ANL A, #00001111B           ; mask unused bits
CJNE A, #00001111B, ROW_3 ; key row 3, find col.
LJMP K2                     ; if none, false input,
```

```
; repeat
ROW_0: MOV DPTR, #KCODE0   ; set DPTR=start of row 0
 SJMP FIND                 ; find col. Key belongs to
ROW_1: MOV DPTR, #KCODE1   ; set DPTR=start of row
SJMP FIND   ; find col. Key belongs to
ROW_2: MOV DPTR, #KCODE2   ; set DPTR=start of row 2
 SJMP FIND                 ; find col. Key belongs to
ROW_3: MOV DPTR, #KCODE3   ; set DPTR=start of row 3
FIND: RRC A                 ; see if any CY bit low
JNC MATCH                   ; if zero, get ASCII code
INC DPTR                    ; point to next col. addr
SJMP FIND                   ; keep searching
MATCH: CLR A                ; set A=0 (match is found)
 MOVC A,@A+DPTR             ; get ASCII from table
 MOV P0, A                  ; display pressed key
LJMP K1
; ASCII LOOK-UP TABLE FOR EACH ROW ORG 300H
KCODE0: DB '0','1','2','3'; ROW 0
KCODE1: DB '4','5','6','7'; ROW 1
KCODE2: DB '8','9','A','B'; ROW 2
KCODE3: DB 'C','D','E','F'; ROW 3
END
```

4.8. Interfacing 7(Seven) Segment Display to 8085 Microprocessor

An output device which is very common is, especially in the kit of 8085 microprocessor and it is the Light Emitting Diode consisting of seven segments. Moreover, we have eight segments in a LED display consisting of 7 segments which includes '.', consisting of character 8 and having a decimal point just next to it. We denote the segments as 'a, b, c, d, e, f, g, and dp' where dp signifies '.' which is the decimal point. Moreover, these are LEDs or together a series of Light Emitting Diodes. We have shown the internal circuit comprising of a display of seven segment is as shown in Fig 15.

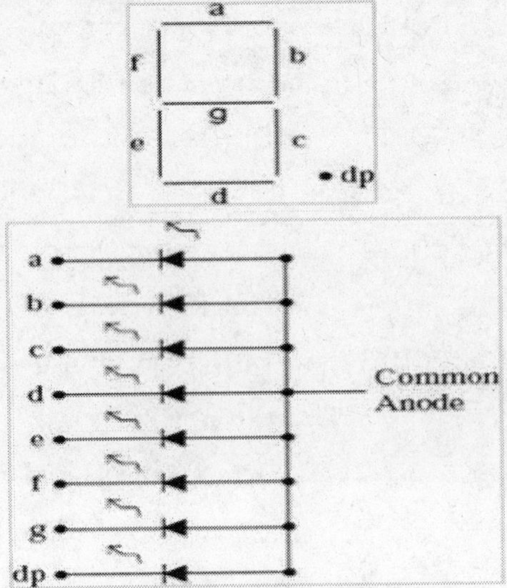

Fig.4.15. 7-segment display of LED

There are two types of 7-segment LED: They are the common anode type and the common cathode type. We have discussed the common anode-type which is 7 segmented Light Emitting Diode. In the LED which is common anode and is 7-segmented, here we connect all the eight LED anodes together and the eight external pin is brought to display. And this pin gets connected to a DC supply of +5 Volt. The cathode ends of the eight segments are brought out on the pins of the display.

The use of 74373 latch for interfacing a 7-segment display is shown in the following Fig.

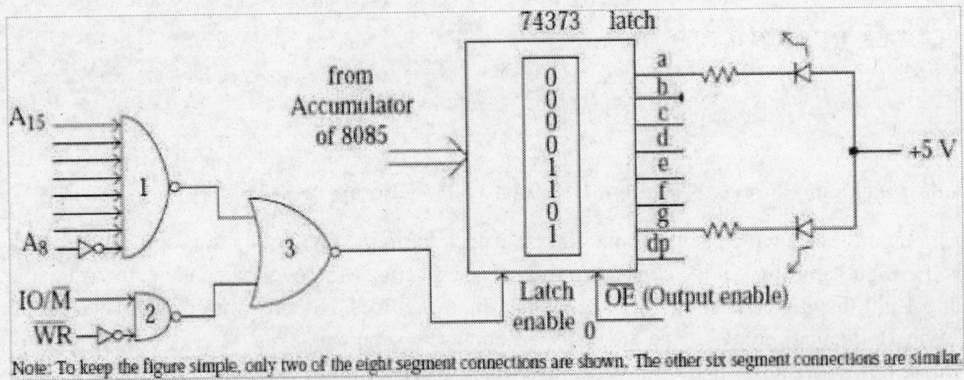

Fig.4.16. 74373 latches for interfacing a 7-segment display

In the 74373 latch is used as an I/O mapped I/O port with the port address as FEH. This could be easily verified from the chip select circuit used in the figure. The following instructions

Are to be executed to display character '3' on the 7-segment display. The corresponding program to send 0DH to the port FEH will be MVI A, 0DH OUT FEH

Using MVI instruction we are initializing Accumulator (A) with Byte 0DH i.e. 0000 1101. Then it will be sent to the port FEH by the instruction OUT.

4.9. Interfacing ADC with 8085 Microprocessor

The Analog to Digital Conversion is a quantizing process. Here the analog signal is represented by equivalent binary states. The A/D converters can be classified into two groups based on their conversion techniques.

In the first technique it compares given analog signal with the initially generated equivalent signal. In this technique, it includes successive approximation, counter and flash type converters. In another technique it determines the changing of analog signals into time or frequency. This process includes integrator-converters and voltage-to-frequency converters. The first process is faster but less accurate, the second one is more accurate. As the first process uses flash type, so it is expensive and difficult to design for high accuracy.

The ADC 0808/0809 Chip

The ADC 0808/0809 is an 8-bit analog to digital converter. It has 8 channel multiplexer to interface with the microprocessor.

This chip is popular and widely used ADC. ADC 0808/0809 is a monolithic CMOS device. This device uses successive approximation technique to convert analog signal to digital form. One of the main advantage of this chip is that it does not require any external zero and full scale adjustment, only +5V DC supply is sufficient.

Let us see some good features of ADC 0808/0809

- The conversion speed is much higher
- The accuracy is also high
- It has minimal temperature dependence
- Excellent long-term accuracy and repeatability

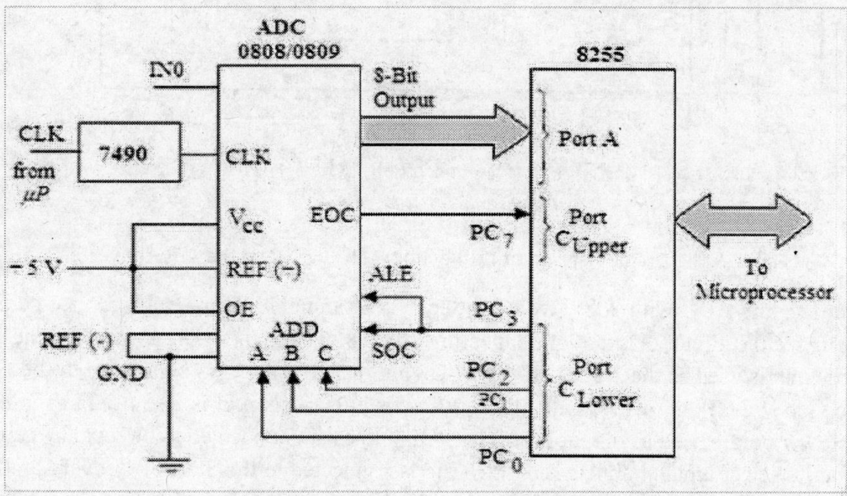

Fig.4.17. The functional block diagram of the ADC 0808/0809 Chip

- Less power consumption

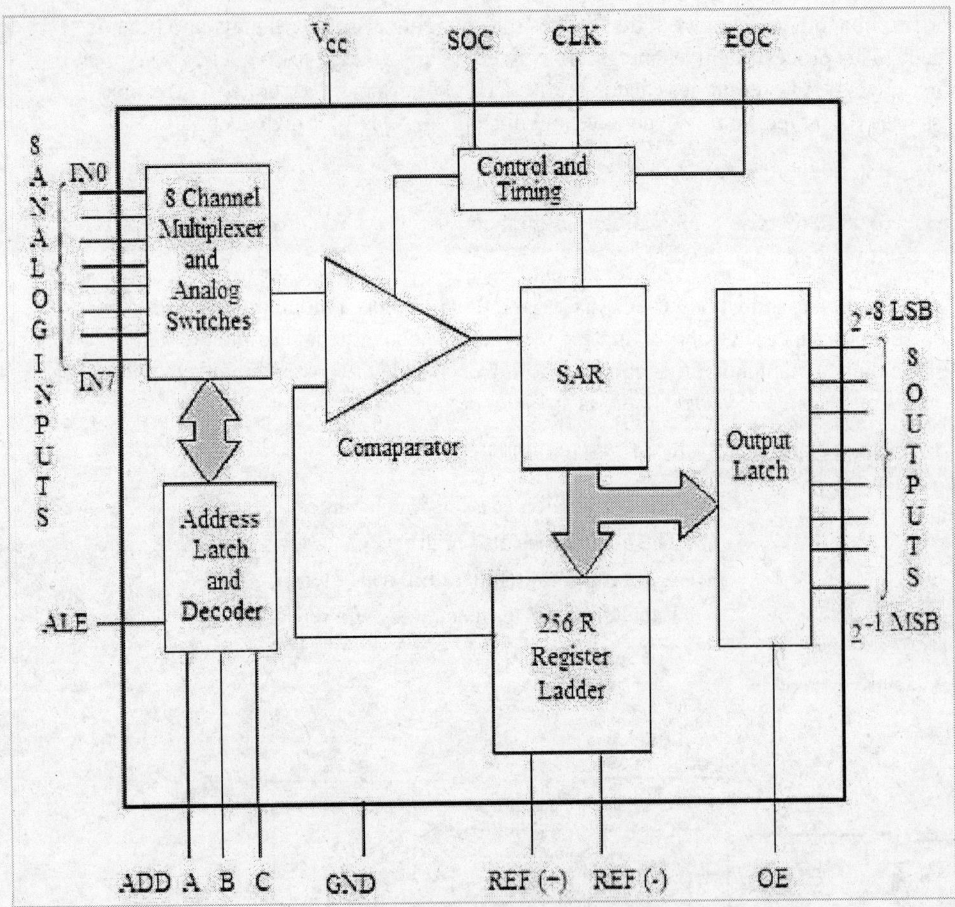

Fig.4.18.The circuit diagram of connecting 8085, 8255 and the ADC converter

To interface the ADC with 8085, we need 8255 Programmable Peripheral Interface chip with it. Let us see the circuit diagram of connecting 8085, 8255 and the ADC converter. The PortA of 8255 chip is used as the input port. The PC7 pin of Port Cupper is connected to the End of Conversion (EOC) Pin of the analog to digital converter. This port is also used as input port. The Clower port is used as output port. The PC2-0 lines are connected to three address pins of this chip to select input channels. The PC3 pin is connected to the Start of Conversion (SOC) pin and ALE pin of ADC 0808/0809. See the QR code for more on interfacing.

more on 8085

Program

MVI A, 98H; Set Port A and C_{Upper} as input, C_{Lower} as output

OUT 03H; Write control word 8255-I to control Word

Register

XRA A; Clear the accumulator

OUT 02H; send the content of Acc to Port C_{Lower} to select

IN 0

MVI A, 08H; Load the accumulator with 08H

OUT 02H; ALE and SOC will be 0

XRA A; Clear the accumulator

OUT 02H; ALE and SOC will be low.

READ: IN 02H; Read from EOC (PC7)

RAL; Rotate left to check C7 is 1.

JNC READ; If C7 is not 1, go to READ

IN 00H; Read digital output of ADC

STA 8000H; Save result at 8000H

HLT; Stop the program

4.10. Interfacing 8253 (Timer IC) with 8085 Microprocessor

The Intel 8253 is programmable Interval Timers (PTIs) designed for microprocessors toper form timing and counting functions using three 16-bit registers. Each counter has 2 input pins, i.e., Clock & Gate, and 1 pin for "OUT" output. To operate a counter, a 16-bit count is loaded in its register. On command, it begins to decrement the count until it reaches 0, then it generates a pulse that can be used to interrupt the CPU.

Features of 8253S

- It has three independent 16-bit down counters.
- It can handle inputs from DC to 10MHz.
- These three counters can be programmed for either binary or BCD count.
- It is compatible with almost all microprocessors.
- 8254has a powerful command called READ BACK command, which allows the user to check the count value, the programmed mode, the current mode, and the current status of the counter.

4.11. Interfacing 8253 with 8085

From the following picture, we can see that the data bus D7-0 of 8085 is connected to the data pins D7 to D0 of 8253. So, the higher order address bus is used as decoder input to select the chip and the A8 and A9 of 8085 are connected to the pin A1 and A0 respectively to select the counter.

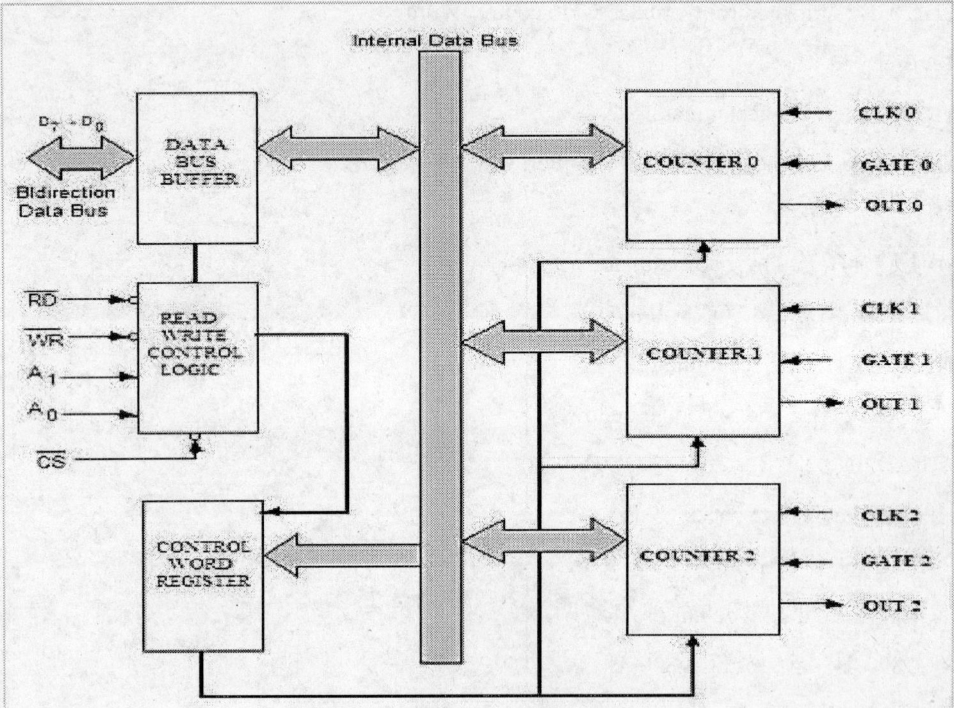

Fig.4.19: The block diagram of 8253

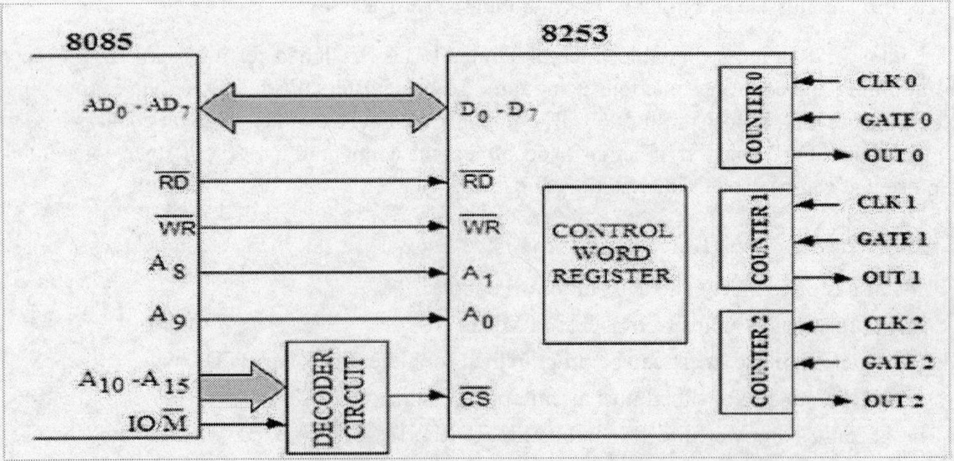

Fig.4.20: Interfacing 8253 with 8085

In the next diagram, we can get the chip select logic of 8253. In that diagram, we can easily find that when A3-2 and A7-5 are at logic 0 and A4 at logic 1, then only the chip select CS pin of 8253 will be enabled.

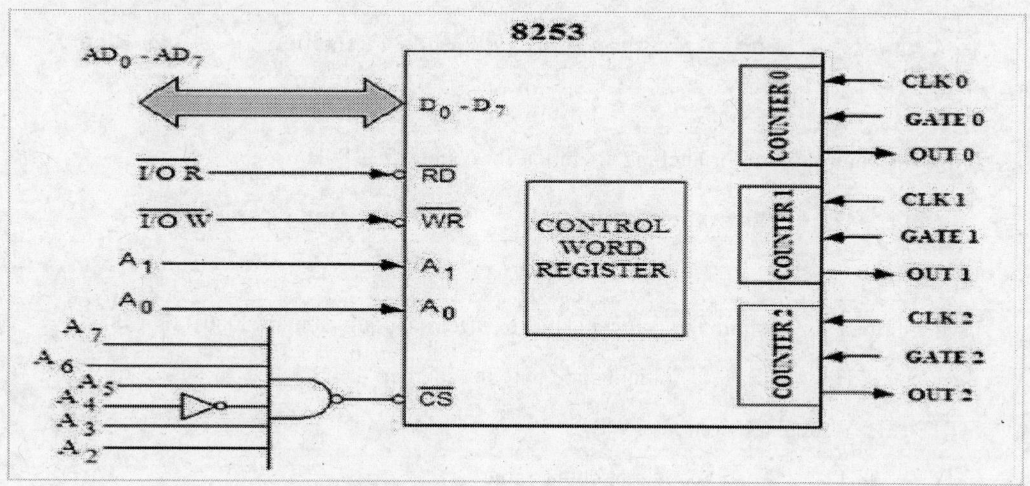

Fig.4.21: Chip select Logic of 8253

Table 4.6. To show how the counter is being selected by using A1 and A0 pins of 8253.

$\overline{CS}$								HEX Address	Counter Selection
A_7	A_6	A_5	A_4	A_3	A_2	A_1	A_0		
0	0	0	1	0	0	0	0	10H	Counter 0
0	0	0	1	0	0	0	1	11H	Counter 1
0	0	0	1	0	0	1	0	12H	Counter 2
0	0	0	1	0	0	1	1	13H	Control Word Register

By using the IN and OUT instruction the counter selection and Control Word Register (CWR) setup can be done. If the Accumulator is holding content to load CWR, then by using OUT 13H the CWR will be set. Similarly, by using IN instruction we can get the value of counter value, like IN 11H will get the value from counter 1 and so on.

So, the following four steps are needed for counter operations:

- Initialize 8253 chip
- Load Control word register with Control Word value
- Load Lower Order count value
- Load Higher Order count value

Let us see a program to load counter 2 in mode 1 with a count value 500010 in mode 0. Also, read the count value on a fly.

At first, to initialize the 8253, the Control word will be B2H

Counter 2		Load LS and then MS		Mode 1 selection			0 for Binary
1	0	1	1	0	0	1	0

Now the control word for latching operation for counter 2 is 80H

Counter 2		Latching Option		Don't Care			
1	0	0	0	0	0	0	0

We will load 500010 into the counter. The hexadecimal equivalent of 500010 is 1388H.

```
MVI A, B2H; Load B2H as initialization byte for counter
OUT 13H; Write ACC content CWR
MVI A, 88H      ; Load LS byte of count value
OUT 12H         ; Send to Counter 2
MVI A, 13H      ; Load MS byte of count value
OUT 12H         ; Send to Counter 2
MVI D, 00       ; clear the register D
L1: MVI A, 80H  ; Set a with control word 80H of counter 2
OUT 13H         ; Write Acc content CWR
IN 12H          ; Read LS value of counter value
MOV B, A        ; store LS value to B
IN 12H          ; Read MS value of counter value
ORA B           ; OR LS and MS to set Z flag
JNZ L1          ; if Z flag is not set, jump to Loop
HLT             ; Halt the program
```

4.12. Interfacing Stepper Motor with 8085

Stepper motor is an electromechanical device that rotates through fixed angular steps when digital inputs are applied. It is suitable for precise position, speed and direction control which are required in automation system.

The angle through which stepper motor rotates with a fixed angle for each digital data is called step angle.

Different stepper motor has different step angle. The more frequently used stepper motor has step angle of 0.9 degrees and 1.8 degrees.

Depending on the sequence applied to stepper motor, it can be classified in two category:

1. 4- Step sequence or full step sequence
2. 8- Step sequence or half step sequence

Calculations:

1. Total no. of steps=

Ex: = 200 steps are required to complete one rotation

2. Total no. of repeated steps=

Ex: = 50 repetition of sequence = (32) in Hexadecimal.

4-Step sequence:

- In this type of functioning, the following 4 binary sequence/code are used for rotation: (Considering step angle= 1.8 degrees)

Table4.7. 4 binary sequence/code are used for rotation

4- Step sequence binary pattern	HEX code	Comments			
A	B	C	D		
1	0	1	0	0AH	Sequence for Clock wise rotation
1	0	0	1	09H	
0	1	0	1	05H	
0	1	1	0	06H	
0	1	1	0	06H	Sequence for anti-clockwise rotation
0	1	0	1	05H	
1	0	0	1	09H	
1	0	1	0	0AH	

8-Step Sequence:

- In this type of functioning, the following 8 binary sequence/code are used for rotation: (Considering step angle= 0.9degrees)

Table4.8. 8 binary sequence/code are used for rotation

4- Step sequence binary pattern	HEX code	Comments			
A	B	C	D		
0	1	0	1	05H	Sequence for anti-clockwise rotation
0	0	0	1	01H	
1	0	0	1	09H	
1	0	0	0	08H	
1	0	1	0	0AH	
0	0	1	0	02H	
0	1	1	0	06H	
0	1	0	0	04H	

Table 4.9. Chips select Logic

Chip select address lines	Address lines to select port	HEX address	Selected I/O						
A7	A6	A5	A4	A3	A2	A1	A0		
1	0	0	0	0	0	0	0	80H	PORT A
1	0	0	0	0	0	0	1	81H	PORT B
1	0	0	0	0	0	1	0	82H	PORT C
1	0	0	0	0	0	1	1	83H	Chip select register

Table 4.10. Program in Look-up table

D7	D6	D5	D4	D3	D2	D1	D0
IO/BSR	MA	MA	PA	PCU	MB	PB	PCU
1	0	0	0	0	0	0	0

LABEL	OPCODE	OPERAND	COMMENT
	LXI	SP,2800H	Initialize Stack pointer
	MVI	A, 80H	Initialize 8255
	OUT	83H (CWR)	
	MVI	B, 32H	Initialize repeated count
REPEAT:	LXI	H, 2100H	Initialize 4-step sequence
	MVI	C,04H	Initialize 4-step sequence from look up table
BACK:	MOV	A,M	
	OUT	80H (PORT A)	Sends data to Port A
	CALL	DELAY	Provide time interval between steps
	INX	H	Increment look up table
	DCR	C	Decrement 4-step count
	JNZ	BACK	Is count= "00"? if no then jump to BACK
	DCR	B	Is count= "00"? if yes then decrement repeated count
	JNZ	REPEAT	Repeated count is repeated for further rotation
	HLT		

Control word Format:

- In the above program in look up table if the 4-step sequence for clock wise then stepper motor will rotate in clockwise direction and if the 4-step sequence for anti-clock wise then stepper motor will rotate in anti-clockwise direction.

- Speed control of stepper motor is achieved by writing program to rotate stepper motor continuously in delay program. We can change the delay between two steps and thus change the speed of stepper motor.

Interfacing diagram of Stepper motor with 8085

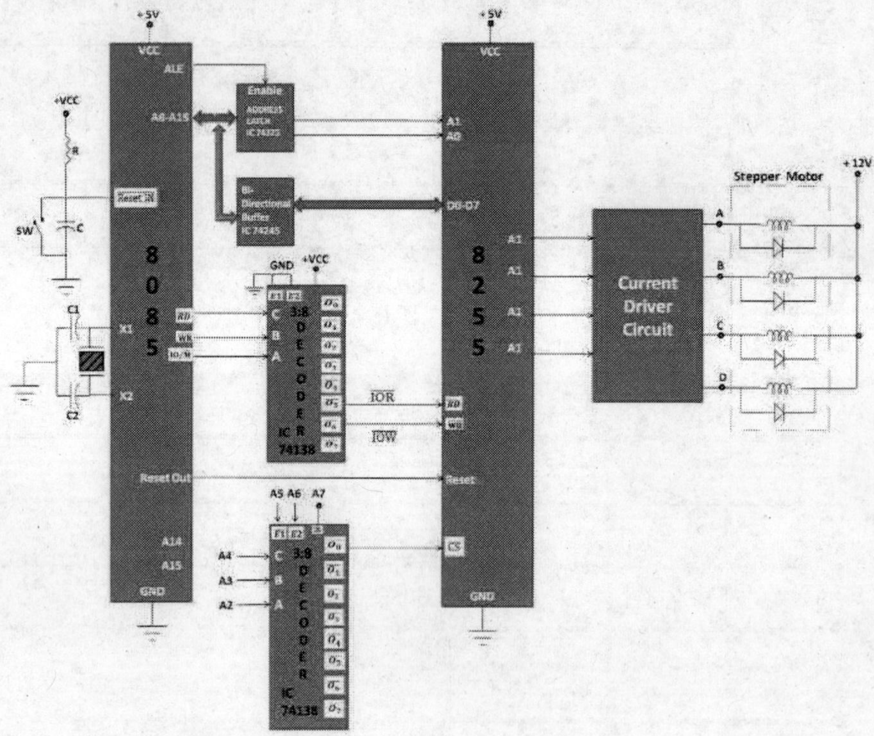

Fig 4.22: Interfacing diagram of Stepper motor with 8085

Review Questions and Exercise

1. The 8051 microcontroller is of ___pin package as a ______ processor. a) 30, 1byte b) 20, 1 byte c) 40, 8 bit d) 40, 8 byte

2. The SP is of ___ wide register. And this may be defined anywhere in the ______. a) 8 byte, on-chip 128 byte RAM. b) 8 bit, on chip 256 byte RAM. c) 16 bit, on-chip 128 byte ROM d) 8 bit, on chip 128 byte RAM.

3. After reset, SP register is initialized to address________. a) 8H b) 9H c) 7H d) 6H

4. What is the address range of SFR Register bank? a) 00H-77H b) 40H-80H c) 80H-7FH d) 80H-FFH

5. Which pin of port 3 is has an alternative function as write control signal for external data memory? a) P3.8 b) P3.3 c) P3.6 d) P3.1

6. What is the Address (SFR) for TCON, SCON, SBUF, PCON and PSW respectively? a) 88H, 98H, 99H, 87H, 0D0H. b) 98H, 99H, 87H, 88H, 0D0H c) 0D0H, 87H, 88H, 99H, 98H d) 87H, 88H, 0D0H, 98H, 99H

7. Match the following:

1) TCON	i) contains status information
2) SBUF	ii) timer / counter control register.
3) TMOD	iii) idle bit, power down bit
4) PSW	iv) serial data buffer for Tx and Rx.
5) PCON	v) timer/ counter modes of operation.

a) 1->ii, 2->iv, 3->v, 4->i, 5->iii.

b) 1->i, 2->v, 3->iv, 4->iii, 5->ii.

c) 1->v, 2->iii, 3->ii, 4->iv, 5->i.

d) 1->iii, 2->ii, 3->i, 4->v, 5->iv.

8. Which of the following is of bit operations? i) SP ii) P2 iii) TMOD iv) SBUF v) IP a) ii, v only b) ii, iv, v only c) i, v only d) iii, ii only

9. Serial port interrupt is generated, if ____ bits are set a) IE b) RI, IE c) IP, TI d) RI, TI 10. In 8051 which interrupt has highest priority? a)IE1 b)TF0 c)IE0 d)TF1

10. Write a program to turns the lamp on and off by energizing and de-energizing the relay every second.

11. A switch is connected to pin P2.7. Write an ALP to monitor the status of the SW. If SW = 0, motor moves clockwise and if SW = 1, motor moves anticlockwise.

12. Write a program to generate a sine wave using DAC 0808.

References

[1] M. Ali Mazidi, J. Gillipsie Mazidi, Rolin D. McKinlay. The 8051Microcontrollers and Embedded System. 2nd ed. New Jersey, Pearson Prentice Hall, 2006.

[2] Santanu Chattopadhyay. *Embedded System Design.* 2nd ed. PHI Learning Private Ltd. New Delhi, 2016.

[3] Manish Patel "Question Paper with Solution the 8051 Microcontroller Based Embedded...." Question Paper with Solution the 8051 Microcontroller Based Embedded..., www.slideshare.net, 1 Mar. 2001, https://www.slideshare.net/manishpatel_79/question-paper-with-solution-the-8051-microcontroller-based-embedded-systems-junejuly-2013-vtu

Chapter 5

External Communication Interface

Key features of Module – 5

- Different types of Communication Protocols.
- Detailed introduction about Serial Peripheral Interface (SPI) and inter-Integrated Circuit Bus (I2C)
- Introduction and Interfacing to Protocols like Bluetooth and Zig-bee

Pre-requisites

- Basics of Computers
- Basics of Means of communication

Module – 5 Outcomes

- Students should be able to understand the different types of communications and communication protocols
- Students should be able to know about the Serial Peripheral Interface (SPI) and Inter-Integrated Circuit Bus (I2C)
- Students should be able to know about the Interfacing to Protocols like Bluetooth and Zig- bee

This chapter gives an overview of the types of communications and communications protocols and also discussed the working principle of communications protocol like RS232, RS485. And here discussed about the introduction of Serial Peripheral Interface (SPI) and Inter-Integrated Circuit Bus (I2C). Introduction and Interfacing to Protocols like Bluetooth and Zig-bee are discussed.

5.1 Synchronous and Asynchronous communication

The key difference between synchronous and asynchronous communication is synchronous communications are scheduled, real-time interactions by phone, video, or in-person. Asynchronous communication happens on your own time and doesn't need scheduling.

5.2 RS232 Serial Communication Protocol:

One of the oldest, yet popular communication protocol that is used in industries and commercial products is the RS232 Communication Protocol. The term RS232 stands for "Recommended Standard 232" and it is a type of serial communication used for transmission of data normally in medium distances. It was introduced back in the 1960s and has found its way into many applications like computer printers, factory automation devices etc. Today there are many modern communication protocols like the RS485, SPI, I2C, CAN etc

1. What is a serial communication?

In telecommunication, the process of sending data sequentially over a computer bus is called as serial communication, which means the data will be transmitted bit by bit. While in parallel communication the data is transmitted in a byte (8 bit) or character on several data lines or buses at a time. Serial communication is slower than parallel communication but used for long data transmission due to lower cost and practical reasons.

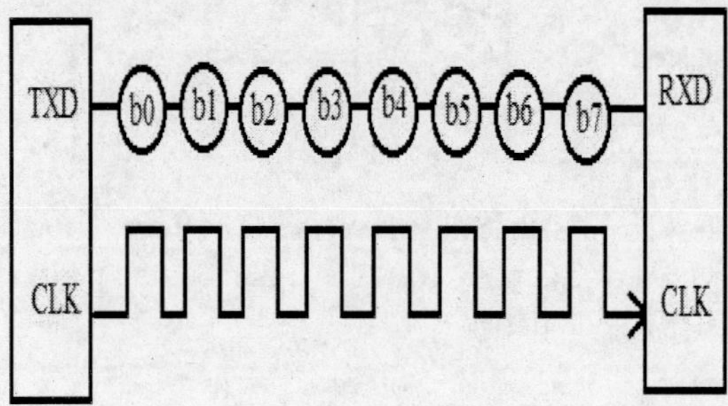

Fig. 5.1. serial communication

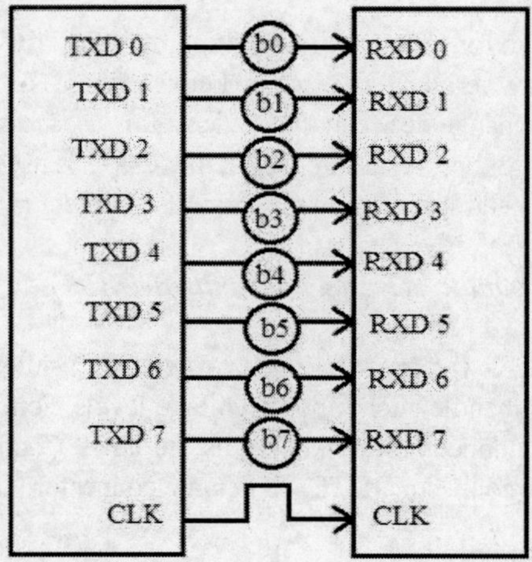

Fig. 5.2. Parallel communication

5.2.1 Modes of Data Transfer in Serial Communication:

- Asynchronous Data Transfer – The mode in which the bits of data are not synchronized by a clock pulse. Clock pulse is a signal used for synchronization of operation in an electronic system.

- Synchronous Data Transfer – The mode in which the bits of data are synchronized by a clock pulse.

5.2.2 Characteristics of Serial Communication:

- Baud rate is used to measure the speed of transmission. It is described as the number of bits passing in one second. For example, if the baud rate is 200 then 200 bits per Sec passed. In telephone lines, the baud rates will be 14400, 28800 and 33600.
- Stop Bits are used for a single packet to stop the transmission which is denoted as "T". Some typical values are 1, 1.5 & 2 bits.

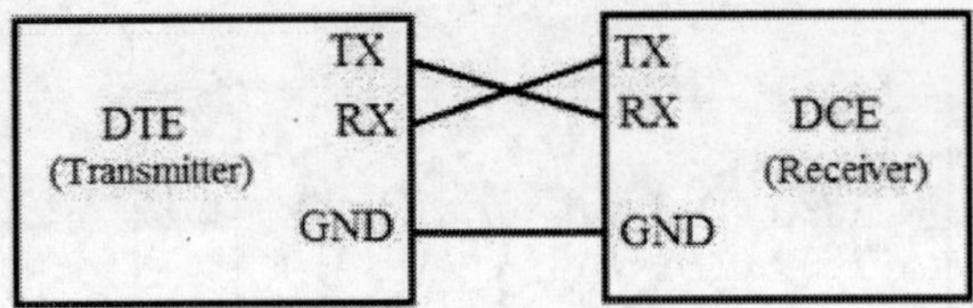

- Parity Bit is the simplest form of checking the errors. There are of four kinds, i.e., even odd, marked and spaced. For example, If 011 is a number the parity bit=0, i.e., even parity and the parity=1, i.e., odd parity.

Fig.5.3. Data transmission process on the RS232

5.3 What is RS232?

RS232 is a standard protocol used for serial communication, it is used for connecting computer and its peripheral devices to allow serial data exchange between them. As it obtains the voltage for the path used for the data exchange between the devices. It is used in serial communication up to 50 feet with the rate of 1.492kbps. As EIA defines, the RS232 is used for connecting Data Transmission Equipment (DTE) and Data Communication Equipment (DCE).

5.3.1Universal Asynchronous Data Receiver &Transmitter (UART)

It used in connection with RS232 for transferring data between printer and computer. The microcontrollers are not able to handle such kind of voltage levels, connectors are connected between RS232 signals. These connectors are known as the DB-9 Connector as a serial port and they are of two type's Male connector (DTE) & Female connector (DCE).

5.3.2 How RS232 Works?

RS232 works on the two-way communication that exchanges data to one another. There are two devices connected to each other, (DTE) Data Transmission Equipment& (DCE) Data Communication Equipment which has the pins like TXD, RXD, and RTS& CTS. Now, from DTE source, the RTS generates the request to send the data. Then from the other side DCE, the CTS, clears the path for receiving the data. After clearing a path, it will give a signal to RTS of the DTE source to send the signal. Then the bits are transmitted from DTE to DCE. Now again from DCE source, the request can be generated by RTS and CTS of DTE sources clears the path for receiving the data and gives a signal to send the data. This is the whole process through which data transmission takes place.

Table 5.1. The complete process of data transmission

TXD	TRANSMITTER
RXD	RECEIVER
RTS	REQUEST TO SEND
CTS	CLEAR TO SEND
GND	GROUND

Example: The signals set to logic 1, i.e., -12V. The data transmission starts from next bit and to inform this, DTE sends start bit to DCE. The start bit is always '0', i.e., +12 V & next 5 to 9 characters is data bits. If we use parity bit, then 8 bits data can be transmitted whereas if parity doesn't use, then 9 bits are being transmitted. The stop bits are sent by the transmitter whose values are 1, 1.5 or 2 bits after the data transmission.

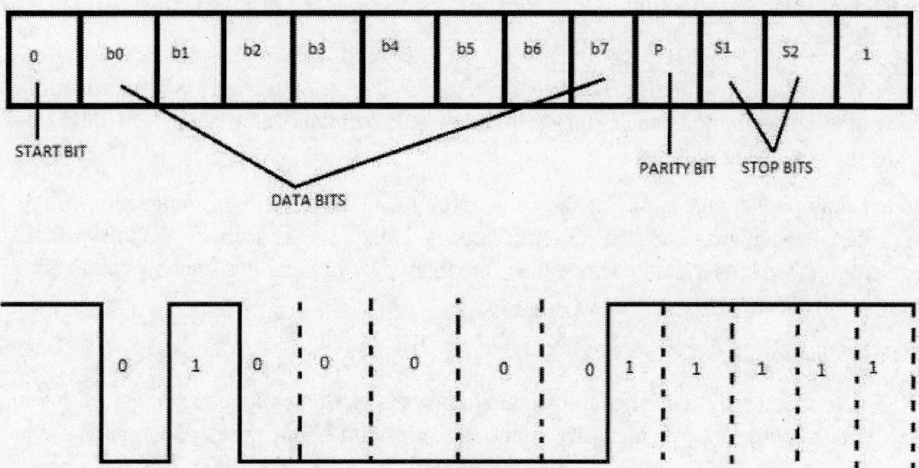

Fig.5.4. The data transmission in RS232

Without interruption any number of bits can be sent or received in a continuous stream. With I2C and UART, data is sent in packets, limited to a specific number of bits. Start and stop conditions define the beginning and end of each packet, so the data is interrupted during 4

5.4 RS485

RS485 is a standard defining the electrical characteristics of serial lines for use in serial communications systems. It is essentially a form of serial communication.

It is known for being able to be used effectively over long distances and in electrically noisy environments. Due to this and it being able to transmit data over long distances, the RS485 is used commonly as a protocol for POS, industrial and telecom. The RS485 is also common in computers, PLCs, microcontrollers and intelligent sensors in scientific and technical applications.

RS485 is used more industrially where many devices need to be interconnected together for a system. However, Arduino and Raspberry Pi hobbyists also use it for some of their projects when multiple peripherals need to be linked to the board.

5.4.1 How RS485 works?

In RS485 standard, data is transmitted via two wires twisted together also referred to as "Twisted Pair Cable". The twisted pairs in RS485 gives immunity against electrical noise, making RS485 viable in electrically noisy environments.

RS485 at its core with 2 wires allows half-duplex data transmission. This means data can be transmitted in both directions to and fro devices one direction at a time. By adding another 2 wires, making it a 4 wires system, it allows data transmission in both directions to and fro devices at the same time, also known as full-duplex. However, in a full-duplex setup, they are limited to a master and slave communication where slaves cannot communicate with each other.

5.4.2 Advantages of RS485

RS485 main advantages as compared to other serial communication are tolerance to electrical noise, lengthy cable runs, multiple slaves in one connection, and fast data transmission speed.

RS485 has many advantages over other standards, especially when it comes to applications in noisy industrial environments. The design of RS485 is targeted towards it being tolerant and forgiving to noise and long cable runs with the twisted pair cable arrangement. It allows cable lengths up to 1,200m/4000feet.

Another major advantage is that there can be more than one slave in the connection. Up to 32 slaves can be connected in the system. This is great for Supervisory Control and Data Acquisition (SCADA) systems where there are many devices and it also comes at a very low cost to implement.

5.4.3 Applications of RS485

RS485 is used in many computer and automation systems. Some of the examples are robotics, base stations, motor drives, video surveillance and also home appliances. In computer systems, RS485 is used for data transmission between the controller and a disk drive. Commercial aircraft cabins also use RS485 for low-speed data communications. This is due to the minimal wiring required due to the wiring configuration requirements of RS485.

RS485 is however most popularly used in programmable logic controllers and factory floors where there are lots of electrical noise. RS485 is used as the physical layer for many standards and proprietary automation protocols to implement control systems, most commonly Modbus.

Modbus is the world's most popular automation protocol in the market. Developed by Modicon, Modbus enables different devices from different manufacturers to be integrated into the main system. Most Modbus implementations use RS485 due to the allowance of longer distances, higher speeds and multiple devices on a single network.

Modbus devices communicate using a Master-Slave technique where only one device (the Master) can initiate transactions (AKA queries). The other devices (the slaves) respond by giving the requested data to the master, or by taking the action requested in the query. This whole system allows manufacturing facilities to control their devices remotely and also set-up automation.

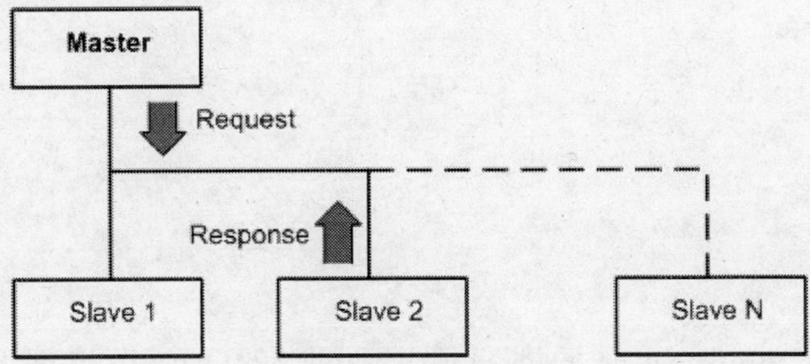

Fig.5.5.Modbus Protocol.

5.5 Introduction to Serial Peripheral Interface (SPI)

SPI is a common communication protocol used by many different devices. For example, SD card reader modules, RFID card reader modules, and 2.4 GHz wireless transmitter/receivers all use SPI to communicate with microcontrollers.

One unique benefit of SPI is the fact that data can be transferred transmission.

Devices communicating via SPI are in a master-slave relationship. The master is the controlling device (usually a microcontroller), while the slave (usually a sensor, display, or memory chip) takes instruction from the master. The simplest configuration of SPI is a single master, single slave system, but one master can control more than one slave (more on this below).

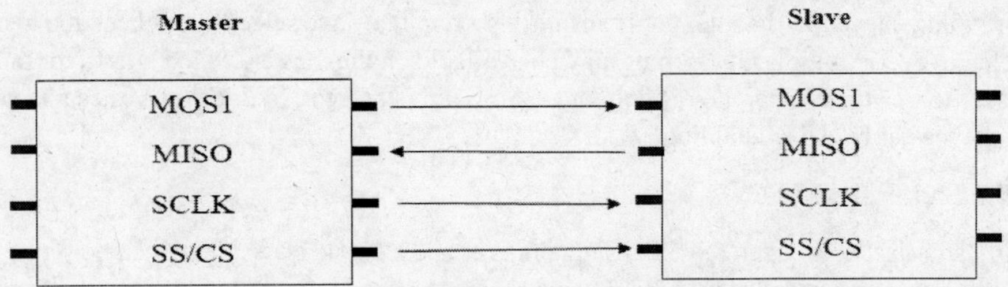

Fig.5.6. Single master, Single Slave System

MOSI (Master Output/Slave Input) – Line for the master to send data to the slave.

MISO (Master Input/Slave Output) – Line for the slave to send data to the master.

SCLK (Clock) – Line for the clock signal.

SS/CS (Slave Select/Chip Select) – Line for the master to select which slave to send data to.

Wires Used	4
Maximum Speed	Up to 10 Mbps
Synchronous or Asynchronous?	Synchronous
Serial or Parallel?	Serial
Max # of Masters	1
Max # of Slaves	Theoretically unlimited*

5.5.1 How does SPI work?

THE CLOCK

The clock signal synchronizes the output of data bits from the master to the sampling of bits by the slave. One bit of data is transferred in each clock cycle, so the speed of data transfer is determined by the frequency of the clock signal. SPI communication is always initiated by the master since the master configures and generates the clock signal.

Any communication protocol where devices share a clock signal is known as synchronous. SPI is a synchronous communication protocol. There are also asynchronous methods that don't use a clock signal. For example, in UART communication, both sides are set to a pre-configured baud rate that dictates the speed and timing of data transmission.

The clock signal in SPI can be modified using the properties of clock polarity and clock phase. These two properties work together to define when the bits are output and when they are sampled. Clock polarity can be set by the master to allow for bits to be output and sampled on either the rising or falling edge of the clock cycle. Clock phase can be set for output and sampling to occur on either the first edge or second edge of the clock cycle, regardless of whether it is rising or falling.

SLAVE SELECT

The master can choose which slave it wants to talk to by setting the slave's CS/SS line to a low voltage level. In the idle, non-transmitting state, the slave select line is kept at a high voltage level. Multiple CS/SS pins may be available on the master, which allows for multiple slaves to be wired in parallel. If only one CS/SS pin is present, multiple slaves can be wired to the master by daisy-chaining.

MULTIPLE SLAVES

SPI can be set up to operate with a single master and a single slave, and it can be set up with multiple slaves controlled by a single master. There are two ways to connect multiple slaves to the master. If the master has multiple slave select pins, the slaves can be wired in parallel like this as shown in Fig.5.7.

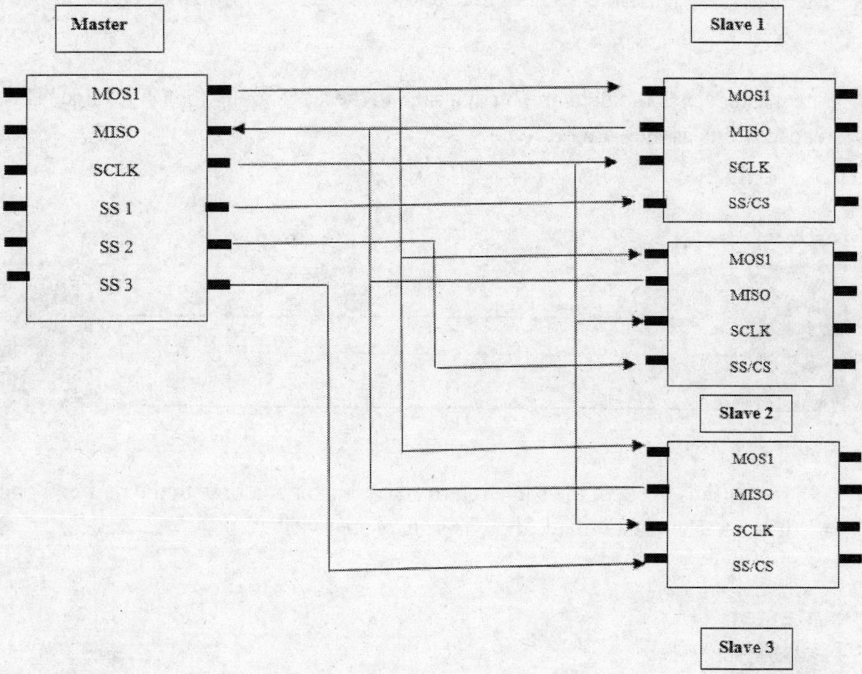

Fig.5.7.Connection of Multiple Slave with Single Master.

MOSI AND MISO

The master sends data to the slave bit by bit, in serial through the MOSI line. The slave receives the data sent from the master at the MOSI pin. Data sent from the master to the slave is usually sent with the most significant bit first.

The slave can also send data back to the master through the MISO line in serial. The data sent from the slave back to the master is usually sent with the least significant bit first.

5.5.2 Steps of SPI Data Transmission

1. The master outputs the clock signal:

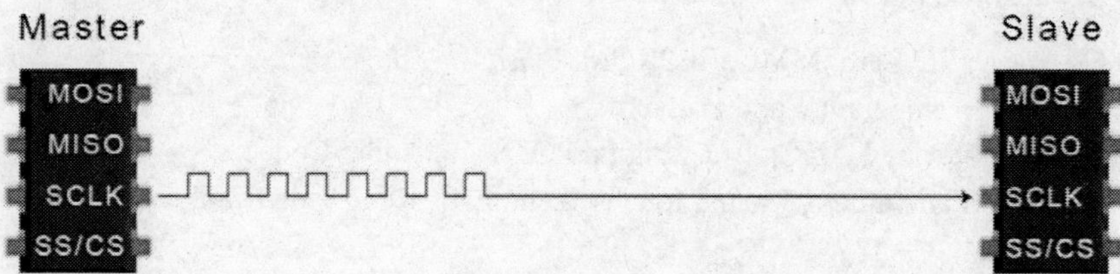

2. The master switches the SS/CS pin to a low voltage state, which activates the slave:

3. The master sends the data one bit at a time to the slave along the MOSI line. The slave reads the bits as they are received:

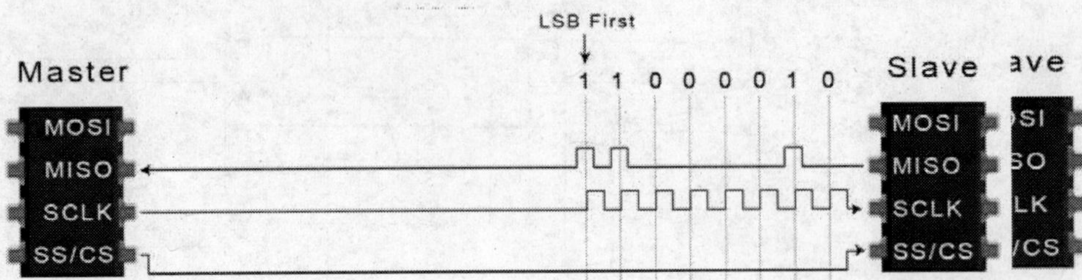

4. If a response is needed, the slave returns data one bit at a time to the master along the MISO line. The master reads the bits as they are received:

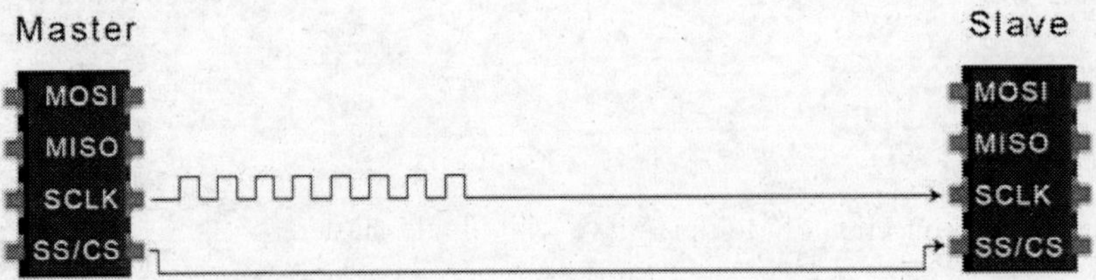

5.5.3 Advantages

- No start and stop bits, so the data can be streamed continuously without interruption
- No complicated slave addressing system like I2C
- Higher data transfer rate than I2C (almost twice as fast)
- Separate MISO and MOSI lines, so data can be sent and received at the same time

5.5.4 Disadvantages

- Uses four wires (I2C and UARTs use two)
- No acknowledgement that the data has been successfully received (I2C has this)
- No form of error checking like the parity bit in UART
- Only allows for a single master

5.5.5 Applications of SPI

- Memory: SD Card, MMC, EEPROM, Flash
- Sensors: Temperature and Pressure
- Control Devices: ADC, DAC, digital POTS and Audio Codec.
- Others: Camera Lens Mount, touchscreen, LCD, RTC, video game controller, etc.

5.6 Inter-Integrated Circuit Bus (I2C)

I²C or I2C is an abbreviation of Inter-Integrated Circuit, a serial communication protocol made by Philips Semiconductor (now it is NXP Semiconductor). It is created with an intention of communication between chips reside on the same Printed Circuit Board (PCB). It is commonly used to interface slow speed ICs to a microprocessor or a microcontroller. It is a master-slave protocol, usually a processor or microcontroller is the master and other chips like RTC, Temperature Sensor, and EEPROM will be the slave. We can have multiple masters and multiple slaves in the same I2C bus. Hence it is a multi-master, multi-slave protocol.

5.6.1 I2C Interface

It needs only two wires for exchanging data and ground as the reference.

- SDA – Serial Data
- SCL – Serial Clock
- GND – Ground

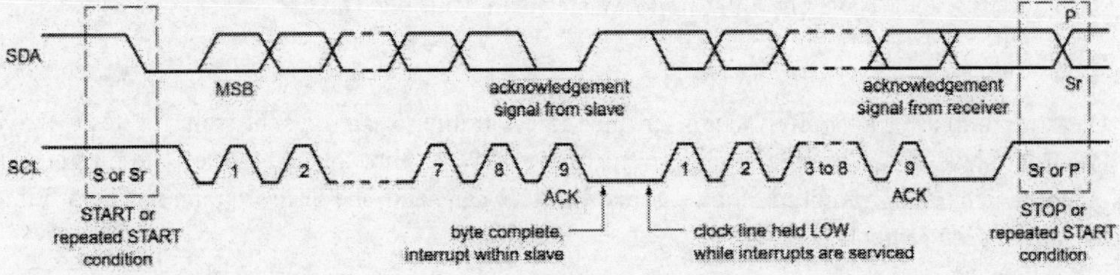

Fig.5.8. Data Transfer using the I2C Interface

5.6.2 I2C Protocol

I2C protocol is more complex than UART or SPI protocols as it using only 2 lines (one for clock and one for data) for to and for communication. But usually, we don't need to worry about it as in most of the device's hardware itself will take care of these things.

Data Transfer on the I2C Bus

Start Condition

I2C start condition is issued by a master device to give a notice to all slave devices that the communication is about to start. Thus, start condition triggers all slave devices to listen to the data in the bus. To issue start condition, the master device pulls SDA low and leaves SCL high. In the case of multi-master I2C there is a possibility that 2 masters wish to take ownership of the bus at the same time. In these cases, the device which pull down SDA first gains the control of the bus

Address Frame

Address frame is always sent just after the first start condition during every communication sequence. In this master devices specifies the address of the slave device to which the master wants to communicate. There are basically 2 types of addressing 7-bit addressing and 10-bit addressing. In the 7-bit addressing mode, master sends address first (MSB first) followed by read/write (R/W) indicating bit (0 => Write, 1 => Read).

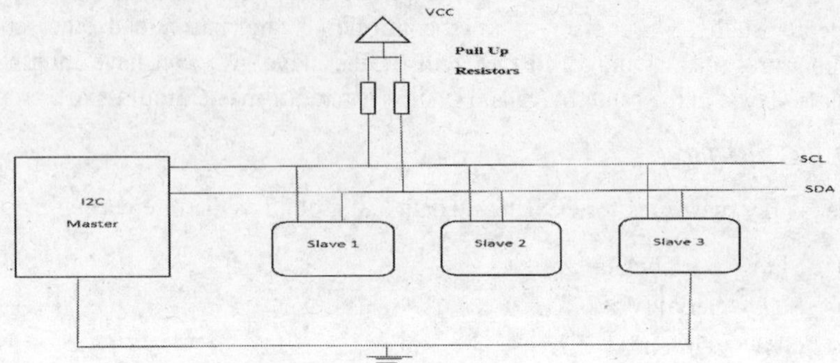

Fig.5.9. Single Master with Multiple Slaves

Data Frames

Data frame(s) are transmitted just after the address frame. It can be sent from master to slave OR from slave to master depending on the above R/W bit through SDA line. The master will continue generating required clock signals. Devices can send one or more than one data frame as per the requirements.

Stop Condition

Master device will generate stop condition once all data frames has been sent/received. As per I2C standards, STOP condition is defined as a LOW to HIGH transition on SDA line after a LOW to HIGH transition on SCL, with SCL HIGH. So, SDA should not change status when SCL is HIGH to avoid false stop condition.

Repeated Start Condition

During an I2C communication, sometimes a master wants to send a specific command to a slave device and read back response right away. In this situation there is a possibility that another master (in case of multi-master bus) takes the control of the bus. To avoid these conditions I2C protocol defines repeated start condition.

In normal cases I2C master will send start condition, address + R/W bit, send or receive any number of bytes and mark the end by a stop condition. During repeated start condition, master will send START CONDITION instead of stop condition and will keep the control over the bus. Master can send any number of start condition using this method. Irrespective of the number of start conditions, transfer must be end by exactly one stop condition.

Clock Stretching

We have seen that master device determines the clock speed in I2C communication. This avoid the need of synchronizing master and slave exactly to a predefined baud rate. But there can be some situations when I2C slave device is not able to cooperate with clock signals given by master. Clock stretching is the mechanism used to slow down master device for slave device to complete its operation.

I2C slave device is allowed to hold down the clock signal when it needs master to slow down on the 9th clock of every data transfer before the ACK stage.

Acknowledge (ACK) and Not Acknowledge (NACK)

Each byte of data in I2C communication includes an additional bit known as ACK bit. This bit provides a provision for the receiver to send a signal to transmitter that the byte was successfully received and ready to accept another byte.

5.6.3 I2C Configurations

We can make I2C configurations basically in 2 ways.

Single Master I2C Bus

This is the simplest I2C bus configuration. Single master in the bus is responsible for all communications taking place in the bus. It will be providing necessary clock required for the communication with slave devices. The master device will specify the address of the particular slave device to which it needs to write data or from which it needs to read data. Only that particular slave device will respond for this.

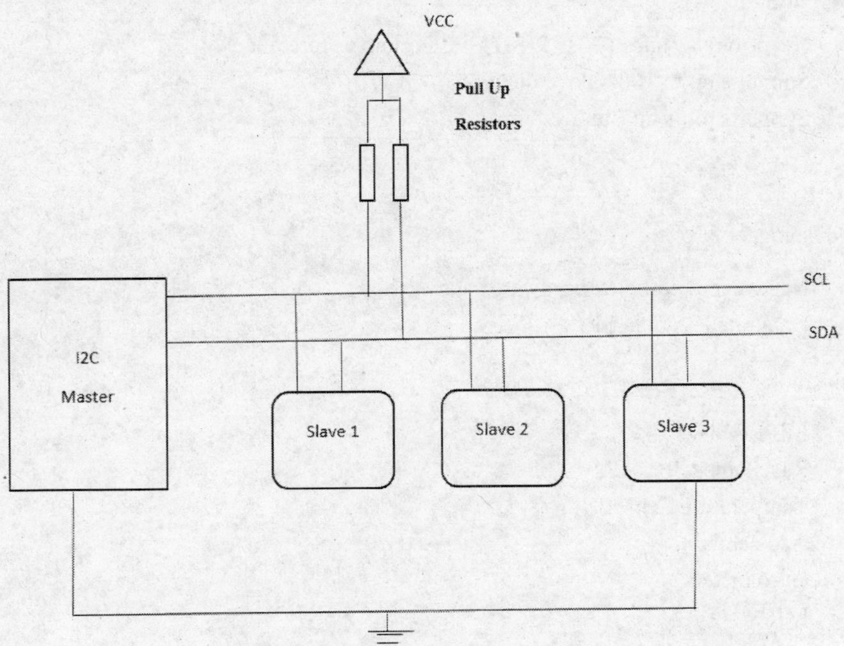

Fig.5.10. Single Master I2C Bus

Multi-Master I2C Bus

In this case there will be more than one master device. Any master device is allowed to start communication or use the bus whenever it is required. If a master in a multi-master bus transmits a HIGH, bus see's that the line is LOW (means another device is pulling down), it has to halt the communication because another device is using the bus.

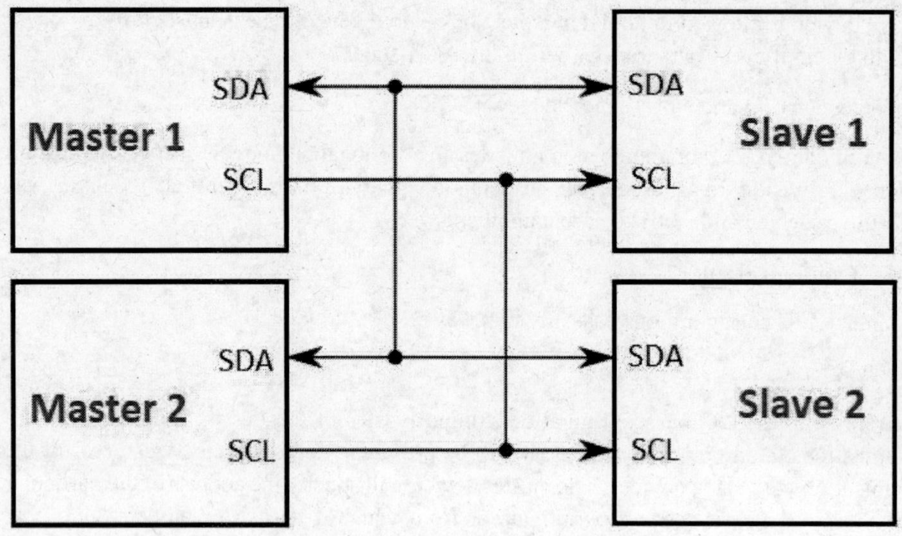

Fig.5.11. Multi - Master I2C Bus

Advantages

- Needs only 2 lines (SCL & SDA) + Ground as reference
- Supports up to 1008 slave devices
- Supports multi-master system

Disadvantages

- Needs more complex hardware
- Data rate less than SPI

Applications

- EEPROMs
- Real Time Clock ICs
- Temperature Sensors
- Accelerometers
- Gyro meters
- LCDs

5.7 What is ZigBee Technology?

ZigBee communication is specially built for control and sensor networks on IEEE 802.15.4 standard for wireless personal area networks (WPANs), and it is the product from ZigBee alliance. This communication standard defines physical and Media Access Control (MAC) layers to handle many devices at low-data rates. These ZigBee's WPANs operate at 868 MHz, 902-928MHz, and 2.4 GHz frequencies. The data rate of 250 kbps is best suited for periodic as well as intermediate two-way transmission of data between sensors and controllers.

ZigBee is a low-cost and low-powered mesh network widely deployed for controlling and monitoring applications where it covers 10-100 meters within the range. This communication system is less expensive and simpler than the other proprietary short-range wireless sensor networks as Bluetooth and Wi-Fi

ZigBee supports different network configurations for the master to master or master to slave communications. And also, it can be operated in different modes as a result the battery power is conserved. ZigBee networks are extendable with the use of routers and allow many nodes to interconnect with each other for building a wider area network.

5.7.1 How does ZigBee Technology Work?

ZigBee technology works with digital radios by allowing different devices to converse through one another. The devices used in this network are a router, coordinator as well as end devices. The main function of these devices is to deliver the instructions and messages from the coordinator to the single end devices such as a light bulb.

In this network, the coordinator is the most essential device which is placed at the origin of the system. For each network, there is simply one coordinator, used to perform different tasks. They choose a suitable channel to scan a channel as well as to find the most appropriate one through the minimum of interference, allocate an exclusive ID as well as an address to every device within the network so that messages otherwise instructions can be transferred in the network.

Routers are arranged among the coordinator as well as end devices which are accountable for messages routing among the various nodes. Routers get messages from the coordinator and stored them until their end devices are in a situation to get them. These can also permit other end devices as well as routers to connect the network;

In this network, the small information can be controlled by end devices by communicating with the parent node like a router or the coordinator based on the ZigBee network type. End devices don't converse directly through each other. First, all traffic can be routed toward the parent node like the router, which holds this data until the device's receiving end is in a situation to get it through being aware. End devices are used to request any messages that are waiting from the parent.

5.7.2 ZigBee Architecture

ZigBee system structure consists of three different types of devices as ZigBee Coordinator, Router, and End device. Every ZigBee network must consist of at least one coordinator which acts as a root and bridge of the network. The coordinator is responsible for handling and storing the information while performing receiving and transmitting data operations.

ZigBee routers act as intermediary devices that permit data to pass to and fro through them to other devices. End devices have limited functionality to communicate with the parent nodes such that the battery power is saved as shown in the figure. The number of routers, coordinators, and end devices depends on the type of networks such as star, tree, and mesh networks.

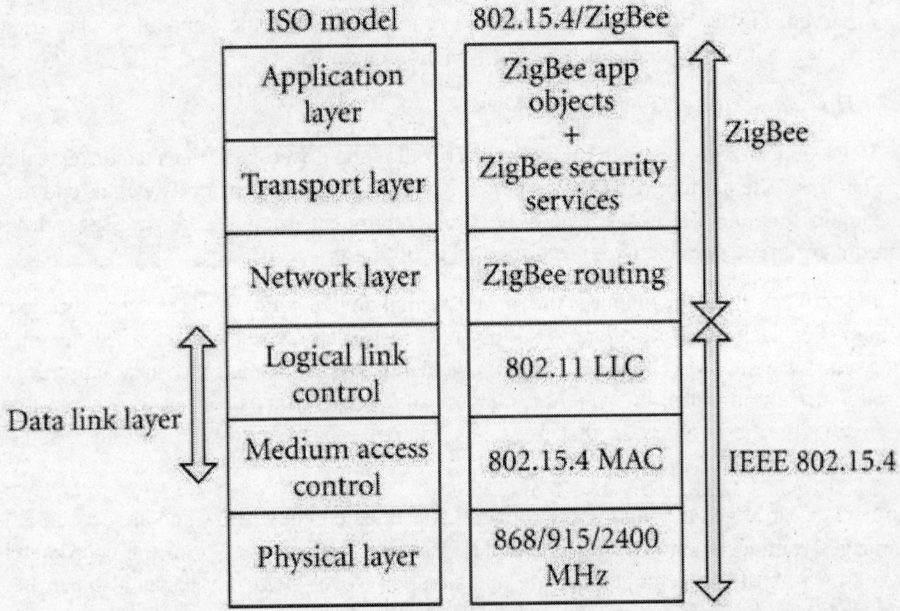

Fig.5.12. IEEE 802.15.4 and ZigBee role in the ISO/OSI stack.

ZigBee protocol architecture consists of a stack of various layers where IEEE 802.15.4 is defined by physical and MAC layers while this protocol is completed by accumulating ZigBee's own network and application layers.

Physical Layer: This layer does modulation and demodulation operations upon transmitting and receiving signals respectively. This layer's frequency, data rate, and a number of channels are given below.

MAC Layer: This layer is responsible for reliable transmission of data by accessing different networks with the carrier sense multiple access collision avoidances (CSMA). This also transmits the beacon frames for synchronizing communication.

Network Layer: This layer takes care of all network-related operations such as network setup, end device connection, and disconnection to network, routing, device configurations, etc.

Application Support Sub-Layer: This layer enables the services necessary for ZigBee device objects and application objects to interface with the network layers for data managing services. This layer is responsible for matching two devices according to their services and needs.

Application Framework: It provides two types of data services as key-value pair and generic message services. The generic message is a developer-defined structure, whereas the key-value pair is used for getting attributes within the application objects. ZDO provides an interface between application objects and the APS layer in ZigBee devices. It is responsible for detecting, initiating, and binding other devices to the network.

5.7.3 ZigBee Operating Modes and Its Topologies

ZigBee two-way data is transferred in two modes: non-beacon mode and Beacon mode. In a beacon mode, the coordinators and routers continuously monitor the active state of incoming data hence more power is consumed. In this mode, the routers and coordinators do not sleep because at any time any node can wake up and communicate.

However, it requires more power supply and its overall power consumption is low because most of the devices are in an inactive state for over long periods in the network. In a beacon mode, when there is no data communication from end devices, then the routers and coordinators enter into a sleep state. Periodically this coordinator wakes up and transmits the beacons to the routers in the network.

These beacon networks are work for time slots which means, they operate when the communication needed results in lower duty cycles and longer battery usage. These beacon and non-beacon modes of ZigBee can manage periodic (sensors data), intermittent (Light switches), and repetitive data types.

5.7.4 ZigBee Topologies

ZigBee supports several network topologies; however, the most commonly used configurations are star, mesh, and cluster tree topologies. Any topology consists of one or more coordinators. In a star topology, the network consists of one coordinator which is responsible for initiating and managing the devices over the network. All other devices are called end devices that directly communicate with the coordinator.

This is used in industries where all the endpoint devices are needed to communicate with the central controller, and this topology is simple and easy to deploy. In mesh and tree topologies, the ZigBee network is extended with several routers where the coordinator is responsible for staring them. These structures allow any device to communicate with any other adjacent node for providing redundancy to the data.

If any node fails, the information is routed automatically to other devices by these topologies. As redundancy is the main factor in industries, hence mesh topology is mostly used. In a cluster-tree network, each cluster consists of a coordinator with leaf nodes, and these coordinators are connected to the parent coordinator which initiates the entire network.

Due to the advantages of ZigBee technology like low cost and low power operating modes and its topologies, this short-range communication technology is best suited for several applications compared to other proprietary communications, such as Bluetooth, Wi-Fi, etc. some of these comparisons such as range of ZigBee, standards, etc., are given below.

5.7.5 Which Devices use ZigBee?

The following list of devices supports the ZigBee protocol.

- Belkin WeMo
- Samsung SmartThings
- Yale smart locks
- Philips Hue
- Thermostats from Honeywell
- Ikea Tradfri
- Security Systems from Bosch

- Comcast Xfinity Box from Samsung
- Hive Active Heating & accessories
- Amazon Echo Plus
- Amazon Echo Show

Instead of connecting every ZigBee device separately, a central hub is required for controlling all the devices. The above-mentioned devices namely SmartThings as well as Amazon Echo Plus can also be used like a Wink hub to play a vital role within the network. The central hub will scan the network for all the supported devices and provides you simple control of the above devices with a central app.

5.8 What is Bluetooth?

Bluetooth was created under the IEEE 802.15.1 standard, which is used for wireless communication via radio transmissions. Bluetooth was first introduced in 1994 as a wireless replacement for RS-232 connections.

Bluetooth connects a wide range of devices and establishes personal networks in the unlicensed 2.4 GHz spectrum. The device class determines the operating range. Many digital gadgets, such as MP3 players, mobile and peripheral devices, and personal computers, use Bluetooth.

Unlike previous wireless technologies, Bluetooth provides high-level services such as file pushing, voice transmission, and serial line emulation to its network and devices.

A scattered ad-hoc topology is the name given to the Bluetooth topology. It defines a Piconet, a small cell that consists of a group of devices connected in an ad-hoc manner.

Bluetooth ensures data security and privacy when in use. It employs a 128-bit random number, a device's 48-bit MAC address, and two keys: authentication (128 bits) and encryption (256 bits) (8 to 128 bits). Non-secure, service level, and link level are the three modes of operation.

5.8.1 How does Bluetooth Works?

Bluetooth Network consists of a Personal Area Network or a piconet which contains a minimum of 2 to a maximum of 8 Bluetooth peer devices- Usually a single master and up to 7 slaves. A master is a device that initiates communication with other devices. The master device governs the communications link and traffic between itself and the slave devices associated with it. A slave device is a device that responds to the master device. Slave devices are required to synchronize they're transmit/receive timing with that of the masters.

In addition, transmissions by slave devices are governed by the master device (i.e., the master device dictates when a slave device may transmit). Specifically, a slave may only begin its transmissions in a time slot immediately following the time slot in which it was addressed by the master, or in a time slot explicitly reserved for use by the slave device.

The frequency hopping sequence is defined by the Bluetooth device address (BD_ADDR) of the master device. The master device first sends a radio signal asking for a response from the particular slave devices within the range of addresses. The slaves respond and synchronize their hop frequency as well as a clock with that of the master device.

Scatter nets are created when a device becomes an active member of more than one piconet. Essentially, the adjoining device shares its time slots among the different piconets.

5.8.2 Bluetooth Architecture

The Bluetooth architecture uses two networks like Piconet and Scatter-net

Piconet Network

Piconet is one kind of wireless network that includes one main node namely the master node as well as seven energetic secondary nodes are known as slave nodes. So, we can declare that there are eight active nodes totally which are arranged at a10 meters distance. The message between these two nodes can be done one-to-one otherwise one-to-many.

Communication can be possible only among the master and slave but the communication like Slave-slave cannot be possible. It also includes 255 parked nodes which are known as secondary nodes. These cannot communicate until it gets altered to the active condition.

Scatter-net Network

The formation of the Scatter-net Network can be done through various piconets. On one piconet, a slave is present which acts as a master otherwise it can be called primary within other piconets. So, this type of node gets a message from the master within one piconet & transmits the message toward its slave in another piconet wherever it works like a slave. So, this kind of node is called a bridge-node. In two piconets, a station cannot be master.

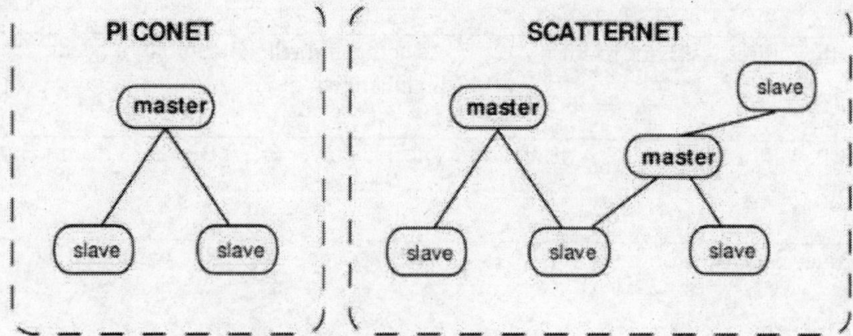

Fig.5.13. Node Diagram of Piconet and Scatter-net Network.

Table 5.2. Difference between ZigBee and Bluetooth

Bluetooth	ZigBee
The frequency range of Bluetooth ranges from 2.4 GHz – 2.483 GHz	The frequency range of ZigBee is 2.4 GHz
It has 79 RF channels	It has 16 RF channels
The modulation technique used in Bluetooth is GFSK	ZigBee uses different modulation techniques like BPSK, QPSK & GFSK.
Bluetooth includes 8-cell nodes	ZigBee includes above 6500 cell nodes

Bluetooth uses IEEE 802.15.1 specification	ZigBee uses IEEE 802.15.4 specification
Bluetooth covers the radio signal upto 10meters	ZigBee covers the radio signal upto 100 meters
Bluetooth takes 3 seconds to join a network	ZigBee takes 3 Seconds to join a network
The network range of Bluetooth ranges from 1-100 meters based on radio class.	The network range of ZigBee is up to 70 meters
The protocol stack size of a Bluetooth is 250 Kbytes	The protocol stack size of a ZigBee is 28 Kbytes
The height of the TX antenna is 6meters whereas the RX antenna is 1meter	The height of the TX antenna is 6meters whereas the RX antenna is 1meter
Blue tooth uses rechargeable batteries	ZigBee doesn't use rechargeable batteries
Bluetooth requires less bandwidth	As compared with Bluetooth, it needs high bandwidth
The TX Power of Bluetooth is 4 dBm	The TX Power of ZigBee is 18 dBm
The frequency of Bluetooth is 2400 MHz	The frequency of ZigBee is 2400 MHz
Tx antenna gain of Bluetooth is 0dB whereas the RX -6dB	Tx antenna gain of ZigBee is 0dB whereas the RX -6dB
Sensitivity is -93 dB	Sensitivity is -102 dB
The margin of Bluetooth is 20 dB	Margin of ZigBee is 20 dB
Bluetooth range is 77 meters	The ZigBee range is 291 meters

Review Questions and Exercise

1. Can devices be added and removed while the system is running (Hot swapping) in I2C and SPI?
2. Is it better to use I2C or SPI for data communication between a microprocessor and DSP?
3. How to set SPI bus speed in the master device?
4. What will happen if two SPI slaves same time communicate with Master (two Cs pins are high)?
5. Is it better to use I2C or SPI for data communication from ADC?
6. How to set SPI bus speed in the master device?
7. Does SPI need a baud rate?
8. What happens when mode fault is enabled in SPI (Serial Peripheral Interface)?
9. What are the limitations of the SPI interface?
10. What Is The Zigbee Alliance?
11. What Is The Goal Of The Zigbee Alliance?
12. What Are The Typical Applications Promoted By The Zigbee Alliance?
13. Which Zigbee Alliance Members Are Active In Residential And Building Automation?
14. Which Zigbee Alliance Members Are Active In Industrial Automation?
15. Which Zigbee Alliance Members Are Active In Automated Metering?
16. What Are The Various Zigbee Application Profiles?
17. What Is The Zigbee Commissioning Framework (zcf)?
18. What Are The Various Zigbee Certification Mechanisms?
19. Is It Possible To Deploy Zigbee Networks In Sub-ghz Bands?
20. What Is The Typical Battery Lifetime Of Zigbee End Devices?
21. Is It Possible To Have Battery-powered Zigbee Routers?
22. Does The Zigbee Coordinator Represent A Single Point Of Failure?
23. How Is Addressing Performed In Zigbee?
24. Define IP Spoofing?
25. Define Cabir Worm?
26. Name few applications of Bluetooth?
27. Why can Bluetooth equipment integrate easily in TCP/IP network?
28. Is it possible to connect multiple Bluetooth hubs?
29. What is FCC and how does it relate to Bluetooth?
30. How does Bluetooth fit in with WiFi?
31. Under what frequency range does Bluetooth work?
32. Do Bluetooth devices need line of sight to connect to one another? List the differences between Bluetooth and Wi-Fi IEEE 802.11 in networking.
33. What is Bluetooth SIG?
34. How many devices can communicate concurrently?
35. How secure a Bluetooth device is?
36. What kind of encryption will be used for Bluetooth security?
37. What is the range of Bluetooth transmitter/receivers?
38. Which technology is used to avoid interference in Bluetooth?
39. What is RJ-45?

References

[1] M. Ali Mazidi, J. Gillipsie Mazidi, Rolin D. McKinlay. The 8051Microcontrollers and Embedded System. 2nd ed. New Jersey, Pearson Prentice Hall, 2006.

[2] Santanu Chattopadhyay. *Embedded System Design*. 2nd ed. PHI Learning Private Ltd. New Delhi, 2016.

[3] Manish Patel "Question Paper with Solution the 8051 Microcontroller Based Embedded…." Question Paper with Solution the 8051 Microcontroller Based Embedded…, www.slideshare.net, 1 Mar. 2001, https://www.slideshare.net/manishpatel_79/question-paper-with-solution-the-8051-microcontroller-based-embedded-systems-junejuly-2013-vtu

Chapter 6

Introduction to Advanced Processors and Concepts

Key Features of the Module

- Introduce readers to some advanced processors
- Key architectural features and concepts
- Instruction-level parallelism
    - Pipelining and superscalar execution
- Cache-memory concept and cache organization
- Concept of virtual memory and memory address translation
- architectural features of 286, 386, 486 and Pentium
- CISC and RISC processors and their differences
- Introduction to ARM processor and ARM-based microcontrollers
- GPIO configuration of ARM microcontrollers and interfacing

Pre-requisites

- Digital Electronics
- Processor basics

Module Outcome

At the end of the course students should be able to

- explain the architectural features of advanced processors such as instruction level parallelism-pipeline and superscalar execution
- explain the concept of cache and its role in the memory subsystem, virtual memory, memory address translation
- understand the internal architecture of the advanced processors, 286, 386, 486 and Pentium
- understand the architecture of ARM-based microcontrollers, concept of GPIO
- interface ARM MCU with external hardware and write interfacing programs

In this chapter we will discuss the important features of some advanced processors and the architectural innovations that have taken place namely, in 286, 386,486 and Pentium. In most of the advanced processors pipelining, superscalar execution, cache memory, concept of virtual memory and memory mapping are most important features. So, we proceed first with the concept of pipeline and superscalar execution. Then we talk about virtual memory, address translation or mapping of virtual memory to real physical memory, cache memory and their organizations. With these important architectural concepts, we proceed towards some advanced processors with their key architectural features. Next, we discuss on the basic features of RISC and CISC processors, a comparison of RISC with CISC is also narrated. A brief introduction to ARM Processors followed by ARM microcontrollers will be illustrated next together with GPIO configuration and interfacing.

6.1 Pipeline vs. Superscalar processing

Advanced processors include many features in their architecture to enhance the performance. These include incorporation of *cache memory* (for both instruction and data), pipelined processing, superscalar execution, RISC/CISC features etc. As pipelining and superscalar processing are the characteristic features in most of the advanced processors, so in the beginning of the chapter the concepts of these two features will be illustrated first.

Pipelining is a technique which allows the processing of several instructions in a partially overlapped manner. Pipelining can be easily carried out for a sequence of instructions which are same or similar in nature that employ a single execution unit. However, all the common steps in instruction processing can also be pipelined such as, instruction fetching (IF), instruction decoding (ID), operand loading (OL), execution (EX) and write back or operand storing (OS). The pipelined execution is very much similar to assembly line of a manufacturing unit where many products are in various stages of manufacturing at the same time. In a non-pipelined processor, the instructions execution follows a fixed sequence as depicted in Fig. 6.1a. Whereas, a pipelined execution unit allows each individual task of fetching, decoding etc. to be taken up independently by a separate sub unit (stage) of the pipeline processor as shown in Fig.6.1b. This is called instructions overlapping-where one instruction may be in fetch stage, while other instruction may be in decode stage while some other may be in execution stage etc. Here, up to five instructions can be overlapped with such a five-stage pipelined execution unit. Of course, performance delay may occur as in case of I_4 which takes EX stage for two consecutive cycles. Similar problem occurs for branch instructions like I_7 (as in Fig.6.1b) where the outcome of I_7's EX step must be known before the location of next instruction (I8) to be processed.

Superscalar execution: A microprocessor's effective MIPS (million instructions per second) can be increased or CPI (cycles per instruction) can be reduced (to less than 1) by replicating various instruction processing units so that several instructions can be processed simultaneously. This makes it possible to start the processing of or issue two or more instructions simultaneously or in parallel. Thus, the instructions can be completely overlapped as shown in Fig 6.1c. Processors with this capability are said to be superscalar. Pipelining and superscalar execution both fall under the category of *instruction-level parallelism.*

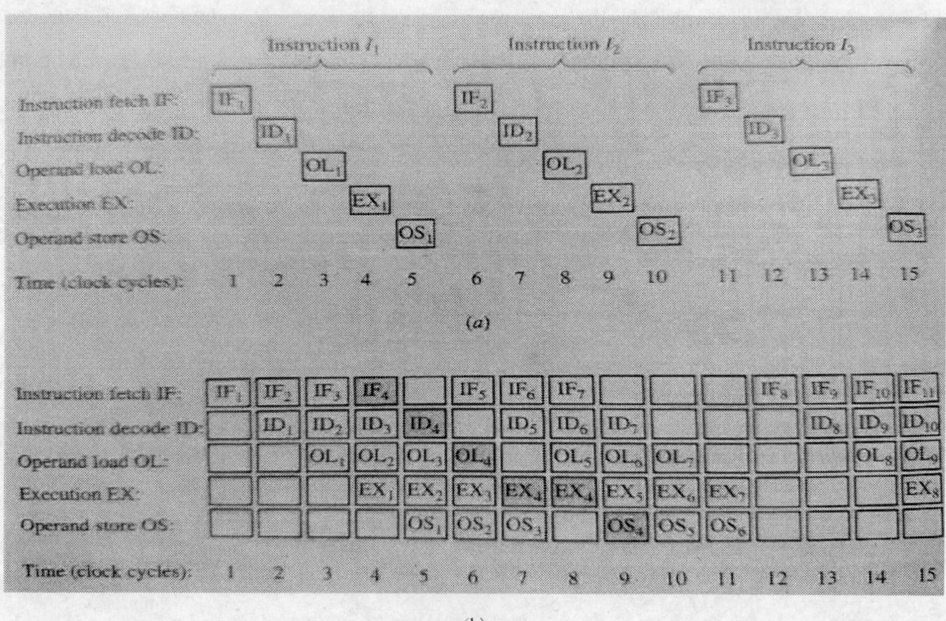

(b)

IF	ID	EX	MEM	WB				
IF	ID	EX	MEM	WB				
	IF	ID	EX	MEM	WB			
	IF	ID	EX	MEM	WB			
		IF	ID	EX	MEM	WB		
		IF	ID	EX	MEM	WB		
			IF	ID	EX	MEM	WB	
			IF	ID	EX	MEM	WB	
				IF	ID	EX	MEM	WB
				IF	ID	EX	MEM	WB

i ↓ t →

(c)

Fig.6.1 (a) Nonpipelined processing (b) Pipelined Processing (c) Superscalar processing [In figure, i =>instruction, t =>time]

6.2 Cache and Virtual Memory Concept

The memory subsystem of a digital computer is organized in a multi-level hierarchical manner. Controlling the various parts of its hierarchy also takes place in a very different fashion. Cache and main memory form a distinct sub-hierarchy whose main goal is to support CPU in accessing instruction and data with a minimum delay. Hardware controllers usually manage this sub-hierarchy. Usually the cache memory and the main memory acts like a single memory M to the user program. Similarly, the main memory and the secondary memory form another two-level sub-hierarchy. The interaction between the two is however managed by the operating system and as such it is not transparent to the system software but somewhat transparent to the user program. *Virtual memory* is a concept and is applied when the main memory and secondary memory appear to a user program like a seamless, single large addressable memory. There are some obvious reasons for bringing the concept of virtual memory. These are as follows:

- To free the user programs from the burden of storage allocation and to permit efficient sharing of available memory space among different users.
- To make the user programs independent of configuration and capacity of physical memory. As such it allows seamless overflow into the secondary memory when the main memory capacity is exhausted.
- In order to achieve very low access time and cost per bit with a memory hierarchy.

A memory system is usually addressed by a set of *virtual or logical* addresses (V) derived from the identifiers specified in an object program. The set of abstract locations that a program reference is the program's *virtual address space*. A set of *physical or real* addresses R identifies the physical storage locations which is fixed in each memory unit M. Therefore, an efficient mechanism is needed to translate/map this virtual address space to real physical address known as *addressing mapping* of the form, $f: V \rightarrow R$ which is the key to successful design of a multilevel memory. This address assignment and translation is carried out at various stages of the program, specifically,

- While writing the program by a programmer.
- During the program compilation by the compiler.
- While initial program loading by the loader.
- During run-time by the memory management unit.

Real physical addresses were explicitly specified by the programmers in early computers, which had neither hardware nor software support for memory management. But with modern computers, programmers normally deal with virtual addresses. Specialized hardware and software within the computer automatically determine the real physical address required for program execution.

Caches

Cache memory is a fast, small size intermediate memory placed between CPU and main memory in the memory subsystem. It is used to reduce the time of access to external memory by the CPU as specified earlier and limit the access time to single cycle. They appear both as a small on-chip memory with CPU and also as a off-chip cache that uses fast SRAM technology in the two-level cache organization. When a memory request is generated, the request is first presented to the cache memory, and if the cache cannot respond, the request is then presented to main memory.

- **Hit:** if a cache access finds data present in the cache memory, as in Fig.6.2
- **Miss:** if a cache access does not find data, then it forces to access data from the main memory

A cache serves as a buffer between CPU and the main memory in the two-level organization. It also acts like a buffer in the memory management unit such as translational look-aside buffer (TLB) which is specialized cache that permits fast translation of memory addresses. Even data buffers in the high-speed secondary memory devices such as in hard disk drives are also known as cache.

Cache Organization

Basically, a cache memory has two principal components. These are cache data memory and cache tag memory. Memory words are stored in *cache data memory* which are grouped into small pages known as *cache blocks or lines.* The contents of the cache's data memory are nothing but the copies of a set of main memory blocks. Each cache block is marked with its block address also called as *tag.* So, the cache knows which part of the memory space the block belongs. The collection of tag addresses that are currently assigned to the cache are stored in a special memory known as *cache tag memory* or *directory.* Thus, the time required to check the tag address and access cache's data memory must be less than the main memory access time in order to improve the performance of a processor.

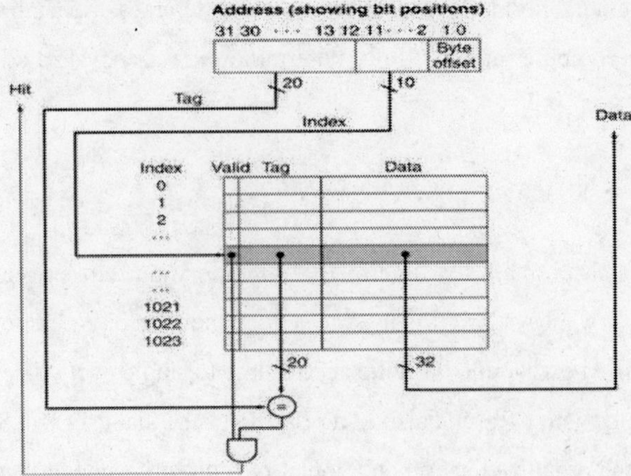

Fig 6.2: Cache memory organization and data access mechanism [Courtesy: Virtual Lab, IITKGP]

Cache memories can be organized in many ways. Based on the way of access it can be of the following two types,

- Look through cache
- Look-aside cache

In *look-aside* design, cache and main memory are directly connected to the system bus. Here the CPU initiates a memory access by placing a real address A_i on the memory address bus at the start of a memory read or write cycle. The cache immediately compares A_i with tag address residing in the tag memory. If it is a match, cache hit occurs and the access is completed without the involving M_2 (main memory). If no match, then it is a miss and the access is directed to M_2. A block of data B_j that includes the target address is transferred from M_2 to M_1(known as block replacement) and is completed in a single short burst. So, in case of cache miss and consequent block data transfer the system bus remains unavailable for IO operations.

Look-through cache is a faster but a more costly organization, where the CPU communicates with the cache via a separate (local) bus which is isolated from the system bus. Thus, the system bus is available for use by other units such as IO controllers. A look-through cache allows the local bus linking M_1 and M_2 to be wider than the system bus, thereby speeding up cache-main memory transfer. Typically, a block replacement takes single clock cycle.

It can also be categorized based on the memory-mapping technique used. In associative or content addressing mapping technique permits the input tag (as initiated by CPU in the memory address) to be compared simultaneously with all the tags present in the cache-tag memory. This is of course feasible in small cache and TLBs. So, a number of low-cost alternative ways have been developed for the limited use of associative addressing. Following caches fall under this category.

- Direct-mapping
- Associative mapping
- Set-associative mapping

Again, caches can be also organized based on the instruction and data they deal with separately or in a unified manner and according categorized as,

- Unified cache
- Split cache (I-cache and D-cache)

For more details on the cache organization and associated memory mapping readers may refer [1]. Keeping these architectural concepts in mind, in the next few subsections, we now look forward to some of the advanced processors and their architectural features.

6.3 80286 Microprocessor

80286 Processor is popularly known as 286 processor introduced by Intel in 1982 and composed of 132K transistors with n-MOS process technology. It has the following salient features.

Key Features

- It has 16-bit Data bus and 24-bit address bus
- 80286 does not have multiplexed address/data bus
- Addressed Memory size or address space of 16MB
- First processor with memory management unit with enhanced memory protection capabilities
- 80286 has memory management capability that maps 2^{30}(1GB) of virtual address
- 80286 can be operated in real mode as well as in protected virtual address mode
- Segmentation in protected mode is different from the real mode
- Backward compatible
- Clock speed is higher (max 12.5MHz) and hence time of execution of some instructions are as low as 250ns.

- It has few more instructions compared to its predecessor 80186 and has faster execution time.
- 80286 is a high-performance processor. Six times the performance of the standard 8086. The power consumption is also less compared to 8086
- It is a multiuser processor and having multi-tasking capabilities
- 80286 has three high-level instructions such as BOUND, LEAVE and ENTER

6.3.1 Architecture of 80286

80286 is an advanced, high-performance processor which is designed specially with additional capabilities for multi-user and multitasking systems. The 80286 has built-in memory protection that supports operating system, task isolation as well as program and data privacy. 80286 is much faster compared to 8086. A 12 MHz 80286 provides a processing speed of about six times faster than the 5 MHz 8086. The 80286 has a memory management capability that can map 2^{30} (one gigabyte) of virtual address space per task into 2^{24} bytes (16 megabytes) of physical memory. 80286 is also compatible with 8086 and 8088 processors (instructions). The Architecture of 80286 Microprocessor has two operating modes: *real address mode* and *protected virtual address mode*. In real address mode, the 80286 is object code compatible with its predecessor 8086, and 8088 software. In protected virtual address mode, the 80286's source code is also compatible with 8086, 8088 software. In both the modes 80286 can operate at its full performances and execute all instructions of the 8086 and 8088 processors. The internal architecture of 80286 is shown in the block diagram of Fig. 6.3. The CPU of 80286 consists of the following:

- Address Unit (AU)
- Bus Unit (BU)
- Instruction Unit (IU)
- Execution Unit (EU)

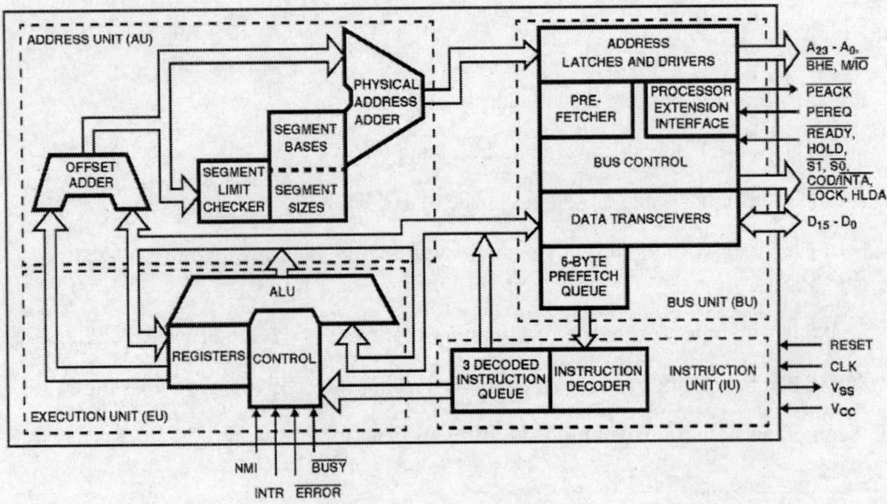

Fig. 6.3: Internal block diagram of 80286 [Courtesy: Slideplayer]

Address Unit (AU)

The address unit (AU) determines the physical address of instructions and operands which are stored in memory. Like 8086 processor, it computes the 20-bit physical address from the content of the segment register and 16-bit offset. The addresses so computed by the address unit are used to specify different peripheral devices such as memory and I/O devices. The physical addresses computed by the address unit are then sent to the Bus Unit (BU) of the CPU.

Bus Unit (BU)

The bus unit also known as bus interface unit interconnects the 80286 processor with memory and I/O devices. 80286 has a 16-bit data bus, a 24-bit address bus, and a control bus. The bus interface unit is responsible for performing all external bus operations. It consists of latches and drivers for the address bus, which transmit the physical address A_{19}-A_0. This 20-bit address facilitates all the memory and I/O devices for read and write operations. Bus unit is used to fetch instructions from the memory and are kept in a queue for faster execution. *Instruction pipelining* uses this concept. As the instructions are prefetched, so the processor will not wait for the current instruction to be completed rather it will decode the next instruction from the instruction queue and make it ready for execution. The prefetch module in the bus unit performs the task of prefetching. The bus interface unit has a bus controller which controls the prefetch module. The fetched instructions are arranged in a 6-byte prefetch queue. This way, the CPU prefetches the instructions to enhance the speed of execution.

Instruction Unit (IU)

Instruction unit or the instruction decoder receives the instructions from the prefetch queue and the instruction decoder decodes them one by one. The decoded instructions are then latched onto a decoded instruction queue. The IU can decode a maximum of 3 prefetched instructions and loads them into decoded instruction queue for execution by execution unit.

Execution Unit (EU)

The decoded instructions are then fed to a control circuit of the execution unit. This unit executes the instructions received from the decoded instruction queue. It consists of the register bank, arithmetic and logic unit (ALU) and control unit. The register bank is used to store data as a scratch pad. The register bank can also be used as special-purpose registers. The ALU is the core of the EU which performs all the arithmetic and logical operations and sends the results either to the data bus or back to the register bank. The control unit controls the overall operation of the execution unit.

The 80286 series of processors contain all the basic set of registers, instructions, and addressing modes of 8086. Moreover, the 80286 processor is upward compatible with its predecessors 8086, 8088, and 80186 CPU's. It has altogether fifteen registers grouped into four groups as shown in Fig.6.4. These are,

- General purpose registers
- Segment registers
- Base and Index registers
- Status and Control registers

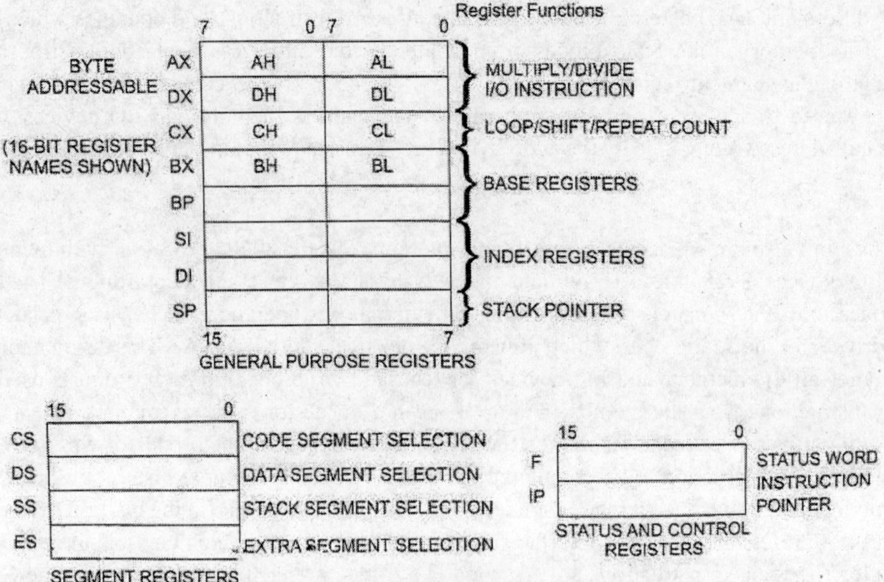

Fig. 6.4: Register Set of 80286 Processor [Courtesy: EEGUIDE]

General-Purpose Registers: These eight 16-bit general-purpose registers which are used to store operands of arithmetic and logical instructions. Four of these (AX, BX, CX, and DX) registers can be used either as 16-bit words or can be split into two separate 8-bit registers.

Segment Registers: There are four 16-bit special-purpose registers in 80286 which are used to select the segments of memory that are immediately addressable for code, stack, and data.

Base and Index Registers: These are four general-purpose registers which can also be used to determine offset addresses of operands in memory. Usually, these registers hold base addresses or indexes to particular locations within a segment. Any specified addressing mode determines the specific registers used for operand address calculations.

Status and Control Register: There are three 16-bit special-purpose registers in 80286 which are used for record and control of the 80286 processor. The instruction pointer contains the offset address of the next sequential instruction to be executed.

Flag Word Register: The flag word register records the specific characteristics of the result of arithmetic and logical instructions. The flag register bits D_0, D_2, D_4, D_6, D_7, and D_{11} are modified as per result of the execution of arithmetic and logical instructions. These are called status flag hits. Bits D_8 and D_9 control the operation of the 80286 within a given operating mode and these bits are called control flags. The flag register is a 16-bit register. Figure 6.5 shows the flag register of 80286.

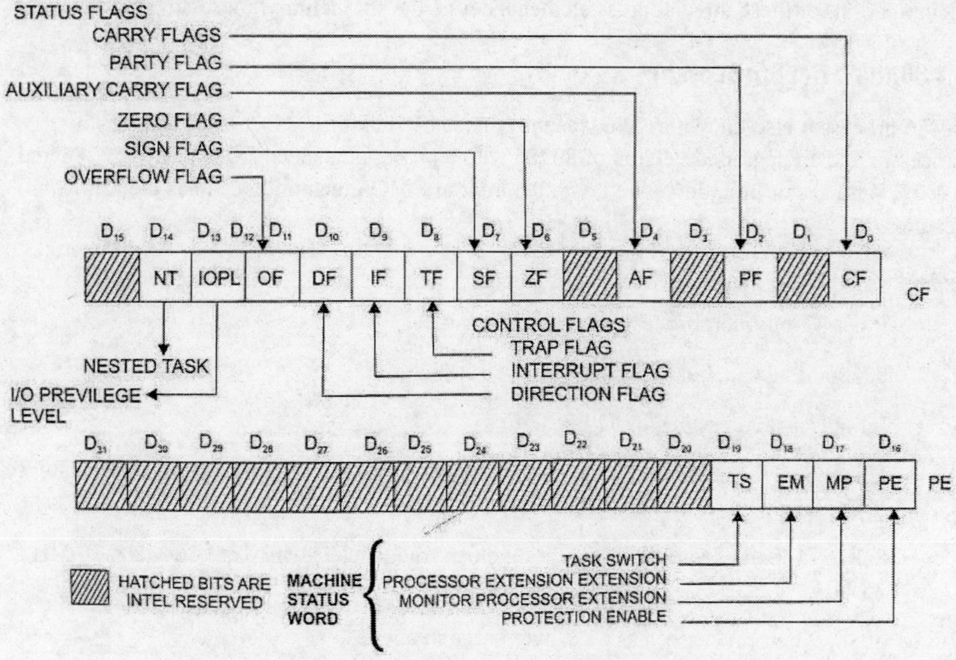

Fig 6.5: Flag registers of 80286 [Courtesy: EEGUIDE]

6.3.2 Addressing modes

The 80286 processor has eight addressing modes for the instructions to access operands from memory. The eight different addressing modes of 80286 microprocessor are as follows:

- Register operand mode
- Immediate operand
- Direct mode
- Register indirect mode
- Based mode
- Indexed mode
- Based indexed mode
- Based indexed mode with displacement

The first two operating modes are related to the register and immediate operands. The remaining six modes are provided to specify the location of an operand in a memory segment. A memory operand address consists of two 16-bit components, namely, segment selector and offset. The segment selector is supplied by a segment register either implicitly chosen by a segment override prefix. The offset is determined by summing any combination of the following three address elements.

- The displacement (8- or 16-bit immediate value)
- The base (content of the BX or BP)
- Any carry out from the 16-bit addition is ignored; eight-bit displacements are sign extended to 16-bit values

Combinations of these three address elements define the six memory addressing modes.

6.4 80386 Microprocessor

80386 processor also known as 386 was introduced by Intel in 1985. It is the first 32-bit processor and an upgraded version of 80286 with a processing speed twice that of 80286 and has 275K transistor in it, developed with 0.8 micron CMOS technology. It has the following features.

Key Features

- It is a 32-bit microprocessor with a 32-bit ALU.
- 80386 has a data bus of 32-bit.
- It holds an address bus of 32 bit.
- It supports physical memory addressability of 4 GB and virtual memory addressability of 64 TB.
- 80386 supports a variety of operating clock frequencies, which are 16 MHz, 20 MHz, 25 MHz, and 33 MHz.
- 80386 Microprocessor has a 16-byte prefetch queue.
- It offers 3 stage pipeline processing: *fetch, decode* and *execute*. As it supports simultaneous fetching, decoding, and execution inside the system.
- 80386 has dedicated hardware that gives multitasking capability.
- Microprocessor has memory management unit with a segmentation unit and a paging Unit.
- It supports 3 operating modes: real, protected, and virtual real mode.
- The 80386 can run 8086 applications under a protected mode in its virtual 8086 mode of operation.

6.4.1 Architecture of 80386 Processor

The detailed architectural diagram of the 80386 processor is depicted in Fig. 6.6. Its internal architecture consists of three different major sections, namely, the Central Processing Unit (CPU), the Memory Management Unit (MMU) and the Bus Interface Unit (BIU).

Central Processing Unit (CPU) The central processing unit consists of an Execution Unit (EU) and an Instruction Unit (IU). The Execution Unit EU has altogether sixteen registers- eight general-purpose and eight special-purpose registers. These registers are used for data-handling and calculating the offset addresses. The Instruction Unit (IU) is used to decode the instructions opcode (one byte) as received from the 16-byte instruction code queue. This is followed by arranging them into a 3-instruction decoded-instruction queue. After decoding opcode bytes of instructions, the information is then passed to the control section to provide the necessary control signals. The powerful barrel shifter present in the EU increases the speed of all shifts and rotate operations. While the multiply or divide logic implements the bit-shift-rotate algorithms to complete the instruction execution a within minimum time. The 32-bit multiplication/division operations can also be executed within one microsecond by the multiply/divide logic.

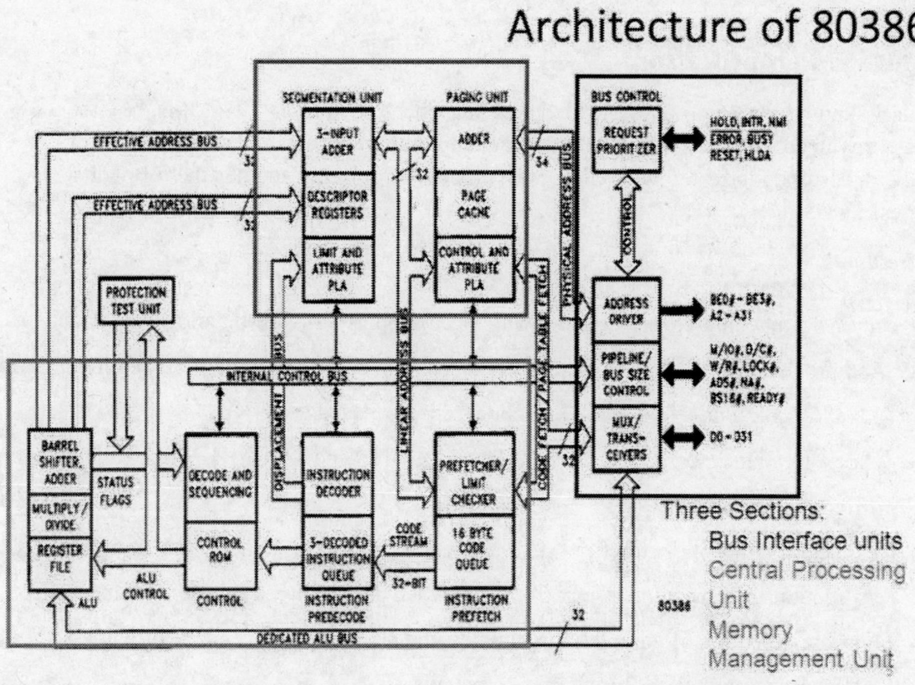

Fig. 6.6: Internal Architecture of 80386 [Courtesy: EEGUIDE]

Memory Management Unit (MMU)

The Memory Management Unit (MMU) consists of a Segmentation Unit (SU) and a Paging Unit (PU).

Segmentation Unit (SU) The segmentation unit uses two address components, namely, the segment address and offset address to locate and share code and data. The segmentation unit allows a maximum size of 4 GB segments. The segmentation unit has four-level protection mechanisms to protect and isolate the system's code and data from the application programs. The 'limit and attribute PLA' is used to check segment limits and attributes at segment level to keep away from invalid accesses to code and data.

Paging Unit (PU) The paging unit organizes the physical memory in terms of pages of 4 KB size each. The paging unit always acts under the control of the segmentation unit. Each segment is divided into pages. The virtual memory is also arranged in terms of segments and pages by the memory management unit. The paging unit usually converts linear addresses into physical addresses. The 'control and attribute PLA' is used to check the privileges at the page level. Each page always maintains the paging information of the task.

Bus Interface Unit (BIU) The bus interface unit interfaces the 80386 processor with memory and I/O devices. To fetch instructions and transfer data from code prefetch unit, the processor provides address, data and control signals through BIU. The code prefetch is used for fetching instructions from the memory while BIU is not executing any bus cycle (i.e. idle). The bus control section has a 'request prioritizer' to decide the priority of the various bus requests. It also controls the bus access. The address driver is used for bus enable signals BE_3-BE_0 and address signals A_{31}-A_0. The pipeline and bus size control units handle the related control signals.

6.5 80486 Microprocessor

Popularly known as 486 processor which was introduced by Intel in 1989. It is the first processor with an in-built floating-point processing unit on the same chip. It consists of 1200K transistors, fabricated with CMOS IV process technology and has the following features.

Key Features

- It is a 32-bit complete architecture which can support 8-bit, 16-bit and 32-bit data types.
- 486 processor has 8 KB unified, level 1 cache for code and data included in CPU. In advanced versions of the 80486, cache size is increased to 16 KB.
- Clock frequency of 25 MHz, 33 MHz, 50 MHz and 100 MHz are available with different versions of 80486.
- Execution time of instructions is significantly reduced. Load, store and arithmetic instructions are executed in just one cycle when data is already present in the cache.
- For fast execution of complex instructions, the 80486 has a five-stage pipeline.
- 80486 processor has a 32-byte prefetch queue.
- The 80486 processor has multiprocessing support capability.
- RISC feature is incorporated in 80486.
- Clock-doubling and clock-tripling technology has been incorporated in faster versions of Intel 80486 CPU.
- Power management and System Management Mode (SMM) of 80486 is a standard feature of the processor.

6.5.1 Architecture of 80486

A simplified architecture of Intel 80486 processor is shown in Fig. 6.7 whereas the detailed internal architecture is shown in Fig. 6.8. The architecture of 80486 can be divided into following three different sections,

- Bus interface unit (BIU),
- Execution and control unit (EU), and
- Floating-point unit (FU).

read more on adv processors

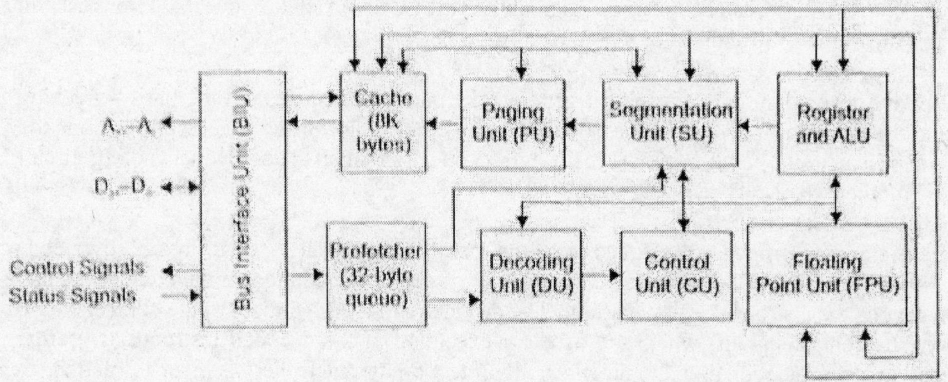

Fig. 6.7: Simplified architecture of 486

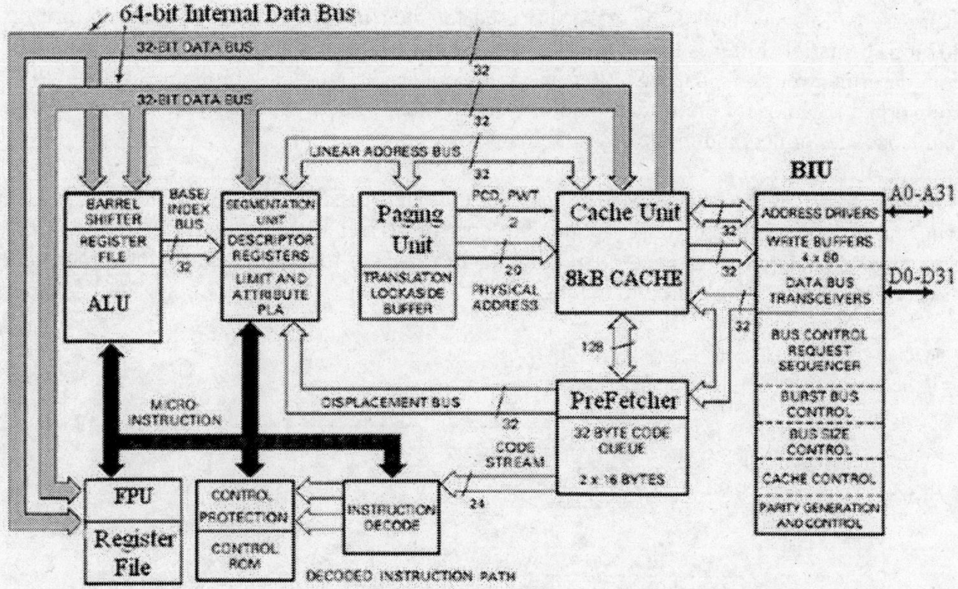

Fig. 6.8: Internal Architecture of 80486 [Courtesy: EEGUIDE]

Bus Interface Unit (BIU): The bus interface unit organizes all the bus related activities of the processor. The address driver is connected to an internal 32-bit cache unit and also with the system bus (also 32 bit). The data bus transceivers are connected between the internal 32-bit data bus and system bus. The write data buffer is a queue of four 80-bit registers and is able to hold the 80-bit data which will be written to the memory. Due to pipelined execution of the write operation, data must be available in advance. To control the bus access and operations, the following bus control and request sequencer signals $\overline{ADS}$, W/$\overline{R}$, D/$\overline{C}$, M/$\overline{IO}$, PCD, PWT, $\overline{RDY}$, $\overline{LOCK}$, $\overline{PLOCK}$, $\overline{BOFF}$, $\overline{A20M}$, BREQ, HOLD, HLDA, RESET, INTR, NMI, $\overline{FERR}$ and $\overline{IGNNE}$ are used.

Execution Unit (EU) and Control Unit (CU): The burst control signal updates the processor that the burst is ready. This signal works as a ready signal in the burst cycle. The $\overline{BLAST}$ output shows that the previous burst cycle is over. The bus size control signals $\overline{BS16}$ and $\overline{BS8}$ indicates dynamic bus sizing. The cache control signals $\overline{\text{KEN}}$, FLUSH, AHOLD and $\overline{\text{EADS}}$ are used to control the cache control unit.

The parity generation and control unit generate the parity and carries out the parity-checking during the processor operation. The boundary scan control unit of the processor performs the boundary scan tests operation to ensure the correct operation of all the components of the circuit on the mother board.

The prefetcher unit fetches the codes from the memory and arranges them in a 32-byte code queue. The function of the instruction decoder is to receive the code from the code queue and then decode the instructions sequentially. The decoder unit then fed them to the control unit to derive the control signals, which are used for execution of the decoded instructions. Before execution, the protection unit should check all protection norms. If there is in any violation, an appropriate exception is generated.

The control ROM stores a microprogram to generate control signals for execution of instructions. Register banks and ALU are used for their usual operation as they perform in 80286. The barrel shifter is used to perform the shift and rotate algorithms. The segmentation unit, descriptor registers, paging unit, translation look aside buffer and limit and attribute PLA are worked together for the virtual memory management. These units also provide protection to the opcodes or operand in the physical memory.

Floating–point Unit (FPU): The floating-point unit and register banks or FPU communicate with the bus interface unit (BIU) under the control of memory management unit (MMU), through a 64-bit internal data bus. Generally, the FPU is used for mathematical data processing at very high speed as compared to the ALU.

6.5.2 Registers and Flag Register of 80486

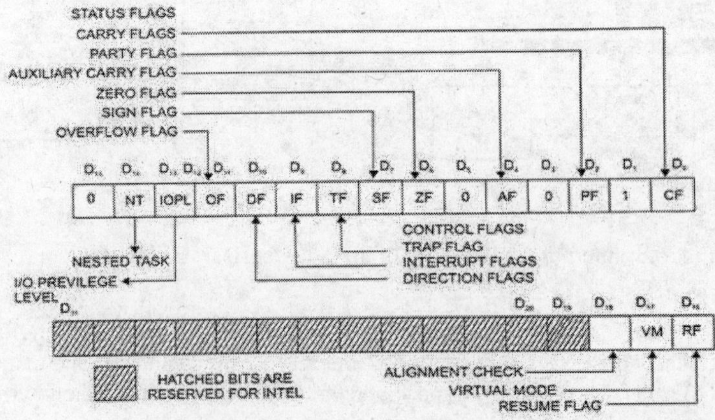

Fig.6.9: Flag Registers of 486 [Courtesy: EEGUIDE]

The registers of the 80486 processor are same as the 80386 processor, except for the flag register. Figure 6.9 shows the flag register. As compared to the flag register of 80386, the flag register of 80386 has only one additional flag called alignment check flag or AC flag. The D_{18} position of the flag register is AC flag as depicted in Fig. 6.9. When the AC flag bit is set to '1', there is an access to a misaligned address and an exception (fault) will be generated. The alignment faults are generated only at privilege level 3.

6.6 Pentium Processor

The fifth-generation processor in the 8086 series is 80586 which is renamed as Pentium Processor. It was developed by Intel in 1993 and represented by P5. It consists of 3.1 million transistors, uses 0.8-micron BiCMOS technology and has the following feature.

Key Features

- Pentium runs at a clock frequency of 60 MHz to 233 MHz.
- Pentium has two 8 Kbyte L1 cache (for instruction and data), but there is no L2 cache.
- Similar to 486 processor but with 64-bit data bus
- Wider internal datapaths: 128-bit and 256-bit wide
- Pentium has a 32-bit address bus, therefore provides a 4Gb physical memory space
- It has two instruction execution units
- It is a superscalar processor
- It has two independent integer pipelines and a floating-point pipeline
- Includes a branch prediction unit

6.6.1 Architecture of Pentium

Pentium processor is an advancement over its predecessor 80386 and 80486. Pentium bring about some modifications in its cache structures, width of the data bus, numeric coprocessor with enhanced speed along with two integer processors. It has two on-chip cache-one for data and the other for instructions. Each cache is of 8Kb size. As it uses dual integer processor, so two instructions can be executed simultaneously in one clock cycle. Advanced version of Pentium processor is *Pentium Pro* which is comparatively faster. This is because Pentium Pro allows scheduling of 5 simultaneous instructions in order to get executed. Along with level-1 cache i.e., 16K-byte like Pentium, it has a level-2 cache that is 256K-byte size. Moreover, Pentium Pro has an error detection and correction capability. The error correction unit offers correction of single-bit error and detection of two-bit error. With additional four address lines, the Pentium Pro offers 64 Gb of accessible physical memory.

The Pentium is a 32-bit processor. It has a 32-bit address bus and a 64-bit data bus. The internal and external data buses are connected through the on-chip caches. Figure 6.10 shows a simplified architecture of Pentium processor whereas Fig. 6.11 shows a detailed internal architecture which consists of 8K byte code cache, 8K byte data cache, Translation Look-aside

Buffer (TLB), Branch Trace Buffer (BTB), Integer pipelines U and V, floating-point pipeline, Microcode ROM, and Control Unit (CU).

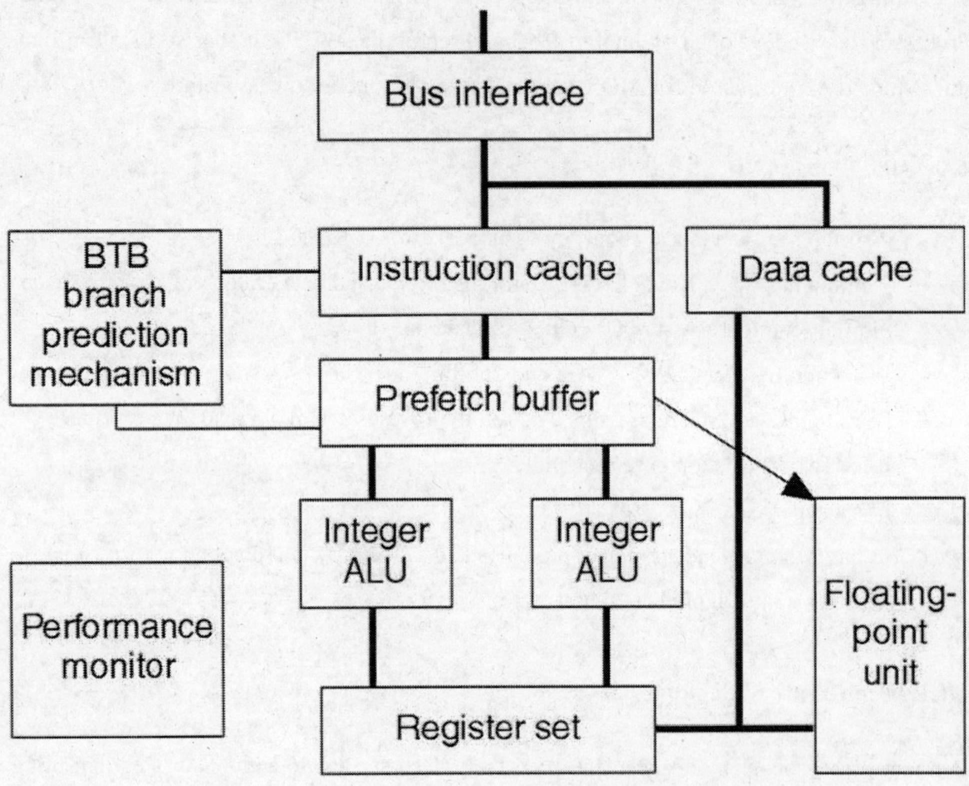

Fig. 6.10: Internal Architecture of Pentium Processor [Courtesy: Computer.org]

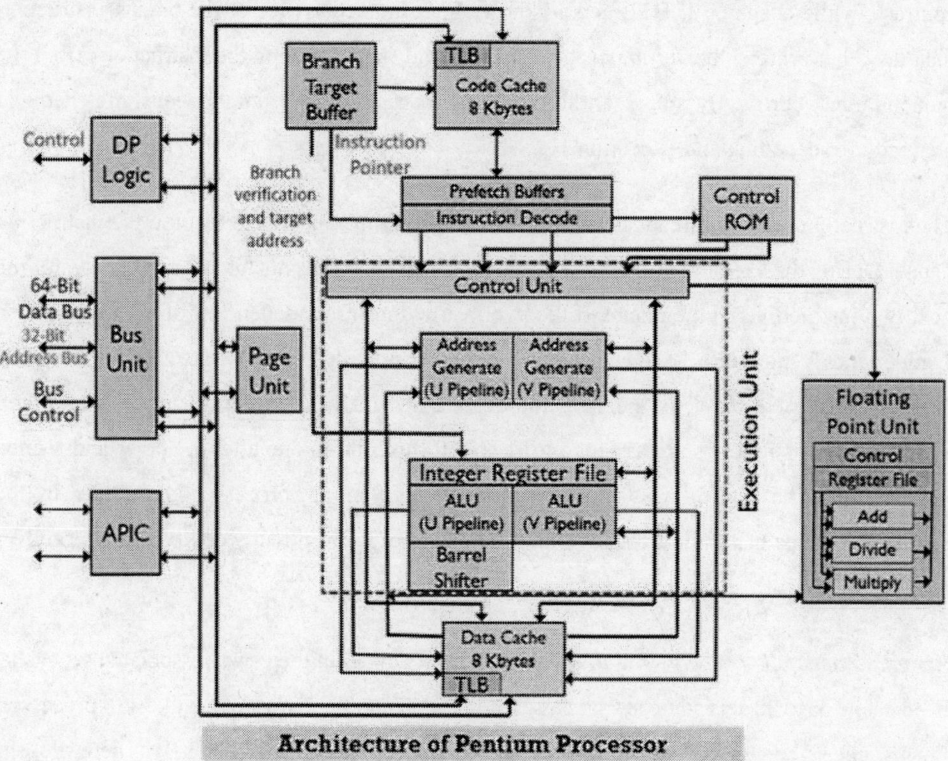

Fig.6.11: Detail Architecture of Pentium [Courtesy: Electronicdesk]

The bus interface unit of the processor sends the control signal and fetches the code and data from external memory and I/O devices. The size of the external data bus is 64-bit through which burst read and burst write-back cycles can be performed. The paging unit in the architecture provides optional extensions of around 2 to 4 Mb page sizes.

In order to load the instructions into the execution unit, code cache, branch target buffer and prefetch buffers work together to accomplish the task. The code cache or the external memory holds the instructions from where codes are fetched. While the branch target buffer holds the address of the respective branch and the TLB (translational lookaside buffer) within the code cache converts the linear address into the physical address which is used by the code cache.

This processor contains pairs of prefetch buffers having a size of 32-byte that combinedly operate with branch target buffer. Both the buffers operate independently but not at the same time. One of the prefetch buffers starts fetching the instructions in a sequential manner till the time branch instruction has not occurred. However, as soon as the branch instruction is fetched by the prefetch buffer, the BTB then check for the branching operation. Once it is checked by BTB that branch has not occurred then linear fetching of instruction will resume. On the contrary, while checking if BTB gets to know about the occurrence of the branch instruction then the other prefetch buffer in pair gets enabled and starts fetching the instructions from the branch target address. By doing so, the branching instructions get simultaneously fetched and are ready for decoding and execution.

The instruction fetch unit reads the instruction one at a time and stores them in the instruction queue. During the execution of an instruction, the processor does not sit idle and checks for the next two instructions in the queue. If the two instructions are independent of each other, then U-pipe and V-pipe are assigned instructions individually so that execution can occur simultaneously. However, in the case, the queued instructions are dependent on each other, then both the instructions are assigned to U-pipe for execution one after the other and V-pipe remains idle. The controlling of the operations of the Pentium processor is provided by the control ROM that has a microcode within it. The control ROM directly controls U-pipe and V-pipe.

Both data and code cache within the processor is organized in the 2-way associated set cache. Each cache has 128 sets and each set has 2 lines which are 32 bits wide just like 486 processor. Each cache is connected with its own Translation Look-aside Buffer (TLB). Therefore, the paging unit of the Memory Management Unit (MMU) can rapidly convert linear code or data addresses into physical addresses The LRU (Least Recently Used) mechanism handles the cache replacement. As we can see clearly in the above figure that the code cache makes a connection with the prefetch buffer by a bus of size 256 bit, thus 256/8 i.e., 32 bytes of opcode can be buffered in one clock cycle. The data cache has two ports that are used to simultaneously deal with two data references. The execution unit within the Pentium processor contains two integer pipelines namely, U-pipe and V-pipe. Each one has its separate ALU. There are five stages in which these pipelines operate, namely, prefetch, decode-1, decode-2, execute, writeback. The U-pipe is responsible for executing all integer as well as floating-point instructions while V-pipe executes simple integer operations.

6.6.2 Branch Prediction

Branch prediction consists of a Control Unit (CU) and a Branch Target Buffer (BTB). The function of control unit and branch target buffer are as follows:

Branch Target Buffer (BTB): The BTB is used to store the target address and statistical information about the branch operation. Hence, the branch prediction is able to predict branches and cause the Pentium to use the most likely target address for instruction fetching, thus enhancing the execution performance. Any misprediction causes penalty and pipeline flushes the wrongly processed data.

Control Unit (CU): The control unit controls the five-stage integer pipelines U and V, and the eight-stage floating-point unit. In the architecture of Pentium Processor, the integer pipelines are used for all instructions which does not involve any floating-point operations. Therefore, the Pentium can transmit two integer instructions in the same clock cycle and performance of the processor is improved. Such an execution comes under **superscalar architecture**, Figure 6.12 shows the superscalar organization of the Pentium processor.

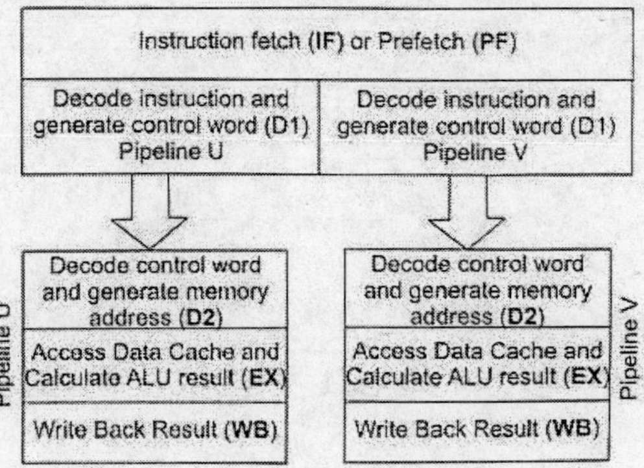

Fig.6.12: Superscalar processor organization in Pentium

The first four stages of the floating-point pipeline execution overlap with the U pipeline. The parallel operation of the integer and floating-point pipelines is possible only under some specified conditions. If the clock frequency of Pentium is same as 80486, then the Pentium floating-point unit is able to execute floating-point instructions 3 to 5 times faster than 80486. This is possible because of on-chip hardware multiplier and divider present in the floating-point unit with quicker algorithms that can be incorporated in the micro-coded floating-point unit.

The Pentium has a microcode support unit to perform complex functions. The support unit controls the pipelines with the microcode. Actually, this unit controls and utilizes both the pipelines together. Therefore, complex microcode instructions run very fast on a Pentium than on a 80486.

6.6.3 Integer Pipelines U and V

As already mentioned that Pentium processor has two integer pipelines, called U and V and a floating-point unit. Hence it falls under the category of superscalar processor. The U-pipeline is capable of handling the full instruction set of the Pentium processor but the V-pipeline has limited handling capability. The V-pipeline is able to handle only simple instructions without any microcode support. The V-pipeline is used to execute 'simple integer instructions' such as load/store type instructions and the FPU instruction FXCH, but the U-pipeline executes any legitimate Pentium instructions. Actually, architecture of Pentium processor uses a set of pairing rules to select a simple instruction which can go through the V pipeline. When instructions are paired, initially the instruction is issued to the U-pipe and then the next sequential instruction is issued to the V-pipe.

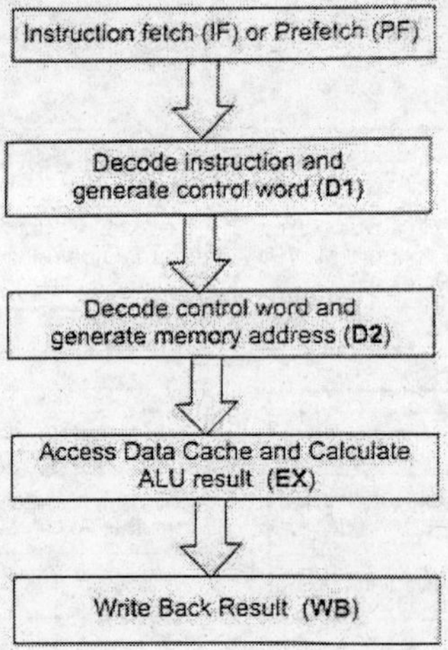

Fig. 6.13: Integer pipeline of Pentium

There are two integer pipelines and a floating-point unit in the Architecture of Pentium Processor. Figure 6.13 shows an integer pipeline. Each integer unit has the basic five-stage pipeline as given below:

- Prefetch (PF)
- Decode-1 (D1)
- Decode-2 (D2)
- Execute (E)
- Write Back (WB)

Superscalar Processing

The internal architecture of Pentium processor has been designed on the basis of superscalar execution. In superscalar architecture, two or more instructions are executed in parallel. Figure 6.11 shows the superscalar architecture of Pentium. There are two independent integer pipelines as depicted in Fig. 6.13. In the PF and D1 stages, the microprocessor can fetch, decode instructions and generate control words. In this stage, decoded instructions issue them to two parallel U and V pipelines. For complex instructions, D1 generates micro-coded sequences for U and V pipelines. Several techniques are used to resolve the pairing of instructions.

6.6.4 Floating-Point Unit

The 80486DX CPU is the first processor in which the 80387, math co-processor has been incorporated on-chip to reduce the communication overhead. The 80486 CPU contains a floating-point unit, but that is not pipelined. The architecture of Pentium processor has been designed for incorporating on the chip numeric data processor.

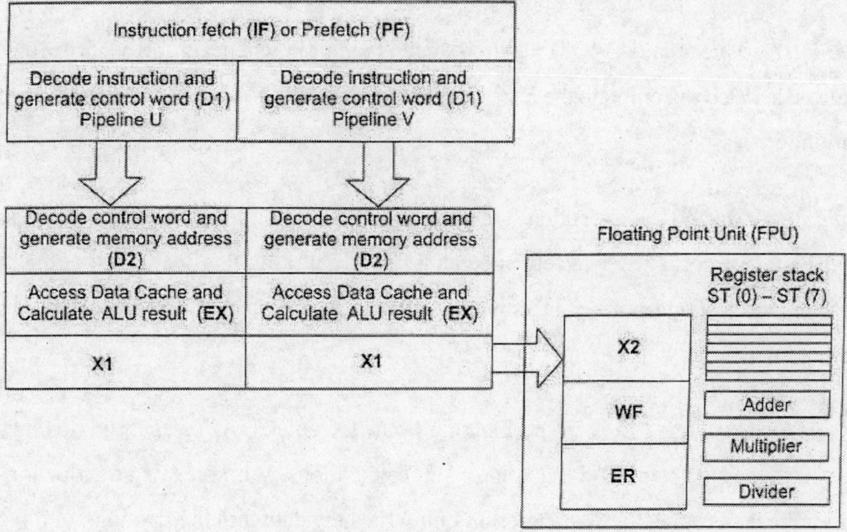

Fig.6.14: Floating-Point unit of Pentium

The Floating-Point Unit (FPU) of Pentium has an eight-stage pipeline as shown in Fig. 6.14. The eight pipeline stages are

- Prefetch (PF)
- Decode-1 (D1)
- Decode-2 (D2)
- Execute (dispatch)
- Floating Point Execute-1 (X1)
- Floating Point Execute-2 (X2)
- Write Float (WF)
- Error Reporting (ER)

The first five stages of the pipeline are similar to the U and V integer pipelines. During the operand fetch stage, the FPU fetches the operands either from the floating-point register or from the data cache. The floating-point unit has eight general-purpose floating-point registers. There are two execution stages in Pentium such as the first execution stage (X1 stage) and the second execution stage (X2 stage). In the X1 and X2 stages, the floating-point unit reads the data from the data cache and executes the floating-point calculation.

Prefetch (PF) The prefetch stage is same as the integer pipeline of Pentium processor.

Decode-1 (D1) The decode-1 (D1) pipeline stage is also same as the integer pipeline of Pentium processor.

Decode-2 (D2) The decode-2 (D2) pipeline stage is required whenever the control word from D1 stage is decoded to complete the instruction decoding. In this stage, it is the integer pipeline of Pentium processor.

Operand Fetch During the execution stage (E), the floating-point unit accesses the data cache and the floating-point register to fetch operands. Before writing the floating-point data to the data cache, the floating-point unit converts internal data format into appropriate memory representation format.

Floating Point Execute-1 (X1) In the Floating Point Execute-1 (X1) stage, the floating-point unit executes the first steps of the floating-point calculations. While reading the floating-point data from the data cache, the floating-point unit writes the data into the floating-point register.

Floating Point Execute-2 (X2) During the Floating Point Execute-2 (X2) stage, the floating - point unit execute the remaining steps of the floating-point computations.

Write Float (WF) In the Write Float (WF) stage, the floating-point unit completes the execution of the floating-point calculations and then writes the computed result into the floating-point register file.

Error Reporting (ER) In the error reporting (ER) stage, the floating-point unit generates a report about resulting floating point operation and any special situations occurred which it updates in the floating-point status.

6.6.5 Register Set of Pentium

The register set of Pentium processor are shown in Fig. 6.15(a) and 6.15(b). It has the same register set as that of 80386 processor, but it has two new registers CR4 and TR12 are added in the register set of Pentium processor as depicted in Fig.6.15 (b).

The control register CR4 controls the Pentium processors extensions for virtual-8086 mode operation. The CR4 register is also used for supporting the debugger which can support up to 4 Mbyte pages. The test control register TR12 enables the selective activation of new features of Pentium processors such as branch prediction, and superscalar operation, etc.

In flag register EFLAG of Pentium three new flags are also added. Two flags are used to support virtual 8086 mode operation and the third flag indicates if the processor supports the CPU ID instruction. When the processor sets and clears the ID flag, it can execute the CPUID instruction.

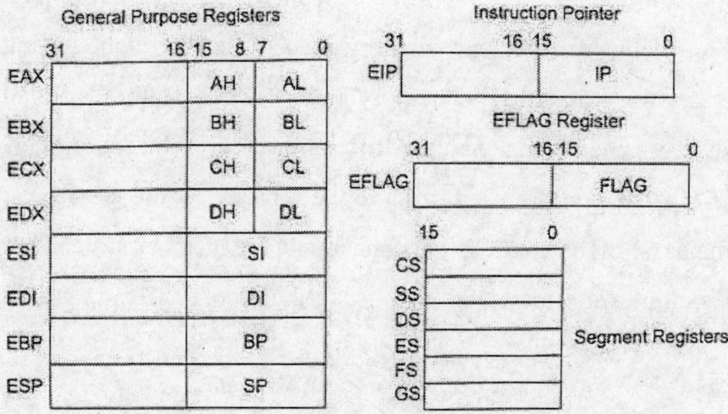

Fig.6.15: (a) Registers of Pentium Processor

Control Registers
31 1615 0
CR4
CR3
CR2
CR1
CR0

Debug Registers
31 16 15 0
DR7
DR6
DR5
DR4
DR3
DR2
DR1
DR0

Test Registers
31 16 15 0
TR12
TR7
TR6

	15 0	31 0	19 0
TR	TSS Selector	TSS Base Address	TSS Limit
LDTR	LDTSS Selector	LDT Base Address	LDT Limit
	IDRT	IDT Base Address	IDT Limit
	GDTR	GDT Base Address	GDT Limit

Fig.6.15: (b) Control and Debug Registers of Pentium

6.6.6 Memory Subsystem in Pentium

The memory subsystem of the Pentium processor consists of the CPU registers, main memory, cache memory and secondary memory. The main memory unit is 4G bytes in size as in the case of 80486 microprocessor. However, the main difference in Pentium lies with the width of memory data-bus. The Pentium uses 64-bit data bus to address the memory which is organized in eight banks each with a capacity to store 512M bytes of data as shown in Fig. 6.16. As a double precision floating point number is 64-bit wide, so with a 64-bit memory data bus Pentium is able to retrieve floating point data just in one cycle. Thus, enhancing its performance over 486 processor. The range of memory location vary from 00000000H to FFFFFFFFH in Pentium. Active low Bank Enable signals (BE7bar to BE0bar) are used to enable each memory bank. Each such memory bank is 8-bit wide. These memory banks allow access to one byte, two-byte, word or double word in one memory read cycle. So, eight separate write strobe signals are necessary for writing to the memory banks. A new feature is added in Pentium to enhance its capability to check and generate parity for the address bus during certain operations. The AP and APCHK-bar pins are used to serve these tasks. As the memory system is 32-bit whereas Pentium has 64-bit data bus, so to connect with the memory system Pentium uses a set of bidirectional multiplexers to convert 64-bit data bus into a 32-bit data bus to access the memory banks.

Cache memory in Pentium is again different from its predecessor 486. The 486 processor uses a unified cache whereas Pentium uses a split cache. That is, it uses a separate instruction cache and data cache each of 8K byte size for storing the instruction and data respectively. Thus, avoiding any cache conflict and enhancing performance over 486 processor.

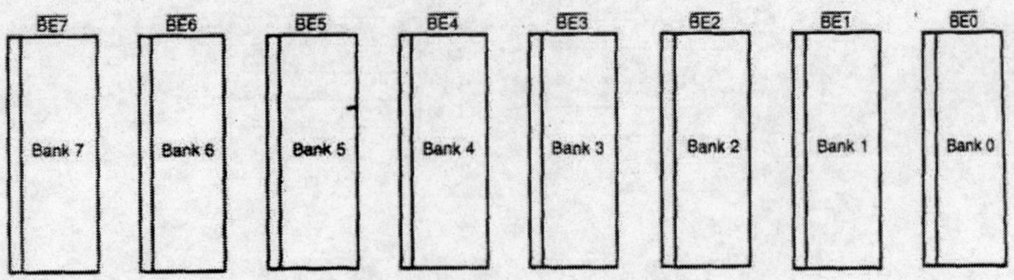

Fig. 6.16: Register banks of Pentium

Memory Management Unit

The memory management unit of Pentium is compatible with its predecessor 386 and 486 processors. Many of it features are remained unchanged. Difference is in its paging unit and a new system management option termed as the memory management mode. Usually, the paging table becomes too large when the system contains a large memory. In Pentium paging works with 4M-byte memory pages which dramatically reduces the complexity to a single page table. Thus, no page table entry is needed in the linear address (unlike a 4K-byte paging) which eventually is converted to a real physical address. The leftmost 10 bits of the linear address as in Fig.6.15 selects an entry in the page directory which ultimately addresses a 4M-byte memory page (a real physical memory). The CR3 in Fig.6.17 holds the root address.

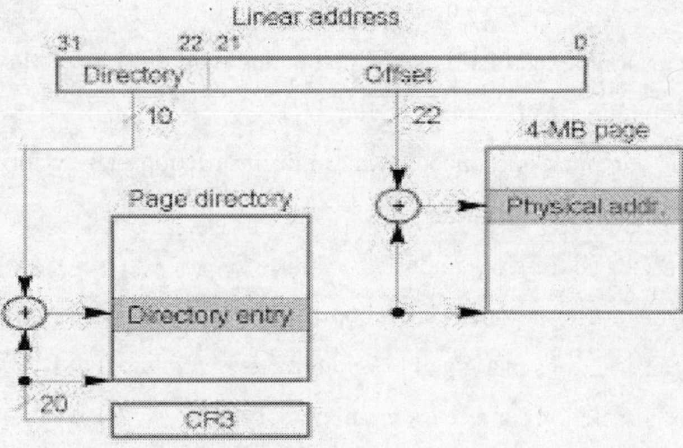

Fig. 6.17: Address translation in Pentium from linear to real physical address with no page table

The system memory management mode (SNM) is of the same level as protected mode, real mode, and virtual mode but it has the privilege to function as a manager. The SNM is not to be used as an application or a system-level feature. It is intended to be used for high-level system functions such as for power management and security in most of the Pentiums. The task of SNM is accomplished via a new external hardware interrupt applied to the SMI-bar pin of the Pentium. When SMI-bar is activated it disables all other interrupts that are normally handled by user applications and operating system. The return for the SNM interrupt is accomplished by the new instruction RSM which returns the program control from the memory management mode to the interrupted program. Interested readers may refer [2] for more on this topic.

6.7 CISC Architecture

CISC stands for Complex Instruction Set Computer. The design of the CISC processor is based on an approach so as to complete the whole operation in few lines of the assembly language code. Most of the Intel processors from 8086 to Pentium belong to CISC architecture, although they have intelligently added some of the RISC features also. While RISC processor uses the approach of increasing internal parallelism by executing a simple set of instructions in a single clock cycle. While he major goal behind the design of CISC is to have such an instruction set that works well with the tasks and data structures of Higher-Level Languages. The important features of CISC architecture are highlighted below.

CISC Features

- They have a variable instruction set which includes simple to complex instructions
- Requires a complex instruction decoding
- The task of compiler is reduced as a single instruction can perform the tasks like, loading, evaluating and storing
- Supports various addressing modes
- Requires more cycles per instruction compared to RISC
- Number of instructions in a given program are less compared to RISC
- Almost any instruction can access main memory
- The operations can be performed in the memory itself thus requiring lesser number of general-purpose registers
- Less support to instruction level pipelining compared to RISC
- Instructions have variable lengths
- It has a complex addressing modes
- It uses microprogrammed control thus more flexible compared to RISC
- Finds applications in general-purpose computers

6.8 RISC Processors

RISC is an acronym for Reduced Instruction Set Computer. As the name implies such a processor has a small but an efficient set of instructions to execute any task or user program. Its design is based on *one instruction per cycle* approach. It is basically a *load-store* architecture. RISC architecture is based on the design principle of simplified instructions that can carry out less but fast operations in each cycle thereby improving the performance. Thus, RISC offer a simplified hardware with lesser chip area and shorter design cycle. ARM series of processors, IBM PowerPC, SUN-Sparc are some of the RISC processors. Following are the important features of this architecture.

Features

- It is a load-store architecture, therefore data operations can not be performed directly in the memory
- Most RISC instructions involve register to register operations that are internal to CPU
- Designed to perform single cycle operation thereby making efficient CPU utilization
- It offers maximization in operating speed; this resultantly reduces execution time.
- It has a fixed length, small set of instructions with uniform format thereby making the design simple.
- The instruction length is fixed thus supports pipelining
- Uses hard-wared control unit which is very fast compared to microprogram control in CISC
- Control unit is not flexible
- As the compiler plays a big role to convert complex instructions into many simple instructions, therefore the performance of the processor depends on compiler.
- As a RISC processor consumes less power and they are high performing in nature so very much useful for low power, battery-operated portable applications.

6.9 RISC Vs CISC

There are a few characteristics features that distinguishes RISC from the CISC. Following gives a brief comparison between the two.

1. RISC uses simple instructions whereas, CISC uses complex instructions.
2. RISC thus requires more number of instructions to complete the task whereas, CISC requires relative lesser instructions.
3. RISC has uniform instruction format whereas, CISC has a variable format.
4. RISC typically has a single cycle execution (CPI=1), whereas, a CISC usually requires more than one cycle to complete execution (CPI>1).
5. Memory access is limited to Load/Store instructions in RISC, whereas, almost any instruction can access main memory in CISC
6. RISC uses hard-wared control (rigid) whereas, CISC uses microprogrammed control (flexible).
7. RISC processors are heavily pipelined whereas, CISC provides lesser support to pipeline architecture because of complex instruction.
8. RISC processors are much faster compared to CISC (typically 2 to 4 times).

6.10 Architecture of ARM Microcontrollers

ARM microcontrollers use ARM processor as its central processing unit in the chip together with RAM, ROM, timing units and IO ports. Although ARM series of processors are general-purpose processors but because of their low cost, low power, high performance and small size they have been widely used today for portable and embedded applications. So before proceeding any further, we discuss first the architectural features of ARM.

6.10.1 ARM Processors

One of the most popular RISC processors is the ARM microprocessor. ARM belongs to a family of processors with the acronym, Acorn RISC Machine which was developed by Acorn Computers Ltd, Cambridge in UK in 1980s to act as CPU of a personal computer. Subsequently, the family name had been changed to Advanced RISC Machines. ARM cores are licensed to business partners so as to develop and fabricate new microcontrollers around the same processor cores. The design of ARM family of processors aimed at reducing the size, lowering the cost and to have low-power, intended for applications such as portable computers, video games, portable digital assistants etc. ARM has progressed through many generations initially with 26-bit in Version-1, to 32-bit in Version-2 and Version-3 (ARM6 &ARM7). Today we have ARM processors of Version-8 with ARM11, ARM Cortex-A50. In 2022, ARM launched in its new version (v9) *ARM Cortex-X2, Cortex-A710 and the Cortex-A510* chips for smartphones, laptops and smart home devices.

Key Features

- ARM is a 32-bit processor but it also has 16-bit variant called THUMB
- It operates on 32-bit data
- It has a 32-bit address bus
- Basically, it is a Load/store architecture with limited access to main memory
- It has a small instruction set and uniform instructions allowing high code density in its program memory when used as microcontroller
- It has a large uniform register file
- Maximum size of the memory is 4Gb (2^{32}bytes) for ARM6 which are byte addressable
- Applies instruction level parallelism (3-stage pipeline architecture) to achieve the goal of executing *one instruction per clock cycle*
- Memory and IO share the same address space

- Uses memory-mapped IO

Organization of the CPU

The CPU and its organization in ARM processor is shown in Fig. 6.18. It has a 32-bit ALU and a large register file consisting of 32-bit general-purpose registers. It has several modes of operation including user mode, supervisory mode and four other special modes associated with interrupt handling. In the user mode, there are sixteen 32-bit user addressable registers, R0-R15 in the register file. Where, R15 is also acts as the program counter PC, so also the current program status register designated as CPSR. R14 also acts as the link register to keep the return address whenever a subroutine is called. The other name of R13 is stack pointer register. Some other additional registers are there in the register file which are not visible to the user and are used in other operating modes. The ALU is designed to perform the basic arithmetic operations on 32-bit integers. It employs combinational logic circuits to perform arithmetic addition, subtraction and a sequential shifter and add method for multiplication. A powerful shifter circuit performs multiplication and division. A separate address incrementor circuit implements address-manipulation operations such as PC=PC+1. In order to have a direct interaction between data and control registers, ARM has an unusual feature of placing PC and status register in the register file, although they are part of the PCU.

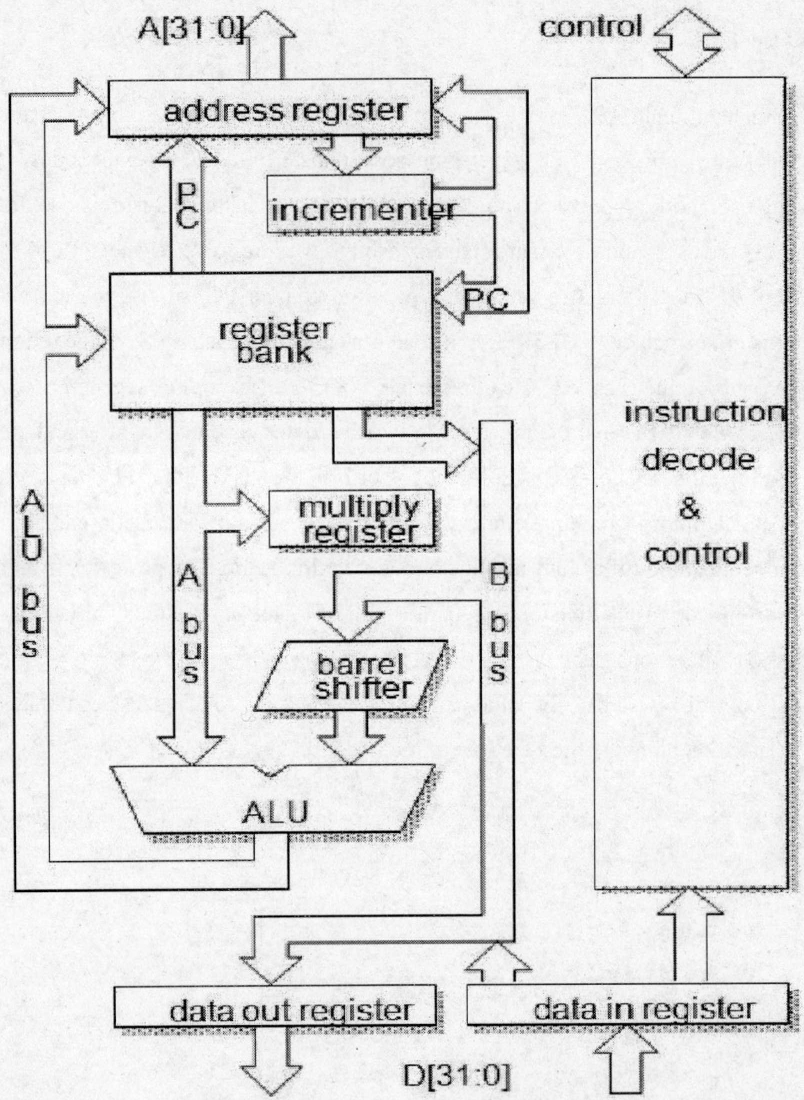

Fig. 6.18: ARM 6 Architecture [Courtesy: ResearchGate]

Apart from these, ARM6 has 32-bit instructions with a variety of formats and addressing modes. There are about 25 main instructions, each of which can operate on 32-bit operands or even with 8-bit operands. Operands and addresses are stored in registers which can be referred by short, 4-bit names. Thus, allowing a single instruction to have as many as four operands (max). The available address space is shared between memory and IO devices (known as memory-mapped IO), considering IO, just like a memory. Hence, load/store instructions used for memory transfers can also be used for IO operations. ARM6 has four status registers, namely N (negative), Z(zero), C (carry), V (overflow) and such ARM instructions can be conditionally executed, thereby increasing the instruction set to a large number. For example, *MOVCC R1, R2*. This instruction will be executed if C=0, then R1=R2. Further, it uses a powerful shifter known as the barrel shifter to perform bitwise shifting for multiplication and divisions. Each bit of shifting to the left implies multiplying the number by 2 and each beat of shifting to the left indicates divide by 2. For example, *MOV, R1, R2, LSL#2*. It means, left-shift R2 by 2-bit positions (multiply by 4) and then copy to R1 (i.e. R1=R2x4). It implements instruction-level parallelism by introducing a three-stage pipeline (fetch, decode and execute) architecture to enhance the performance up to one instruction per cycle.

Processor Modes

The ARM has six operating modes:

- User (unprivileged mode under which most tasks run)
- FIQ (entered when a high priority (fast) interrupt is raised)
- IRQ (entered when a low priority (normal) interrupt is raised)
- Supervisor (entered on reset and when a Software Interrupt instruction is executed)
- Abort (used to handle memory access violations)
- Undef (used to handle undefined instructions)

ARM Architecture Version 4 adds a seventh mode:

- System (privileged mode using the same registers as user mode)

Apart from 32-bit operations, ARM allows a THUMB processor mode which supports 16-bit instructions, thereby increasing the code density however, with a reduced performance for some low-end applications. Usually, a very small amount of RAM is accessible with a datapath of 32-bit in embedded hardware. Rest of it is accessed by a 16-bit path. Therefore, it is logical to use 16-bit thumb code and wider instructions can be placed in a memory which is accessible by 32-bit. ARMTDMI was the first processor to have thumb instruction decoder. Besides, *ARM and THUMB mode* of operations, there is yet another mode known as the *JAZELLE* which allows the execution of JAVA bytecode in hardware. It is most prominently used in mobile phones so that the execution speed of Java EM games can be enhanced. The Java virtual machine performs the complicated operations in software whereas Java bytecodes are usually run on hardware. The first processor to use Jazelle was ARM926EJ-S. One of the most advanced form of ARM microcontrollers is the ARM Cortex, developed using ARMv7 processor. Cortex family is again divided into following three categories,

- ARM Cortex-A series
- ARM Cortex-M series
- ARM Cortex-R series

Cortex family of processors use Embedded C language for programming and Keil compiler for execution purpose. Although most of the ARM based microcontrollers use high-level language for programming but it is necessary to look at the assembly level instructions and programs to understand the high performance and capability of ARM architecture.

ARM Instructions

Although there are 25 main instructions in ARM6 for performing data processing (Arithmetic/logic Operations), data movement and program control operations, ARM7 and other higher versions have a few more instructions which allows tasks like, block memory data transfer, load/store multiple, and coprocessor data processing. These additional instructions making ARM7 more suitable as microcontroller. Table 6.1 shows the instruction set of ARM7TDMI. Incidentally, ARM7TDMI also has 25 main instructions. Normal load/store instructions allow data transfer between a single register and a memory location whereas load/store multiple instruction allows multiple registers can be loaded with memory contents. For example,

- LDR R0, R1
- LDR R0, [R1]
- STR R0, R1
- STR R0, [R1]

are some single register load/store instructions. Whereas, instruction of the type,

- LDMIA R1, {R2, R3, R5}
- STMIA R9!, {R2, R3,R5}

are some load/store multiple instructions. In LDMIA, IA specifies increment after. There are another option IB, which implies increment before. {R2-R5} is an alternative way to specify four registers R2, R3, R4, R5. The symbol '!' indicates auto-incrementation of memory locations specified by R9. The list of destination registers may contain any or all of R0 to R15.

LDMIA R1, {R2, R3, R5} => R2= mem[R1],
R3=mem[R1+4],
R5=mem[R1+8]

Block memory data transfer operations are usually performed using LOOP instructions.

For example, a block of memory containing 128 bytes are to be transferred from memory location (source) R9 to a destination specified by R10. Whereas, R11 indicates the end address of the source, then this transfer can be performed by using the following LOOP,

```
Loop:   LDMIA   R9!, {R0-R7}    //Each register holds 32bits or 4bytes, loading 32 bytes
        STMIA   R10!, {R0-R7}   //store 32 bytes
        CMP     R9. R11         //comparing start and end address of source
        BNE     Loop
```

Thus, to transfer 132 bytes block data, the loop will run only 4 times as each register can store 32 bits or 4bytes and R0-R7 indicates a total of eight register. So, each time 32 bytes of data transfer will take place. Thus, to transfer 132 bytes, the loop will run for 4 times.

Table 6.1: The ARM7TDMI instruction Set

Sl. No.	Mnemonic	Instruction	Action
1	ADC	Add with carry	Rd= Rn +Op2+ Carry
2	ADD	Add	Rd: = Rn +Op2
3	AND	AND	Rd:= Rn AND Op2
4	B	Branch	R15 := address
5	BIC	Bitwise Clear	Rd := Rn AND NOT
6	BL	Branch with Link	R14 := R15, R15 := address
7	BX	Branch and Exchange	R15 := Rn,T bit := Rn[0]
8	CDP	Coprocessor Data Processing	(Coprocessor-specific)
9	CMN	Compare Negative	CPSR flags := Rn + Op2
10	CMP	Compare	CPSR flags := Rn - Op2
11	EOR	Exclusive OR	Rd := (Rn AND NOT Op2) OR (op2 AND NOT Rn)
12	LDC	Load coprocessor from memory	Coprocessor load
13	LDR	Load register from memory	Rd := (address)
14	LDM	Load multiple registers	Stack manipulation (Pop)
15	MCR	Move CPU register to coprocessor register	cRn := rRn {<op>cRm}
16	MLA	Multiply Accumulate	Rd := (Rm * Rs) + Rn
17	MOV	Move register or constant	Rd : = Op2
18	MRC	Move from coprocessor register to CPU register	Rn := cRn {<op>cRm}
19	MRS	Move PSR status/flags to register	Rn := PSR

20	MSR	Move register to PSR status/flags	PSR := Rm
21	MUL	Multiply	Rd := Rm * Rs
22	MVN	Move register negative	Rd := 0xFFFFFFFF EOR Op2
23	ORR	OR	Rd := Rn OR Op2
24	RSB	Reverse Subtract	Rd := Op2 - Rn
25	RSC	Reverse Subtract with Carry	Rd := Op2 - Rn - 1 + Carry

6.10.2 ARM Microcontroller Pinout

The pin diagram of ARM7 based microcontroller LPC2148 is shown in Fig.6.19. It is a trademark chip of Phillips (NXP semiconductor). In the development of different microprocessor-based applications, the designer of embedded systems and SOC (system on chip) use different processor cores, libraries, and tools. Out of these ARM7 is one of the best processors for embedded system designers. It has become so much popular in the last few years. It is easily available in the market. This global ARM7 processor technology has developed many microcontrollers such as LPC2144, LPC2146, and LPC2148, etc. But LPC2148 microcontroller is the most famous microcontroller which has been used currently in different applications such as in automatic braking systems and mobile phones etc.

The LPC2148 microcontroller consists of 64 pins and the group of these pins are called a port. It consists of two ports and registers. These ports could be used as input or output ports therefore the pins of these ports are called **GPIO** *(general purposes input-output)* pins. Following are the details of pins in the chip.

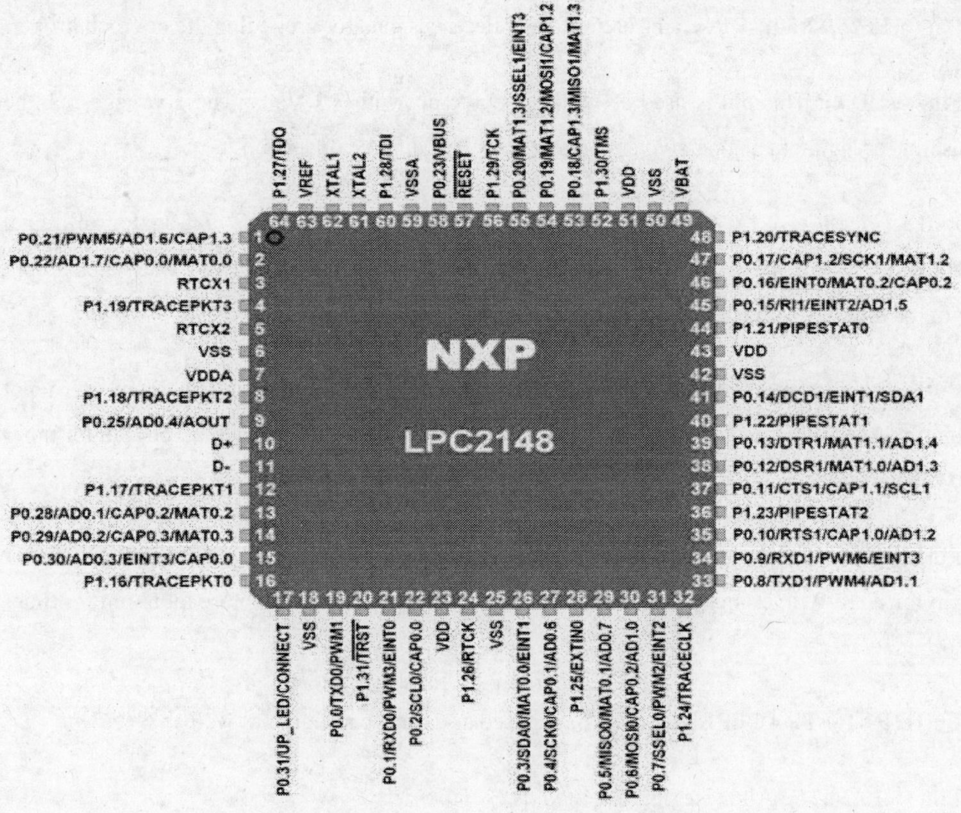

Fig.6.19: LPC2148 Pin Diagram

Pin1 (P0.21/PWM5/AD1.6/Cap1.3): It is a general-purpose pin and can be used for four multiple ways such as it could be as input output data pin, as a pulse width modulation generator, as an analog to digital converter and as a capture input for timer l channel 3.

Pin 2 (P0.22/AD1.7/CAP0.0/MAT0.0): This can also be for used for four purposes. First, as P0.22 it can be used for input output data pin, second, as AD1.7 it can be used as analog to digital converter with ADC 1, input 7. Third, as CAP0.0 it can be used to capture input for timer 0 and channel 0. Fourth, as MAT 0.0 it can be used to match output for timer 0 and channel 0.

Pin 3 (RTC X1): Pin3 is used as input pin for RTC oscillator circuit.

Pin 4 (P1.19/TRACEPKT3): Pin 4 can be as *GPIO pin* so also as 3-bit input output pin for inner pull up.

Pin 5 (RTCX2): Pin 4 is used as output pin for RTC oscillator circuit.

Pin (6,18,25,42,50): These pins are used as references pins for grounding the microcontroller.

Pin7(VDDA): This pin is used as voltage source pin with 3.3 Volts. These voltages can be useful for digital to analog conversion and analog to digital conversion.

Pin13 (P0.28/AD0.1/CAP0.2/MAT0.2): This pin is used as a *GPIO pin,* analog to digital converter pin for ADC-0 input 1, capture input pin for timer 0 channel 2 and as a match output pin for timer 2 channel 1.

Pin14(P0.29/AD0.2/CAP0.3/MAT0.3): This pin can be *used as a GPIO pin,* converter input pin for ADC-0 input 2, capture input for timer 0 channel 3 and as a match output pin for timer 0 channel 3.

Pin15(P0.30/AD0.3/CAP0.3/EINT3/CAP0.0): This pin can be *used as GPIO pin,* converter pin for ADC-0 timer input 3, external interrupt with input 3 and as capture input pin for timer 0 channel 0.

Pin16(P1.16/ TRACEPKT0): This pin is used as a trace packet pin as well as *GPIO pin.*

Pin(17,19,20,21): All these pins are *used as GPIO pins.*

Pin17 is used as UP_LED pin, Pin19 is used as a transmitter output for UART0 and as a pulse Pin20 is used as a reset pin for JTAG interface. Similarly, the pin21is uses as receiver input for UART0, also as PWM generator for output 3 and external interrupt with input 0.

Pin(22,24,26,27,28,29,30): These are *GPIO pins.*

Pin22 is used as clock input output, pin 24 is used as CLK output during JTAG interface. Pin 26 is used as matched output for timer 0 channel 0 and as external interrupt for input1.Pin 27 is used as a serial clock for transferring data from master bus to slave bus and as a digital converter ADC-0.6 for input 6. Pin 28 can be used as external trigger input with inner pullup. Pin 29 is used as MISO for transferring data form mater to slave bus and used as a converter ADC-0 with input 7. Pin 30 is used as MISO output and as a capture input for timer 0 channel 2.

Pin(23,43,51): These pins are used for suppling input voltages to internal core and input output ports.

Pin(31,32,33): These pins are *used as GPIO pins.*

Pin 31 is used as SSEL0, PWM2 and as external interrupt for input 2. Pin 32 is used as a trace CLK for standard input output port with inner pull up. Similarly, pin 33 is used as transmitter TXD1 for UART1 and as a pulse width modulator PWM4

Pin(34,35,36,37): Pin 34,35,36 and 37 *are GPIO pins.*

Pin 34 can be used as input receiver such as RDX1 for UART1, as output pulse modulator such as PWM6 for output 6, as an external interrupt pin for input 3. Pin 35 can be used as a request pin for sending request to UART1, as a capture input pin for timer 1 channel 1, as an anlage to digital converter ADC-1 for input 1. Pin 36 could be used as a 2-bit pipeline status pin for standard input output port. Pin 37 can be used as a clear input pin for UART1, as a capture pin for timer 1 channel 1 and as a clear output input pin for 12C bus observer.

Pin(38,39,40,41): Pin 38,39,40 and 41 could be *used as GPIO pin.*

Pin 38 can be used as an output data terminal ready pin for UART1, as match output pin for timer 1 channel 0 or as an analog to digital converter ADC-1 for input1. Pin 39 can be used as an input data terminal ready pin for UART1 or an output match pin for terminal 1 channel 1 and as a converter ADC-1 for input 4. Pin 40 can be used a bit-1 pipe line status pin for standard input output port. While, Pin 41 be used as input data carrier detector pin for UART1, as an external interrupt pin for input 1 and as an input output open drain pin for 12C bus observer.

Pin(44,45,46,47): These pins are also *used as GPIO pin.*

Pin 44 is used as a bit-0 pipe line pin for standard input output port. Pin 45 can be used as an input ring pointer pin for UART1, as an external interrupt pin for input 2 or as a pulse width modulator generator ADC-1.5 for input 5. Pin 46 can be used as external interrupt pin for input 0, as a match output pin for timer 0 channel 2 and as a capture input pin for timer 0 channel 2. Pin 47 can be used as capture input pin for timer 1 channel 2, as a serial CLK pin for sending output from master but to slave bus.

Pins 49, 50, 51, 57, 59, 61, 62, 63 have their usual functionality as specified in the pinout. Rest of the pins work in a similar manner as specified earlier. For more details, interested readers may refer https//microcontrollerslab.com.

6.10.3 GPIO configuration

Most of the pins of I/O ports in LPC2148 have more than one function i.e. they are multiplexed with different functions. Any pin of the LPC2148 can have a maximum of 4 functions. Hence in order to select any one of the four functions, two corresponding bits of the PINSEL register are needed. So, a 32-bit PINSEL register can control 16 pins with 2-bits to control each pin. PINSEL0 controls PORT0 pins P0.0 to P0.15, PINSEL1 controls PORT0 pins P0.16 to P0.31 and PINSEL2 controls PORT1 pins P1.16 to P1.31.

The default function of all the Pins is GPIO. But it is a good programming practice to specify "PINSEL0=0" in order to select the GPIO function of the Pins.

GPIO function is the most frequently used functionality of the microcontroller. The GPIO function in both the ports are controlled by a set of 4 registers: IOPIN, IODIR, IOSET and IOCLR.

IOPIN: It is a GPIO Port Pin Value register and can be used to read or write values directly to the pin. The status of the pins that are configured as GPIO can always be read from this register irrespective of the direction set on the pin (Input or Output).

The syntax for this register is IOxPIN, where 'x' is the port number i.e. IO0PIN for PORT0 and IO1PIN for PORT1.

IODIR: It is a GPIO Port Direction Control register which is used to set the direction i.e. either input or output of individual pins. When a bit in this register is set to '0', the corresponding pin in the microcontroller is configured as input. Similarly, when a bit is set as '1', the corresponding pin is configured as output.

The syntax for this register is IOxDIR, where 'x' is the port number, accordingly, IO0DIR is for PORT0 and IO1DIR is for PORT1.

IOSET: It is a GPIO Port Output Set Register and can be used to set the value of a GPIO pin that is configured as output to High (Logic 1). When a bit in the IOSET register is set to '1', the corresponding pin is set to Logic 1. Setting a bit '0' in this register has no effect on the pin.

The syntax for this register is IOxSET, where 'x' is the port number, so, IO0SET is meant for PORT0 and IO1SET for PORT1.

IOCLR: It is a GPIO Port Output Clear Register and can be used to set the value of a GPIO pin that is configured as output to Low (Logic 0). When a bit in the IOCLR register is set to '1', the corresponding pin in the respective Port is set to Logic 0 and at the same time clears the corresponding bit in the IOSET register. Setting '0' in the IOCLR has no effect on the pin.

The syntax for this register is IOxCLR, where 'x' is the port number i.e. IO0CLR for PORT0 and IO1CLR for PORT1.

An important point to be remembered here is that since the LPC2148 is a 32-bit microcontroller, the length of all the registers mentioned is also 32-bits. Each bit in the above-mentioned registers is directly linked to the corresponding pin in the microcontroller i.e. bit 'a' in IO0SET corresponds to Pin 'a' in the PORT0.

Moreover, registers in LPC2148 follow Big Endian format. So, bit 0 is the LSB on the extreme right of the register and bit 31 is the MSB on the extreme left of the register.

Also, when reset, all the pins are set as GPIO pins and the direction of each pin is set as Input. For more details refer [3].

6.11 Interfacing LED with LPC2148 MCU

We can write a high-level program to interface LED devices and to turn on/off the LEDs. First, the PORT1 pins are configured as outputs using IO1DIR register. Then in an infinite loop, the pins (or LEDs connected to them) are turned ON using IO1SET register and turned OFF using IO1CLR register. A delay is introduced between the turning ON and OFF of the LEDs using a "for" loop, so that the blinking of LEDs is visible. Figure 6.15 shows the LED connections to ARM-based MCU. The ARM7 LPC2148 advanced development board has eight numbers of point LEDs, connected with I/O Port lines (P1.16 – P1.23) to make port pins high.

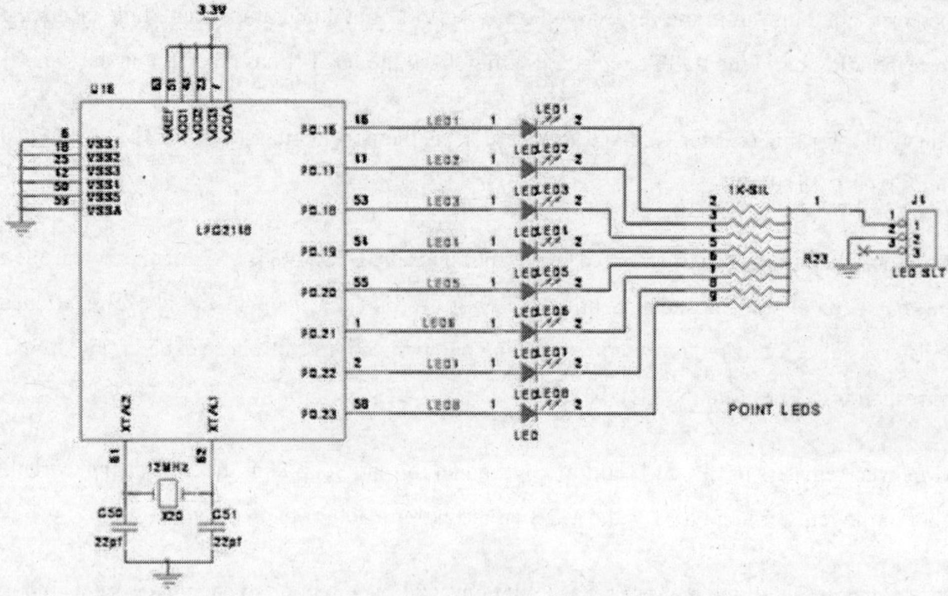

Fig.6.20: Interfacing LED to Microcontroller {Courtesy: Pantech Prolabs]

The following program will blink the LEDs repeatedly that are connected to PORT1 pins of the MCU.

```
#include <lpc214x.h>

int delay;

int main (void)

{

PINSEL2 = 0x00000000;

IO1DIR = 0xFFFFFFFF; // All the pins of PORT1 are configured as Output

while (1)

{

IO1SET = 0xFFFFFFFF; // Set Logic 1 to all the PORT1 pins i.e. turn on LEDs

for (delay = 0; delay<500000; delay++)

IO1CLR = 0xFFFFFFFF; // Set Logic 0 to all the PORT1 pins i.e. turn off LEDs

for (delay = 0; delay<500000; delay++)

}
```

```
return 0;

}
```

Summary

In this chapter, we have gone through the architectural features of some of the advanced processors. We have understood what is instruction pipelining and superscalar execution. We have also seen their differences. Then we have introduced the concept of cache memory-why it is so important in enhancing the performance of a processor. That is why cache is a unique feature in advanced processors. We have come across the terms-cache hit, cache miss and penalty. We have also noted the classification of cache memories, cache organization. Concept of virtual memory and memory mapping are also explained. Next, the architectural features of Intel family of advanced processors, namely, 80286, 80386, 80486 and Pentium are explained thoroughly with diagrams, considering their CPU, register sets, instructions, addressing modes, address translation and memory management. Then, a detail architectural concept of one of the most popular RISC processor-the ARM processor is explained before discussing on ARM microcontrollers. We have also provided a clear concept of RISC and CISC processors and compared the two architectures. ARM7 based microcontrollers have been explained next with pin diagram. GPIO and configuring the GPIO is explained next. Finally, how to interface a ARM microcontroller with LED devices is then explained with a circuit diagram as well as with a high-level program.

Review Questions

1. What do you mean by instruction pipelining?
2. What is superscalar execution?
3. In superscalar processor CPI can be less than 1. Say 'Yes' or 'No'.
4. Compare between pipelining and superscalar execution.
5. What is a cache memory?
6. Define cache tag, cache hit and cache miss penalty.
7. How can you classify cache memories?
8. Define virtual address and address mapping.
9. How do you find 80286 different from 8086 processor?
10. First 32-bit processor is 286/386/486 or Pentium. Pick the correct answer.

11. Concept of virtual memory and memory management unit was first introduced in which Intel processor?
12. Which of the Intel processor has 5 stages of pipeline?
13. Pentium is a pipeline or a superscalar processor?
14. What is the size of the cache in Pentium? Is there any L2 cache in Pentium?
15. Write the full form of ARM.
16. How many instructions are there in ARM6 and how many status registers?
17. Why the architecture of ARM is called a load/store architecture?
18. Can ARM6 processor perform load/store multiple instruction?
19. What is a THUMB mode of operation in ARM?
20. Which of the ARM series processor is useful for ARM based microcontroller design?
21. How many pins are there in LPC2148? How many ports are it?
22. What is GPIO? Which register is needed for configuring GPIO?
23. How to set GPIO port as input or output?

REFERENCES

1. John P. Hayes. *Computer Architecture and Organization.* McGraw-Hill International Editions, 1998
2. Barry B. Brey. The Intel Microprocessors, Architecture, Programming and Interfacing. PHI, 2004, 6th Edition, Copyright 2003.
3. https://www.electronicshub.org/arm-gpio-introduction

Appendices: Experiments and Laboratory Manual

Appendix A

List of Laboratory Experiments

Experiments to be conducted in the Microprocessors and Microcontrollers Laboratory are:

1. **Configuration and Usage of Integrated Development Environment**
2. **Implementation of Arithmetic and Logical Operations to Verify Different Addressing Modes**
3. **Interfacing of LED and 7-Segment Display**
4. **Interfacing 16X2 Liquid Crystal Display**
5. **Interfacing 4X4 Hex Keypad**
6. **Interfacing of DC Motor to Explore Variable Speed**
7. **Interfacing of Stepper Motor to Explore Variable Speed**
8. **Interfacing of ADC**
9. **Interfacing of DAC**
10. **Implementation of Communication by Using RS-232 Standard**
11. **Implementation of I2C Protocol**
12. **Interface of LEDs with GPIO of ARM7TDMI Processor**

Appendix B

Installation guidelines and introduction to IDE

1. **Aim:** To configure and use integrated development environment for 8051 microcontroller.
2. **Objective:** This experiment can be done in two steps.
   - Download and install the required Integrated development environment (IDE) i.e Keil C51 µVision in this case.
   - How to configure it for simulating the code for a given case.

Keil C51 Development tools

There are several integrated development environments (IDEs) available for 8051 microcontroller programming.

- **Keil µVision** is a popular IDE for 8051 development that includes an assembler, linker, and debugger. It also includes a simulation environment for testing code before it is uploaded to the microcontroller.
- A unique feature of the Keil µVision IDE is the Device Database™ which contains information about more than 3500 supported microcontrollers. When you create a new uVision project and select the target chip from the database, uVision sets all assembler, compiler, linker, and debugger options for you. The only option you must configure is the memory map.

Install Keil C51 software for accessing Keil µVision IDE:

Step 1:

Download Keil C51 development tools from official website:

https://developer.arm.com/Tools%20and%20Software/Keil%20PK51

Step 2:

Double click on the .exe file downloaded from the above link.

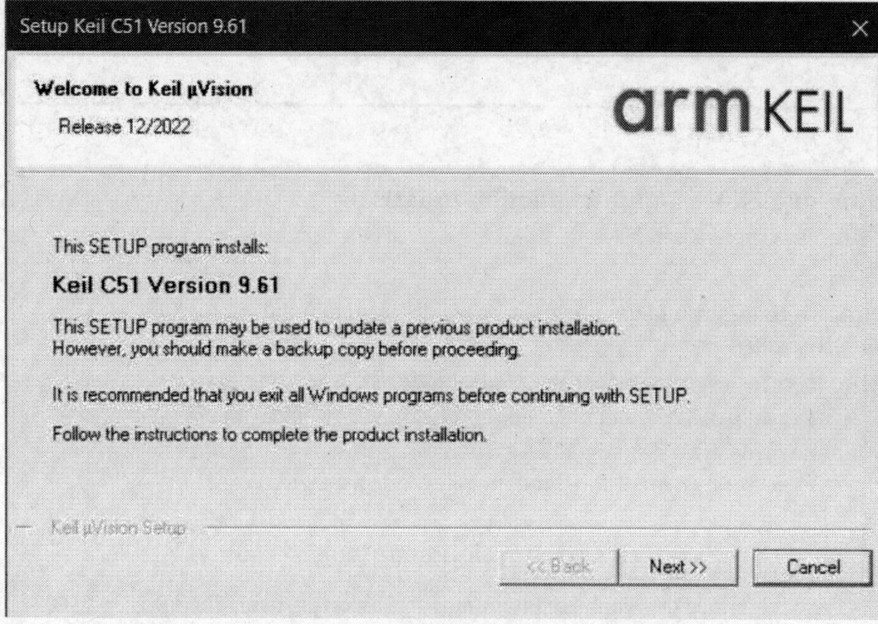

Click on Next tab to proceed to installation.

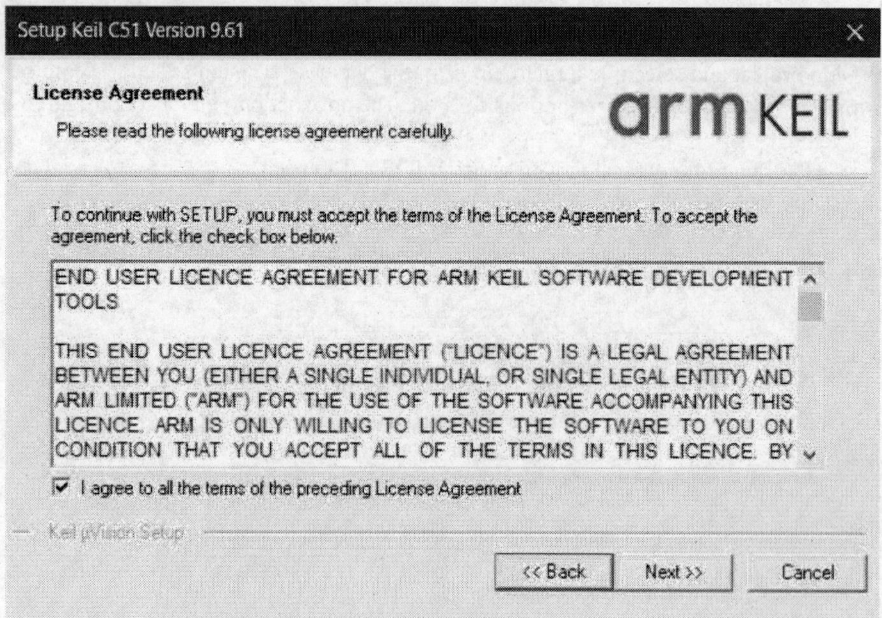

Read the terms of the preceding License Agreement and check the box then click on Next tab.

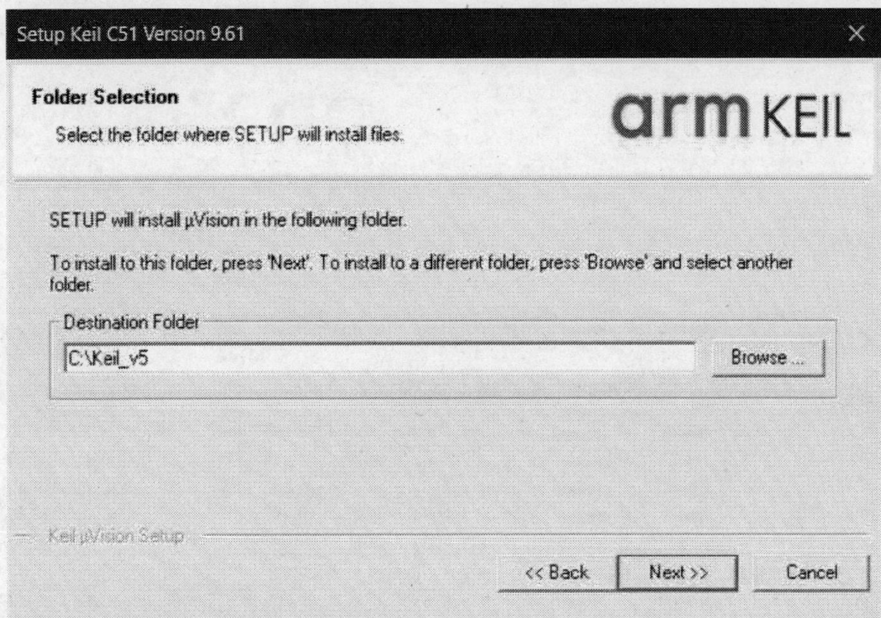

Select the folder to install the setup.

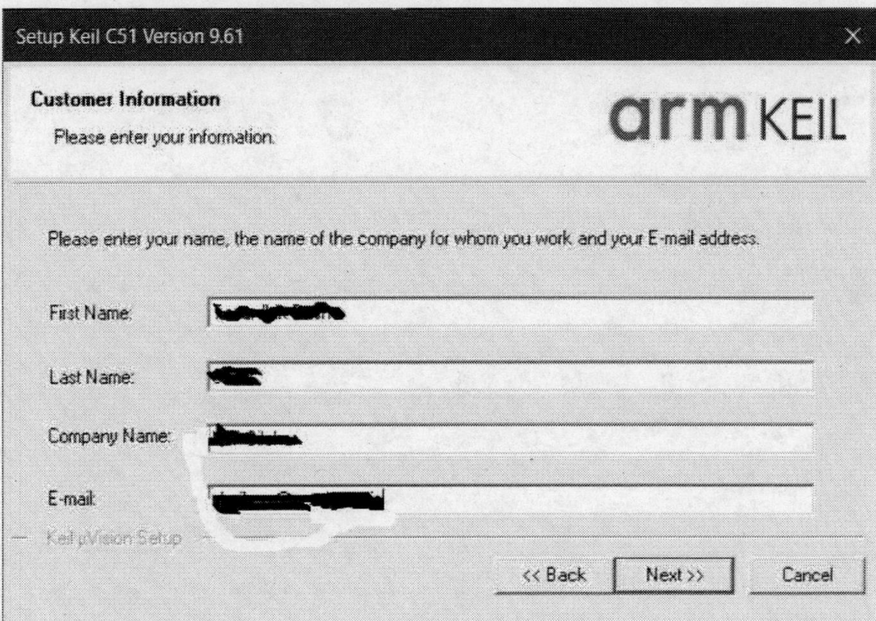

Fill up the required details to move on to the next step.

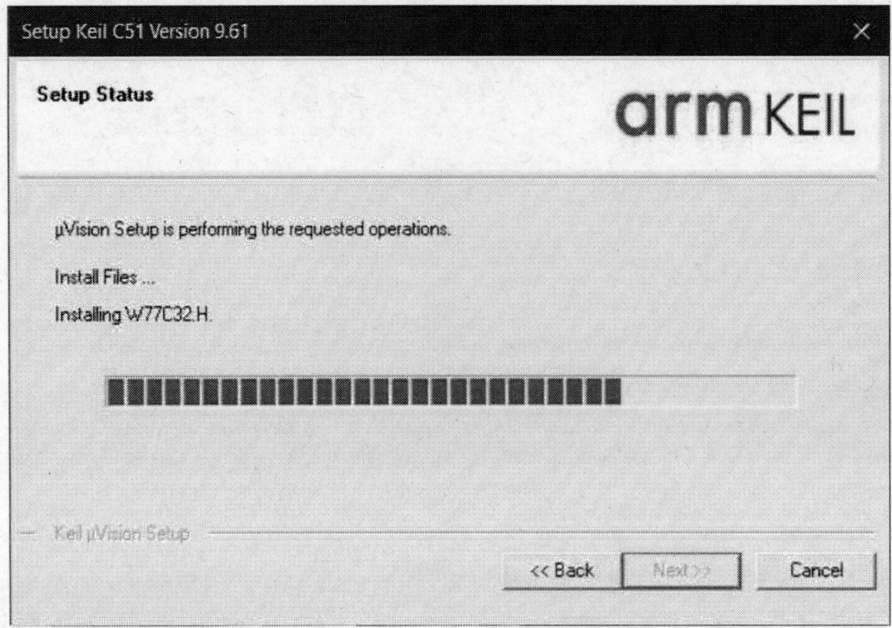

It will take two to three minutes for the installation to complete.

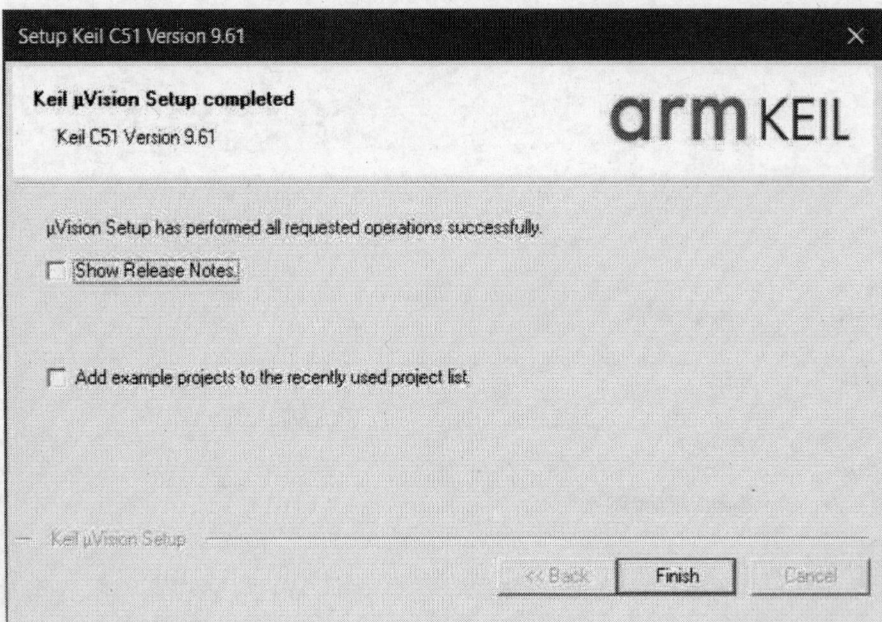

At last Finish the installation window will appear as shown.

So, the installation of the Keil µvision is successfully completed.

Set Up Keil C51 for 8051 Microcontroller Simulations

The 8051 is a powerful microcontroller. Keil C51 Integrated development environment (IDE) is used to write and test code before embedded into microcontroller.

- To transfer code from the PC to the flash memory (a process also known as "burning"), generating the hex file is essential.
- To create this file from assembly-level code or any other high-level language like C you need an IDE that has a compiler that will do this job for you.
- Keil µvision C51 IDE is used for writing code for 8051. It's a free IDE for 8051 related embedded development and is a very popular simulation platform as well.
- You can simulate the code written in the IDE to see the transfer of data in memory locations and registers making it a great tool for simulation. It has advanced debug capabilities too that makes it extremely powerful for testing.

To generate the hex file the IDE follows the following steps:

- It generates a .asm file and sends it to the assembler.
- The assembler generates two files from this. A .lst file and a .obj file.
- In the next step, a process known as "linking" connects the .obj file to others.obj files
- Conversion of the object files to a .hex file.

The hex file can then be burnt into the flash memory of the 8051 using an ISP hardware programmer.

Step 1: Click on the Project dropdown menu and then click on New µvision Project.

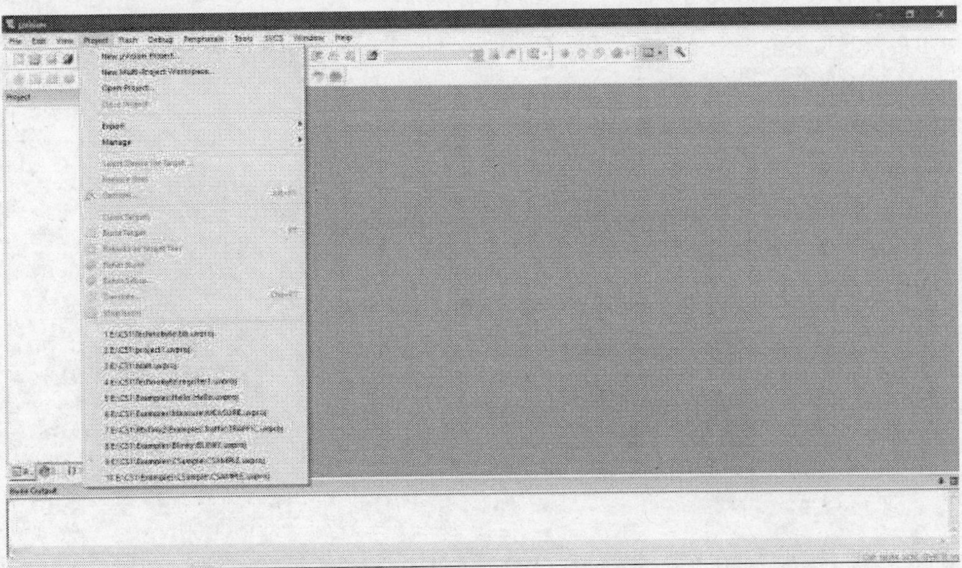

Step 2: Create a new folder at any suitable location on your computer where you wish to keep all project files. In our case it is \thispc\desktop\8051. Create a new project file at this location and click on Save.

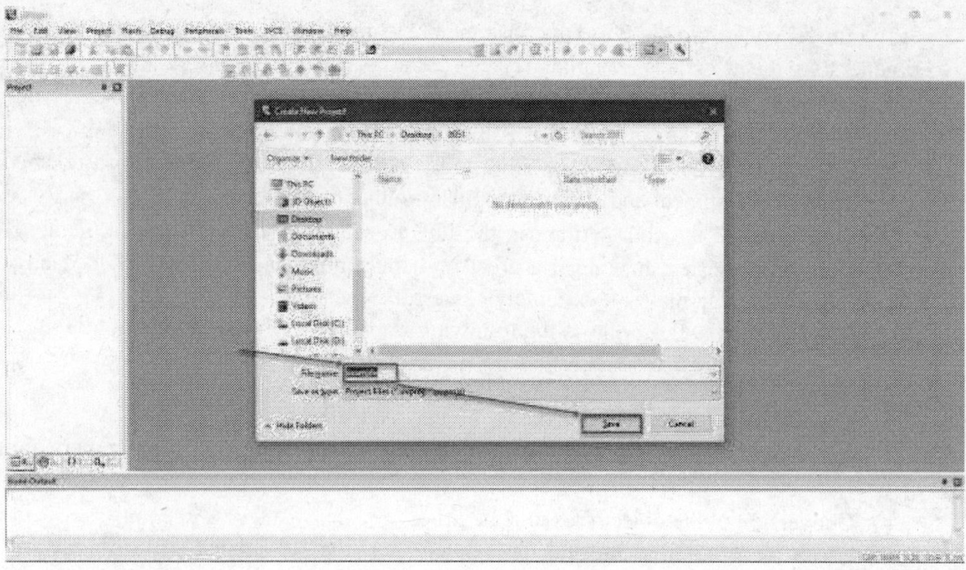

Step 3: Select the microcontroller of your choice in the new pop-up window. In our case, it is the **AT89C51**. Now press Ok.

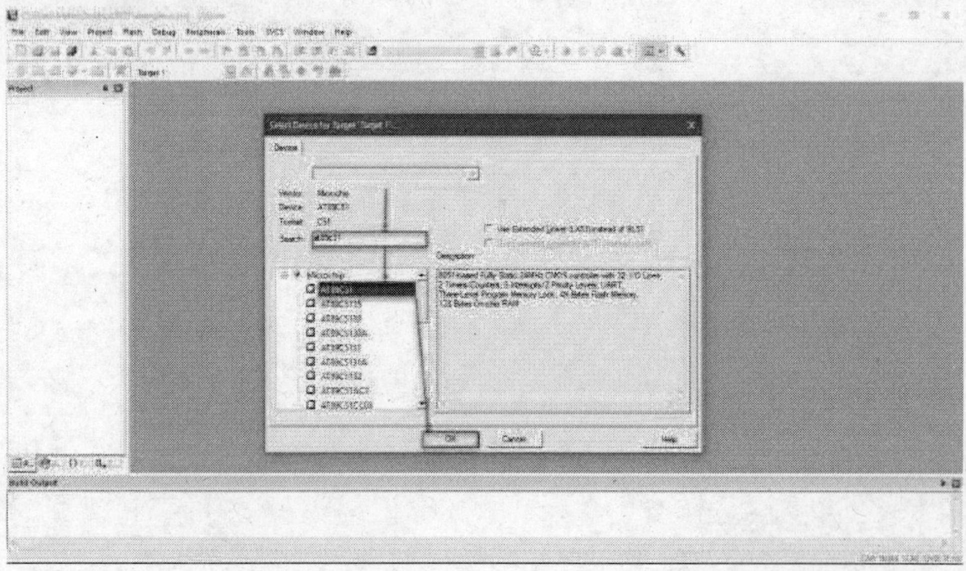

Step 4: Click on NO in the pop-up window that appears next. We will do this step manually.

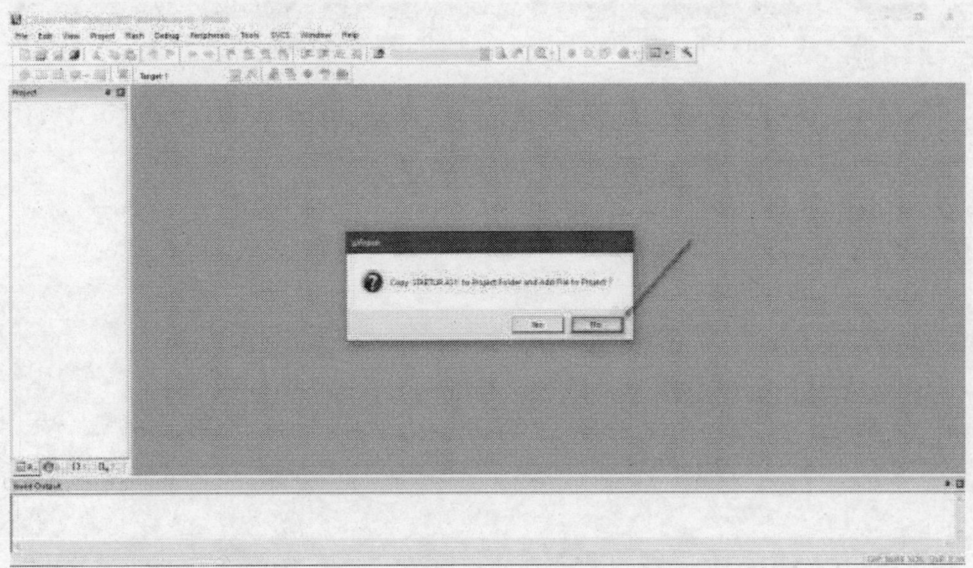

Step 5: Create a new file by clicking on the new file button in the top right corner.

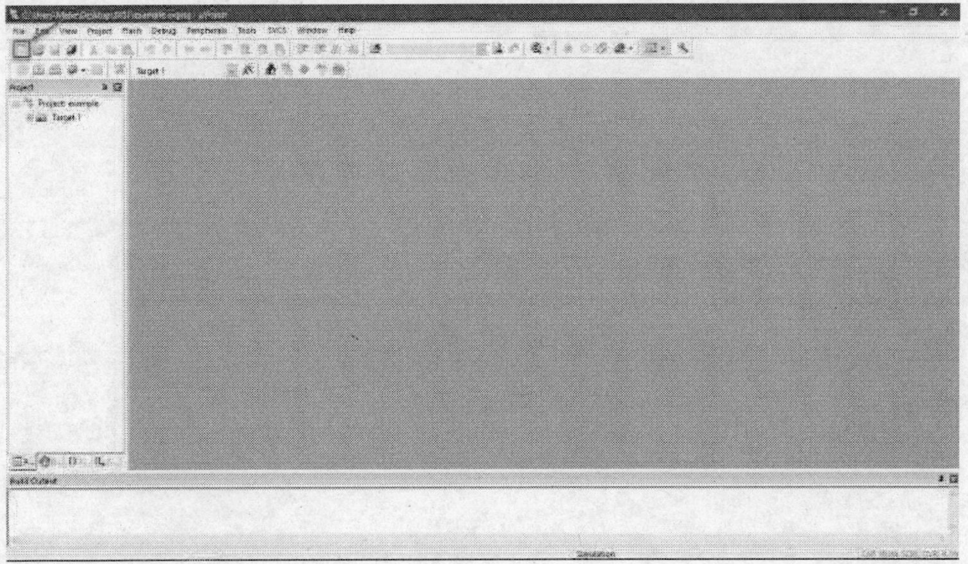

Step 6: Write your code in the newly created file.

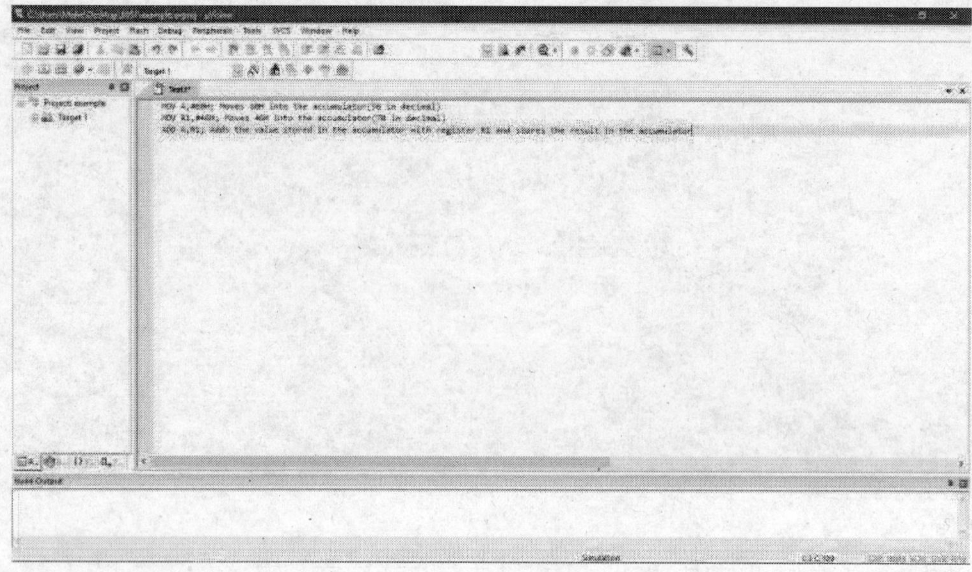

Step 7: Save the file in your Project folder. The extension to be used is .c for c code and .asm in case of assembly-level code. As we are using assembly-level code we use .asm here.

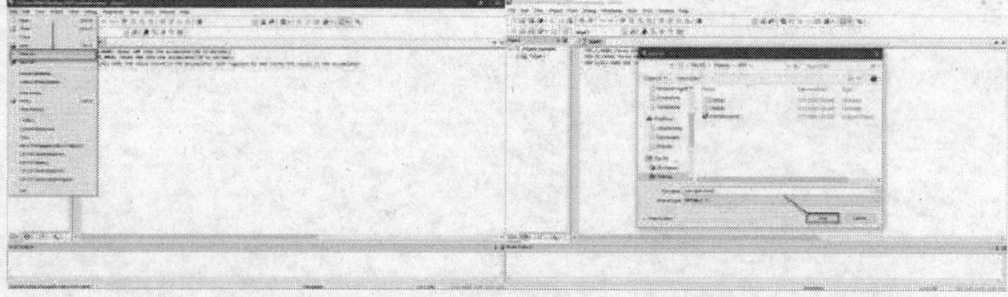

Step 8: Click on the expand (plus) sign next to Target 1 and then right-click on Source group 1. In the options box, click on Add Existing files to Source group 1. This adds the new file that contains your code to your Project file.

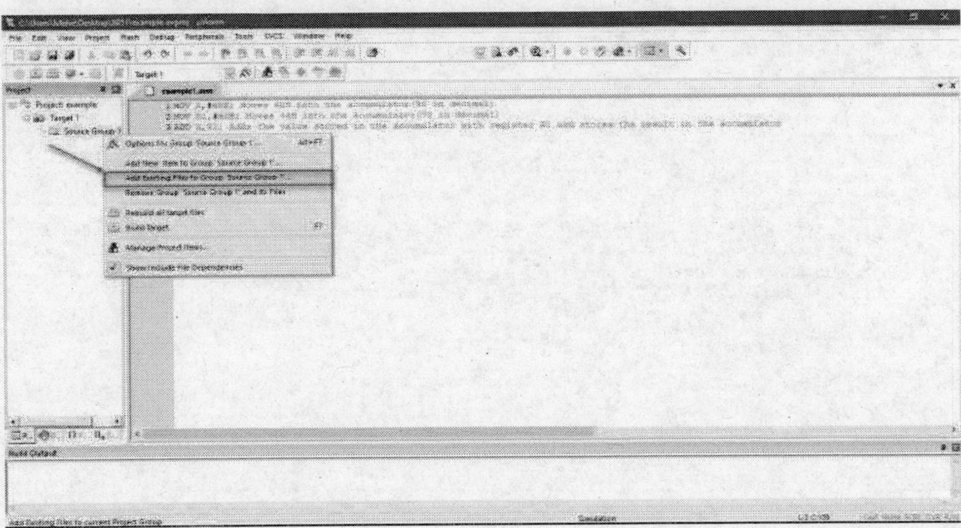

Step 9: Select the file you created and add it here. Now you have a Project file with its constituent code files. All the other files that will be generated will be present in this Project folder.

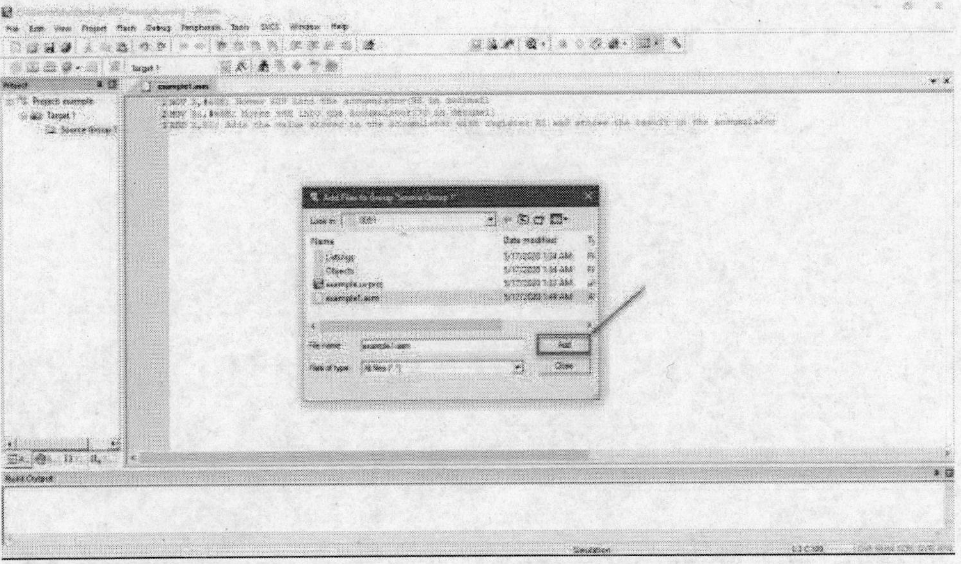

Step 10: Right-click on Target 1 and then select Options for Target "Target 1".

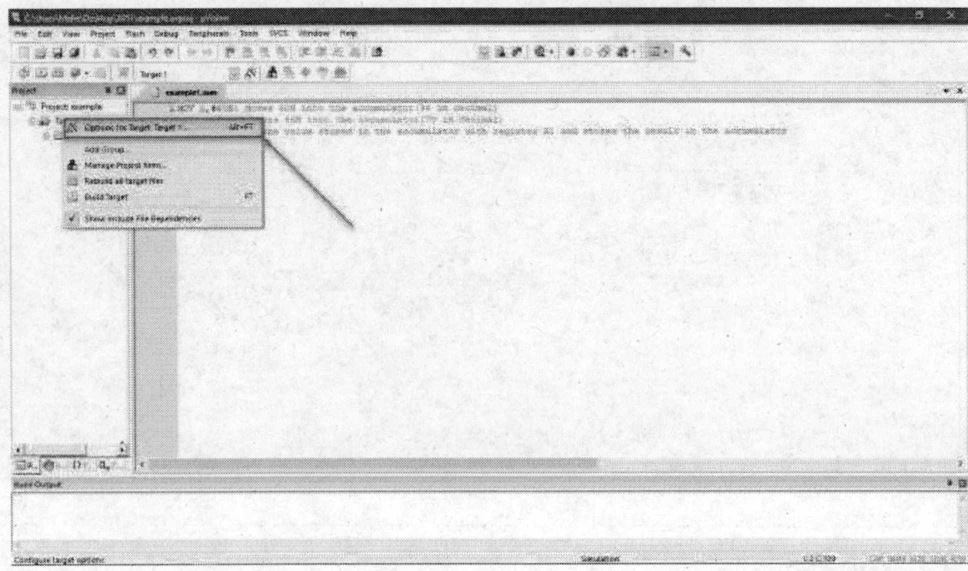

Step 11: In the new dialog box, click on the Output tab and then check the box in front of the Create hex file option.

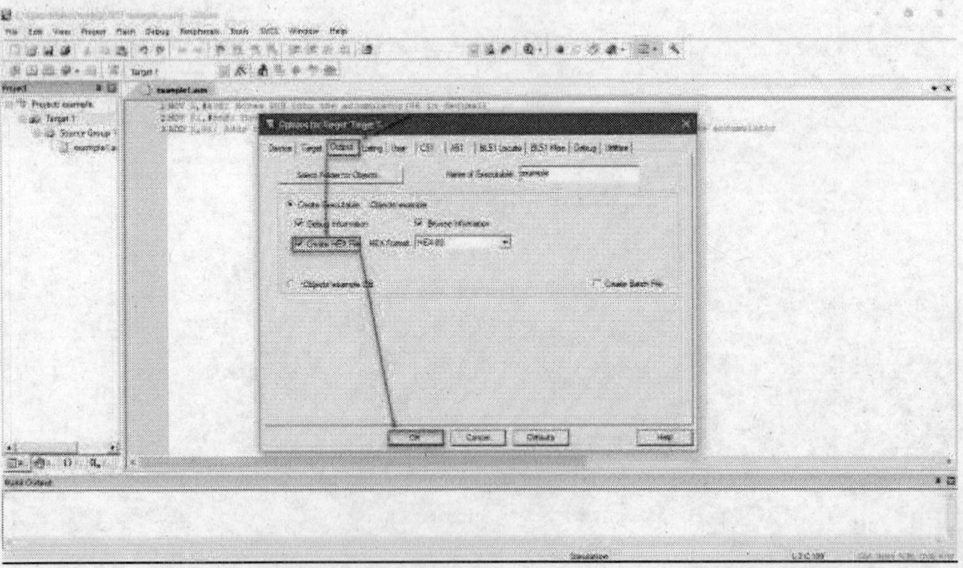

Build the project by pressing F7 on your keyboard and if there are no errors in your code the hex file will be in the objects folder of your project folder.

Simulating code using Keil µvision:

As mentioned earlier we can use Keil to simulate our code. Let's do that by clicking on the magnifying scope symbol in the toolbar.

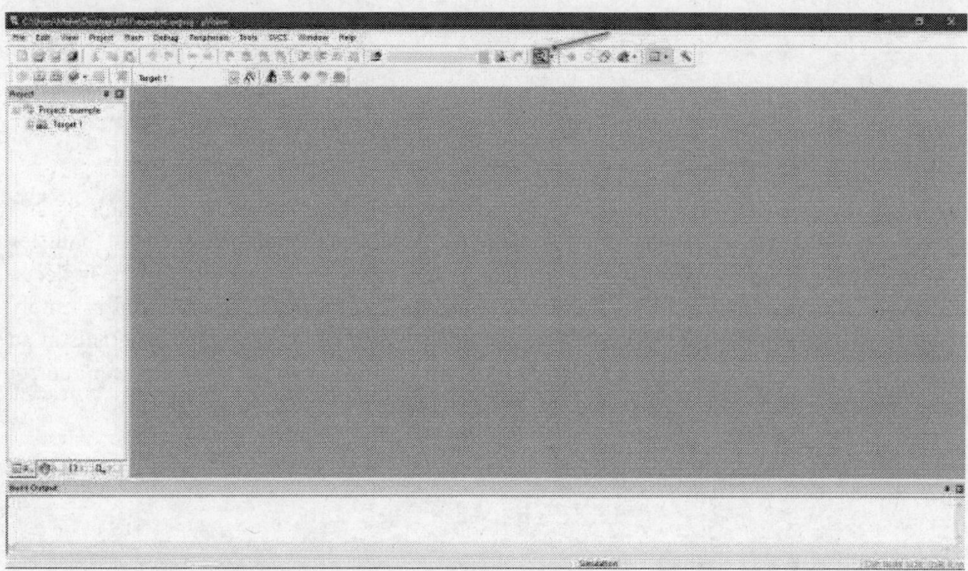

Once you click here after compiling your code you can see a step-by-step execution of your code.

Conclusion:

Now you can learn assembly language programming/embedded C with 8051 without actually needing a kit. Just take up any sample programs, compile them, and run the simulation tool. This is a great exercise in learning the working of instructions from a close perspective.

APPENDIX C

Laboratory Manual

In the following, a detailed systematic procedure for carrying out laboratory experiments 2 to 12 are given. Assembly language programs as well as corresponding Hex codes (both for 8085/8051) are given for most of the experiments in a ready to use manner for the students. However, experiment 12 is to be performed using Keil Software, thus written in assembly language. These experiments are already tested and verified by executing the programs in an appropriate microprocessor or micrcontroller kit. The hardware and/or software requirement for performing each of the experiments are also specified.

EXPERIMENT # 2

1.1 Name of the Experiment: *To verify Different Addressing Modes*

1.2 AIM: Implementation of Arithmetic and Logical Operations to verify different addressing modes

1.3 Equipment needed: Power Supply, adapter, Microprocessor Trainer Kit

1.4 *Program to illustrate Immediate Addressing, Register Direct and Implicit Addressing with Arithmetic operation*

Assembly Language Program			*Hex Code*
MVI B, 4FH	//immediate address	06H	
			4FH
MVI C, 78H	//Immediate address	0EH	
			78H
MOV A, C	//Register direct		79H
ADD B	//Implicit address		80H
STA 2080H	//memory direct		32H
			80H
			20H
HLT			76H

Program Execution

Before executing the program, we need to load the hex codes in memory locations in a sequential manner. For example, if the starting address is 2000H where code 06H will be loaded, then the memory locations for the rest of the codes will be 2001, 2002, 2003, 2004,

2005, 2006, 2007, 2008, 2009 where 04F, OE, 78, 79, 80, 32, 80, 20, 76 will be loaded and saved. Then we need to instruct microprocessor for specifying the starting address. This is done by loading 2000H. And then once the Execution Key is pressed, the microprocessor loads 2000H in the Program Counter and the program control is transferred from the Monitor program the user program. The result will be available at 2080H location (which is 4F+78=C7).

1.5 *Program to illustrate Indirect addressing*

Assembly Language Program	Hex code
LXI H, 2050H //immediate	11
	50
	20
MOV A, M //Indirect address	7E
ANI 0FH //immediate	E6
	0F
STA 2060H //memory direct	32
	60
	20
HLT	76
2050	08
2060	00

Program Execution

Just like previous program, we first load the hex codes to memory locations in a sequential manner. We can start with 2040H to save 11. Similarly, rest of the codes will be saved in memory locations 2041, 2042, 2042, 2043, 2044, 2045, 2046, 2047, 2048 and 2049 respectively. Moreover, memory location 2050 will store an initial value of 08H and in 2060, result will be stored which initially contains 00H. We then instruct the microprocessor to execute. Before that we need to load starting address, which is 2040H. And then once the Execution Key is pressed, the microprocessor loads 2040H in the Program Counter and the program control is transferred from the Monitor program the user program. The result will be available at 2060H (which 08 AND 0F = 08H).

1.6 **Conclusion**: Results are verified in microprocessor kit. This implies that the addressing modes are correctly implemented in the program.

EXPERIMENT # 3a

1. **Name of the Experiment:** Interfacing LEDs for Displaying Binary Data
2. **Hardware needed:** one 8-input NAND gate, one NOR gate, and a 7475 D-type latch with 8085 trainer kit
3. **Objective:** To interface LED output port for displaying binary data from accumulator
4. **Circuit Diagram**

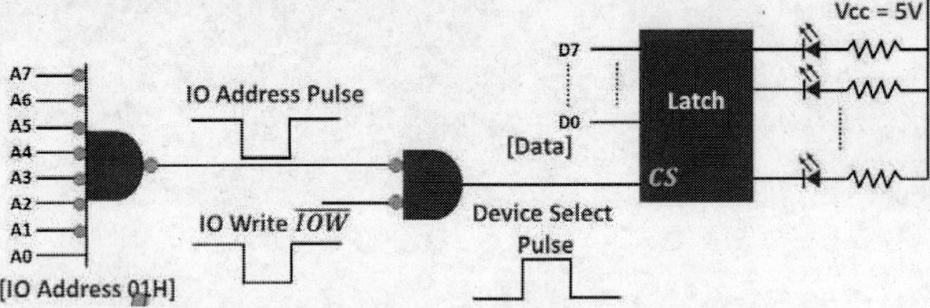

5. **Circuit Operation**

Lower-order address lines of the 8085 are used to generate the enable signal for the D-latch. For this, address bus A_7-A_0 is decoded with an 8-input NAND gate. The output of the NAND gate goes low only when all the inputs are high i.e. when the address is FFH (or 01H as specified in the diagram). The output of the NAND gate is next combined with the IOW-bar control signal with a NOR gate to generate the select pulse or the enable signal, IOSEL for the D-latch. In the meantime, the contents of the accumulator have been put on the data bus. The IOSEL pulse activates the D-latches and the data are now latched and displayed in the LED device. bus

6. **Program**

Mnemonics	Hex code
MVI A, DATA	3E
	DATA
OUT FFH	D3
	FF
HLT	76

7. **Program Execution**

Once the program is executed, LEDs will glow as per the binary data. LED will glow with 1 and remain OFF with a binary 0.

8. **Conclusion:** The LEDs thus got interfaced with 8085

EXPERIMENT # 3b

1. **Name of the Experiment**: Interfacing seven segment display with 8085
2. **Hardware requirement:** NAND gate, NOR gate, NOT gate, Latch, 7-segment displays, limiting registers

3. **Circuit Diagram:**
   (a) interfacing 8085 with 7-segment display

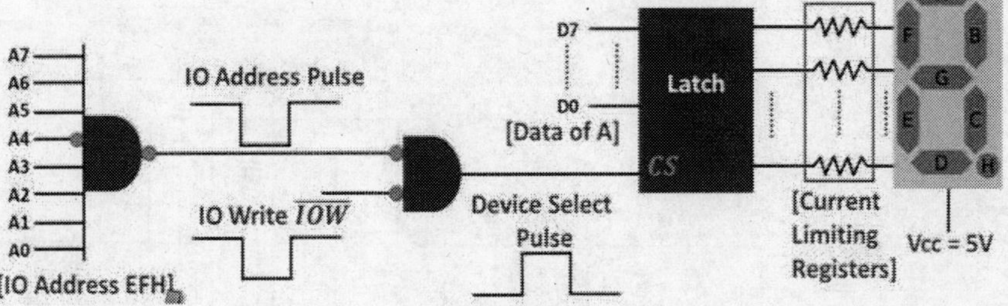

4. **Program:**

Mnemonics	Hex Code
MVI A, DATA	3E
	DATA
OUT EFH	D3
	EF
HLT	76

5. **Program Execution**: Once the program is executed, LEDs will glow as per the binary data. LED will glow with 1 and remain OFF with a binary 0.

6. **Conclusion:** Seven segment display devices got interfaced with 8085

EXPERIMENT # 4

1. **Name of the Experiment**: Interfacing 16x2 Liquid Crystal Display with 8051.
2. **Hardware requirement:**
   - AT89C51 (8051 Microcontroller)
   - 16X2 LCD Display
   - 11.0592MHz Crystal
   - 2 X 33pF Capacitors
   - 2 X 10 KΩ Resistors
   - 1 KΩ X 8 Resistor Pack
   - 10 KΩ Potentiometer
   - 330Ω Resistor
   - Push Button
   - 10µF/16V Capacitor
   - 8051 Programmer
   - 5V Power Supply

- Connecting Wires

3. **Circuit Diagram:**

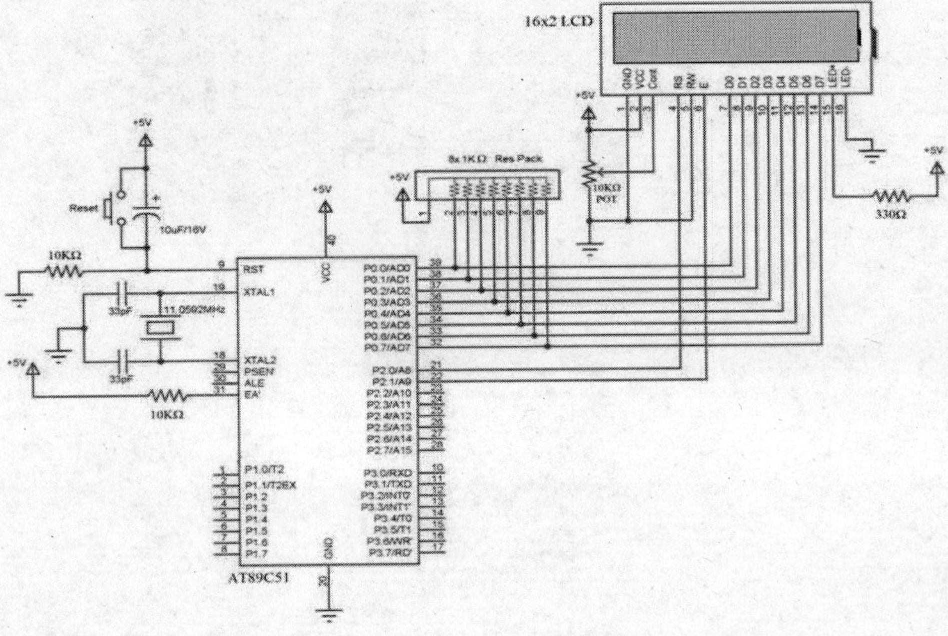

4. **Program:**

0000	HERE: MOV A, #38H
0002	ACALL CMND
0004	MOV A, #0FH
0006	ACALL CMND
0008	MOV A, #06H
000A	ACALL CMND
000C	MOV A, #01H
000E	ACALL CMND
0010	MOV A, #080H
0012	ACALL CMND
0014	MOV A, #' '
0016	ACALL DISP
0018	MOV A, #'H'
001A	ACALL DISP
001C	MOV A, #'E'
001E	ACALL DISP
0020	MOV A, #'L'
0022	ACALL DISP
0024	MOV A, #'L'
0026	ACALL DISP
0028	MOV A, #'O'
002A	ACALL DISP
002C	SJMP HERE
002E	CMND: MOV P2, A
0030	CLR P3.5

0032	CLR P3.4
0034	SETB P3.3
0036	CLR P3.3
0038	RET
0039	DISP: MOV P2, A
003B	SETB P3.5
003D	CLR P3.4
003F	CLR P3.3
0041	SETB P3.3
0043	RET
	END

5. **Execution and Results:**

After executing the code, we can observe the text string shown in the 16x2 LCD display "Hello".

We can also write a program in C for interfacing LCD to 8051 microcontroller.

EXPERIMENT # 5

1. **Name of the Experiment**: Interfacing 4x4 Hex Keypad with 8051.
2. **Hardware requirement:** 8051 AT89S51 microcontroller, 4x4 Hex keypad, capacitors, resistors, 7 segment LED display and power supply.
3. **Circuit diagram:**

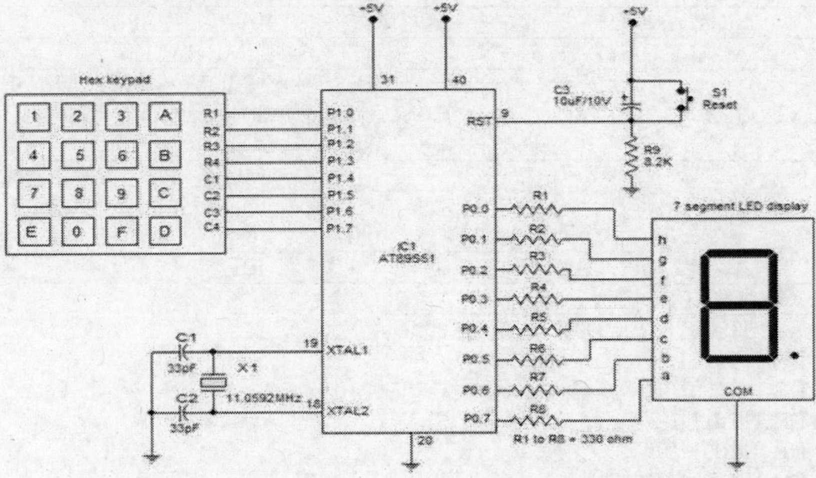

4. **Program:**

MOV DPTR, #LUT // moves starting address of LUT to DPTR	CLR P1.2
MOV A, #11111111B // loads A with all 1's	JB P1.4, NEXT9
MOV P0, #00000000B // initializes P0 as output port	MOV A, #8D
BACK: MOV P1, #11111111B // loads P1 with all 1's	ACALL DISPLAY

CLR P1.0 // makes row 1 low	NEXT9: JB P1.5, NEXT10
JB P1.4, NEXT1 // checks whether column 1 is low and jumps to NEXT1 if not low	MOV A, #9D
MOV A, #0D // loads a with 0D if column is low (that means key 1 is pressed)	ACALL DISPLAY
ACALL DISPLAY // calls DISPLAY subroutine	NEXT10: JB P1.6, NEXT11
NEXT1: JB P1.5, NEXT2 // checks whether column 2 is low and so on...	MOV A, #10D
MOV A, #1D	ACALL DISPLAY
ACALL DISPLAY	NEXT11: JB P1.7, NEXT12
NEXT2: JB P1.6, NEXT3	MOV A, #11D
MOV A, #2D	ACALL DISPLAY
ACALL DISPLAY	NEXT12: SETB P1.2
NEXT3: JB P1.7, NEXT4	CLR P1.3
MOV A, #3D	JB P1.4, NEXT13
ACALL DISPLAY	MOV A, #12D
NEXT4: SETB P1.0	ACALL DISPLAY
CLR P1.1	NEXT13: JB P1.5, NEXT14
JB P1.4, NEXT5	MOV A, #13D
MOV A, #4D	ACALL DISPLAY
ACALL DISPLAY	NEXT14: JB P1.6, NEXT15
NEXT5: JB P1.5, NEXT6	MOV A, #14D
MOV A, #5D	ACALL DISPLAY
ACALL DISPLAY	NEXT15: JB P1.7, BACK
NEXT6: JB P1.6, NEXT7	MOV A, #15D
MOV A, #6D	ACALL DISPLAY
ACALL DISPLAY	LJMP BACK
NEXT7: JB P1.7, NEXT8	DISPLAY: MOVC A, @A+DPTR // gets digit drive pattern for the current key from LUT
MOV A, #7D	MOV P0, A // puts corresponding digit drive pattern into P0
ACALL DISPLAY	RET
NEXT8: SETB P1.1	
LUT: DB 01100000B //Look up table DB 11011010B //starts here DB 11110010B DB 11101110B DB 01100110B DB 10110110B DB 10111110B DB 00111110B DB 11100000B DB 11111110B DB 11110110B DB 10011100B DB 10011110B DB 11111100B DB 10001110B	

```
    DB 01111010B
        END
```

5. **Program execution and Results:**

After executing the code the key which is pressed will be shown in the seven segment LED display connected to it.

EXPERIMENT # 6 & 7

DC Motor Speed Control with 8051 and Stepper Motor Clockwise and Anti Clockwise Rotation

PART NO: PS-ACC-DC-STEP PS-ADD-ON, card (from Pantech ProLab, Chennai) has facility to interface Stepper motor and DC motor. User could evaluate motors features with easily with the interface card. Separate PBT connectors for motors terminations. Motor could be driven by h-bridge drivers. All motor lines and power lines are terminated by the 20pin connector.

SPECIFICATIONS

• Stepper Motor o (Angle control / Clockwise/ Counter-clockwise)

• DC Motor controlled with PWM Control

o Direction and speed control

• Motor control line and Power lines terminated at box connector

• 20-pin FRC Cable o To connect host boards (Microcontroller/Processor)

CARD FEATURES

• 5V Stepper Motor

• 5V DC Motor

• Motor Driver Unit

• Terminal connectors

• 20-pin Box Connector

STEPPER MOTOR

• Step Angle (o) : 1.8

• Motor Length (mm) : 34

• Holding Torque (g.cm) : 1300

• Lead Wire (NO.) : 6

• Rated Current (A) : 0.3

- Phase Resistance (ohm) : 40
- Phase Inductance (mH) : 20
- Rotor Inertia (g.cm 2) : 20
- Motor Weight (Kg) : 0.18

DC MOTOR

- Voltage : 6.0V (Range: 1.5 - 12.)
- Speed : 2,700(ŸA10%) rpm (No)
- Current : 0.02A (No)
- Torque : 5.88 mN. M

KIT INCLUDES

- Motor Interface Card (with Stepper/DC Motor)
- Interface Cable

HARDWARE DESCRIPTION

- STEPPER MOTOR Bipolar Stepper Motor driven by h-bridge driver, facility to connect external power supply to the motor. 5V Stepper Motor speed, direction (clockwise/counter-clockwise) and angle rotation through user program.
- DC MOTOR 5V DC Motor speed has controlled through PWM signal. Motor can run both clockwise/counter clockwise, Motor speed controlled by varying ENA (duty cycle) signal through the program.

IN 8051 WE HAVE SINGLE 8255

- J1 8255

PORTS	ADDRESS
Control port	4003H
PORT A	4000H
PORT B	4001H
PORT C	4002H

PROCEDURE:

- Connect a 20 Pin FRC cable between the 8051 Trainer Kits J1 port (middle port) and the DC MOTOR/STEPPER MOTOR CARD.
- Connect a DC motor at the MG1 connector or connect a Stepper Motor in J4.
- Connect USB/PS2 keyboard on 8051 Microcontroller. Type and execute the DC Motor or Stepper Motor program.
- Now the DC Motor or the Stepper Motor is running

Experiment 6: DC MOTOR INTERFACE WITH 8051

AIM: To interface the DC motor with 8051 and to run the DC motor at various speed

PROGRAM:

ADDRESS	OPCODE	MNEMONICS
9100	74 80	MOV A,#80
9102	90 40 03	MOV DPTR,#4003
9105	F0	MOVX @DPTR,A
9106	74 06	START: MOV A,#06H
9108	90 40 01	MOV DPTR,#4001
910B	F0	MOVX @DPTR,A
910C	12 19 11	LCALL DELAY
910F	80 F5	SJMP START
9111	78 FF	DELAY: MOV R0,#FF
9113	79 FF	LOP: MOV R1,#FF
9115	D9 FE	LOP1: DJNZ R1,LOP1
9117	D8 FA	DJNZ R0,LOP
9119	22	RET

RESULT: Execute the program. Now we can see that the DC motor run.

Experiment 7: Stepper Motor Control for CLOCKWISE ANTI CLOCKWISE ROTATION using 8051

AIM: To interface the stepper motor with the 8051-trainer kit and to run a stepper motor in both the direction

PROGRAM

ADDRESS	OPCODE	MNEMONICS
9100	74 80	MOV A,#80
9102	90 40 03	MOV DPTR,#4003
9105	F0	MOVX @DPTR,A
9106	78 32	**START** : MOV R0,#32
9108	90 92 00	**CLKWI** : MOV DPTR,#9200
910B	A9 82	MOV R1,82
910D	AA 83	MOV R2,83
910F	31 26	ACALL ROTAT
9111	D8 F5	DJNZ R0,CLKWI
9113	31 41	ACALL DELAY
9115	78 32	MOV R0, #32
9117	90 92 50	**ANCKWI**: MOV DPTR,#9250
911A	A9 82	MOV R1,82
911C	AA 83	MOV R2,83
911E	31 26	ACALL ROTAT
9120	D8 F5	DJNZ R0, ANCKWI
9122	31 91	ACALL DELAY
9124	80 E0	SJMP START
9126	7B 04	**ROTAT**: MOV R3,#04
9128	E0	**REPT** : MOVX A,@DPTR
9129	90 40 00	MOV DPTR,#4000

912C	F0	MOVX @DPTR,A
912D	7C 03	MOV R4,#03
912F	7D 01	**LOP3** : MOV R5,#0A
9131	7E FF	**LOP2** : MOV R6,#FF
9133	DE FE	**LOP 1** : DJNZ R6, LOP1
9135	DD FA	DJNZ R5, LOP2
9137	DC F6	DJNZ R4, LOP3
9139	09	INC R1
913A	89 82	MOV 82,R1
913C	8A 83	MOV 83,R2
913E	DB E8	DJNZ R3, REPT
9140	22	RET
9141	7C 03	**DELAY** : MOV R4,#03
9143	7D FF	**LP3** : MOV R5,#FF
9145	7E FF	**LP2** : MOV R6,#FF
9147	DE FE	**LP1** : DJNZ R6, LP1
9149	DD FA	DJNZ R5, LP2
914B	DC F6	DJNZ R4, LP3
914D	22	RET

ORG 9200H

9200 03060C09 DB 03H, 06H, 0CH, 09H

ORG 9250H

9250 090C0603 DB 09H, 0CH, 06H, 03H

END

RESULT: Execute the program. Now you can see that the stepper motor runs in a clockwise and anti-clockwise direction.

Steps for executing the program:

1. After the last instruction, press the **"Enter"** key two times.
2. To execute the program press **"G"** from the keyboard and enter the initial address of the program i.e. **9100** and then press **"Enter"** key.

EXPERIMENT # 8

1. **Name of the Experiment**: Interfacing an A/D converter with 8085 using the Interrupt
2. **Objective**:
   - To interface a typical 8-bit A/D converter with 8085 using status check
3. **Hardware requirements**:
   - one 8-bit A/D converter (SAR) with input voltage 0 to 5V range, with active low START-bar and DR-bar)
   - one 3:8 decoder, 74LS138

- 4-input NAND gate, 2-input NAND gates and inverters
- Two Tri-state Buffer

4. **Circuit Diagram**: Figure below shows the circuit for interfacing a typical ADC with 8085 using Status Check. When the active low pulse is sent to START-bar and DR-bar goes high, the ADC output goes into high impedance state. The rising edge of the STAR-bar pulse initiates the conversion. When the conversion is complete, the DR-bar goes low and the digital output are available on the output lines that can be read by the microprocessor.

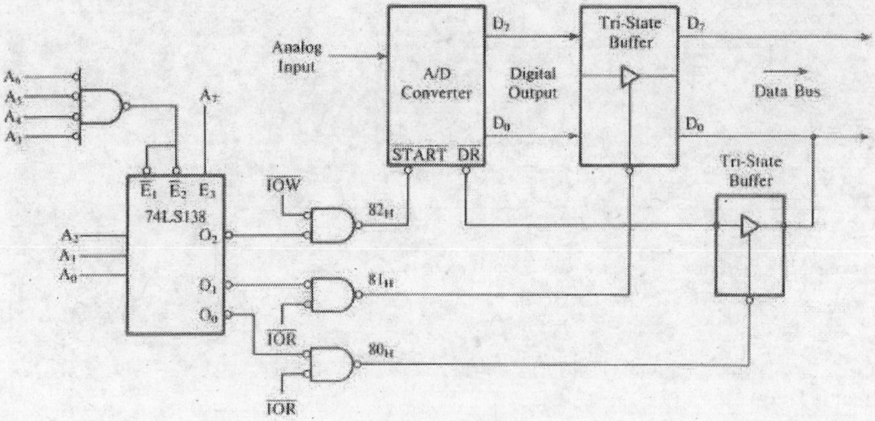

5. **Program**

```
OUT 82H      ; Start conversion
TEST: IN     80H      ; Read Data Ready Status
RAR          ; Rotate D0, into carry
JC    TEST   ; If D0 = 1, conversion is not yet complete
             ; go back and check
IN  . 81H    ; Microprocessor will read output and save
;it in accumulator.
RET
```

6. **Results:** Analog input to ADC will get converted to digital output available at the D7:D0 pins of the ADC will be read by 8085 and found in accumulator.

EXPERIMENT # 9

1. **Name of the Experiment:** Interfacing 8-bit D/A Converter with 8085
2. **Objectives:**

- To design an output port with address FFH and to interface 1408 D/A converter that is calibrated for 0 to 10V range
- To write a program and execute it to generate a continuous waveform

3. **Hardware requirements:** one 8-input NAND gate, one 2-input NOR gate, one 74LS373 latch, 1408 DAC, 2 registers of 2.5K

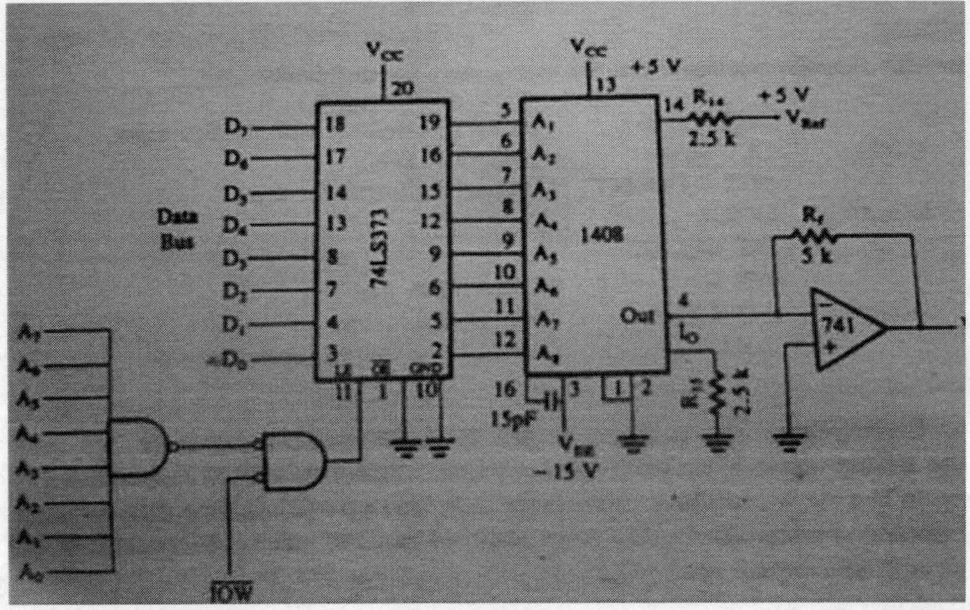

4. **Circuit Diagram**

   The circuit diagram of D/A conversion is shown in Figure below. The 1408 is an 8-bit D/A converter compatible with TTL and CMOS logic, having a settling time of 300 ns. It has 8-input lines with A1 as MSB and A8 as LSB unlike the convention used in the data bus of 8085 (where D7 is MSB and D0 is LSB). It requires 2mA reference current for full-scale input and two power supplies, V_{CC} = +5 V and V_{EE} =-15 V. 74LS373 is a 8-input D-latch for storing the input data from processor data bus.

5. **Program**

Mnemonics		Meaning
	MVI A, 00H	Load accumulator with first input
D2A:	OUT FFH	Output to DAC
	MVI B, COUNT	Set up Reg. B for delay
DELAY:	DCR B	
	JNZ DELAY	
	INR A	Next input
	JMP D2A	Go back to output

6. **Results and waveform**

   The program continuously put 00 through FF to the D/A converter. The corresponding analog output of the DAC starts from 0V and increases up to 10V as a ramp. When the accumulator contents go to 0, the next cycle begins and the ramp signal is generated continuously.

7. **Conclusion:** A DAC has been successfully interfaced with 8085 to generate a Ramp Signal continuously.

EXPERIMENT # 10

1. **Name of the Experiment**: Implementation of serial data transmission using RS-232 standard.
2. **Objective**: To implement serial data communication between two 8051 microcontrollers using RS-232.
3. **Hardware Requirement:** Two 8051 microcontroller kits, and one RS-232 cable.
4. **Procedure:** Suppose, the letter "E" is to be transferred serially at 9600 baud continuously using 8051. Use 8-bit data and 1-stop bit.

Through the PC hyper terminal window (serial window), set 9600 BAUD rate. After executing program with PS2 KIT press 'B', set 9600 baud the rate value

- Connect the two microcontroller kits using an RS-232 cable.
- Enter the transmitter program in 1st microcontroller kit and the receiver program in 2nd microcontroller kit.
- Run the receiver program first in kit-2 and then run the transmitter program in kit-1.
- After executing the transmitter program, reset the kit and then go to location 8700H.

5. The transferred data "Yes" (ASCII value) are stored from 8400H onwards in kit-2.

INPUT in Transmitter Kit: **910F:** **45**

Transmitter Program:

Memory Location	Hex Code	Mnemonics
9100	75	MOV TMOD, #21H
89		
21		
9103	75	MOV TH1, #0F5H
	8D	
	F5	
9106	75	MOV SCON, #52H
	98	
	52	
9109	75	MOV PCON, #00H
	87	
	00	
910C	D2	SETB TR1
8E		

910E	74		MOV A, #45H
	45		
9110	31		ACALL TRANS
	14		
9112	80	HALT:	SJUMP HALT
	FE		
9114	F5	TRANS:	MOV SBUF, A
	99		
9116	30	WAIT:	JNB TI, WAIT
	99		
	FD		
9119	C2		CLR TI
	99		
911B	22		RET

INPUT in RECEIVER KIT: **9200:** **45**

Receiver Program:

9100	75		MOV TMOD, #21H
	89		
	21		
9103	75		MOV TH1, #0F5H
	8D		
	F5		
9106	75		MOV SCON, #52H
	98		
	52		
9109	75		MOV PCON, #00H
	87		
	00		
910C	90		MOV DPTR, #9200H
	92		
	00		

910F	D2		SETB TR1
	8E		
9111	30	WAIT:	JNB RI, WAIT
	98		
	FD		
9114	E5		MOV A, SBUF
	99		
9116	C2		CLR RI
	98		
9118	C2		CLR TR1
	8E		
911A	F0		MOVX @DPTR, A
911B	A3		INC DPTR
911C	80	HALT:	SJMP HALT
	FE		

EXPERIMENT # 11

1. **Name of the Experiment:** Implementation of I2C protocol
2. **Objectives:** To implement I2C protocol on 8051 ARM7TDMI microcontroller.
3. **Hardware Requirement:** 8051 microcontroller, I2C compatible peripherals such as sensors, actuators etc., Pull-up resistors of range 4.7 kΩ to 10 kΩ, Cables and connectors, development board, breadboard or PCB, programmer and Power supply.
4. **Procedure:**
   - Assemble the hardware: Assemble the circuit by connecting the 8051 microcontroller, the I2C-compatible peripheral(s), the pull-up resistors, and any other required components to a breadboard or PCB.
   - Write the software: Write the code that implements the I2C protocol on the 8051 microcontroller. The code should include the initialization of the I2C bus, the communication protocol, and any other necessary functions for your specific use case.
   - Compile the code: Use a compiler to compile the code you have written into machine code that can be run on the 8051 microcontroller.
   - Upload the code: Use a programmer to upload the compiled code to the 8051 microcontroller. The programmer will be connected to the computer and the development board, and will be used to transfer the code from the computer to the microcontroller.

- Test the circuit: Power on the circuit and test the communication between the 8051 microcontroller and the I2C device. You can use a logic analyzer or an oscilloscope to monitor the I2C bus and verify that the communication is correct.
- Debug and refine the code: If necessary, debug the code and make any necessary changes to improve the performance and reliability of the communication. Repeat steps 3-5 until you are satisfied with the results.
- Integrate with your system: Integrate the I2C circuit into your larger system, as required.

5. **Program:**

	;Define i2c pins
	SDA EQU P1.0
	SCL EQU P1.1
	;I2C initialization
0000	I2C_INIT:MOV SDA, 1
0003	MOV SCL, 1
0006	RET
	;I2C start condition
0007	I2C_START: MOV SDA, 1
000A	MOV SCL, 1
000D	MOV SDA, 0
0010	RET
	;I2C stop condition
0011	I2C_STOP: MOV SDA, 0
0014	MOV SCL, 1
0017	MOV SDA, 1
001A	RET
	;I2C write
001B	I2C_WRITE: MOV SCL, 0
001E	MOV SDA, C
0020	MOV SCL, 1
0023	RET
	;I2C read
0024	I2C_READ: MOV SCL, 0
0027	MOV SDA, 1
002A	MOV SCL, 1
002D	MOV C, SDA
002F	RET
	;I2C write byte
0030	I2C_WRITE_BYTE: MOV SCL, 0
0033	MOV SDA, C
0035	MOV SCL, 1
0038	JC ACK
003A	RET
	;I2C read byte
003B	I2C_READ_BYTE: MOV SCL, 0
003E	MOV SDA, 1
0041	MOV SCL, 1

0044	MOV C, SDA
0046	RET
0047	ACK: MOV SCL, 0 ; I2C acknowledge
004A	MOV SDA, 1
004D	MOV SCL, 1
0050	RET

6. **Output**
   - Reading data from an I2C device:
     8051 microcontroller can read the data from the peripheral devices and sensors through I2C device.
   - Writing data to an I2C device:
     8051 microcontroller writing data to the peripheral device through I2C then acknowledge can be seen as output that data successfully written.

EXPERIMENT # 12

7. **Name of the Experiment:** Interface of LEDs with GPIO of ARM7TDMI Processor
8. **Objectives:** To interface LED devices with ARM7TDMI microcontroller and to turn on/off the LEDs.
9. **Hardware Requirement:** IC-LPC2148, Point LEDs (8), 1K resistors (8)
10. **Circuit Diagram:** First, the PORT1 pins are configured as outputs using IO1DIR register. Then in an infinite loop, the pins (or LEDs connected to them) are turned ON using IO1SET register and turned OFF using IO1CLR register. A delay is introduced between the turning ON and OFF of the LEDs using a "for" loop, so that the blinking of LEDs is visible. Figure 6.15 shows the LED connections to ARM-based MCU. The ARM7 LPC2148 advanced development board has eight numbers of point LEDs, connected with I/O Port lines (P1.16 – P1.23) to make port pins high.

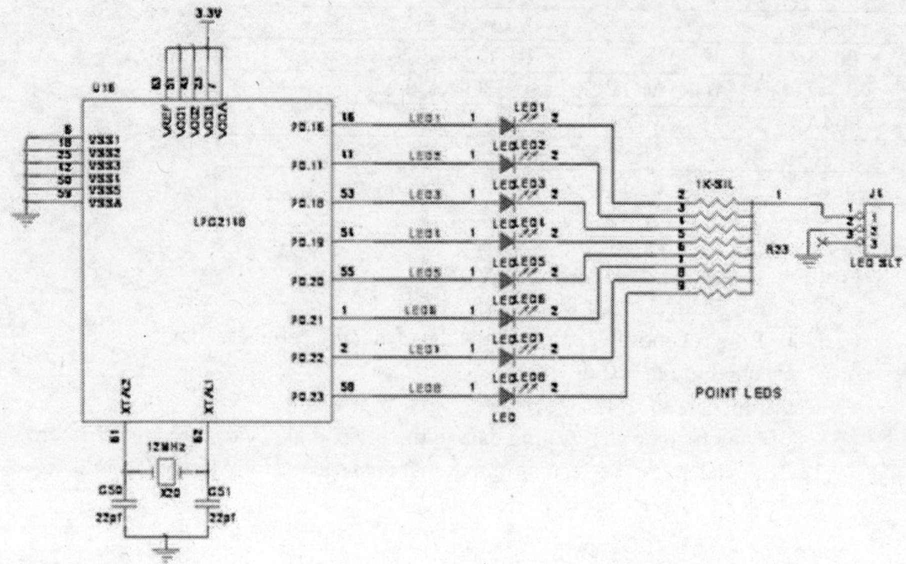

11. **Program**

```
#include <lpc214x.h>

int delay;

int main (void)

{

PINSEL2 = 0x00000000;

IO1DIR = 0xFFFFFFFF; // All the pins of PORT1 are configured as Output

while (1)

{

IO1SET = 0xFFFFFFFF; // Set Logic 1 to all the PORT1 pins i.e. turn on LEDs

for (delay = 0; delay<500000; delay++)

IO1CLR = 0xFFFFFFFF; // Set Logic 0 to all the PORT1 pins i.e. turn off LEDs

for (delay = 0; delay<500000; delay++)

}

return 0;

}
```

12. **Results:** LEDs will glow as per the program.

Annexures

OPCODES (HEX CODES) OF INTEL 8085 PROCESSOR

Sr. No.	Mnemonics, Operand	Opcode	Bytes
1.	ACI Data	CE	2
2.	ADC A	8F	1
3.	ADC B	88	1
4.	ADC C	89	1
5.	ADC D	8A	1
6.	ADC E	8B	1
7.	ADC H	8C	1
8.	ADC L	8D	1
9.	ADC M	8E	1
10.	ADD A	87	1
11.	ADD B	80	1
12.	ADD C	81	1
13.	ADD D	82	1
14.	ADD E	83	1
15.	ADD H	84	1
16.	ADD L	85	1
17.	ADD M	86	1
18.	ADI Data	C6	2
19.	ANA A	A7	1
20.	ANA B	A0	1
21.	ANA C	A1	1
22.	ANA D	A2	1
23.	ANA E	A3	1

24.	ANA H	A4	1
25.	ANA L	A5	1
26.	ANA M	A6	1
27.	ANI Data	E6	2
28.	CALL Label	CD	3
29.	CC Label	DC	3
30.	CM Label	FC	3
31.	CMA	2F	1
32.	CMC	3F	1
33.	CMP A	BF	1
34.	CMP B	B8	1
35.	CMP C	B9	1
36.	CMP D	BA	1
37.	CMP E	BB	1
38.	CMP H	BC	1
39.	CMP L	BD	1
40.	CMP M	BD	1
41.	CNC Label	D4	3
42.	CNZ Label	C4	3
43.	CP Label	F4	3
44.	CPE Label	EC	3
45.	CPI Data	FE	2
46.	CPO Label	E4	3
47.	CZ Label	CC	3
48.	DAA	27	1
49.	DAD B	09	1
50.	DAD D	19	1
51.	DAD H	29	1
52.	DAD SP	39	1
53.	DCR A	3D	1
54.	DCR B	05	1

Sr. No.	Mnemonics, Operand	Opcode	Bytes
55.	DCR C	0D	1
56.	DCR D	15	1
57.	DCR E	1D	1
58.	DCR H	25	1
59.	DCR L	2D	1
60.	DCR M	35	1
61.	DCX B	0B	1
62.	DCX D	1B	1
63.	DCX H	2B	1
64.	DCX SP	3B	1
65.	DI	F3	1
66.	EI	FB	1
67.	HLT	76	1
68.	IN Port-address	DB	2
69.	INR A	3C	1
70.	INR B	04	1
71.	INR C	0C	1
72.	INR D	14	1
73.	INR E	1C	1
74.	INR H	24	1
75.	INR L	2C	1
76.	INR M	34	1
77.	INX B	03	1
78.	INX D	13	1
79.	INX H	23	1
80.	INX SP	33	1
81.	JC Label	DA	3
82.	JM Label	FA	3
83.	JMP Label	C3	3
84.	JNC Label	D2	3

85.	JNZ Label	C2	3
86.	JP Label	F2	3
87.	JPE Label	EA	3
88.	JPO Label	E2	3
89.	JZ Label	CA	3
71.	INR C	0C	1
72.	INR D	14	1
73.	INR E	1C	1
74.	INR H	24	1
75.	INR L	2C	1
76.	INR M	34	1
77.	INX B	03	1
78.	INX D	13	1
79.	INX H	23	1
80.	INX SP	33	1
81.	JC Label	DA	3
82.	JM Label	FA	3
83.	JMP Label	C3	3
84.	JNC Label	D2	3
85.	JNZ Label	C2	3
86.	JP Label	F2	3
87.	JPE Label	EA	3
88.	JPO Label	E2	3
89.	JZ Label	CA	3
90.	LDA Address	3A	3
91.	LDAX B	0A	1
92.	LDAX D	1A	1
93.	LHLD Address	2A	3
94.	LXI B	01	3
95.	LXI D	11	3
96.	LXI H	21	3
97.	LXI SP	31	3
98.	MOV A, A	7F	1

99.	MOV A, B	78	1
100.	MOV A, C	79	1
101.	MOV A, D	7A	1
102.	MOV A, E	7B	1
103.	MOV A, H	7C	1
104.	MOV A, L	7D	1
105.	MOV A, M	7E	1
106.	MOV B, A	47	1
107.	MOV B, B	40	1
108.	MOV B, C	41	1
109.	MOV B, D	42	1
110.	MOV B, E	43	1
111.	MOV B, H	44	1
112.	MOV B, L	45	1
113.	MOV B, M	46	1
114.	MOV C, A	4F	1
115.	MOV C, B	48	1
116.	MOV C, C	49	1
117.	MOV C, D	4A	1
118.	MOV C, E	4B	1
119.	MOV C, H	4C	1
120.	MOV C, L	4D	1
121.	MOV C, M	4E	1
122.	MOV D, A	57	1
123.	MOV D, B	50	1
124.	MOV D, C	51	1
125.	MOV D, D	52	1
126.	MOV D, E	53	1
127.	MOV D, H	54	1
128.	MOV D, L	55	1
129.	MOV D, M	56	1
130.	MOV E, A	5F	1
131.	MOV E, B	58	1
132.	MOV E, C	59	1

133.	MOV E, D	5A	1
134.	MOV E, E	5B	1
135.	MOV E, H	5C	1
136.	MOV E, L	5D	1
137.	MOV E, M	5E	1
138.	MOV H, A	67	1
139.	MOV H, B	60	1
140.	MOV H, C	61	1
141.	MOV H, D	62	1
142.	MOV H, E	63	1
143.	MOV H, H	64	1
144.	MOV H, L	65	1
145.	MOV H, M	66	1
146.	MOV L, A	6F	1
147.	MOV L, B	68	1
148.	MOV L, C	69	1
149.	MOV L, D	6A	1
150.	MOV L, E	6B	1
151.	MOV L, H	6C	1
152.	MOV L, L	6D	1
153.	MOV L, M	6E	1
154.	MOV M, A	77	1
155.	MOV M, B	70	1
156.	MOV M, C	71	1
157.	MOV M, D	72	1
158.	MOV M, E	73	1
159.	MOV M, H	74	1
160.	MOV M, L	75	1
161.	MVI A, Data	3E	2
162.	MVI B, Data	06	2
163.	MVI C, Data	0E	2
164.	MVI D, Data	16	2
165.	MVI E, Data	1E	2
166.	MVI H, Data	26	2

167.	MVI L, Data	2E	2
168.	MVI M, Data	36	2
169.	NOP	00	1
170.	ORA A	B7	1
171.	ORA B	B0	1
172.	ORA C	B1	1
173.	ORA D	B2	1
174.	ORA E	B3	1
175.	ORA H	B4	1
176.	ORA L	B5	1
177.	ORA M	B6	1
178.	ORI Data	F6	2
179.	OUT Port-Address	D3	2
180.	PCHL	E9	1
181.	POP B	C1	1
182.	POP D	D1	1
183.	POP H	E1	1
184.	POP PSW	F1	1
185.	PUSH B	C5	1
186.	PUSH D	D5	1
187.	PUSH H	E5	1
188.	PUSH PSW	F5	1
189.	RAL	17	1
190.	RAR	1F	1
191.	RC	D8	1
192.	RET	C9	1
193.	RIM	20	1
194.	RLC	07	1
195.	RM	F8	1
196.	RNC	D0	1
197.	RNZ	C0	1
198.	RP	F0	1
199.	RPE	E8	1
200.	RPO	E0	1

201.	RRC	0F	1
202.	RST 0	C7	1
203.	RST 1	CF	1
204.	RST 2	D7	1
205.	RST 3	DF	1
206.	RST 4	E7	1
207.	RST 5	EF	1
208.	RST 6	F7	1
209.	RST 7	FF	1
210.	RZ	C8	1
211.	SBB A	9F	1
212.	SBB B	98	1
213.	SBB C	99	1
214.	SBB D	9A	1
215.	SBB E	9B	1
216.	SBB H	9C	1
217.	SBB L	9D	1
218.	SBB M	9E	1
219.	SBI Data	DE	2
220.	SHLD Address	22	3
221.	SIM	30	1
222.	SPHL	F9	1
223.	STA Address	32	3
224.	STAX B	02	1
225.	STAX D	12	1
226.	STC	37	1
227.	SUB A	97	1
228.	SUB B	90	1
229.	SUB C	91	1
230.	SUB D	92	1
231.	SUB E	93	1
232.	SUB H	94	1
233.	SUB L	95	1
234.	SUB M	96	1

235.	SUI Data	D6	2
236.	XCHG	EB	1
237.	XRA A	AF	1
238.	XRA B	A8	1
239.	XRA C	A9	1
240.	XRA D	AA	1
241.	XRA E	AB	1
242.	XRA H	AC	1
243.	XRA L	AD	1
244.	XRA M	AE	1
245.	XRI Data	EE	2
246.	XTHL	E3	1

REFERENCES FOR FURTHER LEARNING

1. John P. Hayes. *Computer Architecture and Organization.* 3rd ed. Singapore: McGraw-Hill International Edition, 1998
2. K.M. Bhurchandi and A.K. Ray, *ADVACNED MICROPROCESSORS AND PERIPHERALS,* 3rd ed. Tata McGraw-Hill, New Delhi, 2013.
3. M. Ali Mazidi, J. Gillipsie Mazidi, Rolin D. McKinlay. The 8051Microcontrollers and Embedded System. 2nd ed. New Jersey, Pearson Prentice Hall, 2006.
4. Ramesh Gaonkar. Microprocessor Architecture, Program ming, and Applications with the 8085. Fifth Edition: Peram International Publishing (India) Private Ltd. 2012.
5. Manish Patel "Question Paper with Solution the 8051 Microcontroller Based Embedded Systems, www.slideshare.net, 1 Mar. 2001.
6. Barry B. Brey. The Intel Microprocessors, Architecture, Programming and Interfacing. PHI, 2004, 6th Edition, Copyright 2003.
7. Kenneth J. Ayala. The 8051 Microcontroller. St. Paul, MN, WEST PUBLISHING COMPANY, 1991
8. Santanu Chattopadhyay. *Embedded System Design.* 2nd ed. PHI Learning Private Ltd. New Delhi, 2016.
9. https://www.eeeguide.com
10. https://www.computer.org
11. https://www.researchgate.net
12. https://www.slideshare.net

CO AND PO ATTAINMENT TABLE

Course outcomes (COs) for this course can be mapped with the programme outcomes (POs) after the completion of the course and a correlation can be made for the attainment of POs to analyze the gap. After proper analysis of the gap in the attainment of POs necessary measures can be taken to overcome the gaps.

Table for CO and PO attainment

Course Outcomes	Expected Mapping with Programme Outcomes (1- Weak Correlation; 2- Medium correlation; 3- Strong Correlation)											
	PO-1	PO-2	PO-3	PO-4	PO-5	PO-6	PO-7	PO-8	PO-9	PO-10	PO-11	PO-12
CO-1	3	2	2	2	1	-	-	-	-	-	-	-
CO-2	3	3	2	2	-	-	-	-	-	-	-	-
CO-3	3	3	2	-	-	-	-	-	-	-	-	-
CO-4	3	3	3	2	2	-	-	-	-	-	-	-
CO-5	3	2	2	2	1	-	-	-	-	-	-	-
CO-6	3	3	3	2	1	-	-	-	-	-	-	-

The data filled in the above table can be used for gap analysis.

Index